MODERN SOUTHEAST ASIA SERIES

James R. Reckner, *General Editor*

WINDOW ON A WAR

Window on a War

AN ANTHROPOLOGIST IN THE
VIETNAM CONFLICT

GERALD C. HICKEY

TEXAS TECH UNIVERSITY PRESS

This book is typeset in Times Roman. The paper used in this book meets the minimum requirements of ANSI/NISO Z39.48-1992 (R1997). ∞

Designed by Barbara Werden

Printed in the United States of America

LIBRARY OF CONGRESS CATALOGING-IN-PUBLICATION DATA

Hickey, Gerald Cannon, 1925–
   Window on a war : an anthropologist in the Vietnam conflict / by Gerald Cannon Hickey.
      p.   cm. — (Modern Southeast Asia series)
   Includes bibliographical references and index.
   ISBN 0-89672-490-5 (cloth : alk. paper)
   1. Vietnamese Conflict, 1961–1975—Personal narratives, American. 2. Montagnards (Vietnamese people) 3. Hickey, Gerald Cannon, 1925– I. Title. II. Series.

DS559.5 .H54 2002
959.704'3'0899593—dc21

                                                    2002004620

02 03 04 05 06 07 08 09 10 / 9 8 7 6 5 4 3 2 1

Texas Tech University Press
Box 41037
Lubbock, Texas 79409-1037 USA
1-800-832-4042
ttup@ttu.edu
www.ttup.ttu.edu

To Catherine

ACKNOWLEDGMENTS

IN THE COURSE of my work in Vietnam between 1956 and 1973, people too numerous to mention lent assistance for which I shall be ever grateful. Some have been explicitly mentioned in previous acknowledgments, and some also have been cited in the text of the present book. I would, however, like to express my appreciation to individuals for their assistance in the preparation and publication of this book. Excellent suggestions for improving the manuscript were made by Joan Allen, George Lovelace, and Rhoda Tripp. Huynh Sanh Thong contributed a scholarly Vietnamese perspective to parts of the text while Roger Donlon carefully went over the events of 6 July 1964 described in Chapter 4. Christopher and Kevin Chambers brought their talents to bear in preparing graphics.

Louis Weisner, George Tanham, Douglas Murray, Mark Bradley, Arthur T. Hadley, and Kevin Buckley were instrumental in moving the manuscript toward publication.

For their roles in realizing the final product—the book—I especially would like to thank Douglas Pike of the Vietnam Center and the staff at Texas Tech University Press for their professional guidance. I also would like to thank Karol Lorenz for her editorial assistance.

A subvention for publication was kindly given by the Albert Kunstadter Family foundation of New York.

Finally, I would like to express my deepest gratitude to the people of

Khanh Hau and the people of the central highlands for their kindness and generosity and for all I learned from them, not only about their worlds but also about the meaning of courage, dignity, hope, and survival.

CONTENTS

ILLUSTRATIONS

MAPS

AID	Agency for International Development
ARPA	Advanced Research Projects Agency
ARVN	Army of the Republic of Vietnam
CAP	Combined Action Platoons
CIDG	Civilian Irregular Defense Group
CORDS	Civil Operations and Revolutionary (Rural) Development Support
FULRO	Front Unifié de Lutte des Races Opprimées (United Struggle Front for the Oppressed Races)
ICC	International Commission for Supervision and Control
IVS	International Voluntary Service
JUSPAO	Joint United States Public Affairs Office
MAAG	Military Assistance Advisory Group (preceded MACV)
MACV	Military Assistance Command, Vietnam
MDEM	Ministry for Development of Ethnic Minorities
MSUG	Michigan State University Group
Mike Force	Mobile Strike Force
NLF	National Liberation Front

SIL	Summer Institute of Linguistics
USAID	U.S. Agency for International Development
USIS	U.S. Information Service
USOM	U.S. Operations Mission
VC	Viet Cong
VNQDD	Viet Nam Quoc Dan Dang (political party)
WRAIR	Walter Reed Army Institute of Research

SERIES EDITOR'S INTRODUCTION

FEW EVENTS IN AMERICAN HISTORY have generated as much emotion, as much division, and as many long-term impacts for American society as our nation's involvement in Vietnam, Laos, and Cambodia in the latter half of the twentieth century. Texas Tech University Press's Modern Southeast Asia Series, of which this work is one of the first two volumes, is intended to facilitate an open dialogue about the Vietnam War and its lessons, with contributions reflecting all points of view.

Though I have never met him, for the past three decades I have known Dr. Gerald C. Hickey through his important study of the Mekong Delta village of Khanh Hau, entitled *Village in Vietnam*. His systematic and authoritative study of that village's internal dynamics provided valuable insight into the very nature of Vietnamese villages throughout the Mekong Delta. It was an important source of understanding for many Americans who served in that region during the war, particularly those assigned duties as advisors to units of the South Vietnamese armed forces.

But *Village in Vietnam,* important though it was (and continues to be), actually was almost peripheral to Gerald Hickey's more important ethnographic studies of the mountain people of South Vietnam, more commonly known as the montagnards. Throughout the years 1956–73, Dr. Hickey systematically collected ethnographic data concerning these people, a truly oppressed minority under the government of the Republic of Vietnam, whose fate it was to be equally oppressed under subsequent Communist rule. As he collected his field research, Hickey grew to be *the* recognized authority on the plight of the montagnards. He also became their advocate, tirelessly reminding the U.S. mission in Vietnam and the South Vietnamese government of their needs and, where possible, protecting their interests.

When Hickey arrived in Vietnam in 1956, he encountered an emerging country with a relative degree of peace seeking to establish a stable government. He was a witness to a great many of the important events of that tragic nation's short history. The nature of his work was field research; therefore, as the insurgency in South Vietnam grew to a full-fledged war, he often found himself on the front lines. He recounts an evening at the Nam Dong Special Forces Camp in July 1964 where he experienced a full-scale Communist attack that was repelled by the outnumbered defenders. Captain Roger Donlon, the special forces commanding officer of the camp, received the first Medal of Honor awarded in Vietnam for his conspicuous gallantry in that defense. Ever the true academic, Hickey remarks that at dawn after that terrible night he immediately searched for his field research notes, which, unfortunately, had been consumed by the fire that destroyed his quarters there.

Hickey was at Ban Me Thuot in January 1968 to conduct interviews for his ethnographic study, and thus was on the scene at the beginning of the Communist assaults we have come to know as the Tet Offensive. He was in Saigon for the "mini-Tet" assault in May 1968, and he saw further action during the Easter Offensive of 1972.

Throughout these trials, Dr. Hickey continued his research into the nature of the montagnard people. He also produced other important studies, including a 1967 report that suggested a way out of the war through "political accommodation" of the National Liberation Front, which he briefed to U.S. and Vietnamese leaders and published as a RAND study. Unfortunately, his "dovish" advice fell on unreceptive ears, as the United States fully backed the government of General Nguyen Van Thieu and thus discouraged the realization of any other than a military resolution of the impasse.

Gerald Hickey's story also includes a cautionary tale for future generations of academics. In 1971, Dr. Hickey sought to return to his alma mater, the University of Chicago, for a year as a visiting scholar, during which he hoped to write up the results of his research into the montagnards. His application was summarily rejected because of his employment in Vietnam by the RAND Corporation. Political correctness, already emerging as a weapon of the left, dictated that an academic who had in any way served the U.S. government in Vietnam could not be granted even the smallest of requests: an externally funded research assistantship. None of the faculty members who voted against Dr. Hickey, we are informed, even took the time to review his extensive record of publications. As Hickey himself comments, "And so the pall of vincible ignorance that long had hung over Vietnam now cast its shadow on the groves of academe."

Regrettably, in today's academia, which proclaims itself free of any prejudice against race, creed, or sexual orientation, there remains one permissible prejudice: it is acceptable, even fashionable to some in "the groves of academe," to be prejudiced against those who served our nation in Vietnam and, by extension, to be opposed to the men and women of this nation's military today. That is most unfortunate.

JAMES R. RECKNER
Texas Tech University

WINDOW ON A WAR

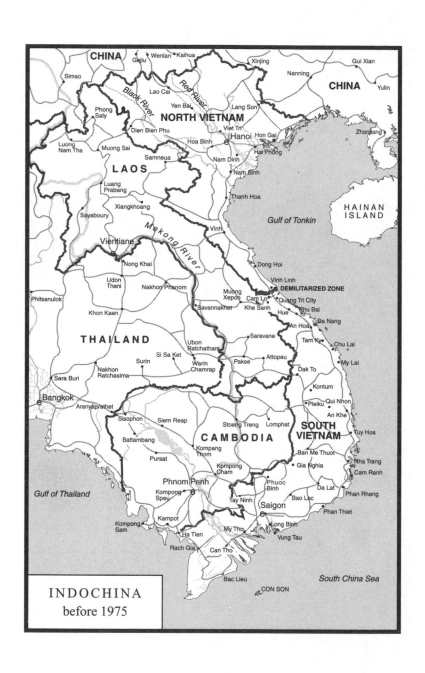

INDOCHINA
before 1975

INTRODUCTION

LITTLE DID I REALIZE, when on 16 March 1956 I arrived in Saigon, I would see through the window a world unlike any I had ever known or ever thought I would know. It was a world that would change dramatically between the day of my arrival and 1 April 1973 when I sailed from Saigon. And little did I realize that between 1956 and 1973 I would witness with an anthropologist's eye the unfolding fury of the Vietnam War, the longest war in American history.

My reason for coming to Vietnam in 1956 was straightforward. In 1951 while a graduate student in anthropology at the University of Chicago I had become interested in the ethnography of Vietnam. This interest was enhanced when in 1953–54 I spent a year in Paris doing library research on the ethnography of Indochina. Although my primary interest was Vietnamese culture, I soon found myself intrigued with works on ethnic groups of the northern and central highlands in Vietnam and Laos. My library research on the northern highlands continued at the University of Chicago where in 1954 I participated in a project on Laos.

The Paris research whetted my appetite for fieldwork—to see firsthand what I had been reading about. But in 1954 Indochina was regarded as a very unstable place so none of the foundations would entertain the idea of supporting ethnographic investigations there. Fortunately, I was offered a position with the new Michigan State University Group (MSUG) to join their staff in South Vietnam.

3

So in March 1956 it was exciting to be at last among the people I had read about, to be doing ethnography. In Saigon (which proved to be a fascinating ethnographic mixture of East and West), on my own time I continued library research at the Société des Etudes Indochinoise in the National Museum, and I soon had the opportunity to interview refugee northern highland leaders from Tai-speaking groups. This research and a field trip to northern Laos later in 1956 provided the basis for my Ph.D. dissertation on historical cultural contact among three groups—the northern Vietnamese, the Tho (also called Tay), and the Black Tai (now called Tai Dam).

What I had not anticipated when I arrived was that I would have a unique ethnographic experience in seeing a new state rise from an old culture. The year 1956 was memorable for a variety of reasons. It was the first year of peace for Vietnam since the beginning of World War II. It also was the first year of independence with President Ngo Dinh Diem's 26 October 1955 establishment of the Republic of Vietnam (better known as South Vietnam). These conditions generated a good deal of elation, excitement, and nationalistic fervor. Confident of the future, the South Vietnamese worked hard and invested in their new nation. They were helped by foreign aid, particularly that supplied by the Americans. Hundreds of thousands of Vietnamese from the north moved south to escape Communist rule and build a new life. Young well-educated Vietnamese returned from France and the United States eager to help South Vietnam take its place among the newly emerging Southeast Asian states in this post-colonial period.

American-Vietnamese relations in 1956 were in many respects at their best. In a setting of peace, Americans and Vietnamese cooperated in coping with the many challenges facing the new nation. Such cooperation was to some extent easy because at first the challenges arose from immediate national needs and contingencies. But unfortunately such cooperation did not eventually lead to any real mutual understanding. This became apparent when the challenge of defining and shaping the new Saigon government arose. The Americans wanted South Vietnam to be a democracy, but the Vietnamese had never known democracy in the American sense. It was an alien concept. Still, strangely enough, it never became an issue of debate between American and Vietnamese leaders. Only a handful of nationalist Vietnamese intellectuals would openly question what "democracy" would be in terms of their history and culture.

Nationalism burns luminously in the Vietnamese soul, a constant theme throughout their history. Nationalism shapes the Vietnamese view of the world and it fuels the forces that in their political arena have through time variously risen, accommodated, fought, fused, splintered, metamorphosed, and fallen. Nationalism provided the spirit for political movements that strove for Vietnamese independence. By 1956, however, it had taken on different shadings in the Vietnam divided by the 1954 Geneva Agreements. In North Vietnam the Viet Minh movement emerged dominant, so by 1956, Vietnamese nationalism had lost its identity as Ho Chi Minh orchestrated it with Marxism to define the whole society. In South Vietnam, post-1954 nationalism still expressed itself in various political movements such as the Viet Nam Quoc Dan Dang, Dai Viet, and Tan Dai Viet parties as well as in Diem's National Revolutionary Party. But none emerged dominant and so by 1956, nationalism in the south was a diffuse, unharnessed force, but nonetheless a force.

Unfortunately, Vietnamese nationalism was never the focus of American leaders in Saigon or Washington. Causation for the American failure in Vietnam will long be discussed and debated, but two causes stand out. One was vincible ignorance—specifically ignorance of Vietnamese nationalism—while the other was the American strategy of making military decisions without regard for their impact on South Vietnamese society.

Vincible ignorance of Vietnamese nationalism could have been overcome through knowledge—learning in the most rudimentary way about Vietnamese culture and history. It never happened because decision-makers in Washington and American leaders in Saigon did not care about Vietnamese nationalism. One result was they tended to project their own American values about political behavior when adjudging Vietnamese leaders' conduct.

In a 1972 discussion about that period, Nguyen Ngoc Tho, who had served as vice president, said none of the American leaders in Saigon or Washington had gained any understanding of President Ngo Dinh Diem or his younger brother and adviser, Ngo Dinh Nhu. On the other hand, he added, President Diem and Nhu never understood any of the American leaders.

In many respects it was inevitable. Ngo Dinh Diem was educated in Hue as one of the last of the Confucian literati. Although he had traveled abroad and spent time in the United States, Diem remained solidly traditional Vietnamese in outlook. There was nothing in this outlook to prepare him to understand American leaders. By the same token there was nothing in the background of American leaders to prepare them to understand Diem.

To Americans, Ngo Dinh Nhu was equally enigmatic. Educated in France, he was steeped in French scholasticism. Drawing on writings of philosopher Jacques Maritain and Emmanuel Mounier, Nhu formulated "personalism," which he attempted unsuccessfully to introduce as a philosophical force in the Diem administration. For the Americans personalism was a murky concept they would never understand any more than they would understand Nhu, but then, Nhu would never understand Americans.

This lack of mutual understanding became increasingly crucial during the 1956–61 period. As the flush of newly found independence began to wane in 1957, rumblings of discontent with Ngo Dinh Diem's administration became more audible.

In Saigon, ever-increasing rumblings arose from political and intellectual circles. Foreign observers attributed this to discontent with Diem's policies and programs and what they considered his authoritarian approach to governing. But from an ethnographic point of view there was a deeper cause that sprang from the Taoist roots of Vietnamese culture. I had become aware that although the Chinese great tradition had brought to Vietnam an amalgam of Taoism, Buddhism, and Confucianism, it was Taoism that proved the strongest influence. Chinese Taoism was transformed as it was overlaid on the Vietnamese Spirit Cult that has its roots in the primordial past. Taoists value the natural, instinctive, primitive qualities or virtues as opposed to those arising from social sanction and education. For Taoists, artificial institutions such as government are wrong, so the Vietnamese view government with an anarchistic eye—they tend to be antigovernment.

The rumblings were not restricted to Saigon. Some arose in rural areas as a result of the multicultural character of the new state. For the first time the Saigon government had to deal with "ethnic minorities" such as the people of the central highlands. These highlanders are Malayopolynesian– and Mon Khmer–speaking people, very different physically and culturally from the Vietnamese. For the Vietnamese they were strangers who were very primitive (dark skinned, scantily clothed, and living in the mountains, a region the Vietnamese dreaded as the abode of evil spirits). The Vietnamese called them *mọi* ("savages" or "slaves").

During my Paris research my ethnographic blood stirred as I read descriptions about the highlanders' fascinating way of life. But reality was overwhelming. From the moment of my 1956 arrival in Ban Me Thuot I was constantly intrigued by the aura of mystery cloaking the mountain country like its persistent mists. Nature, vast, complex, and harboring unimagined secrets, seemed to envelop the mountain people. Their eyes, ears, and senses of smell and taste told them things lost on those whose natural instincts have been dulled by the conceits of "civilization."

Here in their green milieu of forested mountains, sweeping, undulating plateaus, and valleys through which brown rivers flowed, each ethnic group over time had worked out its adaptation to nature and shaped its society so that its members could survive, reproduce, and readapt to whatever changes man, nature, and cosmic forces might impinge upon it. This evolutionary process had resulted in some social-structural differences, but at the same time, adaptation to the mountain country had created among them physical and ideational bonds that had given rise to a common culture, a highlander world.

But the 1957 policies and programs of the Ngo Dinh Diem government threatened to change everything.

As was the case with many newly independent states in post–World War II Southeast Asia, one of the major challenges in South Vietnam was to achieve national integration of the many and varied ethnolinguistic groups. There was a notion, prevalent in many capitals at the time, that in order to achieve this, ties to kin groups, villages, religious sects, and ethnic groups (particularly ethnic minorities) must be replaced by loyalty to the state. Mixing this notion with Vietnamese chauvinism and ethnocentricism, Diem settled on a policy of forcibly assimilating the ethnic minorities (highlanders, Cham, Khmer, and Chinese) into the Vietnamese cultural sphere.

When I encountered young well-educated highland leaders I was struck by how their strong spirit of ethnonationalism was fueling the spread of a pan-highlander ethnic identity (and would soon express itself in organized movements). I found myself sympathizing with their plight as minority people whom the Vietnamese tended to regard as inferior. I also sympathized with their resentment of Diem's efforts at forced assimilation.

With this, the highlanders became for me more than subjects of ethnographic research. Presenting their views in Saigon, I advocated opening communication between the government and highland leaders that could result in a modification of government policy, an accommodation to the highlanders' desire to retain their ethnic identity. Such an approach would, I thought, avoid a worsening conflict and realize government-highlander mutual support in building the new state. My views, however, were ignored or negated and I was discouraged from further work in the central highlands.

In reaction to Diem assimilation policy, ethnonationalist movements formed among the Cham and Khmer Krom. And Chinese resentment of forced assimilation led to a 1957 economic crisis.

But while these rumblings were disturbing, the emergence of Communist dissidence in the late 1950s was more ominous and threatening.

During 1958 and 1959 I was part of a three-man MSUG team that conducted social/economic research in the Mekong River delta village of Khanh Hau. We soon found the Saigon stereotype of plodding, rude farmers who plant the same rice every year was completely erroneous. The villagers were not bumpkins—they were people with more dignity and appreciation of Vietnamese traditions than most Saigon folk. They also were incredibly resourceful, carefully planning new crops on the basis of the market demands and prices and available resources.

I found it constantly fascinating how Taoism mixed with the Spirit Cult to shape the villagers' cosmological view and to play a vital part in villagers' daily lives and in formal religious institutions. Visits to the former royal capital of Hue also revealed the Taoism–Spirit Cult mixture in the high culture of the citadel, heart of the Vietnamese kingdom. The origin of the Spirit Cult was unknown, and my research on it led me into the mysterious depth of "Vietnamese-ness," that is, the heart, the veiled essence of Vietnamese culture. Since linguists have concluded that the Vietnamese language is of the Austroasiatic stock and very likely of the Mon-Khmer family, spirit cults among Mon Khmer–speaking highlanders took on special significance, raising questions about primordial Vietnamese-highlander links.

During the village study we witnessed the advent in the Mekong River delta of Communist dissidence which by the end of the 1950s had intensified throughout South Vietnam. Then in December 1960, the Communists established the National Liberation Front (NLF) in South Vietnam dedicated to overthrowing the Diem government by an armed revolutionary struggle. The NLF was touted as a movement independent of Hanoi so as to create the fiction that the emerging struggle in the South was internal, a civil war.

The existence of the NLF was made public at the end of January 1961. On 28 January 1961, soon after his inauguration, President Kennedy, rising to the Communist challenge, signed the formal counterinsurgency plan. Among other things, the plan called for increased support of the Army of the Republic of Vietnam (ARVN). With this, the Americans were now irreversibly moving down the path of military involvement. Communist "guerillas" became Communist "insurgents," and with insurgency the golden afternoon of the late-1950s vanished.

Early in 1962 while I was a research associate at Yale University teaching and writing my village materials, the RAND Corporation asked me to return to Vietnam briefly with John Donnell, a colleague from the 1950s, in order to learn from highland leaders what they expected of the government. We arrived in Saigon but were blocked from going into the mountain country by a CIA team organizing a highlander village defense (an effort that would result in American military involvement in the highlands with the U.S. Special Forces program). John and I elected to research the newly launched Strategic Hamlet Program that sought to consolidate governmental authority in pacified areas through a defense system and administrative reorganization at the hamlet level.

In the strange and often menacing setting of insurgency, John and I visited a number of villages involved in the program to interview residents and record their views. We found that by and large the strategic hamlets had the potential of bringing security to the rural population, affording an opportunity for the government to organize projects that would demonstrate its concern for the villagers and their problems. But, we noted with examples, when implementation of the program imposed economic and social burdens it had the opposite effect. The sponsoring Department of Defense officials who wanted to attach a rebuttal to our final report considered our findings too negative. But RAND, thanks to its founder, Frank Collbohm, refused on the grounds that with RAND's policy of independence, such a procedure would be an infringement on its right to publish and disseminate its research findings. Rather than heed what we had to say, the Department of Defense had tried to negate our findings just as my findings on the highland situation in 1957 had been negated. As it turned out, the strategic hamlet program was a failure.

By late 1962 American-Vietnamese relations had become very strained.

At the same time, the Communists expanded their struggle against the Diem government and the security situation in South Vietnam deteriorated. The Americans responded with increased military presence. According to former Vice President Nguyen Ngoc Tho, Diem and Nhu began to have grave misgivings about American intentions. Fear that the Americans were going to turn South Vietnam into a battlefield prompted Diem and Nhu to initiate clandestine overtures to the NLF to work out a political accommodation, call a cease-fire, and end the conflict.

Meanwhile, Buddhist rumblings against the Diem government erupted into an armed struggle. At the same time, aware of the Ngo brothers' accommodation with the Viet Cong, certain American leaders in Washington and Saigon decided the brothers had to be removed, so they conceived a plot with Vietnamese generals. The anti-Diem outcries of the international (mostly American) media and the August 1963 government-ordered raids on the Buddhist pagodas played into the hands of the plotters. With President Diem now cast as a villain, the scene was set for him to be overthrown, which he was on 1 November 1963. During the coup d'état, President Diem and his brother Nhu were murdered. Had they lived the Vietnam War might well have been averted.

It is ironic and revealing that Ngo Dinh Diem was the last nationalist leader the Americans supported as president of the Republic of Vietnam.

So in the post-1963 period there unfolded a sad drama in which American and Vietnamese players acted from separate scripts, never communicating and eyeing one another with a mixture of puzzlement and suspicion.

My primary motive in returning to Vietnam in January 1964 with the RAND Corporation was to work again with the highland people both as an ethnographer and as a friend interested in their efforts to preserve their ethnic identity and way of life. I was not surprised to find the highland leaders more deeply involved in ethnonationalistic activities. In September 1964 a new movement organized by highlanders and Cambodians was responsible for mutinies in five Special Forces camps (where twelve-man teams of U.S. Special Forces personnel were stationed). The revolt brought to the mountain country a new era of armed dissidence and at the same time made highlander ethnonationalism a force to be reckoned with in Saigon and Washington. Again I was an advocate of accommodation in playing the role of intermediary between highland leaders and the American mission and to some extent the Saigon government.

Working closely with highland leaders proved to be a fascinating ethnographic experience. They were part of a leadership that had been evolving since the late nineteenth century. It had its roots in the traditional elite centered in chiefs whom the French recognized as intermediaries with local populations. During the Indochina War, in an attempt to win greater support among highlanders, the French established the Collège Sabatier in Ban Me Thuot and provided scholarships to the prestigious Lycée Yersin in Dalat (where Norodom Sihanouk and Emperor Bao Dai had studied). Most of those who benefited were of the elite families, and strong bonds were formed. Although intermarriage among elite families of different ethnic groups was already taking place, these new friendships resulted in an increased number of such marriages. The leadership kin networks I was recording began to expand and it was inevitable that they would link together, producing one vast network extending over a wide territory and incorporating elite families of the major highland groups.

My field research took me to the remote U.S. Special Forces camp called Nam Dong, located in the Katu country (where I had done field research in 1957). There, on 6 July 1964 a force of nine hundred crack Communist troops (supported by emplacements of mortars and 57-mm recoilless rifles) assaulted the small post with its 350 defenders (including an A-Team of twelve Americans and an Australian warrant officer). I found myself facing death for the better part of the night as the unrestrained violence of battle crashed around me. Morning light was rendered stark as it shone on the aftermath of battle with its twisted bodies, blood, wounds, lingering explosions, shooting, fires, black smoke, and eyes that still reflected the nightmare.

The window that had thus far opened on a beautiful, intriguing but increasingly troubled land became a window on a war.

The strange and, in many respects, unique character of the Vietnam War is illustrated by the fact that, unlike most wars in modern history, it had no starting date. There was the insurgency of the early 1960s, which, during the 1965–66 period when American forces became actively involved, became "the war in Vietnam." Soon, however, at some indeterminate time when the effects of the war began to be felt in the United States, everyone began calling it "the Vietnam War." It was the most controversial and the longest war in American history.

Regardless of what the conflict was called, as North Vietnamese forces became involved and American forces increased, it began to exact a heavy toll throughout Vietnam, particularly in the central highlands where the fiercest fighting took place.

As the war swept into the mountain country like a vicious typhoon, the highlanders found themselves "a people in between." The sounds of violence, the appearance of refugees on the roads, and burning villages all signaled the end to the last traces of highland tranquility I had found in 1956.

By the end of May 1965 the U.S. forces in Vietnam surpassed 50,000 and on 18 June the first B-52 raids occurred in the terrace region northeast of Saigon. In September 1965 the U.S. 1st Cavalry Division (Airmobile) arrived at An Khe in the Bahnar country, and the following month in the Jarai country of western Pleiku it engaged North Vietnamese troops in the "battle of Ia Drang Valley." With 1966, other American units such as the 25th Infantry Division and the 101st Airborne Division conducted operations in the highlands, and the U.S. 4th Infantry Division established a large headquarters in Pleiku. By mid June 1967 the American military strength in South Vietnam reached 450,000 while intelligence estimates placed Communist forces at 260,000 including more than 50,000 North Vietnamese. The military use of herbicides, which had begun in 1962, reached a peak in 1966. Some 12 million gallons of herbicide were used throughout Vietnam, many of them in the central highlands.

If American vincible ignorance of Vietnamese nationalism contributed heavily to the advent of the war, the American strategy of making military decisions without regard for their impact on South Vietnamese society boded badly for the outcome of the war. American planners and decision-makers in Washington and Saigon failed to understand that the social, political, economic, religious, and military aspects of Vietnamese society were intrinsically interrelated and had to be understood that way. A decision regarding one aspect had to be based on its effect, its impact, on all of the other aspects. Making military decisions without considering what effects they would have on the society as a whole resulted in ever-spreading disruption that weakened social order and structure, rendering the people war-weary. Through it all, the enduring theme of American-conceived pacification programs was to "win the hearts and minds of the people." Yet the decision-makers (in their wood-paneled offices far removed from the reality of the war) totally ignored the increasingly harmful effects of their war strategy on the people of South Vietnam. They never asked what the war was doing to the hearts and minds of the Vietnamese people. (At a briefing I gave in Washington at the Pentagon, I was making this point and used the word "compassion," which drew a collective wince.) To make matters worse, administrations changed, politicians came and went as did civilian officials, military commanders, and the entire staffs under them. "Experts" deplaned, made pronouncements, and enplaned. New people proposed new strategies and programs, most of which, with different labels, had been tried in the past unsuccessfully.

Some Americans leading the pacification program clung to the misguided notion that generating refugees was a plus for the government, when in fact the increasing number of refugees was an indication of social disruption. Equally ill advised were forced relocations of populations for military purposes (an attempt to create front lines in a war without front lines). The Communists on their part mounted cruel night assaults on villages, breaching weak defenses within minutes and using grenades (and in one case flamethrowers) against the elderly, women, and children huddled in bunkers. Communists shot people working in the fields, forcibly recruited young highlanders, wantonly ambushed buses and private automobiles, and indiscriminately shelled highland towns.

But war is not just a matter of opposing forces engaged in killing and destroying. It sets off a vast array of changes that spread and deepen as the conflict intensifies.

The vast influx of American troops in the highlands, for example, brought changes to many of the highland towns, particularly Pleiku. The tiny settlement I had seen in 1956 by 1966 had a population estimated at 50,000, an upland "boom town," a dismal collection of Vietnamese shacks and flimsy shops. The main part of Pleiku had been transformed into a "G.I. town" with endless bars, snack shops, and steam baths (another designation for brothels). Ironically the American presence also brought huge piles of garbage through which bands of highlanders picked, carrying off in their backbaskets what they could use.

By 1966, it was all too apparent that the fears of Ngo Dinh Diem and his brother Nhu that South Vietnam might be turned into a battlefield were being realized.

Was there any way to prevent the war from continuing? This was a subject I found myself deeply probing with Vietnamese friends, Ton That Tien, Dang Duc Khoi, and Tran Nhu Trang. Totally unaware of the Diem-Nhu accommodation, we agreed that the path to peace lay within the Vietnamese cultural concept of accommodation. Since the war was a political conflict, there would have to be a process of political accommodation by Saigon leaders with the existing nationalist political parties and movements, including those of the religious groups such as the Buddhists, Catholics, Cao Daists as well as those among the minorities—highlanders, Cham, and Khmer Krom, none of whom wanted to be under Communist rule. They would be drawn into a pro-peace coalition government that would include the NLF. It would declare a cease-fire and rely upon international pressure to force the North Vietnamese and Americans to withdraw their troops. Briefings in Washington on this approach elicited incredulity that I would suggest such a thing when our military efforts were going so well. My RAND publication on accommodation (in October 1967), which received wide distribution, went unnoticed.

And so the Vietnam War raged on. It not only raged on, the war also steadily intensified and reached a peak of violence with the early 1968 Communist Tet Offensive which drew the urban areas into the vortex. With this horrendous event the war now enveloped the entire society of South Vietnam. Willingly or unwillingly, everyone participated.

I was in Ban Me Thuot on 30 January when Communist forces attacked the city. Again I found myself in the fury of battle reminiscent of Nam Dong. But at Nam Dong the fighting ended with dawn while the Tet fighting continued in Ban Me Thuot for days and followed me to Nhatrang and Saigon.

Outside of Vietnam, two important events occurred at this time. On 31 March 1968, President Johnson announced that he would not run as a presidential candidate in the November elections. He also called for a partial halt in the bombing of North Vietnam to induce the North Vietnamese to agree to negotiations. On 3 April, the North Vietnamese accepted President Johnson's invitation to establish direct negotiations. This led to the beginning of the Paris Peace Talks on 13 May 1968.

Despite the convening of the Paris Peace Talks, in the confused post-Tet period the American strategy to gain support for the Saigon government in rural South Vietnam continued to be through pacification programs, none of which had thus far been successful. I felt this was because of the American failure to recognize (or admit) that the war basically was political and could only be resolved in political terms within the context of South Vietnam. With the Paris Peace Talks, it seemed to me inevitable that political aspects of the conflict would become a subject of discussion in the negotiations. So, my accommodation approach might become a solution worth considering. I revised and updated the original RAND report.

But to American leaders in Saigon the word "accommodation" carried the connotation of "giving in." Besides, such a risky approach was now considered unnecessary because the solution of the war for Washington and the Mission in Saigon was Vietnamization (which called for systematic withdrawal of U.S. forces while turning over more and more fighting to the South Vietnamese government and army) and the Accelerated Pacification Campaign which they erroneously considered successful. One result was unqualified American support of President Thieu, which meant a continuation of the war. And it also meant that with our disregard for Vietnamese nationalism, we would allow Thieu to suppress systematically nationalist leaders and movements.

One very hopeful development at this time was the 15 June 1971 appointment of Nay Luett as minister for the Ministry for Development of Ethnic Minorities (MDEM). This remarkable man brought new life to the ministry as he pushed for programs to enable the highland people to survive the wartime disruption and preserve highlander ethnic identity. But on 31 March 1972 the Communists launched an offensive that was to have devastating effects in the highlands. In a matter of weeks, many of the highland programs in education, village health, and agricultural extension collapsed when whole ethnic groups fled villages and even their own territories. For months, refugee relief became my primary activity.

By 1972 the American military presence in the highlands had to all intents and purposes ended. Neither the Department of Defense nor RAND was interested in any highland research, and I resisted becoming involved in research for pacification programs. Then I agreed to be part of the National Academy of Science's study of the effects of herbicides in Vietnam. Conducting interviews among highlanders who had been sprayed, I was shocked at the deadly effects of Agent Orange with its dioxin component. Small children developed skin rashes and died, and adults fell ill with abdominal cramps, vomiting, diarrhea, dizziness, and skin rashes. Many domestic animals and wild animals in nearby forests died. Fish with discolored gills floated to the surface of rivers and streams. Crops in fields and gardens wilted and died. In the National Academy of Science President's letter accompanying the Washington distribution of the final report, my findings were deprecated as "Montagnard tales" and "second hand." And so again my findings were negated, but subsequently the deadly effects of Agent Orange on Vietnamese civilians and American military personnel were acknowledged.

When the final herbicide interviews were completed I left the highlands with a deep sadness. The North Vietnamese, South Vietnamese, Viet Cong, and Americans had brought vast death and destruction to the mountain country. At least 200,000 highlanders had died and eighty-five percent of their villages had either been abandoned or destroyed. The ethnolinguistic maps of 1956 were now hopelessly out of date. The Americans, who had used the highlanders, were abandoning them to a dark future. Bishop Seitz had been all too accurate when, in February 1973, he declared to me that the highlanders were "between zero and infinity."

Meanwhile, because my being in Vietnam with RAND had earned me the status of a pariah among many of my academic colleagues, I found myself isolated until a very welcome invitation came from Cornell University professors A. Thomas Kirsch and George McT. Kahin to spend a year in Ithaca as visiting associate professor of Indochinese Studies in the Southeast Asia Program and the Department of Anthropology.

On 16 March 1956 I had seen through the window an intriguing and beautiful country, enjoying peace and hope, but on 1 April 1973 when I sailed from Saigon, it had become a window on a country ravaged by war.

One

A BREATH OF PEACE AND HOPE

THE WORD "EXOTIC" to describe something excitingly strange or
having the appeal of the unknown with connotations of the mysterious,
romantic, picturesque, or glamorous captures the Indochina of 1956. It was
a part of Asia relatively unknown to Americans, a faraway place that at best
stirred vague ideas of India or China. And well it might, because in this
corner of Asia the Chinese great tradition molded the society of the Vietnamese while Indian influences diffusing eastward brought civilization to
the Cambodians and Lao.

I first became interested in Vietnam when in 1951 I met a group of Vietnamese students at Crossroads House near the University of Chicago. The
students, most of whom were Buddhists, had come to the United States on
university scholarships arranged by Father Emmanuel Jacques, a Belgian
priest who had taught in Vietnam for many years. They formed the Vietnamese Students' Association and looked forward to using their training
back home in a new Vietnam. For Professor Fred Eggan's graduate seminar
on Southeast Asia I prepared a paper on the Vietnamese kinship system
using genealogies supplied by the Crossroads students. Then in 1953 I had

the good fortune to obtain through my colleagues, Sally Cassidy and Paule (Pauty) Verdet, a fellowship from the Groom Foundation to do library research in Paris on the ethnology of Indochina. It was a fascinating task and an enlightening one, too, in revealing the cultural/linguistic mosaic of that region. Most of the library materials dealt with cultures and histories of the lowland Cambodians, Vietnamese, and Lao, but there also were works on the vast variety of lesser-known people who inhabited the mountains rising above the deltas, plains, and river valleys. I attended lectures by Claude Levi-Strauss and Georges Condominas. In Paris, Madeleine Tainturier arranged for me to meet some remarkable people such as the philosopher Henri de Lubac and Joseph Folliet. I also found a friend in Romeo Le Blanc who later would be active in Canadian politics and be named governor general of Canada. A fellow University of Chicago student at the Fondation des Etats Unis was Allan Bloom, who in 1987 would publish the brilliant and controversial *The Closing of the American Mind.* The fellowship also enabled me to spend a term in 1954 sampling British anthropology at the London School of Economics.

On returning to the University of Chicago in 1954 I assumed the role of editor for preparation of a monograph on Laos. Under a contract with Human Relations Area Files this project was directed by Professors Norton Ginsburg and Fred Eggan.[1] This prompted me to take Ginsburg's course in economic geography of Southeast Asia and another course on cartography, which proved very useful in my Indochina research.

The Paris research stimulated a deep desire to do field work—to see and study what I had been reading about. But in 1954 Indochina was regarded as a very unstable place so none of the foundations would entertain the idea of supporting ethnographic investigations there. Fortunately, through the intercession of my friend, Father Jacques, I was offered a position with the Michigan State University Group (MSUG). Wesley Fishel, the group's leader, was a close friend of Ngo Dinh Diem, who in October 1955 had become president and proclaimed the Republic of Vietnam, better known as South Vietnam. Mr. Fishel, an intelligent and kind man, had organized the university group on a contract with the U.S. International Cooperation Agency, later called the Agency for International Development (AID), to help the new Republic of Vietnam become a modern state. In Vietnam, MSUG worked closely with AID's United States Operations Mission (USOM). MSUG had a public administration section that conducted research on government ministries to formulate recommendations for improving their efficiency. Some professors also taught at the National Institute of Administration. In addition, there were advisers from Michigan State University's School of Police Administration to help the Saigon government in its public safety efforts. The police advisory section included a small group of CIA personnel who were advising the Saigon government in organizing its version of the FBI. The presence of CIA advisers would later be cited as proof that the MSUG was a CIA front. This was not true.

Early in 1956 I attended orientation sessions for new staff members at the Michigan State University campus in East Lansing. The coordinator for the Vietnam project was Stanley Sheinbaum, a friend from Paris days when he was a Fulbright Scholar. I began Vietnamese language studies with Ton That Tien, a scholar who later would hold a high position in the Diem government and subsequently gain a reputation as a writer on Vietnam. I also met Lynn and Jim Hendry who would soon join me in Vietnam with MSUG and remain close friends.

From New York I flew on a Pan Am stratocruiser (when the flight was delayed, Pan Am took the twenty passengers to Forest Hills Tennis Club for dinner, believe it or not). It was bliss to be back in Paris for a few days and see old friends at a gathering Madeleine Tainturier arranged in her Neuilly flat.

My first stop in Southeast Asia was Bangkok, which in 1956 was very beautiful and exotic. A tone was set en route from the airport at night along a road under thick trees with a wide canal to one side. Moored at the bank were large sampans and in the light of oil lamps women in sarongs moved gracefully as they went about serving evening meals to huddled figures seated on grass mats. The next morning a brazen sun glittered on the bustling Chao Phraya River and sparkled on Buddhist temples (whose roof bells tinkled in the wind) and royal palaces. Sunlight played on the yellow robes worn by Buddhist monks holding begging bowls while they walked in single file. Pedicab rides revealed shady streets lined with canals and wonderful rococo mansions, façades for poorer quarters with wood and thatch houses jammed together. Shops bulged with Thai and Burmese antiques, Thai silks and cottons, and pieces fashioned from celadon, brass, lacquered woods, and teak. Mixed aromas of Thai markets (which held a whole new universe of tropical fruits) dazzled the nose and eyes. The cool lawn in front of the Oriental Hotel facing the river provided a calm setting for cocktails—a respite to savor what the first days in Southeast Asia had brought.

Arriving on a Pan Am stratocruiser, I found Tan Son Nhut airport in Saigon sleepy in the dry-season heat with two Air Vietnam DC-3s parked in front of the small terminal building. Leaving the airport there were fields where cattle grazed and then a relatively short drive on rue de Gaulle under splendid flame trees into the center of the city.

Soon after my arrival in Saigon there were two incidents which Vietnamese interpreted as favorable omens. Peg and Dave Cole kindly provided lodging until I was given an apartment and in the freshness of the first morning I was just about to put on my white short-sleeve shirt when I found on the back of it a large gold scarablike beetle. The houseboy, delighted at this auspicious sign, carefully released the beetle in a flower bed. Then, two days later at a dinner party, as guests chatted at the table, the host's pet cat quietly dragged in a large, beautifully colored gecko lizard, which it placed between my feet. The maid serving dinner discovered it and became very excited at this omen of good luck. Later, I looked out at the garden before going to bed and thought to myself, "If this continues, I'll be overwhelmed by the exotic!"

But the exotic was soon counterbalanced by the prosaic office world of the MSUG public administration section office in an apartment building of faded elegance at the corner of Lagrandière and Catinat. More or less cooled by ceiling fans, the rooms were crowded, but rustling green tamarind trees outside the large open windows provided a balm. And we could take our iced-tea breaks down rue Catinat in the pleasant Café la Pagode where French and Vietnamese ladies came to buy pastries and petits fours. A few weeks after my arrival I was offered an apartment that none of the MSUG staff wanted. It was a fourth-floor walk-up one bedroom with a balcony in a French building behind the Saigon Hospital on Huynh Thuc Khang St. which curved from the traffic circle in front of the central market to Boulevard Charner. My friend, the writer Nguyen Tu, described it as a "back street near the market." There was no telephone. The bathroom had old fixtures and an electric water heater. The narrow kitchen had a small sink and one cold-water tap. Bottled gas fueled the two-burner stove. All drinking water had to be boiled and fresh vegetables were immersed in chlorine before being served. Servants had been trained by the French so even in archaic kitchens they could prepare good French and Vietnamese dishes.

I was very happy to have for the first time my own apartment and immediately I set about arranging office space where in my free time I could work on my ethnographic materials collected in Paris and Chicago. It was then that I began to formulate a study of historical cultural contact among the northern Vietnamese and upland Tai-speaking Tho and Black Tai.

Saigon itself proved to be a fascinating ethnographic mix of East and West. In 1956 the city still strongly reflected French colonial urban planning and Mediterranean influence with vistas of walled villas set in lush gardens and attractive apartment buildings. The rue de Gaulle flame trees signaled careful planning by the French forestry service to bring beauty and shade to each street in the city with an astonishing array of tropical trees (even rubber trees).[2] Under lacy tamarind trees, rue Catinat (streets and boulevards were still called by their French names despite the new Vietnamese names), the main street of Saigon, ran from the rose-brick Romanesque Cathedral of Our Lady to the Saigon River. This attractive street had a variety of shops and sidewalk cafés in front of bars and restaurants. It boasted two venerable hotels, the Continental Palace Hotel, sharing the square with the National Assembly a former opera house, and the Saigon Palace. The newer Hotel Majestic's terrace afforded a wonderful view of life on the Saigon River and the restaurant on the top floor looked down on unexpected paddy fields across the river. As night fell, rue Catinat filled with pedicabs, which everyone called cyclo-pousses, little yellow-and-blue quatre-chevaux Renault taxis, somber black Citroëns, and motor scooters. At Boulevard Bonard, traffic swirled around the fountain in front of the brightly lit Grands Magasins Charner and Auto Hall Bainier near the rococo Hotel de Ville, the City Hall.

French air force pilots, paratroopers in red berets, and Legionnaires, reminders of the Indochina War, strolled down rue Catinat. Legionnaires seemed to favor the London Bar next to the Cinéma Majestic while air force pilots crowded the Croix du Sud café and nightclub. A reminder of the transitional political character was the presence on the Hotel Continental Palace's terrace of the American Military Assistance Advisory Group (MAAG) officers from the Bachelor Officers' Quarters in the nearby Brink Hotel.

French clubs—the Cercle Sportif, Club Nautique, and Boule Gauloise—were the social centers of Saigon society. Restaurants such as Aterbea, l'Amiral, La Paix, Le Paris, Paprika, and Guillaume Tell served excellent French food while lighter fare could be had at cafés Brodard,

Givral, and La Pagode. On rue Catinat, the large Thai Thach grocery store had high shelves filled with imported canned goods, wines, liquors, and brandies and an impressive refrigerated counter displaying hams, sausages, patés, and cheeses. Thai Thach catered to the French as did the smaller Au Petit Saint-Antoine which had a blackboard in front announcing the arrival by Air France of lamb, veal, artichokes, and cheeses. Cavernous Librarie A. Portail carried mostly French books, magazines, and newspapers from Paris along with the local *Journal d'Extrême-Orient* and *Nouvelles de Dimanche.* The Imprimerie d'Extrême-Orient supplied Portail with two scholarly journals, René de Berval's *France-Asie* and the *Bulletin des Etudes Indochinoises* issued by the Société des Etudes Indochinoises located in the library at the National Museum in the Botanical Garden.

Away from the world of boulevards, villas, and attractive apartment buildings were working-class Vietnamese quarters whose populations were swollen by newly arrived refugees from North Vietnam. Unplanned, these quarters were lively jumbles of small wooden houses and shops lining narrow winding lanes. Along waterways such as the Arroyo Chinois as well as under docks and bridges were jerry-built refugee shacks of scavenged wood and palm fronds. Since houses were small, the large families spilled into the lanes where children played, old folks chatted, women nursed babies and prepared evening meals over braziers.

Vastly different from Saigon was Cholon, the twin Chinese city, whose pagodas, temples, associations, and restaurants reflected the population mix of Cantonese, the dominant group, and people of Hakka, Swatow, and Fukien origin. Cholon was a place of narrow bustling streets bordered by masonry shop-houses with balconies and tile roofs. Unlike Saigon's brightly lit, clinical pharmacies, those in Cholon were somber with tall hardwood cabinets whose drawers were filled with dried pungent medical herbs, roots, and barks along with highly prized bones and whiskers of tigers bagged in the central highlands. Groceries had marble counters and chopping blocks over which hung cooked ducks and cuts of pork all lacquered with sauces. Shops selling religious accoutrement were dazzles of red and gold in depictions of deities, altars of varying sizes, and packages of joss and paper money for offerings. One could dine in restaurants ranging from small steamy noodle shops to grander places identified by garish neon signs in Chinese characters and filled with large round tables to accommodate extended families and fraternities of businessmen. Older restaurants were the Arc en Ciel, which still had an antigrenade wire grill (a leftover from the Indochina War) around its terrace, and the Pavillon de Jade with its vast rooms and potted palms. Cholon hotels had a racy fluorescence not found in big Saigon hotels. Some had restaurants in their courtyards where the diners could hear the click of mah-jongg tiles from upstairs game rooms.

Cholon still held vestiges of the turbulent 1954–55 events when Ngo Dinh Diem confronted forces trying to topple him as prime minister. These forces included the reformed Buddhist Hoa Hao and syncretic Cao Daists, both relatively new religious movements with territorial enclaves and private armies. More fearsome were the Binh Xuyen, a band of river pirates who developed a Mafia-like organization that controlled gambling, narcotics, and vice as well as the police and security forces in Saigon. Binh Xuyen leader Bay Vien ran the Grand Monde, a huge gambling casino, and the Hall of Mirrors, Asia's largest brothel. Diem won over Hoa Hao and Cao Daist leaders and in April 1955 his forces clashed with the Binh Xuyen at the Y Bridge near Bay Vien's headquarters, which was destroyed. His enemies vanquished, Diem went on to win the 23 October 1955 national elections and proclaim the Republic of Vietnam. In 1956 the famous Grand Monde stood empty but a few years later its ballroom's bright lights shone again for the Marine Ball given by the U.S. Marine Guards from the American embassy.

Unlike larger and more spread-out cities such as Bangkok, everyone in Saigon lived in relative proximity. This, combined with Saigon's tropical charm, provided for an international society a lively and interesting loose-knit amalgam of varied groups. It did not, however, include many in the sizeable French community dominated as it was by colonials—notably planters and businessmen. They moved in their own long-established circles. Some of them regarded the Americans as intruders and complained that Americans were too nice to drivers and too easy with servants, giving them Sundays off. Frenchified Vietnamese added that the Americans were not as cultured as the French. On the other hand anti-French sentiment was alive among some Americans who felt the French had exploited Indochina for their own ends and had not prepared the people of the colonies for independence. Males with MSUG were advised not to wear walking shorts in downtown Saigon for fear of being identified as French. The largest non-French group was of people posted at foreign embassies who set a tone with an endless round of dinners, luncheons, cocktail parties, and official receptions to which men invariably wore white suits while women's dress varied with nationality.

All embassies had under their umbrellas groups associated with economic, technical, or military aid programs, and relief organizations. While people in these groups were invited to national receptions, they usually formed their own social sets. Most MSUG folks, for example, socialized among themselves and with USOM staff families. With the exception of high-ranking officers the American military advisory group personnel stayed to themselves, but the military opened its clubs to American civilians for dining and seeing occasional movies.

Single people tended to be relatively flexible with open-ended social sets allowing them to move with ease into any of the other groups. Since I did not hold a high-ranking position with the MSUG I fortunately was not expected to attend "official" dinners, cocktail parties, and receptions. When not on field trips, I divided my free time between work on my dissertation and friends.

It was good to find in Vietnam some Vietnamese I had met at Crossroads House in Chicago. I had them to dinner several times and was struck by their intense nationalism and determination to help build South Vietnam into a free and thriving nation.

In 1956, for many Vietnamese the Americans possessed a certain magic. President Diem believed that the MSUG was going to work wonders. One result was if the group wanted to do an administrative study, all doors were open. We were free to interview anybody in any ministry.

I happily accepted the assignment of doing field research on provincial services of Saigon ministries being studied, and this took me mostly by road all over South Vietnam. Field research revealed first hand the intriguing ethnic mosaic I had found in my Paris library research. The Vietnamese dominated the mosaic. But their thousand-year "advance southward" which took them from the Red River delta in the north along the coastal plain to the southern Mekong River delta gave rise to social differences between villagers of the central coastal plain and those of the Mekong River delta. In 1956 Cham populations of central Vietnam and the Khmer population of the Mekong River delta were still struggling to preserve ethnic identity as they had done historically in the face of continued incursions by the ever-expanding Vietnamese population. Then there were the highlanders whom the French called *montagnards* ("mountaineers" or "highlanders") divided into some thirty groups speaking languages either of the Mon-Khmer or Austronesian (Malayopolynesian) stocks, making them linguistic kin of the Khmer and Cham respectively.

Field research also made me aware that in more remote parts of South Vietnam there remained pockets of what local folks called "Viet Minh," not yet using "Viet Cong" (a shortened version of "Việt Nam Cộng Sản" or "Vietnamese Communists") employed by the Diem government.

The first field trips, part of a study of the Ministry of National Education, were in the Mekong River delta. This was the last region to be settled by the Vietnamese in their "advance southward." Called the Nine Dragons River by the Vietnamese, the Mekong was the mainstay of the delta, formed as it was by rich soils carried in constantly turbulent waters rushing from southern China through Burma, Thailand, Laos, Cambodia, and Vietnam finally debouching into the South China Sea.

Market towns serving as provincial capitals reflected the French colonial era with their shaded streets and inevitable rococo province chief's residence surrounded by a garden and a high iron fence. The slightly musty guest quarters had louvered shutters, squeaky ceiling fans, and mosquito nets that effectively kept out any circulating air. Bathrooms had nineteenth-century fixtures and rusty water. Most province chiefs served good Vietnamese fare, although some still served French food, with civet de lapin for some reason a favorite.

Composed of clustered farmsteads, delta hamlets reflected seasonal variations and the annual farming cycle. During the dry season hamlets were green oases in baked paddy fields. Here and there shimmering in the still heat huddled figures under conical hats repaired dikes and bundings. Livestock lazily nibbled grasses by the weathered stone tombs. Then in late April or early May came dramatic change as thunderheads built up in the southwestern sky, moving daily toward the delta. The first rains, heralded by high winds that sent clouds of dust in all directions, came in sheets, whipping foliage, soaking thatched roofs, and conjuring the sensuous smell of wet earth. Farmers with plows pulled by water buffaloes emerged to till the soil. As the rains continued, hamlets became tropical islands in flooded paddy fields. Teams of transplanters moved in rows, bending to plunge rice seedlings into primordial mud, soon transforming seas of rainwater into seas of green paddy.

One delta provincial capital that in 1956 bore signs of the recent

Indochina War was Ca Mau at the extreme southern tip of the peninsula. Reached by a narrow, almost washed-away road, marshy Ca Mau was still in ruins. Blackened walls of the hotel room were pitted with bullet holes and one section of the ceiling was missing. There was no running water or electricity and the torn mosquito netting was mildewed. During interviews there also were brief references to "Viet Minh cadre" still lurking in the marshes. At the only restaurant with passable food, Khanh, my Vietnamese assistant, scowled and said that Ca Mau was "sad," and we would best return immediately to Soc Trang. We stayed, continued our interviews and one evening were treated to a good meal with San Miguel beer by friendly Filipinos of Operation Brotherhood. One of the few other Americans to visit Ca Mau was the writer, Gloria Emerson, who was researching Operation Brotherhood.

MSUG became involved in the South Vietnamese government's program to settle many thousands of northern refugees, so late in May 1956 I visited Cai San in the extreme southwestern corner of Vietnam near the Cambodian border and witnessed the arrival of the first of fifty thousand to be settled in this remote place. During the one-day drive, the Mekong River delta scene changed from endless paddy fields, coconut plantations, and waterways to a vast expanse of grassy plains with the Seven Mountains in the background. After the heat and dust of the drive, the American-aid houseboat moored at the bank of the main canal was a welcome sight. The refugees were being resettled on land that once belonged to wealthy southern Vietnamese who had abandoned it during the Indochina War. American farm-equipment firms donated sturdy plows and tractors and hired young midwestern farmers to till the long-fallowing soil in the early rains.

Cai San had an exhilarating air. Along the main canal the atmosphere was boom-town with shops and houses being built to create new market towns that lured a mixed bag of small businessmen, opportunists of various types, and squatters. Canal traffic was lively. Heavy sailboats were loaded with lumber, ceramic vats, pottery, food products, and other ingredients of new settlements. There were large paddle-boats filled with refugees in their dark northern peasant clothes standing silently on the decks. Amidst them maneuvered simple pirogues that had been issued to each refugee family.

In one new town a Catholic church and school were being built with the priest and parishioners, most of them young girls, carrying baskets of soil for the foundation. The refugee commission provided each farm family a thatched roof supported by thin logs on a low mound of earth. Latania-

Cai San. A newly arrived family of northern refugees stands in the government-supplied frame of their new farmouse, 1956.

palm fronds were distributed to allow the family to arrange its own walls, and trucks delivered papaya and coconut-palm saplings. Standing under his thatched roof a northern farmer expressed his gratitude for being able to bring his family south and have a plot of land. The family, he said, looking out at the sun-baked scene, would complete the house themselves, arrange a kitchen garden, and grow rice and other field crops in the same way southern farmers do. They would use the pirogue the commission gave them to "buy and sell" along the canals.

During subsequent field trips in the Mekong River delta I began to realize that its frontier character no doubt had much to do with the appearance of two innovative southern religious movements—Cao Dai and Hoa Hao.

During a 1916 seance, a spirit identified itself to Ngo Van Chieu as Cao Dai, the symbolic designation for the "Supreme Being." Subsequent spirit messages led to the 1926 declaration of Cao Daism as a formal religion which sought to bring together under the Supreme Being the five branches of the Great Way—Confucianism, Taoism, Buddhism, Spirit Worship, and Christianity. In many respects Cao Daism mirrored the syncretism of Vietnamese culture, and ritual expressions such as kowtowing and offerings of joss, flowers, glutinous rice, small sweet bananas, and rice alcohol were already familiar to all but Christian Vietnamese.

Early in August 1956 a field trip took me to Tay Ninh near the Cambodian border where the "Holy See" of the Cao Dai religious sect was located. Tay Ninh was in the shadow of Black Lady Mountain which rose unexpectedly from the flat plain and was rendered somewhat ominous by clouds hiding the summit. Its rugged slopes were said to harbor dissident Cao Daist troops who, after their 1955 defeat by Ngo Dinh Diem's forces, resorted to banditry.

The center of the headquarters was an extremely colorful temple designed to capture great architectural motifs of the past. Its interior was a litany of bright colors in altars, statues, and gilded thrones enveloped by plaster cobras. A huge depiction of an eye emanating rays of light, symbolizing the Supreme Being, dominated the main altar. Ranked below as saints were Confucius, Buddha, and Lao T'se and at a slightly lower rank, Christ, who appeared later. At the bottom level of the pantheon was a collection of saints drawn from Buddhism, Taoism, and Christianity. Eventually, Sun Yat Sen, Jeanne d'Arc, and Victor Hugo were added.

While walking out of the temple, an elderly lady in a long robe invited us into a nearby building which she explained housed female cardinals and bishops of the hierarchy. A gentle lady of about seventy who identified herself as "head bishop" came forth to greet us. Over tea she told how she had held her position for twenty-seven years and was in charge of the orphanage. Everyone in the headquarters followed a vegetarian regimen, and the head bishop insisted we sample some of them. Soybean seemed to be the principal ingredient, which in the absence of the usual Vietnamese garnishments made the dishes a bit bland.

Hoa Hao, also reformed Buddhism, appeared in 1939 under the leadership of strange and mystical Huynh Phu So, who believed himself to be the reincarnation of Phat Thay Tay An, founder of the Buu Son Ky Huong sect which flourished in the western provinces during the mid nineteenth century. Huynh Phu So attracted attention in the same region with his "miraculous cures," and he also preached a "new Buddhism." This movement thrived in areas along the Mekong and Bassac Rivers which in 1956 were considered insecure because of continued dissidence by a fierce-looking Hoa Hao leader known as "Ba Cut" for a finger joint he cut off in a pledge to fight for Vietnamese independence. On 13 April 1956 Ba Cut was captured. Sentenced to death by a military court, on 13 July he was guillotined in the Can Tho stadium. It was said that his head was carefully hidden to prevent his followers from using it as a rallying symbol.

In the 1956–58 period there still were in the Mekong River delta curious pockets of Khmer Krom, Khmer living in Kampuchea Krom or "Lower Cambodia," reminders that the region had not long before been part of Cambodia. In some predominantly Vietnamese villages were Khmer hamlets with Theravada Buddhist wats. And it was not uncommon to see, in the large river-port town of Can Tho, Theravada monks in saffron robes accepting food offerings at the morning market. One field trip in early April 1956 took me to a very remote coastal Khmer Krom village reached by a very bad road, through thick forest with large colorful birds and monkeys chattering in the trees. The driver took great delight in trying to run over long black snakes that twice slithered across the road. Entering the village we were suddenly transported to a Khmer world. Signs were in Khmer, houses were on pilings, women wore sarongs, and monks at the large wat were garbed in saffron robes. In the school the teacher spoke Khmer to pupils who were learning Vietnamese as a second language.

Two trips in June–July 1956 took me to Nhatrang, a quiet seaport and province capital in central Vietnam on the South China Sea. This part of the coastal plain had been one of the last enclaves of the Cham, whose final defeat by the Vietnamese in 1471 marked the end of the kingdom of Champa, leaving only ruins as mute reminders of Cham high culture.

The first trip in late June was for research on the Ministry of Education. The Air Vietnam DC-3 flew over splendid green mountains and at Nhatrang it circled over the bay where the mountains meet the blue-green sea. In the dry season of central Vietnam the town had a sleepy air with very little traffic on its sandy streets. A landscaped road ran along the wide almost-empty beach lined with shuttered French villas, past the old Hotel Beau Rivage and the nearby Institute Pasteur in a group of charming colonial buildings. North of the beach a sprawling Catholic seminary dominated the headland while to the south a group of white villas that had belonged to Emperor Bao Dai, the last ruler in Hue, nestled amidst the greenery of the headland. Off-shore were islands that resembled mountain-tops rising from the sea.

My assistant Khanh and I stayed at the small Hotel La Frégate with its spartan rooms cooled by ceiling fans. We set to work and after finishing our interviews we swam in the blue-green water of the South China Sea. Back at the hotel I ran into some girls from USOM, and while we were chatting two American army officers from the advisory group stationed in Nhatrang joined us. They kindly drove us to see the Po Nagar temple dating A.D. 1170 by the river in Nhatrang. Standing on a hill, the weathered brick temple was still imposing and held traces of the grace and beauty of classical Cham art and architecture.

The second visit to Nhatrang was on a holiday weekend with a small group of Americans. The weekend held an important date—21 July 1956, anniversary of the Geneva Agreements that ended the Indochina War in 1954. The first part of the document called for a cease-fire with a demarcation line at the 17th dividing Vietnam into two "temporary regroupment areas." An International Commission for Supervision and Control (ICC) composed of Canada, India, and Poland would provide military personnel to monitor the cease-fire. The "Final Declaration" which formed the second part of the Geneva Agreements, concerned political arrangements, and in a vaguely worded passage called for general elections to be held throughout Vietnam on 21 July 1956. None of the participating delegates signed the Final Declaration, making it an unsigned treaty. It had become clear long before this date that the elections would not take place, but 21 July 1956 nonetheless cast a shadow on sunny Nhatrang.

Everyone was in a gala mood in the *couchette de luxe* compartments of the wood-burning train like something out of the old west with its polished brass fittings and high smoke stack. The beds were made and little overhead fans kept the compartment cool. Moving slowly, the train seemed to squeeze its way out of Saigon through a jumble of shacks built almost on the tracks. From the train windows, life in working-class quarters unfolded with people in the light of little oil lamps sitting on mats eating, and bare-bottomed babies running about. In the small train diner, cooking was done on braziers so smoke billowed through the car. After dinner there was bingo using corn kernels as markers.

Beyond Bien Hoa the train passed into thick rain forest, and fronds brushing the louvered windows were reminders of the wild world outside. Dark thick jungle stirred some apprehension because of a recent incident reported by French journalist, François Sully, about an attack on the train by a herd of elephants. It seems that as the herd crossed the tracks the engine bumped a young elephant, angering the bull who trumpeted an attack on the stalled train. Using their trunks, elephants smashed windows, menacing the passengers. When the engineer realized what was happening, he blew the shrill whistle sending the herd scurrying into the forest.

With morning light the train touched the coast at Ca Na where waves crashed among rock formations. At Nhatrang the Minister of Education had arranged for us to stay in Emperor Bao Dai's headland villas, which turned out to have magnificent views of the bay, but the enormous rooms were almost devoid of furniture. American army officers of the military advisory group invited us to go out in their boat to skin-dive in the magnificent coral reefs. After a seafood lunch at Chez François, a small frame seaside restaurant run by a former French soldier who elected to remain in Vietnam, the advisers had to return to their headquarters because of an alert. There were reports that the following day, 21 July, might be marked by uprisings or incursions by Viet Cong operating in the mountains to the west. The dining room at Hotel La Frégate was empty and the hotel owner told us that French residents of Nhatrang had evacuated to two freighters anchored in the bay by the port. We drove through silent streets back to the villas. The servants quarters, which had been lively that day with kids running around, were dark with doors locked. No one responded to knocks. Alone in the Villa Frangipani I went upstairs where a bed, the only furniture, stood in dead center of the room. The one light was over the sink in the bathroom and I left it on. Carefully tucking in the mosquito netting I lay my head on the rocklike pillow. Suddenly the nocturnal silence was broken by soft rhythmic sounds of drums. In the mind of anyone schooled in the Hollywood films of the 1930s and 1940s, such tom-tom sounds suggest messages being relayed. Did they signal the beginning of an uprising? A chilling thought. Should I alert the others? That would necessitate going outside. I pulled back the netting and went to a large window facing the area behind the villas. Below was a small Vietnamese village and light coming from the place where the drum sounds seemed to originate. The ominous mood was suddenly dispersed by muffled sounds of laughter. I felt a sense of relief as it occurred to me that the drums were those used for effect in the popular theater where political parodies were common themes. No doubt one of the traveling theatrical troupes was performing for the villagers. Perhaps the theme that night had something to do with the elections. After all, the joke making the rounds among the Vietnamese wags in

Saigon was that if the elections *were* held, everyone in the South would vote for Ho Chi Minh while everyone in the North would cast ballots for Ngo Dinh Diem.

Finally in September 1956 a field trip took me to the central highlands, abode of the highlanders, people who in my Paris research I found particularly intriguing. On 5 September 1956 for a study of the Ministry of Information my assistant Khanh and I went on Air Vietnam to Ban Me Thuot, the major town on what the French called the "high plateau," where red latosols—"terres rouges"—invited coffee plantations during the colonial period. This is the heart of territory occupied by the Rhadé, one of the largest highland groups, who speak a Malayopolynesian language. I knew from library research in Paris and Saigon that the Rhadé call themselves "Êdê," derived from Anak H'Dê or "Children of H'Dê," a designation taken from a legend identifying H'Dê as ancestress of the Rhadé. This signals women's central role in Rhadé society. Descent is reckoned through the female line (matrilineal descent) which determines membership in the longhouse extended family, the basic social and economic unit in Rhadé society. Women take men in marriage, after which they reside at the wife's longhouse. Children are members of their mother's clan. Women own family property such as the longhouse, domestic animals (including elephants), and fruits of the harvest. The Rhadé farm upland rain-fed rice by the swidden (shifting) method, cutting small trees and brush, which when dry are burned. Using dibble sticks they make holes in the soil and plant the rice seeds. A field is farmed about three years and then left to fallow for at least fifteen years before farming it again.

Shaded by magnificent gnarled old trees, the administrative offices in Ban Me Thuot reflected a French provincial style adapted to the tropics: tile roof, a veranda with rococo touches, French windows, and high ceilings with fans. In the center of the town behind a high wall was the sumptuous hunting lodge of Emperor Bao Dai.[3] It was a large building in a European style (called "le palais" by local highlanders). Nearby was Bao Dai's guest lodge, a large hardwood adaptation of a Rhadé longhouse. Known as the Grand Bungalow, it was now occupied by American military advisers who had turned the garden into a "motor pool."

But it was the Rhadé villages that opened an entirely new world. The villages have about them a certain grandeur that derives largely from their longhouses elevated on pilings, with splendid hardwood frames and topped

Rhadé Kpa sowing upland dry rice in a swidden. Men make holes with dibble sticks, and the women follow to sow, 1956.

by lofty, thickly thatched roofs. In 1956, longhouses, built entirely of materials provided by the physical surroundings, symbolized Rhadé harmony with nature. Some old longhouses were around one hundred meters long and housed a hundred residents related through the female line.

Visiting Rhadé villages I experienced for the first time the unfailing hospitality of the highland people. I also found myself entranced with the rousseauean late afternoon village scene when the air was still and a thin veil of smoke from the evening cooking fires settled amidst the longhouses

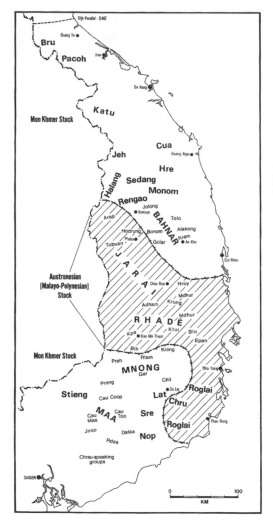

Ethnic Groups of Central
Vietnam

and the backdrop of rich green bamboo groves. Men in loincloths clutching
bush scythes and women wearing only long skirts walked in silence,
returning from the forest and fields with backbaskets laden with wild fruit,
vegetables, and edible flowers. Villagers also gathered by a nearby stream
to bathe, while downstream elephants frolicked in the water, their trunks
sending sprays of water into the air.

After interviewing in Ban Me Thuot we headed south on a winding
road that in places was completely washed away, to the district the French
called Poste du Lac. A small river had to be crossed on a ferry poled by

A Rhadé longhouse, 1956.

men. Then the country became thick with forests and at one point the car skidded into a morass of mud, almost tipping over. Fortunately we were near a village of Mnong Rlam people, who physically resemble the Rhadé, but their language is of the Mon Khmer stock. Good-humored men from the village lifted the car back on to the road. We continued on and suddenly there was the lake for which the district was named: beautiful in a primeval setting of misty mountains.

We interviewed the district information officer who afterward took us to a nearby Mnong Rlam village. Entering the headman's longhouse I was invited to sit on a floor-mat while the host, holding a live chicken over my head, invoked the spirits. He then placed a brass bracelet on my right wrist. Seven elders and the eldest woman did the same, after which I drank rice alcohol from a jar through a bamboo tube. Jar alcohol is prepared using husked and unhusked rice and a mixture of crushed barks and such things as ginger root which in a sealed jar is left to stand for at least a week. When opened, the jar is filled with fresh leaves and water into which is inserted the drinking tube. A "good jar" has the flavor of a smoky cider while a "bad jar" is sour and apt to cause intestinal dolors. One way or other, drinking rice alcohol was something I would do on innumerable occasions during research in the highlands.

The district chief invited us to have lunch of civet de lapin at his house, a somewhat dilapidated chalet by the lake. After lunch he insisted we visit Bao Dai's hunting lodge, located on a promontory above the lake. The dirt road unexpectedly gave way to a concrete drive lined with flowers and ahead loomed an elegant French-style chalet. Inside was a large main room with comfortable furniture and in one corner a small bar. Hung along with walls were game trophies—a gaur head and elephants' tusks. A tiger skin covered the floor before the fireplace. The district chief showed us a sizable generator to supply electricity for lights and air conditioners in bedrooms where neatly curtained windows looked out over the lake. The generator also powered a walk-in freezer for game in the basement.

Leaving Ban Me Thuot we went north by plane to Pleiku, landing at the airstrip near the large Catecka tea plantation. Pleiku town consisted of few Vietnamese shops around a gasoline station run by a man who had known Khanh's father in Hanoi. We stayed in the provincial guest house built on pilings near a village of Jarai Hodrung, a Malayopolynesian-speaking people who resemble the Rhadé in physical appearance and culture. Nearby was a small house occupied by five American military advisers. Although the prevailing idea in Saigon was that all highlanders practiced slash-and-burn farming, Jarai Hodrung near Pleiku farmed paddy fields in volcanic depressions. Some also had relatively large herds of cattle grazing on the grassy plain of the Pleiku plateau.

After interviews we were invited to the Jarai village for a funeral honoring the headman who had died the previous day. Men playing gongs moved rhythmically around the tomb while mourners drank rice alcohol from rows of jars staked to the ground. A buffalo had been sacrificed that morning and tin basins of food were passed around.

That evening at supper the province chief announced he had arranged for Khanh and me to go hunting. Tired after a full day, Khanh and I thanked him and tried to make excuses, but the province chief was adamant. He had ordered a Jeep and enlisted a French-speaking Jarai clerk from his office to take us to the clerk's natal village in the Ia Drang valley west of Pleiku. The province chief provided weapons and spotlights that could be strapped on our heads. He explained that if the lights revealed an animal with white eyes it would more than likely be a tiger. At the village, the Jarai clerk got a young kinsman to act as our guide. The barefoot young man, dressed only in a shirt and loincloth, inspired confidence as he walked in typical montagnard fashion looking straight ahead with head high. Leaving the village we were immediately enveloped by dense forest. The only eyes we spotted were those of small game darting into the brush. Then the wind picked up and rain began to fall. We walked and walked. My London Fog raincoat became soaked, the ground turned into slippery mud, and the spotlight strap on my head seemed to contract. There were sudden slithering movements in the undergrowth. We walked and walked. Suddenly, our silent guide stopped. He spoke to the clerk who turned to me with a somewhat pained look on his face and said, "Monsieur, nous sommes perdu." "Lost!" Khanh exclaimed, "We can't be!" My confidence that the Jarai guide knew every tree and leaf in the forest collapsed. And to make matters worse, they asked me what we should do. Looking around at the dripping trees it was readily clear the only thing we could do was to continue walking until we came upon a village. The rain came in torrents and the next hour seemed an eternity when the spotlights revealed red eyes which the Jarai clerk said were those of water buffalo, a sign that a village was near. In the longhouse we hung our wet clothes by the open hearth, drank some hot water, and rolled up in blankets to fall into exhausted sleep. We arrived back in Pleiku late the following day, and the province chief could not conceal his disappointment at our lack of game.

North of Pleiku, Route 14 ran close to the strange Lake Tenneung, a placid body of water located in a deep depression. According to Jarai legend, a Cham army invading the highlands was drowned in this lake. Beyond the lake, the road entered the twisting Mount Pao pass and descended into the valley where Kontum stood on the bank of the Bla River. Kontum had the look of being a town older than any other in the highlands. It also had a certain charm. Although none of the streets was paved, the row of shophouses by the old market were of weathered masonry and a few had rococo carvings. The tile roofs looked as if they had endured many lashing rainy seasons. The residential section had wide streets, and Vietnamese houses with wattled mud walls painted white or powder blue. Each house was set in a sizable plot, much of which was devoted to extensive vegetable gardens, fruit trees, and patches of flowers.

Adjacent to the town were villages of the Bahnar Jolong and Rengao, Mon Khmer-speaking groups who trace descent through both male and female lines. Some of their rectangular houses built on pilings had wattled walls and tile roofs reflecting Vietnamese influence. In the center of non-Christian villages stood men's houses built on pilings with high, sloping thatched roofs often graced with symbolic decorations. Young unmarried males slept in the men's house, which also served as a gathering place for village men.

North of Kontum loomed heavily forested country where villages suddenly appeared by the road. Twice, long dark snakes, probably pythons or boas, seemed to glide across the road. At Dak To the district information officer accompanied us to a village of the Sedang, Mon Khmer-speakers who had the reputation of being bellicose. Men carried spears, crossbows, and quivers of arrows (some with poisoned arrowheads) which would seem to confirm this, but everyone was friendly. As gongs and drums played, a line of village girls holding hands did a slow dance involving a rhythmic dip. While we drank from jars, the village headman expressed regret we were not armed because in recent months ten people had been killed by tigers. We were considering driving farther north to Dak Sut, but district officials said it was not advisable because of "Viet Minh cadre" in remote forests. Driving back to Kontum in the dark rain I was startled to see suddenly in the headlights a mass of animals with slick black pelts bounding ahead of the Jeep like creatures from the primordial past. As they disappeared into the brush, the Bahnar driver laughed, saying they were wild boars!

At the beginning of October 1956 I combined a highland field trip with an interesting weekend with friends at Cam Ranh Bay. In a 1954 yellow convertible Chevrolet we followed the road the French called the "Mandarin Route" through thick jungle east of Bien Hoa along the edge of the uplands to Ca Na on the South China Sea. One pleasant surprise in traveling along the steamy coast by road was that small thatched Vietnamese restaurants invariably provided cold drinks and tasty sautéed fresh fish. Around the coastal town of Phan Rang were Cham villages, the last enclaves of what had been the kingdom of Champa. Their houses were not much different from those of the neighboring Vietnamese. But Cham women were dressed in long black skirts and the men wore loosely wrapped turbans. Not far from Phan Rang was the impressive Po Rome, a Cham tower restored by the French. Standing on a hill in the desertlike coastal plain, the solid strength of the brick tower was relieved by beautiful stone carvings. The tower commanded awe, but nonetheless it stood sad and abandoned.

Surrounded on three sides by mountains and on the other side by a sandy peninsula, Cam Ranh Bay was magnificent. Passing a large copra plantation with its coconut palms whipped by an off-shore wind, we entered Ba Ngoi which was little more than a large fishing village with one hotel run by Chinese. The stone main building and surrounding pavilions with guest rooms were shuttered. The owner showed us to long-closed musty rooms with sputtering water rustier than usual. Things brightened up when the smiling owner had his staff set a table on the terrace with a view of the bay for an excellent seafood dinner.

In the village the following morning we rented a junk. The crew, with catlike faces and bandanas wrapped around their heads, resembled fabled South China sea pirates portrayed in films. Dropping anchor in shallow water at the peninsula, we climbed the dunes to find sturdy abandoned French military buildings. With unit insignia painted on the walls of what had been lounges and mess halls, the wind-blown buildings were eerie remnants of the former French presence in Vietnam. The Chinese hotel owner had provided a picnic lunch and he explained that although Cam Ranh Bay was a shark-breeding area we could swim close to shore inside coral reefs. In the clear water we were delighted to find starfish of incredibly varied colors and patterns. While examining caves along the shore to find a shady, cool place for lunch we came upon two elderly Cham weaving nets. I remarked that the scene was like a diorama at a museum. Then, one of the Cham astonished us when he smiled and holding up a net said in French, "This is for small game." Canadian and Indian officers of the ICC came to visit us at the hotel (typically the Poles kept to themselves) and took us to an island in their boat.

Sunday afternoon we drove to Dalat through the idyllic upland Danhim valley and had dinner at La Savoisienne, a rustic restaurant run by Madame Grillet, a solemn French lady whose farm provided all of the delicious food. My friends left me at the Lang Bian Palace Hotel, a ponderous building on a hill, where the MSUG station-wagon and my assistant Khanh would meet me the next morning. The only guest in the hotel, I was given a very faded regal suite and when later I went down to the desk I found the whole place dark with no one about. Back in my room I double-locked the door and fell into an uneasy sleep. In the clear morning freshness I was surprised to find on the spacious terrace a table set with silver service for a breakfast of crisp croissants and strong coffee. I savored the cool air and sweeping view while awaiting Khanh and the station wagon to do interviews in Dalat and Blao.

Throughout 1956 and 1957, when not on field trips, I spent a great deal of time in Saigon doing interviews in ministries being researched by the MSUG. Since Saigon was not built as a national capital, ministries were crammed into nineteenth-century colonial buildings. Fans turned lazily in the stuffy rooms, where civil servants huddled at desks piled high with dossiers tied with strings to hold the papers together. Close at hand were little glasses of tea with green plastic lids to keep the flies out. Khanh and I, dressed in white short-sleeved shirts and wearing clip-on ties, were invariably served tepid tea and dry cookies. We hated afternoon interviews because, groggy after a siesta, we found the accumulated heat in the offices intolerable.

After work and on weekends I concentrated on my dissertation and was fortunate to be able to obtain ethnographic information from informants in Saigon. MSUG was affiliated with the National Institute of Administration where there were northern Tai-speaking refugee leaders being trained, so I researched Tho (Tay) culture with Hoang Le Sinh and Black Tai (Tai Dam) society with Cam Van Vui. Dr. Fishel asked me to teach English at the Independence Palace when I was in Saigon. Two of my "students," Doan Them and Nguyen Dang Can of the Presidency, provided information on northern Vietnamese village society.

I had completed a first draft of my dissertation when in early November 1956 my colleague Jim Hendry and I were selected to present papers at the Ninth Pacific Science Conference to be held in Bangkok at Chulalonghorn University. This was highly fortuitous because among those attending were University of Chicago professors Fred Eggan and Norton Ginsburg, principal members of my dissertation committee who had agreed to read the draft and make comments. They kindly took time to read the draft, make border comments, and suggested that I send them the final version. The meetings were exciting and a high point was an invitation by the King of Thailand to a royal garden party at Amphorn Palace. In our white suits we stood in a line while the king and queen (a strikingly beautiful lady in traditional Thai garb) greeted each one.

En route back to Saigon, the Air France DC-3 stopped in Phnom Penh where everyone had to leave the aircraft while it refueled. Taking my dissertation I sipped coffee in the thatched terminal restaurant and chatted with the Vietnamese waiter. When the flight reached Saigon I realized with a cold shudder that I had left the dissertation in Phnom Penh! Before panic set in, I went to the air terminal office where the Vietnamese quickly radioed Phnom Penh. After a sleepless night I was relieved the following day when a telephone call to the MSUG office informed me that the waiter in Phnom Penh terminal restaurant remembered me because we spoke Vietnamese and he would only consign the dissertation to the pilot of the Air France flight arriving in Saigon later in the day. I duly went to Tan Son Nhut airport, thanked the Air France pilot, and brought the dissertation back to the office where I ran off five copies.

The year 1956 was coming to a close and in every respect it had been a year that held a breath of peace and hope. It marked a time when there had been for the most part enthusiastic support of Ngo Dinh Diem and his administration. Although an introverted man, in public appearances he was likable and good humored. He made trips to the countryside, waving at peasants from barges, and he was seen on rue Catinat shaking hands with ordinary folk. Depending on the occasion he was garbed either in a white sharkskin suit (wearing black shoes) or a traditional black tunic. In the American media he was something of a hero and the adjective "doughty" was often used to characterize him.

To mark the first anniversary of Diem's election, his proclamation of the Republic of Vietnam and promulgation of a new constitution drafted by a Constitutional Assembly, the last week in October 1956 was filled with celebrations. In preparation, Saigon was spruced up with buildings freshly painted, flowers and trees planted, and decorative arches built. A U.S. Navy cruiser docked at the Saigon River front, and Americans crowded on board to eat ice cream. The MSUG staff was invited to sit on the reviewing stand for the parade with marching soldiers, tanks, and military bands while overhead zoomed seventy-five fighter planes from an American aircraft carrier in the South China Sea. There were boat races on the river and dragon dances in the streets. In the evening a torchlight parade with floats passed in front of the Independence Palace which, like all public buildings, was alive with strings of colored lights. From the rooftop Paprika restaurant we marveled at the spectacle, particularly the splendid fireworks over the palace.

This was a time for celebration and curiously the French joined in, as if to end their colonial presence in style.

The Cercle Sportif (still a French club) announced it would have a particularly splendid annual grand ball. "A Chinese Village" theme transformed the swimming pool into a lavish mise-en-scène with an elegant Chinese house and junk at one end and a deck for dancing at the other end. Chinese lanterns and colored lights were strung over the pool and temporary extension decks accommodated tables. Men were in black ties and white jackets while women wore ball gowns (some flown in from Paris). A stunning French-Chinese lady in a white ball gown was identified as one of Emperor Bao Dai's last mistresses in Saigon. As champagne was served, a Filipino orchestra played tunes popular in 1956, and dancing stopped when productions were presented. The elegant house served as a set for a scene from classical Chinese opera and as a background for a display of Chinese boxing. The final production was a "Ballet of the Junks" in the pool. Girls wearing flippers paddled small junks to music with Debussy-Ravel touches in a charming aquatic ballet, forming stars and circles. At 3:00 A.M. steaming *soupe gratinée* was served and with first light of dawn the last grand ball ended.

The Société des Etudes Indochinoise sponsored a trip to Phnom Penh, capital of neighboring Cambodia, to celebrate the "Fête des Eaux" when, with rains subsiding, the flow of water in the Tonle Sap reverses to empty into the Mekong River. I joined friends for the trip to Phnom Penh. We expected a rather provincial city like Can Tho, but were pleasantly surprised to find that Phnom Penh was in many ways the most charming city in Southeast Asia with broad boulevards lined with flowering trees and elegant villas. We got a bungalow at the venerable Hotel le Royal and joined the French group from the Société des Etudes Indochinoises at the Club Nautique on the river near the exquisite Royal Palace (flood-lit for the occasion). Gongs and drums sounded along the river bank jammed with Cambodians dressed in their best traditional clothes. As night fell, illuminated barges of all colors and designs moved slowly by.

The following morning there was a tour conducted by André Migot, a respected French savant of Cambodian culture, particularly Buddhism. We visited the Royal Palace and the serene Buddhist Institute where monks in saffron-yellow robes shaded by matching parasols promenaded around the courtyard. The National Museum had a wonderful collection of Khmer art, notably stone carvings from Angkor. The tour ended with refreshments on the terrace of Dr. Migot's large apartment facing the river. That evening held a performance of the Royal Corps de Ballet in their beautiful open pavilion at the palace. Protocol required that ladies wear hats and gloves and men wear white suits. On the final day there were races of long boats, each with fifty rowers, that moved incredibly fast and low in the strong current.

Western cultural events were almost non-existent in Saigon, so everyone greeted enthusiastically the news that the U.S. Information Service's Cultural Affairs Office would sponsor concerts by the opera star Eleanor Steber at the Majestic Cinema, and concert pianist Eugene Istomin at the much larger Dai Nam cinema. Neither house was air-conditioned, and the ceiling fans were ineffective and squeaky. As representative of the International Rescue Committee, Peg Cole gave a garden cocktail party for Miss Steber who was very chic in a Chinese cheong-san which writer Han Su-Yin had her Hong Kong couturière fashion for the soprano. Afterwards a small group of us dined at the elegant Bodega restaurant which had a bar with piano music. When the pianist played "Love is a Many-Splendored Thing," Steber insisted the tune was stolen from Puccini, whereupon she began singing "Un Bel Di" from *Madame Butterfly*. Her fabulous voice could be heard all the way down rue Catinat.

She fared better than poor Eugene Istomin who had to play in the stifling Dai Nam on a baby grand belonging to the Japanese ambassador's wife (who kept a light bulb burning in it to prevent rusting in the Saigon humidity). Before his second concert he was taken to a large Chinese lunch in Cholon. As he played Beethoven his face began to perspire and turn red before he collapsed on the keyboard.

While conducting library research at the Société des Etudes Indochinoises I had the good fortune to meet French anthropologist Pierre-Bernard Lafont who was serving as delegate of the Ecole Française d'Extrême-Orient in Vientiane, Laos. In addition to offering data from his own research among Tai-speaking groups of northern Vietnam, Laos, and Thailand, Lafont suggested I visit the Black Tai at Muong Nam Tha in northern Laos. So in late December 1956 I took leave and flew on Air Laos to Vientiane. In Vientiane, fellow anthropologist Howard Kaufman put me up in a guest room also used by Dr. Tom Dooley, who had a hospital at Vang Vieng. Howard's pet monkey, Gregory, lost no time in rummaging through my belongings. Lafont made necessary contacts to visit Muong Nam Tha near the Chinese border. I wondered why Lafont laughed when he said the only flights to Nam Tha were on Veha-Akat, an Air Laos subsidiary. The full import came when, in the early morning light at a corner of the silent airport, I stood by a 1932 de Havilland "Dragonfly" biplane with two small engines. The pilot, a hardy man who had flown in the French air force, supervised loading of cargo wrapped in woven rattan. Then he bid me and two Lao passengers to follow him in crawling over the cargo to our small seats. We rumbled over the grassy runway and after we were aloft heading northward it was apparent that the aircraft was unable to fly *over* the mountains but instead followed the Mekong River valley. Resigned to my fate, I sat back to enjoy the beautiful scenery.

The plane began to circle as the pilot shouted, "Sayaboury." I looked down to see only coconut palms. We landed on the airstrip, unloaded some cargo, and resumed our flight. At one point the pilot pointed straight out and shouted, "Voilà, Monsieur, un village Meo!" And there in a direct line on the mountainside was a Meo (now called Hmong) village similar to those in French books.

The next stop was Luang Prabang, the royal capital of Laos, and from the air it seemed idyllic. A golden stupa on a hill glittered and nearby stood the beautiful royal palace. Only the tile roofs of many pagodas poked through the splendid greenery hiding the rest of Luang Prabang. The two Lao passengers shook hands with me as they left the plane and the cargo was unloaded. North of Luang Prabang the country seemed wild with mountains, forests, coursing rivers, and very few settlements. The pilot sipped a bottle of "33" beer. In the empty cabin looking down at the vastness below I felt a curious sense of aloneness.

At the Nam Tha airstrip, as the plane taxied to a halt, any feelings of isolation were dispelled by a large crowd of highland people wearing embroidered clothes, varied headpieces, and silver jewelry, and some clutching sabers, rushed up to look in the window. At that moment I asked myself, "What decision in my life resulted in my being face to face with these exotic people?"

The *chau khoueng* (governor) of Nam Tha province, who had been informed of my arrival by Lafont, greeted me and I presented him with Lafont's letter of introduction. In his Jeep, the only vehicle in Nam Tha, he explained that my visit was well timed because every year in December all ethnic groups in the province send delegations to Nam Tha where at a cere-

At the Muong Nam Tha airstrip with members of the Yao (Mien) delegation, 1956.

mony honored by a member of the royal family, they swear an oath (*grand serment*) of loyalty to the king. The governor said the elders in the hill groups want their young men to come to Nam Tha and meet other highland people. He added that everyone comes to the airstrip to see the planes land and take off, a manifestation of the spirits' powers.

The only available accommodation was at what the governor called "le cabaret," which turned out to be a trading post run by a Vietnamese married to a Lao. The guest quarters consisted of a bed surrounded by a curtain in the corner of the main room. On the first morning, the owner's little daughter brought me a steaming glass of water which she said was for brushing my teeth, something that would never happen in a grand hotel. The governor had arranged for a French-speaking older Black Tai school teacher to accompany me on foot to his nearby village where we paid respects to the leaders and began research. The village looked exactly like those in the French monographs, and the people were very friendly. At the end of our interviews they served food and distilled rice alcohol.

The oath ceremony attracted a wide range of ethnic groups each of whom grouped in its own quarters. The school teacher suggested we visit the "chateau du Yao," an elegant designation for a ramshackle structure filled with delegation members. We also visited the Meo, Lolo, Lahu, and Khmu delegations.

Delegates came to the trading post to exchange things they brought with them for goods the Vietnamese sold. One afternoon I saw from the post window men carrying two long poles to which a bronze "Kha drum" was lashed. The men were Khmu and had carried the drum down to the post where they hoped to sell it. I bought the drum. In the evening, highlanders gathered at the post to drink and talk. Late one night I was awakened by an outburst of shouting and gunfire. At breakfast the owner related that a large number of Chinese nationalist troops were installed around the Burmese border to the west where they retained their military organization and farmed. From time to time some came into Nam Tha to drink and carouse as they had the previous evening.

The governor arranged for me to take a Laotian military plane to Luang Prabang which proved to be even more exotic on the ground than it was from the air. The many pagodas and Lao houses on pilings with large verandas were set in a jungle of tropical trees and flowers through which narrow lanes meandered. Elephants moved slowly down the quiet main street which had a few stone buildings with tile roofs. The only guest accommodations in Luang Prabang were at Le Bungalow, a colonial-style building on pilings with a large veranda which attracted women who sold exquisite silk stoles they had woven. During the French period Le Bungalow probably was very pleasant, but by 1956 it had fallen into disrepair. Electricity was very sporadic and although the rooms had plumbing, running water was nonexistent. A "boy" brought jerry-cans of water to the room, and when I inquired about toilet facilities, the manager simply pointed to a nearby overgrown coconut grove. At the bleak bar in the lobby a large old refrigerator held cold drinks, but it was kept locked and the barman had to get the key from the manager to fill each order. One young barman was a Black Tai from the Nam Tha area who liked to discuss his village.

When I arrived, a Canadian ICC military officer who lodged with the Indian and Polish officers at Le Bungalow advised me to take meals in nearby restaurants. It seems the ICC paid its bills at the beginning of the month so the Lao kitchen staff bought copiously at the market. As the month wore on, servings became skimpier until the last week when the dining room closed. The Black Tai barman reported that a new Thai hotel-management expert was arriving from Bangkok and things would improve. The Thai expert arrived and immediately installed himself at a table on the veranda where, daily sporting a succession of splendid Thai-silk shirts, he played cards and drank beer.

In many respects the Bungalow comedy-scene reflected the insouciant atmosphere of Luang Prabang. With the still night, groups of women strolled through the lanes singing in high voices to announce festivals at local Buddhist wats, usually to raise money to make repairs. Luang Prabang wats were handsome structures of carved wood, gilded decorations, and sweeping roofs of colored tiles. For the festival, a wat was lit with masses of candles. Fresh green decorations of fronds and flowered boughs combined with the rich saffron of the monks' robes and gold-silver glitter of women's skirts and shoulder cloths to create an elegantly exotic air. Pretty girls, their hair arranged in chignons, passed among the crowd holding silver bowls for donations. Traditional music played as laughing young people danced in a circle dancing the *lam-vong,* moving in rhythmic steps with graceful hand and arm movements. At one such festival an elderly, slightly tipsy man said to me in French, "We Lao live for festivals, for dancing, drinking," and winking, added, "and for making love!"

After a brief stop in Vientiane I boarded the U.S. Embassy plane to Bangkok. The Hotel Erawan had just opened and after Laos it seemed the epitome of modern luxury with teakwood walls in the rooms and automatic fans in the bathroom. The pool was surrounded by a lush tropical garden and terrace dining room. When I had dinner with Dr. Tom Dooley to talk about Nam Tha, he sniffed and said the hotel was a "Hollywood version of Thailand." Among the hotel guests was an Italian crew shooting a film version of Marguerite Duras's book *The Sea Wall,* starring Silvana Magnani. A French lady from one of the silk shops called my attention to a lanky young man with thick glasses standing in the lobby whom she identified as "the new Jimmy Dean." He was Anthony Perkins, the male lead in the movie.

By and large the South Vietnamese, who were occupied with building their new nation, did not dwell on the Indochina War which had ended in 1954. But early in 1957 the Indochina War was revived in Saigon with production of a film based on Graham Greene's war novel *The Quiet American,* the first American film to be shot in Saigon. Again, plastic bombs demolished cars parked by the Continental Hotel sending male leads Audie

Murphy and Michael Redgrave into action. Peg Cole, who was helping producer-director Joseph Mankiewicz, recruited her husband Dave and me to be extras in a scene where Mr. Redgrave and Bruce Cabot interviewed the Cao Dai pope in Tay Ninh. The scene actually was shot in front of the 1799 traditional Vietnamese-style tomb of Pigneau de Behaine, the redoubtable French missionary instrumental in the rise of Nguyen Anh, who in 1802 unified Vietnam and declared himself Emperor Gia Long. As a "correspondent" dressed in white shirt and scribbling in a small note-book, I was placed next to Mr. Redgrave. In the still afternoon heat the scene was shot endless times, but it gave me a chance to have a nice chat about the theater with the charming Michael Redgrave.

By the end of 1956 I had had the good fortune to be able to conduct ethnographic research in parts of South Vietnam and Laos. Central Vietnam was, however, still terra incognita, so early in 1957 I seized the opportunity to visit the former royal capital of Hue, an intriguing and mysterious city.

My Paris research had touched on the culture of Hue, and in Saigon I sought out works on Hue at the Société des Etudes Indochinoise Library in the National Museum. Before the lunar new year (*têt*) in February 1957, accompanied by two assistants, Miss Hong Phuc (one of the Crossroads group) and Mr. Hue (who had studied in Paris), I flew to Hue, to conduct interviews on the Department of Information. The experience was something of a step back in time. French influence had brought commerce to cities of northern and southern Vietnam, but Hue had no commercial functions, leaving the "traditional" high culture of Vietnam relatively intact. Both Hong Phuc and Hue were from the city so they stayed with their families where they could celebrate Tet. I was given use of the former American consulate, a pleasant French-style country house on a leafy street. We did our interviews and when Tet began I was alone with a refrigerator full of food prepared by the servants.

This afforded an opportunity to wander around Hue and I headed straight to the citadel armed with extensive notes I had taken from two French sources—Louis Chochod's *Hué la mystérieuse* and articles in Léopold Cadière's scholarly journal, *Bulletin des amis du vieux Hué*. When in 1802 Emperor Gia Long declared Hue the capital of newly united Vietnam, he began construction of the citadel, modeled on the Chinese court in Peking. Its layout, based on Taoist geomancy, involves five elements— metal, wood, water, fire, and earth or soil—the auspicious combination of which enables harmony with earthly and heavenly currents. The citadel is divided into three enclosures, each of which contains a "city." Just within the outer wall is the Capital City, and within it the Imperial City and embedded in that is the Forbidden Purple City, residence of the sovereign, Regulator of the World, on whom earthly and heavenly currents converge.

At the southern Noon Gate I marveled at the Belvedere of the Five Phoenixes with its violet-tinted stone and structure of russet hardwood columns, gilt wood, glazed tiles, and moon-gates. There was no one in view. I walked over the Bridge of Golden Waters dividing two stone pools filled with water lilies to the Esplanade of Grand Salutes where gatherings of mandarins greeted the ruler. Then I entered the Palace of Supreme Harmony where the throne room is located. Inside was a dark silent great hall with polished floor and tall antique porcelain vases in front of lacquered columns to which stylized oil lamps were affixed. In a splendid setting of gilded panels and molding in fantastic swirling dragon and chimerical motifs, the red and gold throne on a dais was surprisingly simple.

Walking through the throne room I came upon the famous Golden Door, an exquisite lacquered portal through which only the emperor was allowed to pass. Beyond was a stone gate leading to the Forbidden Purple City where the Royal Palace and other buildings with names such as the Palace of Honor and Palace of Diligence in Government had stood along with archives, concubines' quarters, and a host of other royal abodes. Now, however, all were in ruins, destroyed during the Viet Minh occupation in 1945.

I suddenly wondered how alive the citadel must have been in the past with the ruling family, an army of servants to care for them, and guards to protect them, not to mention the scribes, librarians, medical practitioners, shamans, artisans, musicians, dancers, and actors for the royal theater.

I was relieved to find still intact Taoist temples and shrines as well as the labyrinths of courtyards with their gardens with rocks and miniature trees and tiny lakes, all replicas in microcosm of the great world with its mountains, forests, and limitless oceans. I had read in one of the articles that the royal palace was "cunningly encased" within the labyrinthine courtyards to prevent the whole geomantic layout from being understood. It must remain a secret because to understand the plan of the palace would amount to taking mystical possession of it.

Just outside the citadel walls in the Gia Hoi quarter I came upon a courtyard where men in black shorts were stirring a pasty brown mixture in large pots over blazing fires (I later found out it was a sticky sesame candy only available in Hue). On a narrow street moved a procession of men, hired attendants for a wedding, in brightly colored traditional garb and hats of royal guards some of them clutching lances and triangular-flag standards. Two men carried a large cask of scented rice wine lashed to a pole. At the old Hotel Morin where American military advisers were billeted, I had a drink with one of the enlisted men, Ezra Vogel, who later would become a well-known journalist in Saigon.

My assistant, Mr. Hue, was engaged to a Vietnamese girl from Hanoi who worked with MSUG and she joined him and his family for the Tet celebrations. Hue's father, a doctor, insisted that I accompany them to a ritual introducing the fiancée to Hue's ancestors. We went to the ancestral house, a splendid traditional structure set in a garden and areca-palm grove on the banks of the Perfume River. The servants had opened the louvered doors in front, lit candles, and placed flowers on the altars. On the walls were large scrolls on which the family genealogy was beautifully recorded in the demotic *chữ nôm* characters. I stood to one side and felt transported to the Vietnam of old as I watched my hosts holding joss sticks bow before the altars. Afterwards, as Hue's father explained the entries on the scrolls, we sipped tea and chewed quids of areca and betel garnished with lime.

Some American friends arrived to spend a long weekend. We spent two days in the citadel and dined in small thatched restaurants sampling the special cuisine found only in Hue. Miss Phuc invited us to the house of her brother, Dr. Quynh, head of the Hue Provincial Hospital. Located just outside one of the gates to the citadel, the house, built up to the narrow street, had a rather severe exterior, but the interior, arranged around a courtyard filled with potted plants, was charming with dark hardwood furniture. While partaking of tea and traditional Tet goodies such as candied ginger and fruits, Dr. Quynh recommended we visit the royal tombs.

The following day we boarded Hue's boat to go upstream on the Perfume River to visit the tomb of Emperor Minh Mang (1820–41). En route while passing a curious half-hidden structure on a rock formation our attention was drawn to several long black boats being poled across the river. Standing and sitting on the boats were men and women in tunics of rich colors. Hue explained that the structure was known by the French as "La Pagode des Sorciers," a Taoist temple that at Tet attracted various shamans and people from Hue who wanted to communicate with their

Hue. Gate to Emperor Minh Mang's tomb, 1957.

ancestors. He added that we could stop there on the way back. We continued upstream where the country became hilly and forested with no settlements. At a heavily wooded bank we docked the boat. The overhanging forest enveloped the wide path that led to a weathered traditional stone gate with a pagoda-style arch. Its great wooden doors were half open. Minh Mang's tomb is in the imperial style with courtyards containing lotus-filled pools, steles, shrines, and pavilions. The tomb itself was an enormous circular earthen tumulus.

En route back to Hue we stopped at the Pagode des Sorciers which was reached by stairs cut in the rock formation. In a courtyard where traditional string music played, the splendidly garbed people knelt with sticks of joss in their hands while two young female shamans with heavy make-up and gold earrings swirled around in a dance, bending to accept monetary offerings after which they whispered in the donors' ears. People were ascending another stairway to a higher level, and when I asked a musician if I could go up there he smiled enigmatically. I climbed the stairs to find smaller altars and at one of them a male highlander in a loincloth stood before an

altar flagellating himself with leafy tree branches. Back at the main courtyard the ritual had ended, and the "female" shamans who had changed into
shirts and trousers, were removing their make-up, revealing that they were
young men.

Reflecting on the Hue experience I found it interesting and significant
that while the citadel contained some overtones of Confucianism, Buddhism was absent. Buddhist pagodas were located elsewhere in Hue. The
citadel, its layout, and royal cults centered on Taoist beliefs and practices.
Furthermore, the cult associated with the Pagode des Sorciers was purely
Taoist as were the popular cults I had seen not only in the rural Vietnamese
areas but in Saigon as well. It struck me that while most works on Vietnam
emphasized Buddhism and Confucianism, Taoism clearly deserved more
attention, thought, and ethnographic probing.

Two

RUMBLINGS

BY THE BEGINNING of 1957 the flush of newly found independence had begun to wane. President Diem already faced a growing host of social, political, and economic problems within the context of "nation building." Then, during the year, ominous rumblings warned of a coming crucial time, a challenging time for the Diem administration still in a formative stage. Insurgency in the South fostered by North Vietnam began to rumble the relative calm in rural areas and 1957 marked the beginning of Communist terrorism against Americans which sent waves of fear through Saigon-Cholon. To cope with this threat there was pressing need for effective cooperation with American leaders, but lack of understanding prevented such cooperation.

To make matters worse, some of the social-economic programs Diem began to implement in 1957 set off rumblings of discontent among ethnic minorities (highlanders, Cham, Khmer, and Chinese) who felt their ethnic identities threatened.[1] It was a problem Vietnamese leaders would have to approach with sensitivity based on some understanding of these people who composed part of the new nation's ethnic mosaic. But my continuing research in the highlands was to reveal that not only did Vietnamese leaders lack any understanding of the highlanders, they had no intention of learning anything about them.

As was the case with many newly independent states in post–World War II Southeast Asia, one of the major challenges in South Vietnam was to achieve a national integration of the many and varied ethnolinguistic groups. There was a notion, prevalent in many Southeast Asian capitals at the time, that in order to attain national integration, ties to kin groups, villages, religious sects, and ethnic groups (particularly ethnic minorities) must be replaced by loyalty to the state. Mixing this notion with Vietnamese chauvinism and ethnocentrism, Ngo Dinh Diem settled on a policy of assimilating the ethnic minorities into the Vietnamese cultural sphere. In the case of the highland people, assimilation would relieve the government of any need to gain an understanding of them. Unlike the Chinese, Khmer, and Cham, the highlanders were strangers who by Vietnamese standards were very primitive (dark skinned, scantily clothed, and living in the dreaded mountains). The Vietnamese had no experience administering the mountain country and there already was a shortage of trained civil servants, none of whom wished to serve in the mountains.

My library research had revealed how the highlanders, relatively isolated in their forested mountains, had historically remained aloof from the Chinese great tradition that had molded the society of the Vietnamese and also from the Indian influences diffusing eastward that had brought civilization to the Cham and Khmer. The French established the first urban centers in the highlands during the early part of the twentieth century. Around these centers the colonial government brought an administration in which highlanders assumed clerical and technical roles. The French also launched education and health programs. By and large, the French respected the integrity of highland village society and allowed the traditional ways to pertain (reflected in customs courts where village problems were resolved by highland judges weighing cases on the basis of traditional laws).

My field work gave me an appreciation of the highland world, based as it was on successful adaptation to the mountain country. It was centered on small communities where kinship was primary and resources shared by all. The people respected the integrity of their surroundings, and each society had leaders who served as stewards in preserving it. Villagers farmed slopes and bottomland within the never-ending cycle of rainy seasons followed by dry seasons, of fields planted or fallowing. In nearby streams they drew water, washed clothes, bathed, and fished. The surrounding forests supplied them with game, wild fruits and vegetables, and firewood as well as hardwood, bamboo, and rattan for their houses, artifacts, and wood carvings. Nature sustained them, but at the same time threatened them with unseen otherworldly forces intrinsic to nature itself and to human destiny. Although their religious pantheons varied, all of the highland people tried to keep in harmony with their deities by observing religious prescriptions. Cosmic forces had revealed sets of sanctions, taboos, omens, and signs, and they mandated certain individuals to serve as stewards of religious prescriptions. These stewards also were guardians of moral order expressed in systems of justice wherein respect for individual rights provided a counterpoint to the prevailing concern for group survival. Throughout the highland world were expressions of beauty in art, architecture, music, and dance, all of which took on symbolic meaning within the context of religious prescriptions. In a 1972 conversation concerning Diem's policy for assimilating the highlanders, former vice president Nguyen Ngoc Tho pointed out that, from the time in June 1954 when he became prime minister of the new government south of the 17th parallel, Diem felt that French influence in the central highlands had to be eliminated. The Crown Domain instituted by the French in 1950, which placed the central highlands under Emperor Bao Dai, was in Diem's words a "legal fiction" which only gave the appearance of Vietnamese control. In reality, the French maintained their hegemony over the region, using the Crown Domain to keep the "Kinh" (Vietnamese) out of the highlands so French entrepreneurs could "develop plantations and exploit valuable minerals." It was therefore essential to do away with the Crown Domain as the first step toward integrating the highlands into the national framework. Then the administration of the region would have to be reorganized, after which the "primitive highland people would have to be civilized," i.e., Vietnamized.

Nguyen Ngoc Tho stressed that Diem saw economic development as another means of integrating the highlands into the state and envisaged this taking place in a "progressive way—neither too rapidly nor too slowly." Since the region was sparsely populated, Diem deemed it necessary to move Vietnamese from the overpopulated coastal provinces, where "there is too much sand and not enough soil," into the uplands. The Vietnamese

settlers would have a role in the economic development, and they would
bring Vietnamese culture to the indigenous people.

During the October 1956 week celebrating the new republic, Diem
issued an ordinance initiating a new land reform program for South Vietnam and among other things it provided the basis for "land development"
programs. In addition to resettling northern refugees and people from overcrowded lowland areas, the Land Development Program called for transformation of the agricultural methods and lifestyle of the highlanders. Le
Van Kim, who had been chief of staff for the 4th Infantry ("Montagnard")
Division during the Indochina War, headed the program. On 22 February
1957, at Ban Me Thuot he launched the program with an "agricultural fair"
that featured floats, bands, speeches, highlanders in their "native costumes," and an elephant race. The gala air, however, was shattered when a
would-be assassin broke through the crowd and fired a pistol at Ngo Dinh
Diem. The bullet missed the president, but struck the minister of agriculture, seriously wounding him. The captured assailant was described as a
"Communist agent bent on killing Diem."

Since American aid funds would support the Land Development project
a member of the USOM's Agricultural Division prepared a report recommending that there should be a just policy regarding highland people's land
rights. Sadly, this view did not reflect those of either most American officials in Saigon or some influential foreign advisers to President Diem. One
American official said that the highlands served only as a hideout for hostile guerrillas while Wolf Ladejinsky, an adviser to Diem, described the
central highlands as a wilderness, a game preserve for King Bao Dai,
where none but nomadic tribesmen lived. This ignorance unfortunately
characterized many American leaders' view of the highlands until the end
of the Vietnam War. One fixed erroneous idea was that the highlanders
were "nomadic" people who constantly moved about, indiscriminately
slashing and burning the forests.

I met with Wesley Fishel, head of MSUG, to explain that on the basis of
my research it was apparent that highlanders had well-defined land-tenure
systems. He suggested I gather more information in the highlands, so early
in April 1957 I organized a field research trip into the central highlands
(with Frederick Wickert of the MSUG staff). In addition to researching
land tenure, we also hoped to discuss with highland leaders some ideas for
resolving the land question. The secretary of state at the presidency

approved the field trip, but he recommended that anyone going to the highlands talk only with province chiefs rather than "local people" in order "to avoid any possible misunderstanding."[2]

Riding in a Jeep station wagon with a Vietnamese driver who called himself Masourin, we drove in the early morning mist north from Saigon on Route 13 to reach Route 14, passing through territory that had been described by French explorers in the late nineteenth century. The road, in bad condition because of neglect of the Indochina War years, wound over the dry, rolling country of the Stieng people, passing Mount Bara which rose like a large mound covered with scrubby growth. Northward the road seemed to be swallowed by the massive rain forests of mixed growths that crowded one another in the struggle to reach the sunlight. Tangled vines and orchids clung to the massive hardwood trees in which we watched gibbons and monkeys swing. And we quickly discovered that stopping to stretch invited attacks by leeches. At Trois Frontières (named for the three frontiers of Cochinchina, Annam, and Cambodia that once converged here) there was a weathered monument to Henri Maitre, the French explorer and writer who in 1912 had been slain in a nearby village by the much feared Mnong chief Pu Trang Lung.

Moving out of Trois Frontières, our driver Masourin rolled up his window as he explained that when the fierce highlanders saw him they were sure to let fly with poisoned arrows.

As Route 14 continued northeast in the direction of Ban Me Thuot, there were in the forest Rhadé villages with their rows of longhouses. Children (some of them nude) scampered about, and on the large verandas of the main entrances to the houses, women worked, weaving textiles or husking rice by pounding it in a heavy wooden mortar with a wooden pestle. On the road, highlanders walked single file, and as the vehicle passed, they invariably stopped and bowed, a gesture of respect that the French expected. On the slopes in the dark green forests were odd-shaped patches of brown or black. Here the highland people had cut and burned trees and brush so they might farm the slopes when the rains begin in late April or early May. The last of these fires were sending gray smoke into the air, obscuring the mountains and settling in the valleys. This marks the first phase in the never-ending cycle of cutting, burning, planting, and harvesting of upland rain-fed rice that is at the heart of the mountain people's way of life.

Moving through a forested area south of Ban Me Thuot, Masourin let out a shout as we almost drove over a large snake. Later in Ban Me Thuot an American army captain who was driving behind us said the snake was a cobra and as we passed, it rose to lunge at the rear tire. Entering Ban Me Thuot from the south, we passed Buon Ale-A where the Christian and Missionary Alliance was located. On the hillside by the road stood the three "Italian villas" the Reverend Gordon Smith had constructed in 1950. Looking like villas one might have seen in California or Florida in the 1930s and 1940s, these houses seemed impressive in the setting of a carefully trimmed lawn graced with a large traveler palm.

Wickert and I were received hospitably by the American military advisers, who provided rooms in what had been Bao Dai's guest lodge. Immediately, we began interviewing some of the provincial officials, beginning with the Vietnamese province chief. He lost no time complaining that the highlanders working in the administration were trained by the French and were not literate in Vietnamese (we found out later that several of the highlander civil servants had studied in Hue and Qui Nhon). As a result, the province chief noted, "one Vietnamese clerk is worth three highland clerks." The highlanders, he emphasized, must learn the Vietnamese language and ways (such as wearing Vietnamese clothes). Regarding land tenure, the province chief was annoyed at what he described as the highlanders' belief that they owned all of the land and everything on it. Conflict ensued when Vietnamese sought to settle on land or fish in some of the streams.

Wickert and I met with three highland assistants to the province chief, and they outlined to us the Rhadé land-tenure system which, as expected, was tied in with social organization. With their matrilineal system, the Rhadé trace descent through the female line which determines membership in a clan. All of the clans lay claim to certain territories which are well delineated by geographical features. Within each clan a senior female of the subclan is the steward of local clan land, designating who can farm, hunt, fish, and cut timber so as to prevent abuses of the physical environment. She also punishes moral profanations of the soil (the gravest of which is incest, whether it implicates parent and child, household members, or clan members), affronts to the ancestors. The steward also must walk the land boundaries every seven years and perform prescribed rituals invoking ancestors and spirits associated with nature and farming.

A Rhadé steward of
clan land, 1957.

We visited surrounding villages where information on social organization and land tenure conformed to what the civil servants had reported.
Everyone emphasized that the Rhadé did not claim all of the land but only
certain territories which were well delincated.

Although our interviews were focused on land tenure and other aspects
of Rhadé society, the interviewees invariably began to complain about the
Vietnamese. In mid 1956 northern Vietnamese were settled in two large
villages along Route 14 thirty-two kilometers north of Ban Me Thuot and
there were cases of settlers and Vietnamese squatters moving onto land that
Rhadé villagers had cleared in preparation for planting. The civil servants
complained about discrimination against them in the administration. Both
civil servants and villagers expressed fear that with a large influx of Vietnamese they would soon be outnumbered. The civil servants also reported
that, following the 1954 Geneva Agreements, between five thousand and
six thousand Rhadé had "gone north" with the Viet Minh.

Wickert and I journeyed over an incredibly bad road to Ban Don near
the Cambodian border to meet with Y Keo, judge for the Ban Me Thuot
"customs court" organized by the French to arbitrate conflict on the basis
of Rhadé customs. While displaying his French medals he outlined the

At Ban Don with Y Keo, judge of the Rhadé customs court, and his wife, 1957.

Rhadé land-tenure system, relating it to the kinship system as the others had done. Near Y Keo's house an elephant convoy was gathering to travel to the Boloven plateau in Laos. Y Keo invited us to join, a very tempting invitation which we were sorry to decline.

Back in Ban Me Thuot we were warmly welcomed by the American missionaries, the Reverend N. Robert Ziemer and the Reverend Edward Mangham. We discussed relations between the highlanders and Vietnamese, and the two missionaries outlined some complaints they had received from Rhadé in their congregation. Complaints concerned the claim that Vietnamese were settling on land owned by the Rhadé, the superimposition of a Vietnamese administration on Rhadé villages without regard for indigenous leadership, and what Rhadé considered the arrogant attitude of the Vietnamese in general. The village medical program organized by the French was now totally neglected with empty dispensaries, and neglected also was the education system.

I then met with Father Roger Bianchetti, a member of the Société de la Mission Etrangères de Paris, who was training young highlanders to cultivate coffee and process the beans for sale. He echoed the same views as the

American missionaries concerning the highlanders' complaints about the Vietnamese. Father Bianchetti added that highlanders felt like "conquered people."

In Pleiku the province chief said that relations between lowland and highland people were good, and he himself went to highland celebrations where he ate the food (noting he did this in spite of it not being "sanitary") but he only pretended to drink from the jars. It was, he felt, necessary to show respect (although he admitted that he did not like their habit of going about half naked and he wished that the men would wear trousers instead of the brief loincloth). As to land tenure, the province chief said it was a problem because Jarai only claim land they are farming and move constantly because of their farming methods.

Highland civil servants and villagers reported that farming methods varied from swidden (such as that found among the Rhadé) to permanent paddy farming. A family had usufruct of its swiddens whether they were being farmed or were fallowing. Many of the informants complained about ill treatment by the Vietnamese. Vietnamese soldiers entered villages to steal animals. In the Pleiku market, Vietnamese would pluck fruits and vegetables from highlanders' backbaskets and Vietnamese merchants cheated them. Highland civil servants were relegated to an inferior status by Vietnamese officials.

We were invited to a Jarai village on the plateau some fifteen kilometers from Pleiku for a buffalo sacrifice to thank the spirits for curing a man who had been gravely ill. Arriving in the middle of the night, we heard the haunting sound of gongs rendered dramatic by drumbeats mixed with thunder as lightning flashed over the mountains. People wrapped in mantles against the chilly wind sat around fires and drank from jars. In front of the healed man's longhouse men beating gongs circled a restless buffalo tied to a stake decorated with symbols. At dawn, as everyone gathered around, a husky young man clutching a saber danced around the buffalo which became agitated as the gong music grew louder and more rhythmic. Suddenly the dancer lunged forward to cut the tendons of the rear legs, sending the animal thrashing to the ground. Then another dancer moved in to kill the buffalo with a blow to the back of the neck. After a few moments the buffalo lay still and men with metal basins rushed to collect the flowing blood. Men with sabers dressed out the buffalo, putting certain parts, offerings to the spirits, on a metal platter which was taken into the longhouse.

Children gathered to watch the men cut up the flesh, and the men handed them pieces of the stomach to chew on.

As guests, Wickert and I were accorded the "honor" of having some of the sacrificial buffalo's raw liver to eat. The liver was very tough and very bloody (I could not dispel thoughts of what it might contain). I hoped fervently that something would occur nearby to divert everyone's attention so I could spit the liver into the fire. It didn't happen.

By now, great clouds swelling in the southwestern skies had moved visibly closer until the first rains began in a drama of high winds. On slopes the last of the burning logs and smoldering ashes in the fields hissed as they were dampened. Cracked brown earth softened into mud. Everywhere there was the fragrance of newly wet earth. As the rains beat down, dusty foliage was washed clean. People running with large fronds sheltering their heads sought refuge and naked children scampered out of the houses to frolic and revel in the downpour. The arrival of the monsoon is in many ways an exuberant event because it is not the time to worry about whether the season will bring too much or too little rain or to fret about whether the crops will flourish or fail. It is a time of renewal, of fresh hope.

At the northern edge of Kontum along Route 14, the newly arrived American military advisory team was housed in tents. In the evening they showed movies on an outdoor screen, attracting many Vietnamese and highlanders (who by their reactions clearly sympathized with the Indians in the movies).

The province chief complained about lack of trained highlanders for positions in the administration. One result was that only one of the four district chiefs was a highlander. He also voiced discontent over the way highlanders (whom he described as "lazy") farmed. It was destructive, and he planned to end it by launching a forest conservation program.

We went to pay our respects to Bishop Paul Seitz, head of the Kontum Mission. The bishop came down the steps of the large, rambling Norman-style mission headquarters to meet us. A storm was gathering, and he presented a dramatic figure with his black soutane, graying beard, and penetrating eyes. In his book-lined office we discussed relations between the highlanders and Vietnamese in Kontum. The two groups had lived in proximity for many years in Kontum, and the bishop felt that it had been beneficial for the highlanders. They had retained their way of life but had learned many things from the Vietnamese, such as better gardening and farming methods (he noted that there was extensive permanent field cultivation by highlanders in the vicinity of Kontum). The highlanders, he felt, must develop both socially and economically to avoid being overwhelmed by the more advanced Vietnamese.

As in Ban Me Thuot and Pleiku, highlander civil servants were most cooperative in providing information on their land-tenure systems. The Bahnar and Sedang had village territories in which the residents farmed. Use of this territory (land, streams, and trees) was carefully controlled by village elders. The most impressive highlander we encountered in Kontum was Paul Nur, a man with a brooding air, who was bitter about the Vietnamese treatment of highland people. He was serving as a schoolmaster, and he cited examples of highland civil servants and teachers being accorded second-class status by the Vietnamese. He also said that male villagers were expected to do corvée on roads for twenty to thirty days a year. Although they were supposed to receive forty piasters a day, they never received any compensation.

Traveling northward from Kontum on Route 14, at Kon Horing, a large Sedang settlement and market, the schoolmaster provided information on land tenure. In the vicinity of Dak To the French priests from the Kontum Mission lived in villages and their style of life was little different from that of highlanders around them. In one village the French priest kindly invited us to return that evening to share his meal of wild boar. While dining (we managed to find some dusty bottles of wine in a thatched food store nearby), the priest told how during World War II he had hidden three American flyers. One day, however, he saw Japanese soldiers coming in the front gate and warned the Americans, who fled into the forest. The priest later learned that one had been captured and beheaded, but the other two made good their escape.

In the village, some boys were shooting arrows from a crossbow at the strip of bamboo they had arranged as a target. They insisted I try, and although Wickert laughingly said I "couldn't hit the side of a barn," I took aim and dispatched the arrow through the target. The boys shouted with excitement, wanting me to repeat this feat. Needless to say, I declined, but they insisted I keep the crossbow.

We drove south from Kontum on Route 14 to the juncture of Route 7 near Pleiku and proceeded to Cheo Reo. Route 7 wound down from the plateau in a southeasterly direction through country that was only sparsely forested but had many escarpments and hills. Located at the confluence of the Ayun and Apa Rivers, Cheo Reo was little more than a collection of Jarai villages, most of them established by members of the elite Rcom clan, the first to settle in the area. There were a few small administrative buildings (Cheo Reo was a district headquarters), a school, and some Vietnamese shops built of wattled walls and thatched roofs. We were greeted by Nay Moul, a husky man with a thick, large face (he was one of the first highlanders to join the French army in 1931). He had married Rcom H'ban, daughter of the famed Jarai chief, Nay Nui, who at the end of the nineteenth century had fought the first French to come into the area. Both Nay Moul and Nay Nui were good examples of the Jarai belief that certain individuals are favored by the spirits and consequently predestined to leadership. We gladly accepted Nay Moul's kind invitation to stay at the very large longhouse that Nay Nui had built many years before (the old chief lived across the river with a daughter). While there we gathered information on the land-tenure system, which like the system of the Jarai in Pleiku and the Rhadé, called for land, gardens, and house sites to be passed down through the female line.

While conducting research on French sources in Paris and Saigon, I had become fascinated with accounts of the two powerful Jarai shamans, the King of Water and the King of Fire who possesses a sacred saber said to have remarkable magical powers. Nay Moul related that the King of Fire resided in a village north of Cheo Reo and every dry season he made a tour of villages aimed at bringing rain for crops and warding off epidemics.

We also visited villages and in order to reach one of them we had to disrobe to swim across a river. During a lunch in one of the longhouses an elephant stuck its trunk through a window to beg for food. In another longhouse a woman was preparing a rat to roast and when a baby cried she gave it the severed tail as a pacifier.

From Cheo Reo we returned north on Route 7 to the juncture of Route 19, which we took to the coast. Toward the end of the Indochina War in 1954, the French army Groupe Mobile 100 had suffered a series of Viet Minh attacks on this road. Now, three years later, there still were burned-out hulks of military vehicles almost hidden in green forest growths along the road. Here and there were small concrete memorials to the fallen. We reached Qui Nhon and went south along the magnificent coast via Nhatrang to Saigon, ending a field trip of some 2,500 kilometers.

Since the area around Ban Me Thuot was scheduled to be the site for some of the first Land Development Centers, I decided to focus further land-tenure investigation on some of the Rhadé villages and clans involved. In May 1957 I returned to Ban Me Thuot accompanied by Price Gittinger, a staff member of the USOM Agricultural Division, who was conducting most of the research for the proposed land reform program. At Ban Me Thuot we consulted with Col. Le Van Kim, director of the Land Development Program in the highlands. An alert, intelligent man with considerable wartime experience in the region, Kim was very well aware of the problems involved in his program because of Rhadé land claims. He had become familiar with the Rhadé land-tenure system, so he had formed a committee consisting of himself, several of his Vietnamese officers (who were learning Rhadé), the district chief, and some notables from local Rhadé villages. The Rhadé village of Buon Kroa near Ban Me Thuot was to be the site of the first Land Development Center. When the agricultural fair had been held in February 1957, the committee agreed to pay the village ten thousand piasters for five hectares to use as a demonstration plot to indicate that implementation of the program was beginning.

Gittinger and I met with Rhadé civil servants and village leaders to discuss the possibility of land being sold or leased to the government. The consensus was that the government could take any land not claimed. Clan land, however, was inalienable according to Rhadé tradition, but it might be leased. They pointed out that some French plantations were on clan or village land leased for ninety-nine years (a *bail emphythéotique*). They also noted that most of the land around Buon Kroa belonged to the Eban clan, and the current guardian was an elderly lady named H'deo Eban.

We went to Buon Kroa, and villagers provided an elephant to transport us through the thick forest to the swidden where the villagers were busy planting their crops. We found H'deo Eban sitting amidst some jars of alcohol in the middle of a field being sown that day. Nearby, some men were striking gongs that provided a rhythm for rows of men who moved along making holes with dibble sticks in the reddish soil. Behind them, women followed, stooping to drop seeds from a bamboo tube into the holes. Then, with the solid end of the tube they pushed dirt into each hold and tamped the soil. As we began discussing the land question with H'deo Eban, the gong players and some of the planters came to join the conversation.

H'deo Eban was annoyed because some of the Eban land had been taken for land development and she had never been consulted by Le Van Kim's committee. She and the others pointed out that in the past, payments had been made to land guardians and villages for plantation lands. Since 1954, however, these payments had ceased. One man stated, "The government is stronger than we, so we must do what it wants, just as we had to do what the French wanted." H'deo Eban finally agreed to meet with Kim's committee to discuss leasing Eban land, although she was vague about what the compensation might be. One villager noted that most Rhadé were unfamiliar with cash, and traditionally land was rented for such things as a pig, a large old jar, or a woman's skirt.

Gittinger and I then consulted with various Rhadé and Vietnamese officials (including Y Keo, the judge living in Ban Don). All agreed that a commission of Vietnamese and Rhadé be formed to negotiate with local village notables and clan land guardians to work out the land question. We returned to Saigon and in June 1957 submitted separate reports. Gittinger's report focused on Rhadé land rights, particularly in the Buon Kroa situation. He recommended that Rhadé land claims be honored and, where Vietnamese were to be settled on clan lands, the guardians be given compensation. He also pointed out that failure to resolve such land claims would generate discontent among the highlanders, making them more susceptible to Communist propaganda. In addition, he recommended that "USOM, on its side, should support such a general land tenure accord, and should make it a condition of its continuing support for land development projects."[3]

My report contained the same recommendation concerning the need to resolve highlander land claims, and it also favored the formation of a commission such as the one organized by Le Van Kim. Furthermore it summarized findings on land tenure and related aspects of the various ethnic groups' social organization and agriculture that had been gathered during both field trips. The report also presented some views expressed by the province chiefs and the highlanders regarding the Vietnamese. Included were historical data that had been gathered at the National Museum in Saigon. Since this report was to be sent to President Diem and other government officials, it was decided to have a French version.[4]

According to Wesley Fishel, Diem was very upset by my report, particularly the section about the highlanders' attitude toward the Vietnamese. (Typical of the direct quotations were: "The Vietnamese talk equality, but they don't mean what they say. In their hearts they want to dominate us. They are colonialists. The French were bad at the mouth, but in their hearts they were good."). Diem arranged a flight to Ban Me Thuot, where, fore-warned of his purpose, province officials had some Rhadé notables, dressed in Vietnamese clothes, greet him with a few Vietnamese words. Diem returned to Saigon and told Fishel that the report was inaccurate. The highland people, he said, loved the Vietnamese and desired to emulate them.

But the harshest criticism of my report (and Gittinger's as well) came from Wolf Ladejinsky, a land reform "expert" for Diem. He had been telling Diem that the highlands comprised the richest region in Vietnam. At the MSUG offices he ranted that the report "was the worst ever issued" by the group. "How do you expect the government to deal with these children?" was his comment regarding my recommendation for resolving land claims. I retorted that if he operated on the premise that the highlanders were "children" he would not get far in any dealings with them. Then he added, "They look out the window and say 'I own all the land I see,'" to which I responded that such a statement only demonstrated that he had not read the report. Gittinger's report was withdrawn by USOM and locked in a safe. My report, however, was allowed by Fishel to circulate without changes. Nonetheless, both Gittinger and I were in disfavor (one of the few who supported our views was the French scholar, Bernard Fall). Worst of all, it was quietly agreed in the American mission that the Land Develop-ment Program would move ahead without regard for highlander land claims.

According to Bui Van Luong, it was understood in Saigon that compen-sation to the highlanders for land expropriated by the government (not a lease but a forced sale) would be in the form of a water buffalo or a jar of rice alcohol. Reports from Ban Me Thuot, however, indicated that Le Van Kim was making cash payments for land, and by mid 1957 he had already expended some thirty thousand piasters in Darlac province. This annoyed President Diem and his brother Nhu, who felt there was no need for negoti-ation or compensation. Kim was removed from his post (subsequently he became director of the new Military Academy in Dalat).

The significance of these developments was not lost on a group of young, educated highlanders who felt the policies of the Diem government reinforced rather than reduced their sense of ethnic identity, particularly the common identity of being highlanders. This led to formation of the first indigenous ethnonationalistic movement to appear in the central highlands. Early in 1955, a group of young Rhadé and Bahnar, outraged at Vietnamese discrimination against highlanders and the violation of highlanders' rights by the army, formed Le Front pour la Libération des Montagnards. Most were Christians and they met in Buon Ale-A, site of the American Christian and Missionary Alliance headquarters near Ban Me Thuot. Through 1956 and 1957, growing discontent with the influx of Vietnamese as part of the Land Development Program expanded recruitment of the Front in Ban Me Thuot and Pleiku. Recruitment among educated highlanders also was successful because they either knew one another or knew about one another. Many had attended the same French schools—particularly in Ban Me Thuot and Kontum. In addition, there was an increasing number of marriages taking place among the elite families of the Bahnar, Jarai, Rhadé, Chru, Lat, and Sre.

Early in 1958 the Ban Me Thuot group and another in Pleiku merged and formed the Bajaraka Movement, a name derived from the key letters in Bahnar, Jarai, Rhadé, and Koho. In August, Y Bham Enuol, a Rhadé leader, wrote a letter in French outlining highlanders' grievances. The movement sent the letter to the American, British, French, Indian, and Laotian diplomatic missions in Saigon asking them to intervene with the Vietnamese government on behalf of the highlanders. The reaction of the Saigon government was to arrest some Bajaraka leaders including Y Bham Enuol and Paul Nur (whom I had interviewed in Kontum in 1957). In October the movement sent President Diem a request signed by one thousand highlanders for the release of the prisoners. Movement leaders also organized a demonstration in Ban Me Thuot. An estimated crowd of two thousand streamed into the town from surrounding villages, and a Bajaraka leader addressed them, enumerating the discontents of the highland people. Armored units of the 23rd Division moved in to disperse the crowd. The Bajaraka Movement was forced underground, but Diem's attempts to crush ethnonationalism among the highlanders had failed.

This was a low period but one glint of hope came when Dr. Richard Pittman and David Thomas, Wycliffe Bible translators with the Summer Institute of Linguistics (SIL), came to see me about research among the highland people. In 1956, Dr. Pittman had met with President Diem to explain his program of linguistic studies, preparation of literacy material in vernacular languages, and Bible translation. Diem granted permission for the SIL to begin its project in South Vietnam. The following year Dr. Pittman and David Thomas arrived to organize the project, which was to be sponsored by the University of Saigon. My meeting with Dr. Pittman and David Thomas resulted in a long period of cooperation in highland research.

During 1957, rumblings came from other parts of rural South Vietnam. In reaction to Diem's policy of forced assimilation, movements similar to Bajaraka were forming among the Cham and Khmer Krom. Ever since their "advance southward" had taken them into Cambodian territory in the Mekong River delta, the Vietnamese had been regarded as alien invaders by the Khmer Krom. When Diem abolished use of the Khmer language and did away with Khmer schools, Khmer Krom antagonism deepened. Many Khmer Krom moved to Cambodia, and those who remained in Vietnam sent their children to study in Phnom Penh. One result of this surge of eth-nonationalism was the formation of the Struggle Front of the Khmer of Kampuchia Krom.

In the late 1950s there were reports that a movement called the Front for the Liberation of Northern Cambodia was founded by the Khmer Krom. About the same time there appeared a Front for the Liberation of Champa intended for the Cham populations in the coastal provinces of Central Vietnam and in the Chau Doc and Tay Ninh areas. There are indications that a figure active in the establishment of both movements was Lt. Col. Les Kosem, a Cambodian Cham (also a Muslim) officer of the Royal Khmer Army security forces.[5]

While rumblings among the highlanders, Khmer Krom, and Cham were far removed from Saigon and the Independence Palace, new rumblings began in nearby Cholon because of Diem's policy of integrating the ethnic minorities into the Vietnamese cultural sphere. In August 1956, Diem issued two decrees affecting the Chinese. One removed the special status of Chinese and required them to register as aliens. It also forbade aliens from engaging in eleven types of merchandising. The second decree conferred Vietnamese citizenship upon all Chinese born in Vietnam. As new citizens they were required to obtain new identity cards and adopt Vietnamese names. The decrees set off shock waves in the Chinese community but it brought disunity rather than unity among the Chinese congregations. There were reports that some Chinese fled to Cambodia. When a deadline was set for changing all commercial signs into the Vietnamese language, the elaborate neon and electric bulb signs in Chinese characters that at night turned Cholon into an oriental fantasy went dark.

By the beginning of 1957 the conflict between Diem and the Chinese congregations worsened. There were reports that the Chinese were threatening to withdraw all of their money from the banks. In May there were riots at the Taiwanese consulate by Chinese who demanded that the Taipei government help them. Outside intermediaries stepped in to resolve the differences. The congregations finally attained some unity and Diem agreed to meet with them, setting the stage for an accommodation.

But the most ominous rumblings in South Vietnam accompanied the emergence of Communist guerrilla activities. In 1956 there had been different predictions about future Communist moves in South Vietnam. At the colorful and impressive parade in late October marking the first anniversary of the republic, I was not surprised to see Jack Ryan, one of the brightest and most vocal of the MSUG police advisers, wince and shake his head as the tanks rolled by. Diem and the American military experts agreed that the major threat to security in South Vietnam would be military moves by North Vietnam. Ryan and other police advisers saw Viet Minh cadre remaining in remote parts of the South as potential guerrillas, a threat to security at the village level. Ryan's group said that reliance on tanks and other heavy military machinery would keep the South Vietnamese army on the roads. They advocated using the Civil Guard as a rural police force to cope with the guerrillas. Diem and Lt. Gen. Samuel T. "Hanging Sam" Williams, head of Military Assistance Advisory Group (MAAG), regarded any expanded role of the Civil Guard as a potential barrier to growth of the army. They prevailed. Soon after, the Civil Guard dwindled in size as its police role diminished. And so the tanks rolled down the boulevard.

By and large, during 1956 and early 1957 Communist activities were restricted to recruitment and spreading of propaganda among villagers. Before the end of 1957, however, Communist guerrilla strategy turned to violence against Americans. The last week of October 1957 was marked by celebrations for the second anniversary of Ngo Dinh Diem's election victory. The Colombo Plan conference also was held that week. Just as the conference ended, Communist terrorists exploded a bomb under a MAAG bus and another bomb in front of the Five Oceans Hotel, an American officers' billet in Cholon. These shocking events marked the first Viet Cong terrorist attacks in the capital district and everyone wondered what they heralded. Troops moved in to protect Americans and public buildings.

On field trips thus far, the revelation that Communist cadre lurked in dark corners of South Vietnam was unsettling. One particularly revealing field trip (which also was the most exotic I had made thus far) was in August 1957 and took me to the Katu country in the mountains inland from Hoi An, a coastal port that in the past was called Faifoo. The Katu live in the harshest and least hospitable physical environments of the central highlands.[6] In his 1938 article on the Katu (one of the few sources on them), J. Le Pichon describes the relief of their country as being "very broken, a confusion of mountains" where rivers rush through tortuous valleys cut by innumerable streams with rapids and waterfalls. He adds, "Katu paths, slippery and filled with leeches, push ahead, plunging and replunging into rivers, scaling the steep mountain slopes (the Katu do not ask 'where are you going?' but rather, 'where are you going up to?'). At dawn the cries of monkeys mix with songs of peacocks and chatter of birds, belling of deer, and rustling of thousands of insects, a signal that the hunting hour of the tiger, lord of the forest, is at hand."[7]

Historically the Vietnamese in coastal settlements greatly feared the Katu because of their frequent raids on villages, less to pillage than to kill and obtain human blood for their ritual sacrifices. During the reigns of Minh Mang (1820–41) and Thieu Tri (1841–47), the "blood raids" were so numerous that the royal court was prompted to organize ceremonial presentations of buffalo and other gifts to Katu chiefs in the vain hope of ending the raids. During the French colonial period the only Vietnamese who had contact with the Katu were Vietnamese traders, woodcutters, and those in search of precious oils. But despite their familiarity with the Katu, it was not unusual for these Vietnamese to fall victim to the raids.

In preparation for the field trip I joined my friend the American missionary the Reverend Gordon Smith (who had founded the Ban Me Thuot mission) and Philip Hodgeson of the British Embassy at the Smith's compound in Danang (which everyone still called by its French name, Tourane). A cook and handy-man joined us. Located on a beautiful bay, Danang had faded colonial charm, and the boarded-up Grand Hotel on the Han River lent a ghost-town air. Having already visited the Katu, Gordon knew that blood raids normally do not take place in August, a time when villages experienced food shortages. So he arranged with the priest in charge of the Catholic Relief Service in Danang to obtain rice, which would be accompanied by a Vietnamese nurse in a larger boat. Gordon Smith was an unusual man, deeply concerned with the welfare of the highland people, a missionary with extensive ethnographic interests. His son Douglas was with the U.S. Information Service in Saigon, another son Stan was studying for the ministry, and a third son Leslie was a professional hunter who took Americans hunting in the mountains.

With our bedrolls, food, and other gear we drove in a Land Rover south to Hoi An. There, Gordon contacted Mr. Phuong, a wood vendor who spoke Katu and knew their villages. We boarded two sampans belonging to a hardy woman and her equally hardy daughter. They positioned themselves at the rear of the sampans to pole them against the current and move upstream in the Thu Bon River. Leaving Hoi An, the mountains were covered with somber thick forest. The cook served a lunch of canned meat with bread. Afternoon air became heavy and moist as the women guided the sampans through rapids. Sitting erect in his sampan and wearing a toupee, Gordon Smith looked for all the world like the storied Western explorer in the tropics. Toward dusk we reached a small Vietnamese settlement where we slept in the communal temple. The cook purchased strange brown rice from the villagers. It turned out to be tasteless (the cook insisted it was good for us because it contained "histamine"), so we opened a sack of relief rice for dinner.

Three days later we arrived at Tan My on the Cay River, the last Vietnamese settlement where Katu gathered to trade. The Katu men and women in a trading party were of varied ages. Men wore loincloths while women, with brass earrings and bead necklaces, wore skirts and, unlike most highland women, had tops covering their breasts. The Katu were amused when I photographed an older woman kneeling low to allow a pet monkey to rummage through her hair in search of lice. Then in the morning, Katu boys watched quizzically as we shaved, a strange ritual. From among the Katu, Gordon and Phuong obtained bearers to carry our gear. Leaving the settlement on the narrow winding path, dead bamboo stalks covered the ground, cracking underfoot while the canopy overhead filtered sunlight. Suddenly we were enveloped by jungle vastness of huge trunks, tangled branches, gnarled roots, and an astonishing array of fronds. In the soft earth were animal tracks and on wild banana trees large evil-looking spiders in webs. On the path we met a file of Katu women with backbaskets, followed by men with packs containing compartments for a knife, pipe, some tobacco, and a quiver of arrows for the crossbows they carried. Dripping from the still, humid heat, we came upon and bathed in a flowing brook with cool, clear water, a lustral refreshment.

Finally we reached the village Mr. Phuong identified as A-To, surrounded by a stockade. The gate was closed and along the path were freshly made bamboo symbols, raising the question of whether they were taboo signs. Mr. Phuong went to the gate where a young man informed him that the village was indeed taboo. At Mr. Phuong's behest he summoned the headman. After an exchange, the headman relented, saying we could enter the village and go straight to the men's house for a short time marked by the passage of the sun. The village struck me as grubby compared with other highland villages I had visited. The seven houses on pilings arranged around a carved sacrificial stake were ramshackle. Gardens were skimpy. The village was strangely still, notched log stairs had been pulled up to the entrance verandas, doors were closed, and we could see eyes peering at us through cracks in the walls.

We lapsed into silence as we made our way to the men's house which figures prominently in blood raids. It is here that the men gather to perform a chicken-foot divination ritual to decide on the raid and select a victim. After talking, drinking, and singing all night the raid party leaves at dawn. Strategies for blood raids vary from nocturnal ambushes to seeking a victim in a sleeping village. The raiders dip their long spears into the victim's blood. Afterwards the party returns to the men's house where they remain incommunicado for one month, during which they cannot bathe. Then they emerge to dance around the bloody spears while invoking the spirits.

In the semi-darkness of the men's house with its smell of smoke and walls covered with heads of buffalo that had been sacrificed, the glum-faced headman sat on a mat. Around him was a group of longhaired young men garbed in very brief loincloths and clutching long hardwood spears with sharp blades used in the blood raids. We mustered up smiles and greeted the headman with bows, but his face remained glum. Talking through Mr. Phuong, the chief expressed dissatisfaction at having "Frenchmen" in the village, saying the "Viet Minh" would not like it. He noted there were Viet Minh in the forest, adding that his brother, who had "gone north" was now with them. When the headman mentioned a food shortage, Gordon said that if his men went to Thanh My they could get rice from the boat. The chief, however, shook his head. "The Viet Minh would be angry if we took food from the French."

I always brought American cigarettes on field trips to give as gifts, so I offered some "Hit Parade filter-tips" to the headman. Philip whispered that he hoped the Katu would not choke on the filter-tips. The headman brightened up, took the cigarettes and distributed them to the young men. They puffed away and then eagerly split open the filter tips to find out what they were made of. According to Mr. Phuong they all agreed the tips were full of dried grass.

Back on the trail, Gordon, Philip, and I admitted we had experienced feelings of unease in A-To. With Mr. Phuong guiding we walked to the neighboring village of O-Mo, which had no stockade and a small men's house. Its longhouses (even more ramshackle than those at A-To) were arranged around a sacrificial stake. Smoking his long pipe, the headman welcomed us and explained that survivors of two epidemic-ravaged villages had banded together to found O-Mo. He added that O-Mo was now plagued with more sickness and lack of food. As villagers gathered around us, Gordon distributed large safety pins which the Katu valued as decorations. They touched our clothes, wondered at our watches and cameras, and felt the hair on our arms. We in turn were fascinated with the way the young men combed their long hair and arranged impressive hairdos with boar tusks.

In the main room of the headman's longhouse we arranged our bedrolls and strung mosquito nets from the beams. Sleep did not come easily because the Katu coughed loudly. I finally dozed, only to be awakened by sharp insect bites on the back of my neck. I shined my flashlight to find large black ants on the bedroll. Pulling the mosquito netting aside I was shocked to seen an army of black ants, thousands of them, moving like a conveyer belt alongside the bedroll. Shaken, I rolled out the other side and shouted to Gordon and Philip. Lured by our food, the invading ants were swarming up the pilings. The headman aroused other men who carried pots of boiling water from the open hearths to pour on the ants, finally dispersing them.

When the boat carrying the nurse and relief rice arrived at Thanh My, men from the village carried bags of rice to each longhouse. We accompanied the Vietnamese nurse from the mission who began treating sick villagers, most of them suffering from fevers, abdominal problems, and diarrhea. In one longhouse they unrolled a grass mat which contained a naked emaciated woman, her crotch one red and bleeding sore. After helping tend the sick as best we could we sat with the headman. He gave us basic information about kinship and farming, touching on blood sacrifices. The headman told how three years before in his natal village two people were victims of blood raids.

Back at the Smith's Danang compound, while enjoying Laura Smith's warm hospitality and discussing our findings, we learned that two Katu in the central market were being taunted by Vietnamese because they had long hair. We went there to find a man in his twenties and a boy of about fifteen, who explained that they had come to Danang to trade areca nuts and betel leaves for salt (highly valued in the highlands). The older one had visited Danang before, but it was the first time the boy had left the Katu country. Their ride in Gordon's Land Rover was a frightening experience and the traffic policeman waving his arms mystified them. At the compound the Katu were astonished at running water in the kitchen and glass in the windows (which they refused to touch). They clearly felt at home, however, with the compound pets, particularly Chesty, the gibbon.

The comment of the Katu headman of A-To village that his brother had "gone north" and was now with the Viet Minh in the forest strongly suggested that highlanders trained in North Vietnam might in 1957 be returning to play vital roles in Communist guerrilla cadres. If so it put in a new light earlier information that five thousand to six thousand Rhadé had "gone north" with the Viet Minh. Should these Communist-trained highlanders return as cadres they no doubt would play on highlanders' discontents with Diem's minority policies in spreading propaganda that the Saigon government did not care about them.

At this time I joined the MSUG research faculty at the National Institute of Administration located in a former Catholic girls' school facing the park behind the cathedral. I organized a course in anthropology which attracted very bright advanced students who requested an additional course, but Rector Vu Quoc Thong would not approve it.

During most of the 1958–59 period, I was a member of an MSUG team consisting of Jim Hendry (an economist), and Lloyd Woodruff (a specialist in government) who conducted research in the Mekong River delta village of Khanh Hau. The objectives were manifold since a study was needed to answer many social, economic, and administrative questions about the role of the village in rural development. For me there was primarily the intention of making an ethnographic contribution by adding a description of southern Vietnamese village society to the growing body of information about peoples of the world. I wanted to present the village as a whole—to unfold the fabric of interrelated social institutions that have to do with all aspects of village life, not from a flat, two-dimensional view but to show the changes that have been occurring and continue to occur—and relate it to the greater society of which it is a part.

None of the team ever thought that we would witness the advent of Viet Cong guerrilla activities in the Mekong River delta.

After several months of planning and visiting Mekong River delta villages we selected the village of Khanh Hau, just south of the market town of Tan An. Following protocol, we visited the district chief to obtain his approval. Then we wrote a letter to the village chief explaining what our study would entail and why we were doing it (to inform the Americans about life in a Vietnamese village). Rather than agreeing on common problems to study, we simply agreed to pursue our separate disciplinary paths, discuss our findings, and share our data. The result was stimulating cooperation, some pooling of information, and increased sensitivity to the tools and interests of one another's approach to the study of society.

When we began our village study there was in Saigon a stereotype of southern farmers as "lazy" peasants (the Vietnamese word *nhà quê* was used pejoratively in Saigon, implying ignorant bumpkins) who sat around and planted the same rice every year. We found that Khanh Hau people were hard-working and very resourceful. Drawing on the experience of their ancestors in the historic "southward advance," the farmers had learned to maintain the necessary balance among soil, seeds (adopting some indigenous Khmer varieties of rice), water, sun, and available fertilizers. In time they also selected the artifacts they considered functional—a Khmer plow, a harrow, waterwheels, water scoops, knives, sickles, threshing sledges, baskets, winnowing machines, granaries, and rice mills.

During the dry season farmers planned carefully for the next crop. They cultivated *Oryza sativa* (within this species, five types of early or hasty rice and nine types of late rice) and also four types of the *O. glutinosa* species. One variety called "fox's fang" was highly prized in Southeast Asia. Anticipated market price of rice probably was the factor most often discussed among farmers during the dry season. Prices of the previous year and opinions of successful farmers such as one big landowner and the village chief

A wedding procession led by the groom, the best man, and the bride, identifiable by her large circular hat, 1958.

were heavily weighed. We witnessed innovation as rising prices of fruits and vegetables stimulated some farmers in 1959 to devote portions of farmland to these cash crops.

Unlike most Saigon folks, Khanh Hau villagers were proud of Vietnamese traditions. At first they watched us carefully (one lady later said, "At first I was afraid you might change village ways, but now I'm glad to meet you on the road"). In time we visited every house and were invited to most weddings and funerals. One of the pleasures of conducting research in a southern Vietnamese village was the delicious food. We had traditional Vietnamese tunics and turbans tailored to wear at rituals in the communal temple (several older ladies exclaimed how impressive we looked). Villagers freely offered information on any aspect of their lives. When I asked about transplanting rice seedlings, however, they suggested I do it, which I did.

As research went on, I became increasingly aware that religion in Khanh Hau was an integral part of almost every activity in village society. Léopold Cadière, the Western investigator who more than any other

With Lloyd Woodruff, the village chief (*in front of Woodruff*), the deputy chief (*left*), and a former resident in western clothes, at a ritual in the communal temple, 1958.

plumbed the depths of Vietnamese religious beliefs and practices, likens Vietnamese religion (and he expressly uses the singular) to a dense rain forest in the Annamite Cordillera.[8] With its all-embracing abundance of great trunks, roots, massive foliage, branches, lianas, fronds, flowers, and carpets of moss, the individual is enveloped as is the Vietnamese in the omnipresence of his religion. Implied also is an analogy between the symbiosis of the diverse elements in the forest and the symbiosis of the Buddhist-Taoist-Confucianist great tradition inherited from China with the myriad beliefs and practices of the Vietnamese little tradition, notably the Cult of Spirits.

Interestingly, Cadière concludes, "The true religion of the Vietnamese is the Cult of Spirits," and he adds, "This religion has no history, for it dates to the origins of the race."

Everywhere in the village were symbols and signs of Taoism and also the Spirit Cult. Often the two were intertwined. Taoism defined the villagers' cosmological view based on the tenet that individual destiny is guided by a star, a lucid manifestation of a cosmic force, that shone brightly at the moment of birth. The relationship of this star to other stars affects the cosmic force, augmenting or diminishing it, thus boding good or evil for the individual. Horoscopes permit individuals to prepare for good or bad periods. Soothsayers and the lunar calendar advise prescribed behavior for maximizing the good influence of favorable days and evading bad effects of unfavorable days. The Taoist concept of harmony with universal order is the basis for folk medicine. To cope with imbalances causing ailments the practitioner brings to bear his knowledge of the vital points of the human body which correspond to hours, dates, and numbers of the lunar calendar.

Still, villagers believed that benevolent or malevolent spirits cause good and bad influences as well as ill health so they consulted shamans who use exorcism to heal.

Taoist geomancy provided the means for auspicious layouts of settlements and sites for tombs and houses; nonetheless, prior to construction the Spirit of the Soil was invoked. Before most houses were altars honoring this spirit and the Spirit of Heaven.

When a farmer's fields were prepared for planting he consulted the Taoist lunar calendar for an auspicious day to transplant the seedlings. Prior to sewing his rice seed bed, the farmer performed a simple ritual to the Spirit of Agriculture who also was invoked in rituals associated with the Guardian Spirit of the Village held at the communal temple (*đình*).

One persistent symbol of Taoism in the village was the iniquitousness of Quan Cong, a hero in the Taoist tradition. In the Quan Cong pagoda his cult included a pig sacrifice. He was enshrined in many households and in the two Buddhist pagodas, and had become a popular Cao Daist deity.

In Khanh Hau the primordial Vietnamese beliefs in spirits of the popular oral-tradition had many origins. Some were uniquely Vietnamese while others could be traced to Chinese sources or had been borrowed from the Cham and Khmer with whom the Vietnamese have historically had contact.

My research and field experiences impelled me to probe more deeply into the possible links between the Vietnamese Spirit Cult and similar cults found among highland ethnic groups. French and American linguists have concluded that the Vietnamese language is of the Austroasiatic stock and very likely of the Mon-Khmer family. It is interesting to note that Chinese

An important annual ritual by village leaders pays homage to the Spirit of
Agriculture, 1958.

accounts of Lac society in early Vietnam describe culture traits I found
among the highlanders such as special deities associated with agriculture,
and special offerings are made to them at planting time by both family
groups and the village community. Another practice they share is the levi-
rate (wherein on the death of a man his younger brother has either the right
or the obligation to take the widow as his wife). Interestingly, the Vietnamese communal temple for the Guardian Spirit of the Village, which
appears to be a non-Chinese institution, usually is constructed on pilings as
are the communal men's houses (where many rituals are held) among many
of Mon-Khmer speakers. Sources on Lac culture describe the people as
wearing few clothes, blackening their teeth, chewing betel and areca, using
poisoned arrows, and tilling with hoes of stone. As my highland research
continued in the coming years I would find similar traits among the Mon
Khmer-speaking Bru, Pacoh, Katu, Hre, and Cua in the northern part of the
central highlands.[9]

In July 1958 there arose a second opportunity to visit Hue which proved fortuitous because it put Taoist beliefs and practices I was seeing in Khanh Hau into a historical/cultural perspective. While in Khanh Hau Taoism was expressed at the folk level of household and village, in Hue the Taoist beliefs and practices were expressed on the grand scale of high culture surrounding the figure of the emperor, Regulator of the World, on whom converge heavenly and earthly currents for the benefit of the kingdom. As in the village, Taoism in Hue was mixed with the Cult of Spirits. At the exquisite temple of Nguyen Kim, for example, every spring the Emperor as guardian of agricultural fertility made offerings to the Spirit of the Soil and the Rice Spirit, commanding a high official to plow a furrow symbolizing the onset of the agricultural cycle. Here was a cult ritual similar in essence to some in Khanh Hau as well as agricultural cult rituals among highland groups.

But it was at the Nam-Giao, built in 1808 as an "ensemble des esplanades" outside of Hue, that I found the Taoism–Spirit Cult rituals very reminiscent of those in the village and among the highland people. The Nam-Giao consisted of four masonry esplanades, the bottom one rectangular, the next two square, and the top one round, all of them oriented to the four cardinal points. Here every three years in lavish rituals laden with symbols of the Sun, Moon, Gold, Jade, and the five planets, the Emperor made offerings of sacrificial buffalos to the Spirit of Heaven and Spirit of Earth. Since their currents converge on the Emperor he invited them to partake of the offerings while imploring their blessings and benefits. When I read in French sources about Nam-Giao buffalo sacrifices my mind shot back to highland villages where the sacrifice of buffalos, the most prestigious of offerings, propitiated the spirits so as to bring their blessings and benefits.

When early in 1958 our research team began field work we had not anticipated witnessing the advent of Viet Cong insurgency in the Mekong River delta. Initially the rumblings were muted with Viet Cong activity limited to antigovernment propaganda in some nearby villages. Then, not long after, my friend Nguyen Van Mung, the director of the UNESCO School of Fundamental Education in the village, awoke one morning to find a Viet Cong flag stuck in the ground before his house. Several months later, banners bearing antigovernment slogans were strung in the main hamlet. There were guarded comments by villagers about Viet Cong patrols coming into Khanh Hau and neighboring villages at night to spread propaganda either orally or by tracts. The village Self-Defense Guards, numbering around fifteen, were stationed in the military stockade, and the Hamlet Guard maintained watch posts throughout the village, but after dark the area of security dwindled as it did during the Indochina War to the barbed wire enclosure around the Council House and communal temple.

By the end of 1958 the ever-increasing number of assassinations throughout South Vietnam, of which most victims were civil servants, was attributed by the government to the Viet Cong. Several of the Self-Defense Guards were suddenly arrested, accused of being Viet Cong, and the father of one of the guards was apprehended when some of his neighbors reported that he fed Viet Cong nocturnal patrols. Villagers were shocked at this sudden action, and the village chief protested directly to the province chief, vouching for the good character and loyalty of the three accused. Subsequently the older man was released, but the guards were detained six months.

In December 1958 the team obtained use of a USOM boat with a cabin and armed guards to visit the Plain of Reeds where some Khanh Hau families planned to resettle. Leaving Tan An in the morning, we followed the West Vaico River noting as we moved westward there were fewer and fewer settlements and boats transporting goods. Still, all along the way, men fished from pirogues and sampans. By afternoon the shore was dominated by mangrove swamps and trees heavy with moss. We reached Moc Hoa, a town only about two years old, giving it a frontier look with a new market and some administrative buildings but little else. After meeting with the province chief, we had dinner and returned to the spend the night on the boat. Early in the morning we left Moc Hoa to visit the government-built Ten-Story Tower modeled after the famous tower Nguyen Anh (later Emperor Gia Long) had built around 1778. After the Tay Son rebels slaughtered his family, Nguyen Anh took refuge in the Plain of Reeds and had the tower built to keep watch on possible troops advances by the rebels. In 1959 the Viet Cong blew up the tower. Continuing down waterways toward the Mekong River we stopped at Ap Bac, a hamlet that in early 1962 would be the scene of the first defeat of government forces by the Viet Cong.

Viet Cong activities increased in Khanh Hau through 1959, and when an important annual ritual was held in a hamlet removed from the village center, the village chief and deputy chief were unable to attend because security was lacking. By the end of 1959, government control in some surrounding villages close to the Plain of Reeds had greatly weakened and three of the six hamlets in Khanh Hau were considered insecure even in daytime. The village study ended in December 1959 and we wrote comprehensive reports on our findings.[10] We had collected a good deal of information on Vietnamese culture and we benefited greatly from the human experience of participating in the world of villagers who were welcoming and unfailingly helpful. We also ended the study with great admiration for the industriousness and entrepreneurship of the villagers, but it was readily clear that the economic development taking place in the Mekong River delta was being threatened by the advent of Viet Cong activities orchestrated by North Vietnam.

During 1958 and 1959 most of my time was devoted to research, but periodically I found diversion in visits with a few friends to Angkor Wat, the fabulous temple complex in Cambodia that for centuries had been "lost." We read and discussed the available literature to plan our visits which were exhilarating ethnographic experiences as we savored the incredible reliefs and statues in temples, plazas, and libraries. We marveled at the elaborate water-management systems but were endlessly haunted by the question of why Angkor, this civilized achievement, had been abandoned to jungle growths.

One particularly memorable trip took place in March 1959. It was on the heels of the "Dap Chhuon affair," an attempted coup d'état against Prince Sihanouk by Dap Chhuon, the general in charge of Siem Reap province where Angkor is located. Not far from Siem Reap we were stopped on the road because the queen mother was arriving for a visit designed to restore calm in the troubled province. Accompanied by a large number of troops and police, the queen's entourage of forty cars (she could barely be seen huddled in the rear seat of a long black Cadillac) rolled in front of us. The following day there were ceremonies in the town and as evening fell, thousands of people converged in front of Angkor Wat where food-and-drink stands lit with oil lamps did a lively business. With darkness, lights provided by the French illuminated the temple and statues. Troops in dress uniforms lined the way as the queen arrived and took her place on a throne before the main entrance. As traditional music played on the terrace, court dancers (flown from Phnom Penh) dressed in splendid gold costumes gracefully performed dances based on classical themes.

A happy Cambodian child in the ruins of Banteay Srei, 1958.

Then the atmosphere became very festive and a large movie screen arranged in the midst of the crowd and stands came alive with MGM's "Zeigfeld Follies of 1946." There was Fred Astair and Lucille Bremer dancing in an elegant set to the beautiful Harry Warren ballad "This Heart of Mine." It was fabulous and heartening to seen Angkor Wat alive with Cambodians having a wonderful and carefree time.

By the end of the 1950s, there was in many circles a disillusionment with the Ngo Dinh Diem government. As the president relied increasingly on his family (notably brothers Nhu and Can) and cronies, non-Communist nationalist political leaders and the young educated people who returned to help build the new nation felt more and more shut out. Also, in the face of a growing Communist threat, Diem's strategy was to hit back with force arresting suspected subversives, which brought the criticism that he was becoming dictatorial.

At the same time, the president was becoming less accessible. Following the 1957 assassination attempt in Ban Me Thuot, Diem began to avoid open contact with the public. A symbol of this was increased security around the Independence Palace where lights were installed on the elegant fence posts and a barrier of barbed wire was built along the sidewalk, which became forbidden to the public. There were heavy security measures employed when Diem left the palace to travel, and his route to Tan Son Nhut airport was closed to any traffic, effectively cutting the city in two and resulting in monumental traffic tie-ups.

Serving as director of Vietnam Press, my friend Ton That Tien tried to present a balanced view of the president, emphasizing that he was an honest man, a nationalist dedicated to South Vietnam and its people.

All of these things were true. Although a Catholic, Ngo Dinh Diem was educated in Hue as one of the last of the Confucian literati. Convinced he was destined to rule the Vietnamese people, Diem brought to his presidency aspects of the mandarin system which he believed contained a number of democratic institutions. At the same time he invoked Confucian concepts of social and moral order to form a homogenous and tightly organized society. Diem also was deeply nationalistic (as a young mandarin he espoused nationalism, greatly influencing King Bao Dai).

But Diem was coping with something deeper in the Vietnamese soul. Diem had the unenviable task of trying to rule a population mystically skeptical of government.

My experience in the village, visits to Hue, and endless conversations with Vietnamese friends such as Ton That Thien, Dang Duc Khoi, and Nghiem Tham about the Vietnamese soul set me on the path into the mysterious depths of "Vietnamese-ness," that is, the heart, the veiled essence of Vietnamese culture and character. After almost four years of ethnographic research in Vietnam, the signs along that path pointed to Vietnamese religious beliefs and practices, specifically Taoism.

It was inevitable that Diem would absorb some of the Taoist high culture so prevalent in the Hue citadel where mandarins participated in the elaborate rituals performed by the Emperor. But his experience with high-culture Taoism does not appear to have made him appreciate popular Taoism and its effect on the matter of governing.

Popular Taoism, mixed with the Spirit Cult prevailed in the world of ordinary Vietnamese, particularly the villagers. As H. G. Creel points out, the Taoists harbored a "mystical skepticism" in China and this was true in Vietnam.[11] Taoists emphasize man's oneness with nature. Prior to the

French conquest the Vietnamese had no urban centers. They were rural people embedded in nature. Taoists value the natural, instinctive, primitive qualities or virtues as opposed to those arising from social sanction and education. For the Taoists, artificial institutions such as government are wrong so the Vietnamese view government with an anarchistic eye—they tend to be antigovernment. Vietnamese political "parties," a product of Western influence, always remain "movements" (*phong-trào*), a combination of the words "winds" (*phong*) and "tides" (*trào*).

Ngo Dinh Diem's problem in trying to communicate with the Americans was more intercultural. In a 1972 interview with former vice president Nguyen Ngoc Tho, I asked him if Diem or Nhu understood any of their American counterparts, and he replied, "no." I then specified some of the people such as American ambassadors and his advisers, Col. Edward Lansdale, Wesley Fishel, and Wolf Ladejinski. Mr. Tho simply shook his head and said, "none of them." On the other hand did the American leaders and advisers ever understand Diem or Nhu? "Never."

In many respects it was inevitable that there would be such a lack of understanding. Mr. Diem was a product of the esoteric Hue Confucian-Taoist mandarin milieu. Although he had traveled abroad and spent time in the United States, Diem remained solidly traditional Vietnamese in outlook. There was nothing in this outlook to prepare him to understand American leaders.

On the other hand there certainly was nothing in the background of the American leaders that would have prepared them to understand Ngo Dinh Diem. His nationalist-Confucianist approach to government completely escaped the Americans.

From accounts of friends at the American embassy, officials visiting from Washington were received by Diem, who indulged in a three-hour monologue about the history of Vietnam (and the officials were wisely warned to drink very sparingly the tea that was served). Perhaps his long monologues with the Americans were intended to convey something of the Hue world, to educate them about things Vietnamese. It does not appear to have been successful.

To the Americans, Ngo Dinh Nhu was equally enigmatic, but in a totally different way. Educated in France and graduated from the scholarly Ecole de Chartres, Nhu was a respected archivist. Less imbued with traditional Vietnamese culture, Nhu was steeped in French scholasticism and strongly attracted to the writings of Emmanuel Mounier in his journal, *Esprit,* which drew on the views of the eminent philosopher, Jacques Maritain. Maritain rejected both capitalism and socialism as having materialistic conceptions of life. He advocated a new solution at once personalistic and communal which views human society as the organization of liberties. In the middle ground between capitalism and Communism, personalism advocated the free and harmonious development of the human person not through individual isolation nor blind sacrifice to the omnipotent state but within the context of community (such things as family, church, and trade unions). Nhu brought this concept to Vietnam and although interpretations of it varied considerably, in the mid 1950s, "personalism" with the Vietnamese name *Nhàn Vị* became a philosophical force in the Diem administration although Diem never expounded it himself. Despite the fact that it stressed the idea of respect for the human person, personalism brought about no significant changes in the style of government and there emerged no institutions which translated the concept into the practical life of Vietnamese citizens. For the Americans, personalism was a vague and murky concept they would never understand any more than they would ever understand Ngo Dinh Nhu.

But by the end of the 1950s, Diem had failed to blend nationalism with Confucianism, and Nhu's ideology of personalism had similarly never been orchestrated successfully with nationalism. So the Ngo Dinh Diem government lacked identification and justification.

The year 1959 was coming to a close, the village study was finished, and I had been in South Vietnam almost four years. It was time to return to the United States for a phase of teaching and writing.

On 19 December 1959 I sailed from Saigon on the Messageries Maritimes S.S. *Vietnam* to return to the United States via Europe. The ship moved past the vast Rung Sat mangrove swamp on the way to the South China Sea. I stood on the deck and remembered arriving in South Vietnam on 16 March 1956 to see through the window a clear horizon, a time of peace. Now there were dark signs on that horizon.

Three

INSURGENCY

DISEMBARKING IN MARSEILLES on 9 January 1960, my first impression was how pale everyone looked. Winter faces and winter landscapes after the beautiful tropical seas and exotic ports of call—Singapore, Colombo, Bombay, Djibouti, Suez (a short trip to Cairo), and Port Said. But the almost-perfect voyage came to a sudden end off the coast of Crete. With the Bora blowing down the Adriatic and the Mistral down the Rhone Valley, the Mediterranean was like the North Atlantic at its worst.

After staying with Madeleine Tainturier's brother, Louis, and his wife, Maude, in their apartment located in an old residence next to the park of a chateau, I took the train to Paris (beautiful in the snow) and stayed with Gil Sheinbaum (Stanley's brother) on rue du Dragon. Roy and Lee MacLaren, friends from Vietnam—Lee had been American consul and Roy served at the Canadian Embassy—invited me to visit them in Prague. The Czech visa stipulated that I enter the country on a 15 February train from Vienna. I took a train to Geneva where my friend Ton That Thien was studying for his doctorate, so we had long discussions about Vietnam and the Diem government. In Vienna the rebuilt State Opera, which had been in ruins when last I visited in 1953, provided three nights of beautiful operas (*Der Rosen-*

kavalier, Prince Igor, and *Fidelio*) followed by quiet dinners in a restaurant that had zither music.

The small train rolled across snowy countryside and at the Czech border we faced the Iron Curtain, an astonishing barrier of barbed wire and guard towers. It was one thing to enter the forbidding barrier, but what about leaving? Roy and Lee had a very spacious house which the Communist regime had taken from the owners and bugged for the Canadian occupants. Almost untouched during World War II, Prague was a beautiful city but with a dreary greyness, ugly new "Socialist" architecture, and Russian troops everywhere. There were very few tourists, most of them Russian. At the Hradčany Castle the guide and I were alone in damp splendid rooms and galleries.

It was my first visit to a country under Stalinist Communism and given the Communist threat in Vietnam I found it very chilling. Czechoslovakia had been a relatively democratic nation with an efficient economy before World War II. Now it was a police state burdened with an inefficient bureaucracy. The malaise of the economy was graphically illustrated at a United Arab Republic reception we attended. When the doors to the food tables were opened, badly dressed Czechs, all very high-ranking in the government, literally stormed the tables, immediately grabbing fruit in decorations on roasted lambs and using their hands to pile meat on their plates. When we reached the table only fat and scraps remained. On the way out, a Czech lady dropped her purse sending three oranges down the stairs.

Driving out of Czechoslovakia in the MacLarens' Jaguar, on a stretch of lonely road we suddenly found ourselves engulfed by Russian army tanks on maneuvers and breathed a sigh of relief when we crossed the border into Germany. After the somberness of Prague, rebuilt Nuremberg was glittering and lively.

Late in 1959 I had been offered a teaching post by Sally Cassidy at Monteith College, an experimental institution in Detroit supported by the Ford Foundation. The college was located within Detroit's Wayne State University but was independent of the university's administration. The superb curriculum provided a two-year undergraduate interdisciplinary training in the social sciences. Monteith proved an invaluable experience in teaching, but I found myself with little time to write up my village research.

In the fall of 1960 I received an offer from Frank Lebar of the Human Relations Area Files in New Haven to work with him and John Musgrave on a project to produce an ethnographic compendium of mainland Southeast Asia. Early in 1961 I went to New Haven where I worked closely with Frank Lebar, John Musgrave, and Vickie Suddard in researching published and unpublished materials (including my field notes) on all of the ethnic groups. Yale had a scholarly air (and an exotic one with its secret societies and closed clubs). The Southeast Asia collection at the Stirling Library was fantastic. Professors Karl Pelzer and Harry Benda arranged a research associate and lecturer appointment at Yale University for me to teach in the Southeast Asia Studies Program and have an office in the Hall of Graduate Studies. I fortunately found an apartment in an old house near the university, an ideal setting to work on my village notes and a nice place to invite friends and students on Friday for drinks and snacks.

Throughout the 1961–63 period, I taught and wrote. Alan Bloom, also on the faculty, would lure me away from the typewriter ("You're blackening pages!") for coffee at the nearby Yorkside Café. Vickie Suddard, Ruth McVey (a fellow research associate), John Musgrave, and Huynh Sanh Thong (with whom I was privileged to study literary Vietnamese) read parts of the village manuscript and offered valuable suggestions.

During the New Haven period, events in Vietnam were being reported in the American media with increased frequency. On 3 February 1961 the formal establishment of the National Liberation Front (NLF) was announced (it had been formed on 19–20 December 1960 and made known at the end of January 1961). Its aims were the overthrow of Ngo Dinh Diem and formation of a National Democratic Coalition Administration, which would negotiate with the North to realize a "peaceful reunification." The NLF purported to be independent of Hanoi (this proved to be a fiction).

On 28 January 1961, President Kennedy signed the Counterinsurgency Plan. Up to this point there had been references to Communist guerrillas. Now "insurgents" replaced the word "guerrilla."

By mid 1961 the deteriorating situation in the highlands because of infiltration of "regroupees" (southern Communists who had been trained as insurgents in North Vietnam) was a cause for serious concern in Saigon, prompting the Vietnamese government and the American mission to devise new strategies for maintaining control of the region.

Late in 1961 I was approached by Steve Hosmer of RAND Corporation's Washington office about the possibility of conducting three months of research among the highlanders in South Vietnam. The objective of the study would be to learn from highland leaders what they expected of the Saigon government. Since this held the possibility of helping the highlanders by playing the role of an intermediary between their leaders and the American mission (and perhaps the Saigon government as well) I showed interest. First of all I wanted some guarantee that the American Mission would be receptive to recommendations concerning the highlanders' wants and needs and therefore take up their cause with the South Vietnamese government. This certainly had not been the case in 1958. In addition, I wanted a guarantee that neither RAND nor the Advanced Research Projects Agency (ARPA) in the Department of Defense which was funding the study, would interfere with my research. RAND agreed and recruited John Donnell, a friend from the late 1950s who had served with the U.S. Information Service (USIS). John, who spoke excellent Vietnamese, was completing a dissertation on Nhu's personalism for the University of California at Berkeley.

Early in January 1962 John and I met in Honolulu and flew to Saigon. John arranged through a friend to use a sparsely furnished but charming small villa. Both John and I were somewhat astonished how the advent of insurgency had changed the atmosphere of Saigon. Signs of conflict had replaced the feeling of peace. Rue Pasteur from the airport was crowded with military vehicles and everyone was concerned with "security." Sitting with photographer Howard Sochurek on the roof café on the new Caravelle Hotel we could see near the city flares accompanied by thumps of mortar explosions.

At the ARPA Research and Development Field Unit we were informed that it would not be possible for us to go to the central highlands. It seems the CIA had on 1 November 1961 begun a village defense program at Buon Enao near Ban Me Thuot. It was organized by Gilbert Layton, a retired U.S. Army colonel who had been assigned to the CIA in Vietnam. He had stated adamantly that he "did not want any anthropologists running around asking questions about the montagnards' sex practices."

I felt the colonel's remark said more about him than it did any anthropologist, but it was enough to block our highland research. And so there we were in Saigon at loose ends, but RAND encouraged us to devise an alternate study.

Ngo Dinh Nhu, shaded by a hat, officiating at the opening of the Cu Chi strategic hamlet, 1962.

The current topic of conversation in Saigon was the strategic hamlet program which sought to consolidate governmental authority in pacified areas through a defense system and administrative reorganization at the hamlet level. In each hamlet, the defense system was based on a fortification and a Self-Defense Corps unit numbering from five to twelve men. We decided to look into the program. John knew Douglas Pike at the USIS, who gave us a briefing on Operation Sunrise, a rural pacification program in which the "strategic hamlet" was a key concept. Cu Chi district northwest of Saigon had been selected as the pilot area in the program. Often referred to as the "birthplace of the Viet Minh movement in southern Vietnam," Cu Chi had for all intents and purposes been under Viet Cong control until the spring of 1961.

The Operation Sunrise area was in the transition zone between the Mekong River delta and the central highlands, a sandy dry place of poor soils, devoid of the lushness of the delta or the mountains. With a rented Citroën 15, John and I went to Tan An Hoi, a large village that encompassed Cu Chi district headquarters. We wandered into Xom Hue hamlet, one of the first to be fortified by extensive earthworks with a ditch and rampart both studded with bamboo spears. Some farmsteads had been relocated within the enclosure. On the path villagers returned our greeting and bow in guarded manner. At a small shop farmers were sipping tea and when we politely asked about gardens and field crops they responded slowly at first and then became more talkative when it was apparent we had some knowledge of southern farming. The types of rain-fed rice they farmed were of mediocre quality and none was sold in the market. Insufficient rice supplies were a common problem. The primary cash crop (planted after the rice harvest) was tobacco, a labor-intensive crop, requiring irrigation twice a day. Pests were a problem and since the cost of pesticide was too high for most farmers, they relied on rain to wash tobacco leaves.

On subsequent visits, villagers were more open and welcoming, inviting us into houses for tea. A family celebrating the death of an ancestor insisted we partake of special dishes prepared for the occasion. Reflecting the long Communist control of Cu Chi, villagers at times would use such expressions as "*Diệm-Mỹ*" ("Diem-Americans") for "government," which in the usual Viet Cong parlance was followed by the word *bọn,* or "gang," but that word was carefully deleted. On one occasion they showed us tunnels the Viet Cong had dug under the hamlet.

Without our asking, the Cu Chi villagers complained about the strategic hamlet and Operation Sunrise. Families relocated within the fortification were very dissatisfied. But more widespread was resentment over the amount of time, communal labor, materials, and land they had to contribute. John and I had been told in Saigon and the district that Operation Sunrise corvée laborers were paid ten piasters a day and lunch, but we found that this was not true. One group of men and women said that army units would suddenly appear in the hamlet to round up men to work in Operation Sunrise at Ben Cat. They were neither paid nor fed ("If you didn't quickly grab some food you'd go hungry all day," one farmer said). Farmers in the hamlet pointed out that forced labor at Ben Cat and on their strategic hamlet had taken them away from their fields from forty-five to ninety days between mid December and mid March. So in 1962 they could only grow one-tenth of the 1961 tobacco crop. This, one farmer noted, was a "defeat" for them. Also, when the earthwork fortification was built, farmers lost cultivation land and villagers had to "contribute" bamboo which functions as a "cushion" crop, cut to sell when the harvest is meager. Finally, they could ill afford assessments for purchase of concrete fence posts and barbed wire.

The Viet Minh and subsequently the Viet Cong had gained considerable support among villagers of Cu Chi. One member of the Self Defense Guards pointed out that, although life in the Viet Cong is difficult—living outdoors, sleeping on the ground in all kinds of weather, and carrying precarious food supplies—morale is very high. "There are few deserters. The Viet Cong has loyal members," he added, attributing this to their good leadership and effective propaganda. Viet Cong activities continued around Cu Chi. Villagers reported that on several occasions small bands of Viet Cong removed some of the bamboo spikes and tunneled through the earth mound. In March 1962, during a ritual at the communal temple, a Viet Cong of five or six men fired at the military post and the communal temple, smashing some roof tiles and disrupting the gathering.

While still studying Xom Hue hamlet, John and I decided to visit Trung Lap village located farther northwest of Cu Chi in the Operation Sunrise area. Like Cu Chi, Trung Lap had relatively poor soil and farmers relied on peanuts as their important cash crop. The empty road into Trung Hoa hamlet was lined with thick forest. Trung Hoa was the market center of the area, and one row of shops relied on trade from a nearby Ranger camp. Despite the presence of the Ranger camp it quickly became clear that Trung Lap was insecure. One informant reported that the Viet Cong were greatly feared and the local population was forced to cooperate with them. Whereas in the past, the few well-to-do villagers who accumulated capital bought land, now they moved into Saigon, only returning to the village to collect rent. The informant said that his brother, who held a French baccalaureate, had been killed in a wave of terrorism aimed at intellectuals.

Our feelings of dread worsened when a young teacher we were interviewing leaned forward and said, "You shouldn't be here," adding that the previous night a hamlet chief had been killed and his body thrown into a well.

Driving out the empty road, on an uneven bridge the low-slung car was stalled by a board. I got out and guided John around the board. The thick forest on either side was silent, somber, and after our experience in the hamlet it took on a menacing aura. We breathed a sigh of relief when we reached National Highland No. 1. Several days later, newspapers reported that a South Vietnamese army unit was badly mauled on the Trung Lap road in an ambush by Viet Cong, who had spent a week in adjacent forest preparing for it.

The easternmost strategic hamlets of Operation Sunrise were in the vicinity of Phuoc Le, a market town near the coastal resort of Vung Tao (Cap St. Jacques). In Long Huong hamlet ten households with Viet Cong kin were grouped at one end of the settlement nearest the enclosure. At nearby Tam Phuoc one residential section of the settlement was segregated to isolate families with pro-Viet Cong leanings. Immediately to the east were forested hills where, according to the hamlet chief, the Viet Cong had a "stronghold" with an estimated force of five hundred men.

While driving back to Saigon we approached a town where there was an unexpected back-up of trucks and army vehicles. There had been a fire fight on the edge of the town and bodies of two soldiers in camouflaged uniforms were by the road. They seemed small, like rag dolls flung on the ground. I recalled how in the late 1950s we had often driven through these towns en route to Vung Tau and Long Hai for mindless days on the beautiful beaches. Another time, another world, now gone.

In February 1962 some foreign journalists were writing glowing accounts of Lt. Col. Pham Ngoc Thao, chief of Kien Hoa Province, and his strategy for coping with insurgency. Writing about Thao, Robert Shaplen observed, "In all respects, Thao is one of the most remarkable Vietnamese around, being a conspiratorial revolutionary figure straight out of a Malraux novel and, at the same time, a highly sophisticated and politically astute man, whose talents, if only they were properly channeled, could profitably be used right now."[1] John and I decided to visit Lieutenant Colonel Thao at Ben Tre, the province capital. On the morning of 27 February I rose early as usual to prepare for our departure. While shaving I was shaken by a thunderous explosion nearby. I darted out the back door as another explosion shook the house, black smoke billowed and a Vietnamese air force plane swooped over the high trees before disappearing. Roused out of bed, John joined me in the garden. More explosions and clouds of black smoke. Another plane flew over. Just as it did, an American woman appeared on the second-floor terrace of a next-door villa (occupied by a MAAG officer and his family). She was hysterical and shouted something about "the Japs attacking!" before running back into the villa. John and I sipped some coffee and grabbed our cameras. We figured the target was the Independence Palace and as we hurried in that direction, tanks and trucks full of soldiers came rumbling down the street. The target was the palace and streets around it were closed. I led John through the back door of the weedy garden behind the empty building, former site of the National Institute of Administration. We entered the building and went to the second floor lecture hall where I had conducted my anthropology course. From there we could see smoke rising from ruins of the palace. My heart sank at the thought that President Diem and his family might have been killed. And the elegant second-empire Independence Palace where I had taught English at the presidency in the late 1950s was demolished.

The bombers were two disgruntled air force pilots and while Madame Nhu was wounded, the president and Nhu survived.

Despite the military presence along the roads, I was very happy to return to the Mekong River delta with its fluvial air and green lushness. Set in a sea of coconut groves, Ben Tre was a charming town and we went directly to the province headquarters. The deputy province chief informed us that previously there had been numerous absentee landlords in Kien Hoa, but under the Viet Minh and Viet Cong their holdings had been redistributed with titles for the new owners. When the government assumed control of these areas, villagers refused to turn back land to the original owners.

Col. Pham Ngoc Thao, a man with a military bearing and a face that revealed nothing, received us. From an educated Catholic family, Thao had in 1947 joined the Viet Minh as a resistance leader in the South, and in two years was in charge of the Viet Minh espionage apparatus around Saigon. He broke with the Viet Minh but kept in touch with its leaders in the South. By 1956, Thao had managed to ally himself to Diem and was named province chief in Kien Hoa. In 1962 Thao enjoyed the reputation of being an effective counterinsurgency leader by using his knowledge of Viet Minh tactics to gain the support of villagers in organizing resistance against the Viet Cong.

In his office, Thao explained that fortification of all hamlets with ditches and walls was excessively expensive, so he intended to fortify only those hamlets that had suffered frequent attacks from the Viet Cong.

We were invited to stay at the province chief's house, which typically was large, but unlike houses I had stayed in during the late 1950s it was sparsely furnished and Lieutenant Colonel Thao served very simple Vietnamese food. It was curious to see a machine-gun emplacement in the middle of the flower garden.

John and I visited An Thuan hamlet in An Hoi village across the river from Ben Tre and An Hoa hamlet on the other side of the town. In both places the small number of families living outside clusters were relocated and given a small plot of land for their new houses. At Lieutenant Colonel Thao's behest a Council of Elders, composed of twenty to two hundred members, including women, was created. This body had authority to consult with village and hamlet councils and to criticize their actions, thereby providing an added measure of response to local needs. Lieutenant Colonel Thao also encouraged formation of a Council of Patrons, comprising relatively well-to-do and influential men and women to furnish financial and moral support to community development projects.

From Ben Tre, John and I drove to Sadec on the south bank of the Mekong River where we visited two villages. An important presence in the Sadec area was the Hoa Hao reformed Buddhist sect. In 1945, Huynh Phu So, founder of the sect, visited Binh Tien village and pointed out that in northern Vietnam and in China there were great famines, so he encouraged the farmers to produce more rice to help alleviate the sufferings of those in stricken areas. Although he did not proselytize, many villagers embraced Hoa Hao (in 1962, some 75 percent of the residents were members).

In April 1947, Huynh Phu So arranged to meet Buu Vinh, a Viet Minh commander in the Long Xuyen Province, to mediate some local difficulties between the Hoa Hao and Viet Minh. When Huynh Phu So entered the command post he was ambushed and some witnesses later reported he was hacked to death. Many Hoa Hao adherents believe he is still alive and await his return. But the events generated among the Hoa Hao deep bitterness and anti–Viet Minh sentiment, a sentiment extended to the Viet Cong.[2]

John and I were struck by how clean and orderly Hoa Hao villages were, and farmers made good use of some privately owned tractors which were rented out to prepare the paddy fields. We were welcomed by the villagers and invited to visit a Hoa Hao pagoda completed in 1960. In keeping with Hoa Hao doctrine, a framed red board containing no depictions symbolized Buddha. The pagoda guardian related that during the Indochina War the Viet Minh raided the village, burning the communal house and the Hoa Hao pagoda. At a large lunch in our honor, villagers voiced their anti–Viet Cong sentiment, declaring that if the Viet Cong came into their villages they would drive them out. One village elder added, "The Viet Cong are without religion so they do not have the favor of heaven."

Our final look at strategic hamlets was in Khanh Hau, the village our MSUG team had studied in 1958–59. By 20 April 1962 a ditch had been dug around the two main hamlets and earth from the ditch had been piled into earthworks on which a barbed wire would be mounted. Viet Cong activities in Khanh Hau had increased considerably through 1960 and by October 1961 their cadres were operating openly in the three hamlets east of National Highway No. 4. They would rouse villagers and, guarding them with sticks and machetes, force them to hold demonstrations against the government on the main road, stopping buses and trucks to distribute leaflets. One evening late in 1961, a group of Viet Cong entered a hamlet and summoned four villagers whom they accused of cooperating with the "My-Diem gang." They prepared to execute the villagers, but the gun misfired, and when one villager made a break, the Viet Cong pursued him, leaving the others to escape. Not long after, the police chief was killed ambushing a Viet Cong patrol, and another villager died in a clash between Self-Defense Guards and a Viet Cong patrol. The village chief said that Viet Cong propaganda was "four times more effective than government propaganda." For example, the Viet Cong would visit a young man about to begin national service and point out that if he went into the army he would be taken far from the village and only be allowed to visit his family infrequently whereas if he joined the Viet Cong he would remain in the vicinity (implied was the threat that if he went into the army he would be a Viet Cong target if he visited the village).

An elaborate, almost theatrical, ceremony marked the completion of the Cu Chi strategic hamlet. Homer Bigart of the *New York Times* and I accompanied French journalist François Sully in his Citroën 11. Tanks blocked the highway and flags fluttered over the reviewing stand built for American and Vietnamese military and civilian officials. South Vietnamese airborne troops surrounded the area and groups of young villagers belonging to organizations such as the Republican Youth stood at attention. Ngo Dinh Nhu was guest of honor and would officiate at the ceremony. It struck me that despite the crowds there were no villagers in sight. With camera in hand I walked down a lane and entered a small thatched shop to change my film. The shopkeeper offered me some tea. When I asked where the villagers were, she replied they were told to stay in their houses and throw water on the dusty lane leading to the communal temple because Ngo Dinh Nhu was to visit there.

After the usual laudatory speeches, surrounded by guards, Nhu, sporting a cigarette holder, his face (which had a curious pallor) shaded by a hat, walked to the communal temple. A group of American officers followed. I remarked to a colonel that it was strange that no villagers were present. He replied it was because Mr. Nhu needed protection. "I thought the strategic hamlet was supposed to provide protection." That drew a dark look.

In Saigon, Ambassador Nolting and his wife, Olivia, invited John and me to have lunch at the residence. We discussed the current situation in Vietnam and the ambassador struck us as an intelligent and knowledgeable gentleman.

Before leaving Vietnam I gave Gen. Paul Harkins, head of the newly formed U.S. Military Assistance Command Vietnam (MACV), a debriefing. I said in essence that strategic hamlets had the potential of bringing security to the rural population, but they would not work if they imposed economic and social burdens on the population. General Harkins replied that everyone wanted protection from the Viet Cong, so they would welcome the strategic hamlets.

Back in Washington, RAND arranged for John and me to give debriefings, which turned out to be less than pleasant. As we began our first debriefing at the Pentagon with Harold Brown (who would serve as Secretary of Defense in the Carter cabinet), he swung his heavy leather chair around and looked out the window, leaving us to talk to the back of the chair. Roger Hillsman was upset over a Homer Bigart article about Operation Sunrise he had just read in the *New York Times,* so our briefing, which turned out to agree with what Homer had written, was not well received. Then I gave a debriefing to Marine Gen. Victor "Brute" Krulak who said as he pounded his fist on the desk that "we" were going to make the peasants do what's necessary for strategic hamlets to succeed. Coldly angry, I responded, "You're not going to make the peasants do anything! You'd better realize it right now. They're very tough, independent people, and they have ways of circumventing. You're not going to make them do anything!"

John and I produced a final report.[3] Its evaluation began with the observation that "in the present war, the Vietnamese peasant is likely to support the side that has control of the area in which he lives, and he is more favorably disposed to the side which offers him the possibility of a better life."

We noted, "The strategic hamlet has the initial advantage of extending government control to areas previously considered insecure. In doing so it affords an opportunity for the Vietnamese government to organize at the hamlet and village level projects that are urgently needed and that would demonstrate the government's concern for the villager and his problems." We then noted that "the need for such action is particularly evident in the eastern region, the Operation Sunrise area, where there is some resentment among the rural citizens over the amount of communal labor and materials they had to contribute 'voluntarily' to the strategic hamlet program."

On the basis of our discussions and debriefings with American and Vietnamese officials, John and I knew they firmly believed that the rural population was hostile to the Viet Cong and that it required no more than the hamlet fortification to make people grateful and turn them into solid supporters of the government. We therefore explicitly made the point that the farmers are the backbone of the village warning and auxiliary guard system, and they will only participate in these activities willingly and effectively if they see evidence "that the strategic hamlet to which they have made such heavy contributions in time, materials, land, and reduced secondary crop yields is capable to improving their economic, social, and political welfare beyond the narrower aspect of the greater physical security it offers them."

Our suggestions for improvement of the program emphasized careful planning, taking into account each hamlet's capabilities, peasant attitudes, and local security so as to determine the extent of fortifications and pace of construction. Also, "promises of payment to villagers, be they for labor outside their home areas, for resettlement, or for other purposes, should be kept." Other suggestions included addressing the problem of unemployment and underemployment through a program of public works. In poorer areas, agricultural credit and extension services should be provided or restored. As a result of our talks with Lieutenant Colonel Thao we recommended that the Self-Defense Corps members be given an allowance enabling them to marry and provide for their families.

Our report was duly circulated in Washington, and from the Pentagon came harsh criticism that it was too negative. There was pressure brought to bear on the RAND Washington office to make changes. RAND's response was described in a 1998 RAND Alumni Bulletin Supplement marking the RAND's fiftieth anniversary and honoring Frank Collbohm, first director and president. Steve Hosmer, my first contact with RAND, wrote of how Collbohm "was prepared to resist any policy-motivated infringement of RAND's independence to publish and disseminate its research findings."[4] Hosmer added, "This was driven home to me in 1962, when an important government sponsor contested the findings of two RAND consultants, who had conducted an on-the-spot evaluation of the then newly initiated strategic hamlet program in South Vietnam." Hosmer related that the sponsor considered the consultants' findings too pessimistic and prepared a two-page rebuttal, which it proposed to attach to each copy of the RAND research memorandum documenting the findings. "RAND's response was resolute." Speaking for Collbohm, RAND's vice president in the Washington office "told the sponsor that RAND would never agree to such a procedure, and if the sponsor insisted on such as course, RAND would refuse to perform any future work for the sponsor. The sponsor dropped the matter."

Meanwhile, the CIA's Village Defense Program in Darlac was moving ahead. In February 1962 there had been one full Special Forces A-Detachment (twelve men) deployed in Darlac. This represented the first direct American military involvement with the highlanders. As of April 1962 the Village Defense had been adjudged a success. Roads and villages in the network area had become very secure and the number of highland refugees in the province was considerably lower than in the neighboring provinces. It had been decided, therefore, to enlarge the defense network. This, in turn, necessitated an expansion of the U.S. Special Forces involved in the program.

But there was at this time growing hostility of the Vietnamese leaders toward the Village Defense Program. In a January 1977 interview in Washington, former CIA official Lucien Concin pointed out that Gen. Ton That Dinh, commander of II Corps (with its headquarters in Pleiku) was becoming increasingly uneasy over the expansion of the Village Defense Program. Gen. Le Quang Tung, head of the Presidential Survey Office, functioned as liaison between the CIA and the palace, so it was he, rather than Dinh, who had control over the program. According to Conein, General Tung invited Ngo Dinh Nhu and Ton That Dinh to a "highlander celebration" at Buon Enao. Villagers gathered in traditional clothes, buffaloes were sacrificed, and everyone drank from the jars as gongs played. Conein described how, at one point in the festivities, Dinh took Nhu aside and told him that "the Americans have put an army at my back." He then informed Nhu that the Americans had armed eighteen thousand highlanders (Conein said that this figure was accurate and it also had been a deep secret). Nhu turned his face back to the crowd and wore a "coldly impassive" expression. Clearly the news had come as a shock.

This event led to an attempt by Nhu to gain more control over the Village Defense Program and integrate it into the Strategic Hamlet Program. It also triggered the decision of the CIA to "get out of the program," as Conein put it. In discussing this period with William Colby, who had been station chief and then head of the pacification program in Vietnam and later director of the CIA, he pointed out that since the Bay of Pigs disaster in April 1961, Washington had been very sensitive about the CIA becoming involved in any military or paramilitary operations that might become "another Bay of Pigs." As the Village Defense Program began to expand, it fell into that category. This resulted in a Washington meeting between the CIA (represented by Desmond FitzGerald) and the Department of Defense (represented by Paul Nitze), and in May 1962 it was agreed that complete control of the Village Defense Program and other CIA highland operations would be turned over to MACV in Operation Switchback, to be completed by 1 July 1963. Initially the CIA retained responsibility for both the logistical and operational aspects of the program. The CIA and MACV would coordinate everything with the newly formed Vietnamese Special Forces, which had grown out of the Presidential Survey Office and was commanded by Gen. Le Quang Tung. The Village Defense Program now became the Civilian Irregular Defense Group (CIDG, an acronym subsequently used to describe the locally recruited militiamen). In July 1962 the U.S. Department of Defense decided to transfer complete responsibility for the U.S. Special Forces operations to MACV, thus making the army responsible for American support of the CIDG.

July 1963 marked the end of the CIA involvement in the Village Defense Program, and former CIA officials interviewed expressed considerable bitterness at the military takeover of their programs. (Conein referred to Operation Switchback as "Operation Switchblade."). They emphasized that the CIA concept of the program was that it would be "defensive" in character. Intelligence gathering would be involved, but no offensive operations would be mounted. The program also was political in that it involved winning more highlander support for the Saigon government. Finally, American involvement in the program was minimal, and one reason it was effective is that Americans participating in it were not bound by bureaucratic restraints.

The MACV takeover of the Village Defense Program and turning it into an offensive military operation set the course for future American strategy in Vietnam.

Back in New Haven I continued teaching and working on Khanh Hau village materials. In the fall of 1962 I was privileged to have as a colleague Professor Paul Mus, the distinguished French savant of Far Eastern civilization who had been born in Vietnam and had written *Viêt-Nam: sociologie d'une guerre,*[5] a definitive study of the Indochina war. Professor Mus divided the academic year between the Collège de France in Paris and Yale University. He occupied guest quarters in Berkeley College and after we met he sent a note inviting me to visit him. In the note he said, "My past is in Indochina and your future is in Indochina, so we have the present to share." He sat before the fire where his wife quietly served tea and he talked about his research at the Bayon temple in Angkor Thom. Unfortunately he became ill and returned to France.

In New Haven I followed events in Vietnam with growing concern. It was apparent that the United States was becoming more involved militarily while relations between Washington and the Ngo Dinh Diem government worsened. Diem could no longer trust the Americans or anyone but his family members. Later, in 1964 when I visited the remote Special Forces camp at Kham Duc I was told that in 1962, President Diem had the excellent airstrip built so he could visit Kham Duc. He also had a statue of the Blessed Virgin placed on a nearby hill where he would go and spend days in prayer. It was for him a respite, a brief withdrawal.

By early 1963 it was clear that the Diem regime was headed for trouble. On 2 January there was the military debacle at Ap Bac (where in December 1958 our village research team had stopped after visiting the Plain of Reeds) with 350 Viet Cong standing their ground against a well-equipped government force four times their number. In May there was a clash between Buddhists and police in Hue during which nine of the demonstrators were killed. Buddhist leader Thich Tam Chau demanded compensation for the families of the victims and punishment for those responsible for the deaths. The government, however, rejected these demands. Another monk, Thich Tri Quang, emerged as leader of a new Buddhist movement to confront the government, and on 30 May 1963 a large group of faithful marched in a Saigon demonstration. The situation became more tense on 11 June when an elderly monk burned himself in the center of Saigon to protest the government's treatment of his confreres.

During my 1972 interview with former vice president Nguyen Ngoc Tho he observed how no understanding existed between the Americans and the president and his brother. Then Tho went on to describe how, fearing that the United States was on the road to expanding the war in Vietnam and turning the country into a battlefield, Diem and Nhu had begun to make overtures to the Viet Cong. By early 1963 they were in the process of working out an accommodation with the Viet Cong that would lead to a coalition government and end the conflict. According to Tho, the Americans became aware of this, and it was one of the primary reasons they began to look for some means of toppling the Diem government.

Early in 1963 I was approached by the RAND Corporation about returning to Vietnam with the possibility of continuing research on the people of the central highlands. Insurgency was sweeping the Vietnamese countryside, and there was considerable concern in Washington over possible disaffection of the mountain people who occupied what was now considered a "strategic region."

I was at the time near the end of my temporary appointment in the Southeast Asia Program at Yale University, and there were other academic possibilities. I had completed my portion of the manuscript for *Ethnic Groups of Mainland Southeast Asia*.[6] Yale University Press had accepted the manuscript of *Village in Vietnam* (and about the same time, Jim Hendry published *The Small World of Khanh Hau*).[7]

I faced a decision whether to remain in academe or return to Vietnam. Most of my colleagues advised me to remain at a university and pursue an academic career. An exception was Paul Mus, who had returned to New Haven (and who very kindly agreed to write a foreword for my book). Professor Mus had chosen to take an active political role in trying to end the Indochina war through peaceful negotiations. Sitting before the fire in his Berkeley College rooms, he explained that he felt such a decision should be based on whether or not one chose to participate in the events of history. "We all know the great figures of history, the heroes. They are described in books." But, he added, there also are those whose roles affect the course of events in lesser-known ways. Professor Mus then described how he had

arranged to meet with Ho Chi Minh to discuss a peaceful end to the conflict. At the French post where he was to walk across dried paddy fields to
meet the Vietnamese leader in a forested rendezvous, the troopers were
nervous, distrusting the Viet Minh whom they thought might use the cease-
fire to launch an attack. Properly dressed in a suit and white shirt and carrying his briefcase, Mus walked across the fields and had a "satisfying" meeting with the Viet Minh leader. As Mus was preparing to leave, a young
Vietnamese whispered that he respected Mus as a man of honor. The young
man then told how there were plotters among the Viet Minh who wanted
the French troops to kill Mus which would be a propaganda blow against
the French. The plotters had leaked word to the French post that an attack
was imminent. Mus was accompanied to the edge of the forest. What to do?
If he hesitated he faced grave danger, even death, from the plotters. A big
man, he stood straight, removed his jacket, and holding his arms high,
quickly stepped out of the brush on to the path. Silence. He walked with
firm gait to the French post where he was told the troopers were ready to
shoot at any movement, but when they saw a big man in a white shirt the
order was given to hold fire.

Professor Mus's intent was, I think, to illustrate the elements of drama,
frustration, and peril that such as role might hold. I shall be ever grateful
for his wise words.

In July 1963 I joined the staff of RAND's Washington office. The Vietnamese government approved the highlander study, but Ngo Dinh Nhu
wanted me to go to Paris to research French works on the region. I duly
went to Paris and researched in libraries as I had in 1953–54. When I
returned to Washington, ARPA had not yet provided funds for the highland
project, so RAND asked me to do a study of cross-cultural communication
between American military advisers and their Vietnamese counterparts. I
began gathering background material on military advisers' orientation programs.

In Washington I watched with trepidation the events taking place in
Vietnam. The media had become increasingly critical of Diem with stories
of corruption in his family and his administration. These accusations generated in the United States a rapidly growing anti-Diem sentiment. Diem,
who once had been hailed as a hero and savior of South Vietnam, was now
cast as a villain. Beset and besieged by the Buddhist crisis, Ambassador
Frederick Nolting (whose attempts at maintaining a working relationship

with Diem were misinterpreted as appeasement) went on a prolonged vacation. His close friend, William Trueheart, Deputy Chief of Mission, at first assumed Nolting's approach but suddenly shifted to a stance highly critical of Diem's ability to cope with the Buddhist crisis. This set the stage for moves against the Diem administration. In mid August Nolting was replaced by Henry Cabot Lodge. On 21 August 1963 units of the Vietnamese Special Forces commanded by Gen. Le Quang Tung raided Buddhist pagodas in many cities, jailing thousands of monks, killing some. Three days later there were a series of student demonstrations at Saigon University and more than 4,800 demonstrators were arrested.

These events precipitated a series of planned coups and countercoups that involved Ngo Dinh Nhu, various Vietnamese generals, and some American officials. The coup d'état that brought down the Diem government on 1 November 1963 was led by Generals Duong Van Minh; Tran Van Don; Le Van Kim, whom I had met in 1957 when he was director of the Land Development Program; Tran Tien Khiem; and Ton That Dinh who had served as commander of the Second Corps Area in the highlands. Col. Phan Ngoc Thao, with whom John Donnell and I had stayed in Ben Tre, led the tank assault on Diem's palace (Thao was later revealed to have been a Party member and NLF agent). The coup also involved Ambassador Lodge and CIA's Lucien Conein. As a result of the coup, Ngo Dinh Diem, Ngo Dinh Nhu, and Le Quang Tung were murdered.

Ngo Dinh Diem was the last nationalist president the Americans supported in Vietnam. And one wonders if the American actions against Diem and Nhu were, as Vice President Tho had claimed, motivated primarily to prevent their attempts at accommodation with the Viet Cong. If so, Diem and Nhu in their pagoda raids and the foreign press corps in its anti-Diem rhetoric played into the hands of the plotters. Some journalists have since claimed that had Diem not been overthrown South Vietnam would have fallen to the Viet Cong, but the facts suggest strongly that had Diem and Nhu lived, the Vietnam War might well have been avoided.

On 22 November 1963 I was busy collecting pertinent information on American military advisers' orientations at American University when news broke of President Kennedy's assassination in Dallas. En route back to the RAND office at Connecticut Avenue and K Street, embassies along Massachusetts Avenue were putting flags at half-mast. Washington was in a state of shock. At the RAND office everyone gathered around a small radio. One jaded lady from the Santa Monica office predicted that LBJ would get more results in civil rights than Kennedy ever could, but "LBJ will screw up Vietnam." Finally, she shook her head and said, "And there'll be a hell of a lot more 'Jeannie With the Light Brown Hair' than Poulenc at that goddam White House!" From the apartment at 25th and Pennsylvania Avenue, sounds of helicopters at the White House were ceaseless. With a group of friends from early Vietnam days I stood in front of the White House to watch in silence the cortege with the riderless horse move up Pennsylvania Avenue to the capital. And on the day of the presidential funeral we stood on Connecticut Avenue across from the Mayflower Hotel to view with sadness the procession of an incredible group of mourners making its way slowly to St. Matthew's Cathedral.

Prior to leaving for Vietnam I visited Bernard Fall at George Washington University Hospital where he was recovering from surgery to remove a kidney. He seemed very tired, but as I was leaving he assured me with a smile he'd see me in Vietnam.

On 9 January 1964 I returned to Saigon and a smaller apartment in the same building I had lived in when I was with MSUG. But since Reuters News Service had rented this apartment, it had a telephone, a luxury in Saigon. I had been astonished at the changes in Hong Kong with its amazing new skyscrapers and luxury hotels such as the Mandarin, Hilton, and President. Changes in Saigon were not for the better. All sidewalk cafés were gone because of grenade attacks and most of the elegant French shops on rue Catinat had vanished.

I was reassured, however, when I found that the fascinating little-tradition world of Huynh Thuc Khang Street around my apartment building had not changed. There the folks who lived in the small enclave next to the building where the street crossed Pasteur Street greeted me. The enclave was centered on a narrow, short lane crowded with very small frame shacks. On the Huynh Thuc Khang side were tiny one-room quarters of two cyclo drivers, Phuoc and Sau and their families. Of indeterminate age, Phuoc and Sau were extremely thin and had the weathered look of those who under battered conical hats, in rain or shine peddled their cyclos through the streets, which had become very crowded with traffic. Although I had a Vespa motor scooter I often rode in their cyclos, paying fares Vietnamese would consider prohibitive. My cook and I gave them clothes, and

I paid bills for medicines (such things as artichoke extract) prescribed by the city-hospital clinic for their diagnosed tuberculosis.

At the entrance to the lane lived a man called "Fat Number Three" because of his ample girth, who prepared delicious northern beef-noodle soup (*phở*) which my cook often served for lunch. Fat Number Three's "restaurant" on the sidewalk consisted of some round metal tables and stools over which a tarp had been arranged. Also by the entrance to the lane was a gnarled old banyan tree at the base of which was an altar dedicated to the Five Goddesses who in popular belief descended from the heavens via a tree, an occasion signaled by a meteor streaking into the sky. On the altar the enclave residents faithfully burned joss, placed flowers, lit candles, and on prescribed days made offerings of sticky-rice cakes, clear rice alcohol, and small sweet bananas. The original altar had been simple, but one day a well-to-do lady happened by and stopped to make offerings. Afterwards she apparently experienced good fortune because she returned to make offerings and, with approval of the enclave folks, had the altar painted yellow and red and replaced candles with electric lights, a luxury not found in the enclave homes. On the annual ceremonial observance honoring the Five Goddesses, everyone produced food and soft drinks for a feast to which my cook and I were invited.

The rhythm of a passing day at the enclave was marked by variations in food served. Fat Number Three greeted the dawn with his soup. Around noon, when it was sold out, another enclave resident spread out platters of hot food on a low table before the altar. This attracted workers from the nearby central market area who for a low price got a plate of steaming rice on which fried fish and stir-fried vegetables garnished with bits of meat were ladled. Later in the afternoon the man moved his table around to Pasteur Street where under the trees he served the cold remaining food on small plates to accompany servings of beer, rice alcohol, and Cholon brandy. In 1964 there appeared a group of men who spent most of the afternoon sitting in front of the altar drinking alcohol from bottles as they talked incessantly while snacking on the cold food. They did not seem to be destitute and one, invariably dressed in long-sleeve shirt and tie, read palms in a small shop across from the nearby Hindu temple. When I passed he would salute and greet me in French. One day there was a bombing at the Chinese embassy in the nearby financial district, and it sent everyone running, but the "bottle gang" kept nipping, snacking, and talking, oblivious of it all. A

Chinese lady and a French lady from my building also noticed them and jokingly concluded they were turned-off Viet Cong who were now at loose ends.

RAND had a small office in the MACV Research and Development compound, a group of stone one-story buildings built on the Saigon River by the French military early in the century. A former GI who had taken his discharge in Vietnam served as secretary, typing letters and handling mail. At the compound I met Joe Zasloff, a RAND consultant, who had been in Vietnam in the late 1950s and had just arrived with my friend John Donnell to organize the Viet Cong Motivation and Morale Project funded by ARPA. The main purpose of this project was to interview Viet Cong prisoners and defectors to gain a realistic picture of the movement and motivation behind it. Project teams would travel throughout South Vietnam to gather data on different areas and layers of the Viet Cong movement. Joe obtained use of a MACV-rented French villa at 176 rue Pasteur. The villa, built during World War II, was odd, to say the least. It had a huge living-dining area at the back of which was a stairway winding up to the second floor past long windows with purple stained glass. The instant I stepped into the villa I had the uneasy feeling that there was something wrong with it, that something lurid had occurred there. Later I found out that at night the servants retreated to their quarters behind the villa which they were afraid to enter because it was haunted with ghosts.

On 29 January 1964 the ruling junta that had overthrown Ngo Dinh Diem was toppled in a coup d'état headed by Gen. Nguyen Khanh. According to Nguyen Ngoc Tho, General Minh, who like Diem and Nhu became concerned at the deepening American involvement in Vietnam and intensification of the fighting, had by late 1963 made contact with kinsmen and friends in the NLF to make arrangements for a political accommodation leading to a coalition government and avoid any expansion of the war. But, Tho explained, the Americans found out and were angry. He added, "They (particularly Mr. McNamara) wanted a military solution."

Khanh was supported by General Tran Thien Khiem, who had been involved in the overthrow of Diem and was now commander of III Corps (where Saigon was located), and Col. Nguyen Chanh Thi, a leader of a 1960 mutiny attempt and recently returned from exile in Cambodia. They moved quickly, sending Generals Ton That Dinh, Tran Van Don, and Le Van Kim into house arrest in Dalat. Nguyen Khanh became prime minister,

Gen. Duong Van Minh was appointed head of state, and Southern Dai Viet leader, Dr. Nguyen Ton Hoan returned to Vietnam to become vice-premier. I had met Dr. Hoan in New Haven through my friend Huynh Sanh Thong, a Southern Dai Viet, who returned to become head of Vietnam Press.

On 1 February 1964 General Khanh ordered the immediate release of Y Bham Enuol, a Bajaraka Movement leader who had been jailed in 1959. While Khanh was visiting Cornell University on 6 December 1973, he explained that he felt because of his background as commander of Mobile Group II which in 1954 had been involved in highland operations he understood the region's problems better than most Saigon leaders. Also, as commander of II Corps he had met with Y Bham and other Bajaraka leaders. After he became prime minister, Khanh said that he thought it was time to give highlanders an opportunity to assume some responsibility in the administration. Following his release, Y Bham was named Deputy Province Chief for Highland Affairs in Darlac.

Meanwhile I had begun interviewing American military advisers in Saigon offices and compounds. Conducting interviews in the central highlands would provide an opportunity to visit ethnic groups that previously were not very accessible. On 5 February 1964 an opportunity arose to visit the Special Forces A-Team at Bu Dop in the remote Stieng country close to the Cambodian border where rubber plantations thrived. On an L-20 reconnaissance aircraft that carried two passengers (the Vietnamese camp commander and me) required to wear parachutes, we flew to the dirt airstrip near the Special Forces camp, a small collection of thatched structures surrounded by a fortification. Close by was a village of Stieng who had been relocated to afford protection against Viet Cong wandering through the forest demanding rice and chickens from the villagers.

After settling in one of the huts, I began to interview the twelve members of the A-Team. I also visited the Stieng headman and elders to discuss their society. The Stieng are Mon Khmer-speaking, living in longhouses occupied by kin traced through the male line (patrilineal descent) and they have a form of debt bondage related to costly bride prices.[8] The next day six members of the Special Forces team left with Stieng and Vietnamese CIDG militiamen to patrol along the Cambodian border. That night we were awakened by sounds of small arms and machine guns. As everyone ran to his position, flares lit the camp and out-going mortars boomed. Then there was silence and the next morning there were signs that someone tried to breach the barbed wire perimeter. I returned to the Stieng village and in the afternoon I went with one of the team members to a neighboring rubber plantation. In the 1930s-style house the planter and his wife who served cocktails warmly received me. Sitting in the living room where we talked about French ethnography on the Stieng, the world of the Special Forces camp and Stieng village seemed far away indeed.

At the beginning of March 1964 I accompanied American military officers from the ARPA compound to visit two Gulf of Siam islands, sites of the Junk Fleet, a program wherein local young men from fishing villages were recruited as militia seamen for patrolling coastal areas. While I was interested in interviewing Junk Fleet advisers, the ARPA officers wanted to test military weapons and gear. We flew in a military aircraft to Phu Quoc island which I had visited briefly in 1956 (most of the island was now considered insecure). At the naval base we boarded a Vietnamese navy patrol craft for the five-hour trip to the small island of Panjang. In 1777, with the help of French Catholic priest Pigneau de Behaine, Nguyen Anh, who later became Emperor Gia Long, sought refuge on Panjang to escape from the Tay Son rebels who had killed the rest of his family.

En route, the officers tested the new AR-15 (an early version of the M-16) by shooting at long sea snakes, which, when hit, flew into the air. From a distance the island appeared to be a bright green rock, but when the ship rounded a promontory there was a bay ringed with white coral-sand beach and a backdrop of flowering trees, hardwood, and coastal flora above which rose cliffs. The ship's captain explained that the permanent population was about ten people, but fishermen from central Vietnam spent months on the island to fish and salt their catch before selling it along the coast en route back to their villages. Also, from time to time ocean vessels stopped at Panjang to stock up on the island's renowned well water.

The Junk Fleet had a camp on the beach. My military colleagues lost no time testing gear such as jungle tents and hammocks, and they put on experimental boots to climb the cliffs. Meanwhile, I was called on to help the young American navy doctor with his sick call for the militiamen (whom the Americans called "Junkies"). I noticed during sick call that the Junkies accumulated symptoms. Standing in line the first patient had stomach pains and the next had stomach pains and a headache while the third had both along with diarrhea. And so on. After sick call they produced guitars and began to sing while they exchanged pills. Big green pills, for example, were worth three little red pills. When I asked if they ever took any of the pills they just laughed. Despite the fact that I identified the navy officer as the doctor, the Junkies were convinced (probably because I was older) that I was the doctor, so they set up my hammock and built a fire for me.

Fishermen from central Vietnam brought their day's catch to the beach. There were hammerhead sharks seven feet long, red snapper, grouper, and enormous turtles. Protected by a coral reef, the bay with its crystalline water was an ideal place to swim. That evening, with oil lamps burning, the Junkies served on the beach a wonderful dinner of grilled and steamed seafood with rice washed down with La Rue beer.

The following morning we returned to the Junk Fleet post at the southern tip of Phu Quoc where I interviewed navy advisers. An interview with one adviser, a navy chief, who had the reputation of being unusually adventurous, took place on a junk. We began the interview in the calm of the dock, but as we moved into the Gulf of Siam, seas became very rough and as water sloshed over the side I wondered about the wisdom of interviewing adventurous advisers, but it turned out to be a particularly useful interview because the chief had a lot of experience and ideas.

Additional interviews with Junk Fleet advisers took me to Cam Ranh in central Vietnam. After interviewing, I went to Binh Ba, a small bay island. In the only village on the island, when I explained to the headman that I had done research in a southern farming village, he smiled and responded, "This village is not like a farmer's village because fishing is dangerous." He then said that fishing, fish-sauce production, and some gardening were the only economic activities. French works describe the whale cult among fishermen of central Vietnam.[9] I inquired about it. The headman explained that his fishermen venerate the whale and before going out to sea on long trips they push small model boats laden with offerings into the surf. He invited me to visit the communal temple (*dinh*) where the guardian opened a large red and gold box to reveal a whale jawbone. In the nineteenth century a whale had been beached on the nearby coast. Emperor Tu Duc had decreed that the village would get the head while a village down the coast would get the rest of the whale. On specified days of the lunar calendar the whole village assembled in the temple to make ritual offerings to the whale. Little did I realize that Cam Ranh Bay would soon become the site of a large American naval base.

Prior to leaving Washington in January 1964 I had been contacted by David McK. Rioch, M.D., director of neuropsychiatry at Walter Reed Army Institute of Research (WRAIR) in Walter Reed Hospital who was organizing a study of American military advisors in Vietnam. He had a team composed of psychiatrists and an anthropologist, David Marlowe. We met several times and I agreed (with RAND's approval) to cooperate with them on some nondirective group sessions with advisers. We would employ the nondirective group approach of Carl Rogers, whose methods I had become familiar with at the University of Chicago.

In late March 1964, Dr. Rioch came to Vietnam with a group from WRAIR to visit medical facilities in Nhatrang, Pleiku, Kontum, Danang, and Hue, and he kindly asked me to accompany them. Kontum now had its own airstrip and the main street was transformed with new shops, restaurants, and a modern market. The highlight of the visit was Dr. Patricia (Pat) Smith's hospital in Kontum. Arriving in 1959, Pat's goal was to establish a hospital for charity patients. Initially she practiced medicine in the leprosarium that had been established near Kontum by Sister Marie-Louise of the Sisters of Charity order. When we visited, Pat had her own hospital, filled with highlander patients.

Pursuing my own adviser study, I returned to Pleiku in late April and stayed for a few days northeast of Pleiku town in the Jarai Tobuan country at the Special Forces post at Plei Mrong which had been overrun by the Viet Cong in January 1963. I interviewed A-Team members and visited nearby villages where I learned that unlike other Jarai, the Tobuan did not trace descent through the female line. Also, they had other cultural features such as communal men's houses not shared by other Jarai.

From Pleiku I went to Cheo Reo and the nearby Special Forces post in the Jarai village of Bon Beng. I found Cheo Reo (now a province capital) had grown considerably since 1957 because of the influx of Vietnamese civil servants and military personnel with their families. Also, there were land development centers in the vicinity of Cheo Reo, increasing the market functions of the town. A main street had developed and was lined with shops, most of which were owned by Chinese and Indians. At the Special Forces camp with its Jarai and Bahnar militiamen there were members of the highlander ethnonationalist Bajaraka Movement which had been founded in 1958. Two such members were interpreters, a Rhadé named Y Kdruin Mlo and Kpa Doh, a Jarai, both educated in Ban Me Thuot. Kpa

Jarai strategic hamlets near Pleiku, 1964.

Doh's name became "Pardo" for the Americans. Y Kdruin Mlo always called himself Philippe Drouin, and in the camp the Americans called him "Cowboy" because he favored tight-fighting clothes, a belt with a large brass buckle, and a sizable hat. Philippe was married to the daughter of Jarai leader, Nay Moul, who had extended hospitality to Wickert and me in 1957. Another daughter was married to Bajaraka activist, Nay Luett, who was working as an interpreter for USOM in Cheo Reo.

Nay Luett was born in May 1935 at Bon Me Hing, south of Cheo Reo, to a family of modest means. As a child, he displayed a remarkable brightness, which was interpreted as a manifestation of *kdruh* (charisma attributed to the spirits). This attracted the attention of Nay Moul who arranged with Luett's parents to take the boy to his longhouse at Cheo Reo. Luett studied at the Franco-Bahnar school in Kontum and the Collège Sabatier in Ban Me Thuot before entering the prestigious French Lycée Yersin in Dalat (where Bao Dai and Norodom Sihanouk had studied). Nay Moul arranged a marriage between his daughter and Luett.

Nay Luett kindly offered assistance in gaining information on Jarai culture so we crossed the Apa River to Buon Broai where, in a splendid longhouse, Nay Nui, a famed Jarai chief and Nay Moul's father-in-law, lived with kin. Alleged to be around one hundred and twenty years of age, Nay Nui was blind, and we found him sitting on a mat weaving a fish net. Wearing only a traditional loincloth, he appeared very wrinkled and thin, but he quickly pointed out that he still had all of his teeth. He was indeed old, still he had about him the air of one who in the past had been a great chief.

Family legend had it that at the time of Nay Nui's birth, a large white toad with unusually broad legs appeared near the longhouse. His father grabbed it and put it in the river but it returned the following day. Again it was placed in the river only to come back the next day. After this happened a third time, Nay Nui's father offered a pig and three jars of alcohol to the spirits, and the toad disappeared. The incident was interpreted as a sign that the spirits (kdruh) favored the newborn child. Nay Nui recalled during our visit how as a youth he was able to leap from the ground up to the high platforms (usually six to eight feet in height in the Cheo Reo area) in the front of the longhouses. His daughter told how he once jumped over a row of seven water buffaloes.

Nay Nui remembered the first Frenchmen who appeared in the Cheo Reo area and he described them as "big men with large stomachs and red faces." He also recalled how they tried to assert their authority over the Jarai. Nay Nui joined forces with Oi At, the King of Fire, and they drove the French away. He claimed to have killed one Frenchman during the fighting. Several years later, however, the French returned with more troops. Nay Nui lamented that the Jarai with their crossbows, sabers, and spears were no match for the guns of the outsiders, so they had to accept French rule.

My sister Catherine had sent a box of old costume jewelry she had gathered from kin and friends for me to give highlanders as gifts. I presented Nay Nui a simple gold chain necklace, which his daughter put on him much to everyone's delight.

At the beginning of May 1964 I traveled inland from Quang Ngai to the Special Force camp at Gia Vuc in the Hre country. Even in the wartime 1960s the Re River valley was visually idyllic with its waterway lined with verdant hills and villages perched on low hills amidst terraced jade green paddy fields, great sprays of bamboo, and graceful coconut and areca palms. The overall beauty of the scene provided a welcome contrast to the drab sandbags and barbed wire of the Special Forces post.

After interviewing members of the A-Team I went to visit villages of

A U.S. Special Forces medic treating Hre villagers, 1964.

the Hre, who speak a Mon Khmer language and reckon descent through the male line (patrilineal descent). The villagers were friendly, and in the headman's house we drank from the jars. The headman gave me a crossbow, and I presented his wife with pearl earrings, which she immediately put on. But the next day her fat little son appeared completely naked save for the pearl earrings neatly affixed to a string around his neck.

The idyllic aura of the Hre villages was dispelled when I accompanied the Special Forces medic on his round of sick calls. Malarial fevers were common, as were skin ailments. Lepers were missing fingers and toes. Some people were wasting away with a sickness the medic could not identify. Then there were the refugees who had fled their villages in the mountains. A woman and her two small sons had left home after the husband was killed. By the time they reached the village, malnutrition took the woman and one son, leaving the other son in a dying state. Skin and bones with big black eyes that looked lost, he sat by the hearth. All we could do was give him some medicine and candy. The medic explained that malnutrition was common among refugees, and although the Vietnamese district chief had relief rice, he refused to give it to Hre villagers. The Special Forces had constructed a dispensary in the village, but the Vietnamese would not supply it nor would they provide a teacher for the school that American aid had built.

On our "sick call tour" I witnessed a scarification male puberty practice done informally rather than in a ritual. In this instance a boy sat on the edge of a longhouse veranda while his two friends fashioned with finely ground sawdust a circle about 1½ inches in diameter on the upper part of his leg. Using matches, one of the friends lit the sawdust while the other gently fanned. As the sawdust burned with a white heat the boy looked at us showing not one sign of pain. Then the boy and his friends laughed. When the sawdust had burnt it left a nasty circle of blackened seared flesh. The medic related that these burns inevitably fester, but when he offered to treat them, the boys and their families refused; they wanted the festering burn to become a scar. The medic was told the impressive circular scars were symbols of the individual's strength and bravery, characteristics of the good man.

From Gia Vuc I visited Khe Sanh just below the demilitarized zone in the country of the Bru, a Mon Khmer–speaking group. The Special Forces post established in 1962 was located in an old French fort above Khe Sanh. Khe Sanh itself was a small town of some twelve hundred Vietnamese who lived in houses with tile roofs and wattled walls (the style of central Vietnam) surrounded by gardens and fruit groves. The center consisted of a few shops around a small covered market that was bustling in the morning. A stream ran through the town, and a stone bridge reminiscent of rural France crossed it. Surrounded by misty green mountains, Khe Sanh seemed cut off from the outside world.

Close by were several French coffee estates (the coffee from Kha Sanh was reputed to be the best in Indochina), one of which was run by Félix Polin. He explained that his father, Eugène, had begun the plantation in 1904, building his stone house and also planting the avocado tree, still heavy with fruit, that stood next to the entrance. In March 1964 while driving his familiar yellow Citroën on Route 9, Eugène Polin and M. Llinares, a fellow planter, were ambushed by the Viet Cong. Polin was killed, but Llinares escaped.

There must have been a time when the beauty of Khe Sanh was

enhanced by tranquility, but that time was long gone. By early 1964, fighting around the town in the green forests had prompted Felix to send his wife and children to live in coastal Hue.

When in the early 1960s Communist insurgency brought conflict, the Bru found themselves a people in between, and a grim reminder was the influx of refugees. Most went into other villages, preferring those where they had kin. Huc Van, five kilometers from Khe Sanh, had by May 1964 grown from twenty-five houses to one hundred. Others grouped in refugee villages that sprung up around Khe Sanh. Receiving some help from the government, they were now building new houses, and some were farming in the nearby hills. To the west of Khe Sanh was the Ai Lao pass, the historic invasion route, and there the ruins of the notorious Lao Bao French political prison (which once held Ho Chi Minh) were obscured by the tall elephant grass.

After interviewing in the Special Force post, I visited Bru villages, photographing traditional houses and gathering data on their culture about which there was very little in the ethnographic record. In Bru society the patrilineages (traced through the male line to common ancestor) is the most important social and economic unit. Its head serves as steward of religious prescriptions for preserving harmony with the patrilineage spirit (or spirits) and the ancestors, both protectors of the kin group, who bring good fortune, health, and abundant crops.[10]

Accompanied by Taco, a Bru interpreter, and some Nungs (Tai-speaking highlanders from the Vietnam-China border area who served as mercenaries in the French army and were now hired as security guards by the Special Forces), I went to Lang Troi, a Bru village on the Lao border, where we collected ethnographic data and took photos. Lack of security on the road back forced us to remain in the village for the night. As it turned out there was a divination ritual for an elderly man who suffered from fever and severe coughing. I recorded the daylong ritual in which a shaman officiated and a buffalo sacrifice was held.

After leaving Khe Sanh, I visited other remote Special Forces camps in the central highlands. At A Shau there was a small settlement of Pacoh, people linguistically and culturally close to the Bru. At An Diem (where the French had had a post) there was a village of Katu refugees. From An Diem I returned to Danang and went on to Saigon. My plan was to return to the Katu country after which I would go on to Pleiku to participate in a meeting of WRAIR psychiatrists with American military advisers. So, in Saigon when I packed to return to Danang and the Katu country, I included my only copy of notes from the 1957 trip among the Katu, and also some key interviews I had done with advisers.

I returned to Danang and was able to take advantage of a helicopter flight to the Special Forces camp at Nam Dong in the Ta Rau valley of the Katu country.

Four

VICTORY AT NAM DONG

DESPITE THE TERRIBLE THING that happened there, I suppose I shall always remember the valley of Ta Rau as beautiful. Set in lofty, thickly forested mountains with the meandering Ta Trach River, the valley seemed idyllic and timeless as it passed below the H-34 Marine helicopter that on Saturday, 4 July 1964 took me to the Nam Dong Special Forces camp named for the nearby Vietnamese village.

Ta Rau valley in many respects had a timeless aura because it was a place that had been bypassed in the drama of Indochina history. There is no mention of it in the annals of the kingdom of Champa. Nor did Ta Rau lure any Vietnamese settlers in their "advance southward" along the coastal plain. Vietnamese settlers had preferred the flat coastal plain, well suited to their wet-rice farming. Also, inland valleys such as Ta Rau valley were too much in the mountains which the Vietnamese feared and avoided. Then too, Ta Rau valley was located in the country of the Katu, dreaded "blood hunters."

The arrival of the French in the mid nineteenth century prompted the court of Hue to consolidate its rule over remaining territories. This led to a pacification scheme for upland areas of central Vietnam and a series of forts which eventually served as centers for fostering and controlling trade in such valuable mountain products as cinnamon, elephant tusks, rhinoceros horns, deer antlers, and hardwood. But no forts were built in the valley of Ta Rau.

The French also established military posts in the central highlands, some of them on sites of the earlier Vietnamese forts, but none in Ta Rau. The only French commercial development in the uplands west of Tourane (Danang) was a hill station built on the summit of Bana mountain in the mid 1930s as a refuge for French colonists from the stifling heat of the coastal plain. By 1943 the resort, which had a magnificent view of the coastline, had 130 chalets, two small hotels, a children's swimming pool, and tennis courts. With the Indochina War it was abandoned and by 1964 it was forgotten.

In the late 1950s when the Saigon government moved excess populations from the coastal plain, Nam Dong and the other Vietnamese settlements in Ta Rau valley were founded. So in 1964 Nam Dong was relatively new.

One reason for this visit to the camp was to interview some of the twelve-man team as part of my research on American military advisers. Another reason was to visit the Katu country once more in the hope of gathering additional ethnographic information. I carried with me the one copy of my 1957 field notes on the Katu villages we visited. There was only one copy because they were written in pencil which would not reproduce in any of the machines available in Saigon.

As the helicopter on 4 July banked, I could see on a hill the grouping of wood-thatch buildings that made up the heart of the Nam Dong camp. Nearby on bottom land was a dirt airstrip. To the east were the hamlets of Nam Dong hidden in lush growth. The paddy fields were small, a testimony to the difficulty of farming wet-rice in this place where nature relentlessly encroached.

The helicopter stirred up clouds of dry-season dust as it descended to the pad at the inner gate between two perimeters of barbed wire.

As I walked into the inner perimeter I was greeted by Capt. Roger Donlon, the boyish-looking thirty-year-old commander of Team A-726 who had been informed by the Special Forces B-Team in Danang of my visit. We chatted as Donlon escorted me to the small room in the U.S. command

post which he shared with his second-in-command, Lt. Julian (Jay) Olejniczak called "Lieutenant O." by the team (it turned out he was from South
Chicago), and M. Sgt. Gabriel Alamo. I left my bag and camera case on the
spare bunk and we went to the small nearby mess for coffee. The captain
explained that Nam Dong camp had been opened in March 1963 to provide
protection for the estimated five thousand Vietnamese in the valley villages. His team, which had replaced another team some five weeks before,
had twelve men and an Australian warrant officer, Kevin Conway, who had
fought guerrillas in Malaysia and Borneo. Three members of the team,
Sgts. Gabriel Alamo, Thurman Brown, and Vernon Beeson, were Korean
War vets. To provide security for the camp itself, the Americans had
obtained the services of sixty Nungs (twenty of whom had recently arrived)
under the leadership of Le Tse-tung, who had fought in the French army.
Captain Donlon's counterpart, Captain Lich, the camp commander, had
under him a force of 311 Vietnamese CIDG militiamen recruited in the
Danang area and organized in three "strike companies."

Captain Donlon noted that in addition to patrolling the surrounding area
his team engaged in "civic action," including such things as building
schools and digging wells. In addition, the team had two medics, Sgt.
Thomas Gregg and Sgt. Terrance Terrin who operated a small dispensary in
the camp and visited villages to tend the sick. They were assisted by four
Vietnamese nurses.

Captain Donlon asked one of the medics, Sgt. Gregg, a thin, easy-going
young man, to show me around. Everything reflected the need for effective
defense in this remote post located as it was deep in what the Americans
called "VC territory." Most of the buildings had anti-sniper sandbag walls
around them. Spaced around the inner perimeter were five round sand-
bagged mortar pits at the rear of which were concrete bunkers each with
some five hundred rounds of ready ammunition. Interspersed among them
were Nung machine-gun posts. There also was a huge hole that the previous team had dug for an underground operations center and dispensary.
Donlon's team called it the "swimming pool." The small room where I had
left my bag and camera was at the north end of the command post, a long
wood-and-thatched building that housed quarters for the rest of the team
and an operations center which functioned as an office and gathering place.
South of that was another long structure for the communications and supply rooms. Beyond was the dispensary at the southern end of the inner

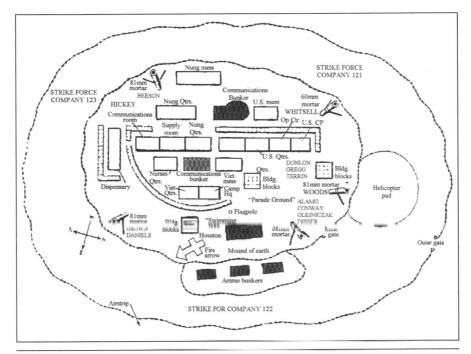

Nam Dong Special Forces Camp

perimeter. Nearby was the camp commander's office and living quarters. On the edge of the inner perimeter were three underground ammo bunkers. The three strike companies were housed in underground quarters between the inner and outer perimeters. Between the "swimming pool" and command post was the "parade ground," an open space save for two piles of cinder blocks made in the camp.

Special Forces camps were busy places with the team members either on patrol or engaged in improving defenses and living conditions. Sgt. Keith Daniels, the communications specialist, for example, was in the midst of building a brick cooking grill. Dinner in the mess was the only time those in the camp would more or less come together to serve themselves some of the daily fare, sit down and eat, exchange some news and views, and then leave. I found that A-team members were happy to have civilian visitors to break the routine and hear what was happening in the world beyond the locale. There was the usual joking back and forth and some remarks about "fourth-of-July fireworks for the VC." When the sun fell behind the mountains, Ta Rau valley was plunged into total darkness. I went to my bunk and changed into the black calico pajamas like those worn by some of the Special Force troopers and the Viet Cong to take notes and sip one allotted drink from the bottle of Scotch that I brought on field trips.

In the morning I arranged through Captain Donlon to begin interviewing members of the team who could spare the time. Over strong coffee, the captain reported the chilling news that the night before, while leading a patrol in villages at the far northern reaches of the valley, Sgt. Michael Disser, youngest member of the team, had radioed, "The villagers are scared, but they won't tell me or my interpreters why." Nonetheless, I agreed to go with Lt. Olejniczak, W.O. Conway, and Sgt. Gregg to visit villages. Capt. Donlon asked if I could find out something about villagers' complaints that herbicides sprayed from aircraft had destroyed some of their rice crops. In the lumbering 2½-ton ("deuce and a half") truck we drove northward down a bumpy road, crossed the Ta Trach River, shallow in the dry season, and continued to a heavily forested area where Katu refugees had a small village. The headman spoke some Vietnamese so I talked with him while Gregg visited sick villagers. The headman complained that an aircraft had swooped over the settlement and sprayed "medicine" which killed some crops. We went to the nearby fields where he said this had happened. It struck me that there was very little damage to the crops or surrounding foliage. An older Vietnamese man approached and identified himself as a hamlet chief. He said that the previous night some men killed the chief of a nearby hamlet, kidnapped another man, then entered a neighboring hamlet where they pushed the chief to the ground and kicked him.

Gregg tended the sick in two more villages before we headed back to the post. As we were crossing the river where it ran through woods, I noticed two elderly Vietnamese men dressed in traditional black tunics and turbans. They had paper models of boats in which they had placed burning joss, and kneeling on the bank they pushed the boats into the slow current. As the boats bobbed they clasped hands and bowed. It was a familiar scene of offerings and invocations to cosmic forces. But I wondered for what purpose?

We picked up some Nungs returning to the camp and then stopped on the edge of a settlement that had sprung up after the camp was established. At a bamboo-thatch shop/bar we stopped to buy beer to take back to the camp. CIDG militiamen from the camp were celebrating a volleyball contest (Captain Donlon had given them money to buy a round of beer). Suddenly a militiaman, his faced screwed up in anger, approached the truck and pointing to one of the Nungs, accused him in salty language of seducing his wife. Other CIDG joined him. There was an angry exchange until the rest of the Nungs stood up and clicked rounds into the chambers of their weapons. The CIDG militiamen backed up and disappeared into the bar. I asked one of the Nungs if the woman was the militiaman's wife and he replied, "No, she was just a whore from Hue."

Inside the bar the atmosphere was cheerful as everyone drank warm bottles of "33" beer. The good-natured lady who ran the bar explained that she was from Can Tho in the south, but her husband was from Danang. She had six children, three of them in the village school.

Back in the camp the mood was solemn. Returning from a three-day patrol, Sgt. Terry Terrin reported that his troopers had found bodies of two murdered village chiefs. I told Captain Donlon what we had seen and heard up the valley and about the incident outside the shop/bar. He had heard about the incident and found out that the CIDG were from Company 122 and an agitator from that unit had caused the disturbance. The Nungs had returned to their area in the inner perimeter while the Vietnamese went back to the Company 122 quarters in the outer perimeter of the eastern sector. But a short time later some of them gathered at the inner perimeter fence near Company 122 where the agitator goaded them into a frenzy of shouting and shaking fists as they threw rocks at the Nungs. Quickly the American team dispersed the Vietnamese CIDG. To quell the conflict Captain Donlon met with Captain Lich and Le Tse-tung, but just as the three got together, a shot rang out. Captain Donlon, joined by Sergeant Alamo, ran toward the fence. It was too late. The Nungs and Vietnamese had hurried to their defense positions and were firing at random. Shots rang out close to the mess hall so I hit the floor and crawled behind the refrigerator, the only solid object in this wood-thatch structure. Holding his weapon high, Sergeant Alamo stood on a mound and slowly put the weapon on the ground. The firing ceased. Captain Donlon got Le Tse-tung to quiet his Nungs. Captain Lich, however, sent word from the Vietnamese mess that he refused to interrupt his dinner, prompting Captain Donlon to go to the mess and insist Captain Lich meet with Le. The commander finally agreed, so he and Le brought their staff officers to a meeting with the American captain. Captain Lich and Le settled on an agreement to quiet their troops and gather for a conference at 8:30.

Meanwhile, some of the Nungs invited me to share their food. They were convinced that the Vietnamese were going to attack Nung guards during the night, prompting their leader to pull almost all of the guards back into the inner perimeter. I went back to the command post where most members of the team were having coffee. I repeated what the Nungs had said, raising the question of how this would affect security. I wondered aloud if all of the incidents might presage an attack on the camp. Captain Donlon said that he had exactly the same feelings. There was a moment of silence and then Sergeant Daniels said, "We can call Danang for a chopper if you want to leave." I looked toward the window. "Thanks sergeant, but it's too late, the sun has just gone behind the mountains."

Then Sgt. Raymond Whitsell, a trim black man with mustache, asked if I wanted a weapon. I said that it probably would be a good idea and asked for a carbine. He replied that they didn't have any carbines, so I accepted an AR-15, which I had learned to fire at the An Diem Special Forces camp.

After dinner I filled out a timesheet that had to be submitted to the RAND Corporation and dropped it in the mailbox at the operations center. Then I sat down with Sergeant Alamo, who had automobile brochures spread out in front of him. He explained that when he got back to Ft. Bragg he planned to order a new car. Sgt. John Houston, a thin, intense man, who had just returned from a patrol, came in and while he talked, threw darts at a board affixed to one wall.

Captain Donlon asked Warrant Officer Conway and me to join him at the 8:30 meeting. With about twenty people gathered, Captain Donlon wisely insisted that the Vietnamese strike force double its outer perimeter guard for the night and secure the airstrip. The Nungs would triple the Nung guards on the inner perimeter. After the meeting I returned to my bunk to take some notes. The ominous news and afternoon incident had made me uneasy. I found out later that members of the team were equally uneasy. That night Sergeant Woods wrote to his wife, "All hell is going to break loose here. We figure that the VC are going to hit us before morning." And in the dispensary Sergeant Terrin told Sergeant Gregg, "I don't think we'll see the sun come up." To which Gregg replied, "I don't either but we'd better get some sleep." I placed my glasses, a flashlight, and the weapon on the dirt floor next to my bunk. Around midnight I awoke and walked outside where Conway was quietly smoking his pipe in a patch of light beyond which was sheer blackness. We chatted a bit and he noted that the dogs were restless. I returned to my bunk to sleep in the great silence of the mountains.

At 2:26 A.M. a massive, resounding explosion that engulfed the mess hall next door in white phosphorous fire shattered the sheer blackness and great silence. The force knocked me out of bed, and in the confused light of dancing flames I put on my glasses and sneakers. There were more explosions and the crackle of gunfire—small arms and automatic weapons. Suddenly, bullets were piercing the bamboo walls. Keeping close to the ground I grabbed my weapon and quickly looked to see Captain Donlon's bunk empty, but Lieutenant Olejniczak was writhing on the floor. "Are you hit?" I blurted, and when he said that he was getting into his clothes, I started to crawl to the entrance. Captain Donlon was just outside by the wall of sandbags and shouted in the din of mortar explosions and gunfire, "It's the VC!" I responded something banal like, "You're telling me!"

Alamo, Donlon, and I started getting ammo and weapons out of the command post and Beeson, Brown, and Olejniczak soon joined us. But it quickly became clear that it was too late—the structure was being swallowed by fast-moving fire. I heard Donlon say something about a flare ship and air strikes. Alamo, Brown, Olejniczak, and Beeson took off for their positions. Donlon motioned me to get under one of the disabled trucks parked nearby. Then one of the Vietnamese interpreters came running out of the explosions and smoke shouting, "The VC are already in the inner perimeter!" Donlon disappeared into the parade ground. Alone, I quickly reasoned that if I got under the truck and a mortar round landed on it the whole thing would collapse on me. (A friend of mine later commented that it wasn't wise to tell a kid brought up in a city to take refuge under a truck.)

Suddenly the command post was a mass of flames, which were rapidly spreading to other buildings in the heat, smoke, and dust of a firestorm. Mortar rounds landed everywhere, grenades exploded, and gunfire filled the air. In a matter of minutes, the camp had become a battlefield. Battle! Unfettered violence sweeping away any rationality or reason as it ascends to a crescendo of death and destruction. For an instant I felt all was lost. But, although adrenalin set my heart pounding, my mind was very clear, and despair quickly gave way to an instinct for survival. So, blocking out the explosions and clutching my AR-15 I ran toward the dispensary at the south end of the perimeter.

Just as I reached the burning supply building a deafening force hit, lifting me off my feet and smashing me against a wall. It was either a mortar or 57-millimeter recoilless rifle round. For an instant I experienced a strange feeling of detachment as if I were outside watching myself. My whole body ached as I lay on the ground trying to catch my breath. I ran my hands over my body to feel for blood or broken bones. Nothing but blood from cuts and bruises. Dragging myself to my feet and still gripping the AR-15, I staggered to the small area between the dispensary and the sandbag wall. Gregg, Terrin, and Daniels were carrying medical chests out of the threatened dispensary. The Vietnamese nurses were shaking with sobs. I said to them in Vietnamese, "Don't be afraid." Suddenly the explosions got louder, and someone said, "Artillery." It wasn't artillery; it was the exploding ammo in the command post and supply room.

With an explosive force, the thatched roof of the dispensary burst into flames. Gregg, Terrin, Daniels, and the nurses quickly dispersed into the smoke of the inner perimeter. Again I was alone and as the heat of the fire intensified I quickly decided that I would best be on the other side of the sandbag wall. I had just placed my weapon on the top of the wall and began to climb over it when Houston grabbed my leg and pulled me back. "See that trench," he said pointing to a spot not far away, "run for it, I'll cover you." I bent over, held my weapon at an angle in front of me and ran zigzag as I had been trained to do in 1944 at the Infantry Replacement Training Center, Camp Roberts, California.

I jumped into the trench and landed on a group of very tense Nungs. Since some of them were firing toward the barbed wire perimeter, I assumed that the Viet Cong were attacking. I raised the weapon to take aim, suddenly realizing that I had only one clip of ammo. By this time flares from our positions were illuminating the surrounding area, and I was astonished to see nothing but forest, eerily immutable in the orange light. No attackers. The older Nung, a leader who had served in the French army, shouted to his men to hold their fire. We both stood up and realized that Captain Lich was in a nearby trench and his men were firing randomly. The Nung leader and I shouted at him in Vietnamese and he replied with a wave of his hand. Then with the din of battle almost drowning us out, we shouted that his men should hold their fire and they did.

Suddenly the firestorm consumed the dispensary in a wave of explosive searing heat. Firebrands showered on us. As we huddled in the trench to avoid being badly burned, the Nung leader offered me a Cotab cigarette, which I accepted, an act that seemed incredibly normal even if I didn't smoke. "You're a professor," he said in Vietnamese, "what are you doing here?" I replied without thinking that I had come to "relax in the mountains," which produced a laugh.

This silly comment broke the tension, and the Nung leader asked about radio messages to Danang. I replied that messages had been sent, an unsubstantiated answer to give me and the Nungs hope that help would come. Suddenly the fire storm consuming the dispensary subsided somewhat but the roar of the flames was replaced by the sounds of battle and I realized fully that at any moment we could face death. It was then that I said prayers.

Over the clatter of automatic weapon fire I could hear Beeson shouting obscenities in his mortar position behind us. The lusty sound of an angry American voice was incredibly reassuring. Unexpectedly the sound of battle fell, and the Nung leader shook his head. Was he wondering if that signaled a final phase in the fighting? I dreaded to think that it might mean that the Viet Cong had taken the inner perimeter. But rising fears were dispelled when Beeson began cussing again as battle sounds burst forth. Suddenly one of the Nungs shouted and pointed toward mortar rounds exploding one after another coming in our direction. The enemy was "walking" the mortar rounds in an apparent attempt to knock out Beeson's position. Like a scene in a World War I movie, we in the trench were right in the path of the exploding shells. All of us quickly crouched and covered our faces with our hands. My stomach contracted but I realized that only a direct hit would get us. In a matter of seconds that seemed an eternity we heard a series of rounds go over and explode somewhere near Beeson's mortar pit.

By this time it was evident that the main thrust of the Communist attack was being directed at the other side, the eastern sector, of the camp. But there was no way of knowing what was going on there. The Nung leader suddenly gave orders to one of the young men, who slid out of the trench and crawled under the strings of barbed wire. The leader then sat down and signaled me to sit, leaving the watch to younger soldiers. He looked skyward and said in an anguished tone, "Where are the airplanes?" My spirits sagged at the thought that perhaps no message had been sent to Danang. I stood up and touched the grasses around the edge of the trench—they would go on growing regardless of what happened to us.

The battle noises would rise and fall in fits of violence accompanied by flashes of exploding shells that sent waves of acrid smoke over the trench. My whole body ached and I felt weary as I looked at my watch —4:00 A.M. Soon after, there was a new sound, and we looked up to see an aircraft that lit the skies with flares. The Nungs let out great shouts and I breathed a sigh of relief. Later in Danang I met the pilot of the flare-ship and he said, "That place sure looked like a furnace," to which I replied, "It felt like a furnace, let me tell you."

The VC knew the flare ship would precede air strikes so their firing began to taper off. Then, Donlon suddenly appeared at the edge of the trench. "Are you OK?" he asked. I was shocked. He had been badly wounded in the leg, left forearm and shoulder, and stomach. His face was cut and blackened by smoke, and his clothes were torn.

"God, Captain, get in the trench, you're wounded!"

"Can't," he said and told us that the inner perimeter was holding, but Alamo, Houston, and Conway were dead. Then he asked if we had enough ammo, to which I responded that I only had part of one clip. "I'll get you more," he said, suddenly disappearing into the smoke and flashing explosions.

The Nungs were exchanging words, and the leader asked me, "When does the sun rise?" I responded that I didn't know, adding that he lived here so he should know. He and the other Nungs laughed. The sounds of battle seemed to taper off a bit. Then, to my great relief, I saw the first morning light on a high rounded mountain peak to the south. I pointed it out and the Nungs repeated back and forth "morning light." It was very faint, but it was dawn, and we knew it would bring a break in the fighting.

As the pale morning light brightened and spread over the mountains the fighting was reduced to small arms fire, sporadic automatic-weapons clatter, and only occasional explosions. When light fell on our position we all stood up and around us Vietnamese militiamen began to get out of their trenches. Captain Lich, wearing a very loud aloha-style shirt, was smiling and waving as if he had led the defense of the camp. The Nungs lost no time going into the outer perimeter and I followed, picking my way past the sandbag wall.

The scene before me was worse than any nightmare I could remember. The whole camp was a blackened smoking ruin and ammo was still exploding. There were bodies and pieces of bodies everywhere—on the cluttered parade ground, in the grasses, and on the wires (I noticed one body clothed in a loud shirt). Charred bodies in the ruins were barely distinguishable. One of the interpreters was burned almost beyond recognition. The smoky air was heavy with the odor of death and destruction. I felt a wave of nausea and got the dry heaves.

There still was shooting all around and then out of the smoke straggled bleeding Vietnamese. Some with desperate looks grabbed my arm asking for help. Others had rags as bandages. My first reaction was to help adjust the bandages to make them more effective, but it was apparent that a great deal more was needed. First, I had to find out how everyone was. Gregg was moving around treating the wounded and he directed me to the cinder blocks on the edge of the parade ground between Whitsell's and Wood's mortar positions, which had become a kind of makeshift command post near where the old one had stood. Still clutching my weapon I ran past the smoking, exploding ruins and felt a great sense of relief at seeing the survivors who were equally relieved to see me.

It was astonishing that any of us survived the long night of death and destruction.

That long night had been heralded by the deadly round of white phosphorus demolishing the mess hall and killing the Vietnamese cooks Onzo and Ding Dong.

Brown, Woods, Conway, Beeson, and Houston shared quarters at the south end of the command post. Sleeping with revolver and holster strapped to his waist, Brown jumped out of bed when the first mortar round hit, grabbed his AR-15, and made for his assigned mortar position east of the dispensary. When he reached the protective wall he saw grenades coming from his own pit. Then a 57-mm recoilless rifle round crashed into the wall, sending him head over heels in a shower of earth and splintered timber. He ran to get grenades at the command post and pitched in to help our salvage effort. When everyone dispersed, Brown, with grenades in hand, started again for his pit when he saw Tuan, one of the interpreters, running toward him. A 57-mm round exploded in front of Tuan. Brown ran to the ditch where Tuan had fallen only to find him dead with his legs gone below the knees. When Brown finally jumped into his mortar pit he glanced up, looking into the barrel of a submachine gun held by one of two VC lying on top of his concrete ammunition bunker. Before he could fire, both VC rolled off. Brown leaped to the edge of the pit and shot them. Wasting no time, he and two Nungs began to fire illumination rounds.

Machine-gun fire woke Beeson, who grabbed his weapon and ran to the command post to help us salvage what we could. When fire swept through the building, Beeson ran back to his quarters, picked up an ammunition belt, and racing between burning buildings reached his mortar pit where the Nungs were already breaking out ammunition.

When the first round of white phosphorus exploded, Woods awoke to see "fourteen thousand different colored flames," and shouted, "For God's sake, what is it?" From a nearby bunk, Conway responded, "I don't know." Woods reached for his pistol as bullets buzzed through the room like a swarm of bees. He grabbed his AR-15 and ammo and clad only in GI drawers began to crawl out the door. The rocks were too much for his knees so he began to run when someone shouted to help get weapons out of the command post. Dragging supplies from the rear of the command post, Woods saw through the window a second round crash into the burning mess hall setting the command post ablaze. Everyone dispersed and Woods ran barefoot through enemy fire to his position overlooking the helicopter pad.

Daniels was jolted out of bed and immediately flicked on the radio and called Danang to report the attack and request an air strike and flare ship. The mortar barrage outside intensified. He strapped on his holster, stuffed his jungle-suit pockets with ammo, and Houston joined him in evacuating radio equipment. Mortar explosions reached the building. Daniels grabbed his AR-15, got out the door, and belly-flopped as far as he could stretch when a mortar round landed on the communications room. Houston was knocked down by the explosion. Coming out of the dispensary, Terrin ran over to help Houston when an explosion knocked him unconscious. He came to in a drainage ditch by the dispensary where Houston had carried him to safety.

With the first explosion Gregg rolled out of bed in the dispensary where he and Terrin had small rooms. He went out the rear door as mortars rained down and gunfire broke out everywhere. In the light of the spreading fires he saw outside the wire fence not twenty yards away six crouched figures moving forward. He raised his AR-15 and pumped away sending the attackers flying backward. Then he ran back to the burning dispensary to evacuate equipment and medicines. He was joined there by Daniels and Terrin and they managed to carry out two iron medical chests used in village sick calls.

Whitsell and Disser shared the supply room and the first crashing explosion jolted them out of their bunks. Heavy small-arms fire and the scary crack of bullets piercing the bamboo walls filled their ears while they crawled through the window. As they ran to their positions a mortar round hit the supply room lighting it on fire. Whitsell reached his position to find his three Nungs (one of them shouting "VC! VC!") positioning the mortar.

In his mortar pit Disser and his six Nungs fired rounds to light up the airstrip to the east of the camp. He peered over the rim of his pit. A horrendous sight! On the side of a hill to the east, muzzle flashes burst from four mortars and a 57-mm recoilless rifle, all dug in and well camouflaged. Light from the illumination rounds revealed hundreds of men moving across the airstrip, some already pushing their way through the grass of the outer perimeter. Heavy fire from hills to the southwest, north, and northwest supported them, and the first wave was no more than thirty yards away. Disser looked over his shoulder to see Conway, the Australian warrant officer, walk down the stairs into the pit with a half-smile on his face. Then he pitched forward, hit the ground, and rolled over. Disser saw a wound, neat and round, almost exactly between his eyes. Just then, Pop Alamo, burned from the command-post fire, jumped into the pit and began picking off VC only a few yards away.

Olejniczak loaded up with smoke grenades, flares, hand grenades, an AR-15, a grenade launcher, and ammunition. After firing three flares, he pitched in to help us at the command post. When everyone dispersed, Olejniczak went to Disser's mortar pit, joining Alamo at the parapet and with his launcher fired grenades among the ammunition bunkers where the VC were advancing. While Disser fired a volley of mortar rounds, Olejniczak tended Conway bandaging his wound and covering him with a poncho, but soon after, Conway died.

Donlon's normal position was in the camp commander's hooch, but it was burning so he left me by the trucks and ran across the parade ground. By the flagpole he was suddenly flung into the air by an explosion. Dazed and missing one shoe he made his way to Wood's mortar pit to help him and two Nungs fire illumination and high-explosive rounds. Suddenly Donlon heard Houston by the "swimming pool" yelling, "They're over here! In the ammo bunker! The VC!" He was kneeling on the inside slope firing into the bunker enclosure. Donlon crawled out of the pit and started toward Houston when a mortar shell crashed a few feet from him knocking him down. He got up and realized that he had lost his pistol belt, the other shoe, and all of his equipment except his AR-15 and two clips. He crawled to Disser's position and asked for more ammunition. As he threw Donlon several magazines Disser told him that Conway and Alamo had been hit.

In the light of the fires Donlon saw movement at the gate, some twenty yards away, so he called to Disser, "Illuminate the main gate!" In the glaring light Donlon saw three VC snaking along a log at the edge of the road on the camp side of the gate. He assumed a kneeling position and fell two of them. The third one began to crawl into the grass and Donlon got him with a grenade. Later it was revealed that the three carried satchel charges of dynamite, entrenching tools, and other demolition paraphernalia.

It was only then that Donlon realized his left forearm was bleeding and there was a shrapnel wound in his stomach gushing blood. His face was cut and powder-burned.

On the mound by the ammunition bunker, Houston hopped back and forth firing continually to give the VC the impression that there was more than one man holding them off. On the other side of the swimming pool Terrin had been supporting Houston with a stream of gunfire. Then Houston fell face down on the mound and when Terrin shouted to him he cried, "I'm hit," but his cry ended in a choking sound. The two VC who got him had breached the inner perimeter between Houston's and Brown's position and hid behind the cinder blocks. Holding his AR-15 in his left hand, Terrin started toward Houston when an explosion laid open his left hand and forearm with hundreds of little pieces of metal and wood. An earlier concussion set his ears and mouth bleeding. With his weapon blown away, Terrin stood perfectly still and was joined by some Nungs who zeroed in on the two VC with carbine fire and grenades. Taking Houston's AR-15, Terrin fired from the hip and pulling a grenade pin with his teeth he threw it, killing both VC. Donlon ran up and said to Terrin, "Get Houston down in the hole!" They maneuvered Houston into the swimming pool, where Terrin examined him and looked up, "It's too late, John's dead."

Daniels had joined Brown in his position where some Nungs were firing projectiles. "Cover me," Brown shouted to Daniels, "They're coming over the fence!" Daniels went to the rim of the pit and took aim. An illumination round threw an orange light on at least a hundred men crawling through the grass. Suddenly a group of ten to fifteen shouted, rose, and made for the fence. Daniels and the Nungs, joined by Gregg, opened fire with their AR-15s. All VC in the first wave fell, but another came, and then another and some got as far as the fence which they climbed in their bare feet. A Nung next to Daniels yelled, wheeled, and fired three shots at the top of the bunker in the rear of the pit. Daniels turned in time to see a VC there, a grenade in his hand, topple backward.

Working his way between the protective wall and the pile of cinder blocks, Donlon heard Gregg shout from Brown's pit and went there. Donlon asked Daniels about the radio message to Danang. It had been received, but where was the flare ship and air strike? Donlon started for Beeson's position where he and the Nungs were firing illuminating rounds followed by high explosives and white phosphorus. Gregg said, "You're wounded, Captain, let me fix you up." But Donlon said to take care of the others and he headed back to Disser's position. For the third time he was knocked down by an exploding round and shrapnel tore into his left leg.

Disser's pit was hell itself. The VC had completely overrun Strike Force Company 122 and were in force at the inner perimeter barbed wire. While the outgoing mortar and automatic-weapons fire kept them down, they were within grenade-throwing distance. The grenades used by the VC in 1964 were the Chinese-made old fashioned "potato mashers" with less explosive power and shrapnel than American grenades. Volleys of five or six grenades began to land near Disser's pit. While Disser fired illuminating and high-explosive rounds, Alamo, bleeding from a shoulder shrapnel wound, worked his AR-15, and Olejniczak used his AR-15 and a grenade launcher. Suddenly Disser yelled as he picked up his AR-15 and fired over Alamo's and Olejniczak's heads. They looked up to see a VC in jacket, bikini, and camouflaged helmet standing on the parapet. He fell backward when Disser fired and a grenade fell from his hand but it didn't go off.

Olejniczak heard a thud as a smoking grenade hit and rolled to his feet exploding like a sledgehammer against his boots. One foot was aching and burning on the bottom, but Olejniczak tightly tied the laces around his bare ankle hoping to stop the bleeding and keep bones together.

Now wounded in the knees, arms, and legs, Disser crouched by his mortar and kept on firing. So many grenades were coming in and exploding with such little damage that the three all but ignored them. Still, even the semiduds were taking their toll, so they retreated to the concrete bunker at the rear where the Nungs were already holed up. A grenade bounced into the bunker, landing in an ammunition box beside Disser. All three dove out, but the blast tore Disser's foot and lower leg. Nonetheless, he crawled back to his mortar and started firing. Slumping on the stairs, Alamo was bleeding badly from a shoulder wound and a fresh hole in his right cheek just below the eye. Olejniczak, a mass of wounds, was sitting in the bunker doorway passing ammunition to Disser. They all knew that it would be a matter of seconds before the VC took advantage of the havoc they had wreaked with their grenade barrages.

Donlon came down the pit stairs in time to be knocked down by an exploding grenade. Shaking off the shock he began firing into the darkness hoping to discourage an attack. Disser, Olejniczak, and the Nungs working as a team yelled and fired one round after another. In desperation everyone began picking up grenades and tossing them out of the pit before they could go off. But everyone knew that it was madness to stay in the pit. So when Disser shouted, "Let's get the hell out of here," they started to leave when an explosion rocked Disser and Donlon who shouted, "Back to the commo trenches!"

Bleeding from face, shoulder, and stomach wounds, Alamo couldn't move so Donlon got one of Alamo's arms around his neck and started to straighten up. A mortar round exploded at the top of the stairs, sending Donlon flying. He could hear himself screaming in what he himself felt was a death wail. He came to with head and shoulder injuries inside the ammunition bunker. Sprawled in the pit, Alamo was beyond help. Donlon picked up the abandoned mortar and carried it to a trench behind Whitsell's position. Covered by Disser and Olejniczak, he ran back three times to Disser's pit for ammunition and Alamo's 57-mm rifle. A grenade exploded and Donlon felt the sharp pain of shrapnel entering his left leg. He ran to Woods's position to get him to fire rounds toward the east where the VC were massed. Yelling at his Nungs to cover him, Woods pounded the area beyond Disser's abandoned pit with a show of mortar marksmanship. Feeling there was so much to do, Donlon suddenly felt weak, tired, and his body ached. And where was the flare ship? Summoning strength, he filled his pockets with flares and ran to the trench where Disser and Olejniczak had been joined by wounded Nungs and Vietnamese. Terrin, despite his wounds, and Gregg were moving through VC fire among the pits and trenches to care for the wounded using supplies from the aid kits they had salvaged from the dispensary.

Donlon tried to reach Beeson's position but a machine gun kept firing at him so he went to Brown's pit. The flare ship finally began to pass over the camp to light up the dark. As the VC fire slacked, Donlon and the others felt a surge of hope, but they knew the attack was not over. Then in front of the pit a loudspeaker sounded a high-pitched excited voice speaking Vietnamese. Tet, one of the interpreters, was there and translated: "He say lay down weapons. VC going to take camp. We all be killed." Daniels, Brown, and Gregg exchanged hard looks of anger and Gregg said, "We'll lay down our weapons when we're too dead to pick them up."

A strange silence followed and then the voice blared out again, this time in English, "Lay down your weapons. We are going to annihilate your camp. You will all be killed." Brown began to adjust his mortar elevation as Daniels indicated where the voice was coming from. Ten rounds of high explosive and white phosphorus produced blasts on a ridge. The voice stopped, but there was the new sound of mortar rounds walking in from the direction of Beeson's position. It was so close they could even hear the *thunk* of the shell firing from the mortar tube. Brown climbed to the edge of his pit and spotted the muzzle flash. Back in the pit he threw two hand grenades that sent a body flying by the mortar—a Vietnamese strike force weapon captured when the VC crept in earlier and slit the throats of half a dozen sleeping militiamen. The loudspeaker began again, so Brown calmly put his mortar into action, saturating the place where the sound was coming from. That was the last of the loudspeaker.

Cut off from everyone, Beeson and his Nungs had settled down for a long hard fight. With only five hundred rounds he fired when he saw a target but he kept his front illuminated and spent time at the rim of the pit using his AR-15. Seven times Beeson was showered with dirt, rocks, and shrapnel from six rounds of high explosive and one of white phosphorus landing on the roof of the bunker or along the parapet. Stunned but unscathed he and the Nungs braced for another round but it never came because Brown had spotted the mortar and silenced it with two grenades.

Whitsell and his Nungs kept firing their mortar and weapons. At one point a Nung at the parapet reeled back with a flesh wound. "VC! VC!" he shouted, pointing to the front just beyond the pit. Then dirt and rocks flew as VC grenades exploded on the pit rim. Whitsell ran over and, not bothering to duck as bullets hit all around, fired his AR-15 into the darkness where he could detect movements of men close by. A VC stood up in a ditch some fifteen yards away to throw a grenade, but a Nung fired quickly and got him.

It was going on 6:00 A.M. and the dawn was breaking. Small-arms fire continued unabated but spaces between VC mortar volleys were longer. Donlon made the rounds and as daylight broke he finally got to Beeson's position where Gregg was treating wounded Nungs. Beeson insisted on bandaging Donlon's shoulder, but Donlon was determined to continue making the rounds to see about ammunition resupply and brace for a possible new attack. There was still firing and a grenade exploded near Donlon, knocking him down. He continued toward Woods's position. Covered with soot, dust, and powder burns, Woods from the knees down was a mass of cuts and bruises, his feet blistered from red ant bites. Donlon spotted some VC behind tree stumps throwing grenades. He pointed them out to Woods who positioned the mortar tube almost straight up and dropped in rounds. The explosions ripped the tree stumps to shreds and the grenade barrages ceased. Now, except for sporadic small-arms fire the battle for Nam Dong was over.

The aftermath brought a mixture of relief, hope, pain, anger, and wonderment. All survivors of A-Team 726 had been wounded, their faces and bodies blackened from explosions and thick smoke. Still, they exuded resolve, the resolve that had brought victory. Sitting amidst the cinder blocks, badly wounded Donlon, Disser, Olejniczak, and Terrin needed medical evacuation to Danang. But they grasped their weapons. Despite his wounds, Donlon talked of reorganizing for a possible new VC assault. Brown and Daniels left with a party of Nungs to start an ammunition check and they found by the ammunition bunker piles of dead VC. Gregg continued to tend the wounded.

I walked over to Disser's mortar pit where the bodies of Conway and Alamo lay and then to the swimming pool where Houston was sprawled. How can those who survived ever express their deep feelings of mourning and gratitude for those who fell saving the camp and everyone in it?

Once over the shock of the post-attack scene, my sense of organization emerged and I asked Gregg what I could do to help. He shook his head as he said that most of the medical supplies were exhausted. We were very short of bandages or material to make bandages. Gregg had a little morphine that he gave Olejniczak who was in dire pain. Gregg noted that the jungle shower was miraculously still standing so we had a small supply of water. We could only carry the wounded CIDG to the parade ground and put bits of wet cloth in their mouths to alleviate the dehydration that battle inflicts. The Vietnamese nurses emerged from their trench near the dispensary and set about treating the wounded as best they could. Co Cuc crawled under the fence to remove needed medical kits from dead VC.

Soon the parade ground was filled with dead and wounded CIDG. Many of Strike Force Company 122 men had their throats slit or had had their necks broken with gun butts. Moving these victims out to the parade ground proved extremely difficult because they had to be kept level. Some of the wounded writhed, moaned, or shouted hysterically while others lay deadly still. I went around and tried to reassure them that planes would come to take them to Danang.

In the midst of this, Beeson yelled something about wounded civilians. Men from the village were carrying them in. They set down a makeshift litter on which a woman lay. She was the lady from the shop/bar where we had beer the day before, and when she saw me she began to shout, "Ong, come here, come here." I rushed over and was shocked to see the blanket over her saturated with blood. She gripped my hand and said, "Tell them to shoot me!"

"No," I replied, "The airplane will come and take you to the hospital at Danang."

"No," she said, bursting into tears and falling back on the litter.

The men had stood back. One of them bent down and in a hushed tone said that the shop/bar was destroyed. She had been shot in the stomach, and her husband and six children were killed. I clutched the poor lady's hand and touched her face. An overwhelming feeling of sadness and weariness descended.

As the sun rose, still dry-season heat steadily intensified. Brown and Daniels spread out a parachute and raised it as a canopy over the cinder block command post. We badly needed bandages, so I went to the ruins of the Nung quarters where they had quietly gathered their wounded. I sought out the leader with whom I had shared the trench and asked if he could send some of his men down to the settlement to find white cloth or anything we could use. The Nungs returned to say that the settlement was in ruins and all they could find was bits of cloth and four bottles of "33" beer. I took the beer over to the command post to give our wounded. They mustered up smiles, but Gregg thought that Donlon shouldn't drink any because of internal wounds.

Word went around that a few of the captured Strike Force Company 122 CIDG escaped the VC and returned to the post. They reported that the VC

Dead Communist sappers by the cinder blocks in the inner perimeter of Nam Dong,
6 July 1964. *Photo by U.S. Special Forces B-Detachment, Danang.*

main force, carrying dead and wounded, was moving along the river to
leave the valley. A small reconnaissance aircraft buzzed around, drawing
fire from VC still in the valley and on the hills. Then an Army Caribou
swooped over the post and despite ground fire dropped radios, medical supplies, and ammunition, which we quickly retrieved. Around eight o'clock
Lieutenant Lu, the district chief, led seventy-five of his civil guard troops
into the camp. He apologized for not coming sooner, because they were
ambushed twice. About 9:30 two Vietnamese Air Force T-28 planes came
into the valley, staying at around five thousand feet and dropping their
bombs on the far side of the ridge to the east, where as far as we knew there
were no VC.

    In the heat we tried to preserve our energy by taking turns resting under
the parachute canopy. It was then that I had a reassuringly normal conversation with Donlon about such things as where we were from. He walked
slowly with me to the front gate, where the VC he had stopped lay. One was
in uniform and had a captain's insignia and handcuffs on his belt. Then
Whitsell took me to see the dead sappers on a mound in the inner perime-

Charred ruins of the Nam Dong camp, 6 July 1974.
Photo by U.S. Special Forces B-Detachment, Danang.

ter. They were husky young men dressed in bikinis of purple iridescent material (burial garb identifying them as a suicide squad), and each had the "cadre" haircut, head shaved with the exception of a patch of hair on the top. Everyone assumed that the troops that attacked us were southern VC who had been trained in the North. But from my experience I knew that southern peasants wore shorts, so their bodies were weathered. The sappers were not weathered.

Taking a break, Co Cuc, one of the nurses, and I chatted in the filtered shade of the canopy and we were joined by Brown. I looked over at the ashes of the command post to see the bent remains of our bunks and it was then I realized I had lost my 1957 field notes, camera, and clothes. But I smiled to myself when I saw, bolt upright in the ashes, the blackened Scotch bottle.

Beeson was on a radio and shouted the news that Marine H-34 helicopters with Special Forces reinforcements were coming in. I looked at the wounded survivors and thanked God they would soon be evacuated to Danang. Gregg led us in lining up the worst of the wounded, and I made sure the lady from the shop was among them. I went over to tell the Vietnamese soldiers to stay off the landing pad because the helicopters were coming.

Back under the canopy, Co Cuc, Brown, and I watched as the line of choppers came over the ridge. The VC opened fire from all around the valley. The first choppers began to turn. I said to Brown, "They must be circling to protect one another from the ground fire."

Brown squinted and snorted, "The motherfuckers are leaving!"

"They can't be!" I responded.

The entire line of Marine choppers turned and went back over the ridge out of sight as we watched in silent disbelief.

Muttering to himself, Brown stalked away. My heart sank as I looked at our own wounded team members and the parade ground. Terrin had lapsed into a depression, while Olejniczak was unconscious. Donlon and Disser were bravely trying to appear normal, but their faces reflected the pain of their wounds.

There was the possibility of another VC attack, so Brown and Daniels began redistributing ammunition. Beeson was shouting on the radio. I went to help Gregg and the nurses tend the wounded. All of us stopped when a U.S. Army Huey came sweeping into the valley with its door-guns blazing. It ignored the VC fire as it made several passes over the airstrip, firing rockets. Then it nipped over a hill where VC were firing and for a moment disappeared. We were expecting the explosion of a crash when the Huey reappeared and flew low over the camp before leaving. The VC volleys ceased.

About an hour later Beeson reported that the marine helicopters were returning, so we got ready again for a medical evacuation. I went again to the landing pad to tell the Vietnamese militiamen to stand back and let the choppers land. The medical evacuation was chaotic. As the helicopters began to descend, dust flew, and suddenly there was VC sniper fire from a hill behind the camp. To make matters worse, Vietnamese CIDG began to storm the chopper, forcing members of the team to brandish their weapons to keep them at bay. The green berets of the Special Forces relief party were a welcome sight as they hit the ground to fan out. They helped us with the wounded, and Woods walked with Donlon to the chopper. We were so busy that none of us paid any attention to VC bullets sporadically kicking up dust on the landing pad.

The first group of helicopters filled with wounded departed. I helped tend the remaining wounded and watched the Special Forces relief team inspecting the ruined camp to set up a defense in case the VC attacked again. When early in the afternoon the helicopters returned, the sniper fire had ceased. All remaining members of A-Team 726 wanted to stay, but the commanding officer of the relief party ordered them to leave. I got on a helicopter that contained the charred body of an interpreter and looked out the door as the bleak ruins of the camp contrasted with the green Ta Rau Valley passing below. When we landed in Danang I boarded a truck with Daniels and Gregg for the ride to the B-Detachment, where Maj. George Maloney, the commanding officer, welcomed us. Marines had come over to the post, and they took us back to their supply room to get clothes, shoes, bags, and toilet articles. After showering and eating, we joined other Special Forces troopers and marines in the small club to drink beer while everyone talked about the battle of the previous night.

A sergeant from the B-Detachment reported that the reason the flare ship had taken so long to reach the camp was because the Vietnamese crew who were on duty could not be found. So a U.S. Army pilot flew the plane, and Special Forces men went along to kick out the flares.

The members of the team and I were given bunks in an empty barracks, and I had the feeling that all of us were glad to be apart from the rest of the B-Detachment. I wanted, after the night of violence and death, to ponder its meaning. Perhaps all survivors of such events wonder why they were destined to survive. It struck me that despite our exhaustion, none of us was eager to sleep. In my case it was fear that the memory of the previous night would haunt me with nightmares. I was thankful that in the next bunk Brown talked reassuringly about the attack and the fact that the VC were not victorious. Exhaustion won out, and I fell into a deep, dreamless sleep.

The following morning after breakfast, Brown went with me to the airport, where I boarded a C-123 for the flight to Saigon. The concierge let me in my apartment. I was glad to see my cluttered office and the view of tile roofs, but I needed further reassurance that reason and rationality exist. Searching through my record collection for music that would touch the soul, I selected Maria Callas's recording of the moving aria "Casta Diva" from Bellini's *Norma*. Before going to the RAND villa on rue Pasteur I stopped at the nearby Cathedral of Our Lady. The calm of the cathedral and

After the battle. Back in Danang with Sergeants Thomas Gregg (right) and Keith
Daniels (left), being welcomed by the B-Detachment commanding officer, Major
George Maloney, 6 July 1964. *Photo by U.S. Special Forces B-Detachment.*

flickering vigil lights provided a balm, a setting for reflection. The battle
was over. We mourn and remember. In Ta Rau valley villagers no doubt
burned fragrant joss sticks for the dead. And life would go on. At dawn
men would go to ready their fields for the new planting season, and women
would fetch water and wood for the daily cooking fires.

Back in my apartment I wrote letters to the widows of Houston and
Alamo.

Within days I debriefed Gen. William Westmoreland and Gen. Richard
Depuy in what had been the MSUG office building on rue Pasteur. When I
described the dead sappers with the comment that I did not think they were
southern Vietnamese, there was no response.

All of the American wounded recovered. Master Sergeant Alamo was
buried in Fayetteville, North Carolina. Sergeant Houston was buried in
Arlington Cemetery. When his wife, pregnant with twin boys, received
news of her husband's death, the shock induced premature birth, and one of
the infants was stillborn. He was buried with his father in Arlington Ceme-

tery. Both Alamo and Houston were awarded the Distinguished Service Cross. Warrant Officer Kevin Conway, the first Australian soldier killed in Vietnam, was buried in Singapore.

On 5 December 1964, at the White House in Washington, Captain Donlon stood at attention as President Lyndon Johnson snapped the ribbon of the Congressional Medal of Honor, the nation's highest decoration, around his neck, making him the first recipient of the Vietnam War. In 1965 an account of the Nam Dong battle was included in Roger Donlon's memoir, *Outpost of Freedom.*[1]

On 16 July 1964, Maj. Edwin T. Nance, commander of Headquarters, Detachment B-410, 1st Special Forces Group, sent a letter of commendation for my role in the defense of Nam Dong to the RAND Corporation in Santa Monica, California.

During the first week of February 1965 I visited Fort Bragg, North Carolina, at the invitation of Roger Donlon and other members of Detachment A-726. The team had a supper, reminiscing about the events of 6 July 1964. The following morning in the presence of Maj. Gen. William P. Yarborough, commanding officer of the Center for Special Warfare and members of Detachment A-726, Capt. Julian Olejniczak read a citation designating me an honorary lifetime member of Detachment A-726. It was for me a very great honor.

On 12 February 1965, Roger Donlon wrote a letter to my mother in Chicago enclosing a copy of the citation along with regards from "all the members of Detachment A-726."

In 1966 I visited the Special Forces camp at Khe Sanh. After a terrible ride through dense fog on a C-123 carrying gasoline and ammo, I walked into the camp to be greeted like a long-lost relative by Co Cuc, one of the nurses at Nam Dong. Over coffee we recounted the events of that horrendous night. At the end of 1966 the Special Forces camp was moved westward to Lang Vei. There, on 8 February 1968, a Communist regiment using artillery, flamethrowers, and nine Soviet PT-76 tanks assaulted the camp. During an American air strike, some bombs were mistakenly dropped on Bru soldiers in the camp, killing many of them. Co Cuc also was killed during the attack.

I kept in touch with Roger Donlon and on several occasions had brief visits with him and his wife, Norma, during which we exchanged impressions and bits of information about the Nam Dong battle. In March 1993 and October 1995, Donlon and his wife visited the site of the Nam Dong camp. Then, late in October 1997, I spent a week with the Donlons at their home in Leavenworth, Kansas, where we reviewed the events. We also contacted by telephone Jay Olejniczak, Mike Disser, Woody Woods, and Ray Whitsell of the A-726 Team and Gerald K. Griffin, captain of the relief team.

There is strong evidence that the Nam Dong attack had been carefully planned and was carried out by a regimental force of nine hundred soldiers. While we in the camp assumed that the attackers were Viet Cong (and used that term in our accounts), there is the strong possibility that the attackers were from a North Vietnamese line regiment. The fact that the soldier killed by Donlon at the main gate was in a regular army uniform and wore a captain's insignia (the Viet Cong wore no insignia) and the sappers' lack of southern weathering would substantiate this.

According to Donlon and Olejniczak, when in June 1964 Team A-726 relieved another Special Forces team at Nam Dong, they and Brown conducted an arms inventory in the CIDG quarters and found a large amount of weapons (including BARs and carbines) and ammunition (including grenades). All were removed to the supply room.

Capture of American weapons and ammunition was a primary goal of Communist forces in 1964. Interestingly, most of the hoard was found in Company 122, where, as it turned out, Communist collaborators were concentrated. The "agitator" in the incident of conflict between the CIDG militiamen and Nungs was from that company. As a result of the incident the Nungs loosened their normally tight security of the airstrip and outer perimeter.

Company 122 on the eastern sector of the camp was in the direct path of the Communist assault. The company was rendered useless in the camp's defense after collaborators cut throats and broke necks of the militiamen.

From post-action reports Olejniczak learned that the battery of mortars pounding the camp (and which was seen by Disser) was in emplacements to the east of the airstrip in the village. The pattern of bombardment suggested the initial targets were the supply room (where the arms had been stored) and the command post (where we slept). A crater analysis revealed that some one thousand mortar rounds had been fired into the post. The CIDG intelligence officer, garbed in a loud shirt to identify himself, was a collaborator and was killed trying to leave the camp during the attack. His was the body I had seen on the wire that morning.

Gerald Griffin related that when the Special Forces relief team arrived at the Danang air base they anxiously waited two hours for the marine helicopters to pick them up. When they reached Nam Dong the evacuation of the wounded and dead took place. The relief team found the Nungs grouped together, but the CIDG militiamen had gone, leaving their weapons. They found some 250 bodies in and around the camp. It was a week before the relief team could gather the bodies for burial.

When in March 1993 Donlon and his wife visited Nam Dong, with approval of local Communist leaders and escorted by Communist military from Hue, they found the campsite overgrown with weeds. The relatively small CIDG cemetery was outside the main gate area, and it was sadly neglected, with headstones (only a few of which had names on them) knocked down and only some G.I. no. 10 coffee cans filled with sand holding the remains of joss sticks.

The Communist cemetery on the ridge was large—Donlon estimated at least four hundred graves. It was very orderly with whitewashed headstones and a central memorial. Donlon tried to convince his Communist escorts that the fallen CIDG deserved respect so their graves should be cared for. Discussing it with him after his first visit I remarked that it was curious that, given the belief in malevolent errant spirits of the neglected dead, any Vietnamese would leave graves unattended. Donlon then related that en route back to Hue there suddenly appeared on the dusty back road a whirlwind that moved to the side of the vehicle. The driver stopped the vehicle and the whirlwind stopped next to it, finally dissipating. They drove back to Hue, Donlon's escort in stony silence.

On their October 1995 visit to Nam Dong, Donlon and his wife found the CIDG cemetery untouched and the Communist cemetery now neglected (Donlon concluded that it was fixed up for his previous visit because they knew he was coming).

In many respects the July 1964 Nam Dong battle foreshadowed the fury of the struggle that would be known as the Vietnam War. As that war, with its modern technology and armament and large armies, drew all of South Vietnam into its vortex and captured world attention, the battle of Nam Dong faded into obscurity. But it should be remembered that we at Nam Dong were vastly outnumbered and outgunned. The Communists had the added advantage of surprise and collusion within the militia ranks. Still, their advantages did not deliver success. They took very heavy casualties and failed to capture the camp. The defenders, notably Captain Donlon; Lieutenant Olejniczak; Warrant Officer Conway; Sergeants Alamo, Houston, Woods, Daniels, Brown, Gregg, Disser, Whitsell, Terrin, and Beeson; and the contingent of Nungs, fought with bravery and held the line. They knew victory.

Five

THUNDERHEADS

INSURGENCY FOR ME became war on that fateful morning of 6 July 1964. For the world beyond Ta Rau valley, however, the conflict was still insurgency and would not become "the war in Vietnam" until mid 1965 when American troops became actively involved. One way or another, in mid 1964 the thunderheads of war were threatening, moving closer by the day, emitting frightening flashes and sounds.

The WRAIR psychiatrists had planned a meeting with American military advisers at Pleiku on 10 July 1964, and on the theory that it would be well to return to work in the highlands, I joined Bill Hausman and Dave Marlowe for the trip. Other than being made very nervous by gunfire one night, the experience in Pleiku proved satisfying. Using group therapy for three days, advisers talked about their relations with counterparts, concepts of the advisory role, their views on pacification, and other subjects. For me it proved valuable in getting patterns of common attitudes and problems which do not come out in individual interviews (although much comes out in individual interviews which does not in group sessions). We repeated these sessions with advisers in Can Tho and then returned to Pleiku for one follow-up session. Afterwards we flew down to coastal Nhatrang where I had an opportunity to visit Roger Donlon at the 8th Field Hospital (the other wounded had been sent to the United States). He was coming along very well and had been awarded the Purple Heart.

After a badly needed vacation in Hong Kong at the new Mandarin Hotel, I returned on 5 August to find Saigon in a state of excitement with news of the Tonkin Gulf bombings. When jet bombers from the 7th Fleet flew over the city, rumors had it that the North Vietnamese or Chinese would conduct air raids in retaliation. Hoa, my cook, reported that there was great fear in his quarter because all houses were of thatching. On 8 August, Gen. Nguyen Khanh declared an emergency. Practice air raid alerts took place but the sirens were not loud enough so no one paid any attention to them. An 11:00 P.M. curfew was declared with sound trucks telling everyone to get off the streets. My quarter near the central market was normally very lively with glittering night clubs and restaurants around the traffic circle. At 10:30 as a misty rain fell, lights began to go out, traffic ceased, and the few pedestrians hurried along the sidewalks.

Signs of war were neither new nor disturbing to Saigon, a city that had always had a life of its own. François Sully, the French journalist who had covered the Indochina War, gave a gala buffet party in his elegant apartment in the Passage Eden building. It was a mixture of diplomats from foreign embassies, Vietnamese ministers, and French rubber planters laughing and chatting with beautiful Vietnamese-French and Chinese-French girls in Parisian gowns. The following evening an American gave a dinner party of Peking food prepared by his jolly beer-sipping cook in the garden while artillery sounded in the background. The political situation at the end of August 1964, with trouble brewing between the Buddhists and Catholics, made it ripe for rumors of a coup d'état against General Khanh. In response to demands for more representative government, Khanh produced a "Provisional Charter" which in effect gave him greater powers. Khanh's move touched off rioting by Buddhists, Catholics, and students. One center of it all was the Cao Thanh Technical School on my street where students blocked streets with barricades. Then as darkness fell, in front of the central market on the other side of my building some ten thousand milled around. An American couple occupied the penthouse in my building so I joined them on the roof to watch. It was quiet that night but the following day, demonstrations throughout the city created a tense atmosphere. Stores closed and the central market shut down. The students were busy piling bricks on the school roof and fashioning weapons. Around 6:00 P.M. en route back to my apartment from the WRAIR lab I found the whole market area blocked off and filled with people. Someone told me that roving gangs had set up a signal system because the Catholics were going to attack. No police or troops were in sight.

I fended my way through the mob and barricades to find my neighbors' servants trembling with fear at the entrance of my building. They said that several students had been brutally killed behind the building. My cook was too upset to prepare dinner, so I escorted him to the barricades. Again we gathered on the roof. Artillery fire sounded at the edge of the city while flares lit up the sky. Around 11:30 gunfire broke out at the market as paratroopers moved in. The mob dissolved into panic. Within half an hour only the paratroopers were left in front of the market and an eerie quiet descended. The next day troops were positioned around the cathedral and pagodas as well as around the Cao Thanh Technical School.

With conflict in the air there was an influx of foreign journalists, a flood that eventually would turn into an inundation. In the American Mission, the Joint U.S. Public Affairs Office (JUSPAO) in charge of public information suddenly came alive to deal with the journalists.

Work with the WRAIR psychiatrists continued with group-therapy sessions held in the advisers' compound at Danang. The sessions were going very well when word came that a typhoon was headed for the coast. The airfield was evacuated. Then on the morning of Sunday, 20 September 1964 came news that a revolt by CIDG highlanders had swept Special Forces camps. Rebels also had seized the radio station in Ban Me Thuot. This was followed by a telephone call from George Tanham of the RAND Corporation who was meeting with Ambassador Maxwell Taylor and Gen. William Westmoreland in Saigon. They asked me to go to Ban Me Thuot.

Early the following morning I boarded a waiting Caribou that bounced in terrible turbulence. At Ban Me Thuot the airstrip was completely empty, and as I watched the Caribou take off I wondered if I had done the right thing in coming into this undefined, potentially dangerous, situation. Gripping my bag I trudged through grasses to the shuttered small terminal. A Vietnamese army truck suddenly appeared and ground to a halt. Relieved when I spoke Vietnamese, the driver offered me a ride to the American advisers' headquarters in Bao Dai's Grand Bungalow. Yes, the driver said as we drove through silent streets, there was a revolt by highlanders. At the

Grand Bungalow Colonel Kersting, the American senior military adviser, said the revolt was carried out by members of a new movement, called the Front Unifié de Lutte des Races Opprimées (United Struggle Front for the Oppressed Races), known by the acronym, FULRO. Violence had struck at Buon Sar Pa and Bu Prang, camps close to the Cambodian border southwest of Ban Me Thuot, and also at Ban Don, the old elephant trading center. There was trouble too at Buon Mi Ga, southeast of Ban Me Thuot. At Buon Brieng, northeast of Ban Me Thuot, a revolt was averted by the quick thinking of the American captain, Vernon Gillespie. Although the radio station had been reoccupied by Vietnamese security police, the revolt was continuing. The rebels still threatened to attack Ban Me Thuot, and their first ultimatum was that all Vietnamese must leave the highlands. Col. John ("Fritz") Freund, deputy senior adviser of the II Corps, had been sent to Buon Sar Pa to deal with the situation.

In a later discussion of these events, Tracy Atwood, an agricultural technician with the International Voluntary Service (IVS), described how he had been visiting the camp at Buon Sar Pa and decided to spend the night. At 1:00 A.M. on the morning of 20 September Atwood was awakened by shouting, screaming, and shooting. At the door he found himself face to face with several CIDG highlanders, one of whom shouted in English, "This is our night! We're going to kill Vietnamese." Atwood witnessed a highlander empty a clip of ammunition into the back of a Vietnamese interpreter. Atwood and the American team members were pushed into a room where Y Dhon Adrong, a Rhadé, came to assert that the camp had been taken over by FULRO. The aim of the revolt was to retake territory the Vietnamese had "stolen" from the highlanders, Cham, and Khmer Krom. After the rebels left there was shooting outside. Team leader, Capt. Charles Darnell, reached the Bu Prang Special Forces team by radio and the commander reported that the Americans still had control of the camp but most of the Strike Force had gone to Trois Frontières to meet FULRO troops coming from Cambodia. By 6:00 A.M. the shooting outside ended. The Vietnamese camp commander was tied to the flagpole, but all of the Vietnamese Special Forces team had been killed and their bodies thrown into the latrine.

At Buon Brieng a different situation unfolded. On the morning of 20 September 1964 Capt. Vernon Gillespie was informed of events taking place at Buon Sar Pa and Bu Prang. Without hesitation, he summoned Y

Jhon Nie, the Rhadé battalion commander, and his four company commanders. Gillespie informed them that a revolt had begun, quickly adding
that he was in charge of the camp. He told the Rhadé commander not to
move against any of the Vietnamese, saying, "To kill them, you'll have to
kill me first." Y Jhon pondered the situation and then suggested to Gillespie
that since he and the American were "brothers" because they had performed an alliance ceremony, they might have another to ally themselves
with Captain Truong, the Vietnamese camp commander. Gillespie agreed.
A shaman was summoned from a nearby village. Dressed in Rhadé loincloths, the three men participated in the alliance ceremony, which involved
the slaughter of a pig and chickens and ceremonial drinking from jars of
alcohol while the shaman placed brass bracelets around their wrists. The
strategy had its desired effect, and a revolt was averted. Howard Sochurek,
a freelance photographer who was in Buon Brieng wrote a detailed account
of the events.[1]

By mid morning of 20 September a total of around three thousand
Strike Force members were in revolt. They had moved on Ban Me Thuot
from Buon Sar Pa, Ban Don (where the Vietnamese were held prisoner),
and Buon Mi Ga (where most of the Vietnamese had been killed). They had
captured the radio station and occupied some nearby villages such as Buon
Enao (the site of the first CIA-sponsored Village Defense Program in
1961). According to Atwood, at about 10:00 A.M. some of the camp leaders
at Buon Sar Pa asked for an American to go with them to Ban Me Thuot.
Captain Darnell volunteered, and they departed in a Jeep. In Ban Me Thuot
they picked up Y Ju Eban, an interpreter for USOM and Bajaraka leader,
after which they went to the house of Y Bham Enuol, another Bajaraka
leader, who got in the Jeep. They returned to Buon Sar Pa. Soon, a Jeep full
of rebel soldiers arrived and took Y Bham down a road in the direction of
Cambodia.

Atwood was still at Buon Sar Pa on 21 September when Col. Freund
arrived by helicopter. Freund met with Captain Darnell and later told the
Americans that "we are going to act like we are in charge here." He mounted the veranda where some of the rebel leaders in the camp had gathered.
Speaking loudly in French, he shook his finger in the face of Y Tlur, the
revolt leader in the camp. Atwood decided to depart and soon after he left
the rebels decided to hold Freund, the American Special Forces team, and
some Vietnamese civilians hostage.

This created a new and tense situation. Vietnamese leaders in Saigon already were rankled at having the FULRO flag flying over the camps. There were reports that, on hearing of the revolts, Premier Khanh blamed the Americans for the trouble, because it was they who had armed the highlanders. General Westmoreland dispatched Gen. Ben Sternberg to Ban Me Thuot to make sure everything was coordinated through Gen. Nguyen Huu Co, II Corps' commander, and Gen. Hoang Xuan Lam, commander of the 23d Division.

I spent the evening of Monday, 21 September putting together some ideas on how to cope with the revolt. On Tuesday 22 September, Howard Sochurek, who had come to Ban Me Thuot from Buon Brieng, and I were on our way to find Rhadé leader Y Blieng Hmok at Buon Pan Lam near the airstrip when we encountered Capt. Barry Peterson, a young Australian officer who had been working with the Village Defense Program and now was organizing young Rhadé into a CIA-sponsored village cadre that had its center at Pleiku. He was accompanied by Y Jut Buon To, a young Rhadé leader, and they led us to Buon Enao, where FULRO troops from Buon Brieng and Buon Mi Ga had set up a local headquarters. They were in the process of improving the defenses, digging new bunkers and trenches. The leader of the camp outlined FULRO demands. They wanted one leader for all the highlanders to represent them in Saigon. They also wanted foreign military and economic aid directly channeled to the highlands. Finally, they desired a special highland military force, trained by the Americans, to provide security in the region. Concerning the events at Buon Mi Ga, the leader said the Vietnamese were slain because of hostility that had built up against them. FULRO, he added, felt that the government had to be goaded into action. "We had to wake the sleeping dog," he concluded.

That afternoon William Beachner, regional director for the Political Section of the U.S. Embassy, and I met with General Sternberg to discuss the situation. Late in the afternoon General Sternberg was called back to report to the American mission in Saigon and he requested Beachner and me to go with him. We arrived around 6:00 P.M. and went straight to MACV to meet with Generals Westmoreland, Stillwell, and Depuy. From there we went to the embassy where Ambassador Taylor, Deputy Ambassador U. Alexis Johnson, Barry Zorthian, head of the Joint U.S. Public Affairs Office, and officials from the Political Section and the CIA. We had a long session, reconstructing events, and after Beachner and I outlined current demands of the FULRO, Johnson said that in his view "all of the points are negotiable." This led to discussion of possible American positions. There was some speculation that the uprising might have been the work of the Viet Cong. Generally, however, the tone of the meeting was that, while this disturbance was of some concern, it was more or less something minor.

Beachner and I returned to Ban Me Thuot the following day. The town was quiet in a dismal rain under low-flying clouds. There was tension because of a report that the FULRO and Viet Cong were going to attack the town. Vietnamese troops were very much in evidence and townspeople had retreated to their shuttered houses. During the night an alert sounded at the Grand Bungalow. I grabbed my weapon and went out the door to the terrace where two pet honey bears were tied to the railing. I bumped into the male honey bear who immediately attached himself with his long claws to my leg. Trying to disengage the damned honey bear I was aware of advisers with weapons running past, the orange light of flares, and the clatter of gunfire. And there I was trying to pry loose the grip of the honey bear who finally let go. At breakfast I told Howard Sochurek about it much to his amusement. Then an officer came by to report that the Grand Bungalow was running out of food. I looked at Howard. "Would you prefer honey bear sautéed or grilled?"

Annoyance with American involvement in the whole affair was apparent with Vietnamese leaders in Ban Me Thuot. Gen. Nguyen Huu Co criticized the American stand of negotiating with FULRO rather than attacking the occupied camps. Other Vietnamese military officers implied that there would not have been any trouble if the Americans had not armed the highlanders. One Vietnamese general expressed the view that the highlanders considered the Americans, like the French, to be superior to the Vietnamese. He stated, "The white man has a certain mystique for the highland people that the Vietnamese do not have."

On 23 September 1964 Gen. William Depuy was sent to Ban Me Thuot to cope with the continuing crisis. At the Grand Bungalow he formed an ad hoc committee that included Beachner and me. Word had come that Y Bham Enuol was willing to meet with government representatives and a favorable reply was sent by General Co. Meanwhile, the hostages at Buon Sar Pa were still being held, although Freund was allowed to have radio contact with the Americans at Ban Me Thuot and a messenger was permitted to go back and forth by helicopter.

The following day Premier Khanh arrived in Ban Me Thuot as an indication of his growing impatience. After he departed in the afternoon, Gen. Le Van Kim and Gen. Ton That Dinh were released from house arrest in Dalat to go to Ban Me Thuot as Khanh's representatives. That evening at their request, General Depuy and I went at 10:00 P.M. through dark silent streets to meet with them and Gen. Hoang Xuan Lam, commander of the 23d Division. Le Van Kim recalled how in 1957 he and I had met in the highlands, and he asked how I thought the uprising could be resolved. Fortunately, I had prepared a written plan, but before I presented it I reviewed briefly some of the background (Diem policies and so forth) that had led to the development of ethnonationalism among the highlanders. Then I outlined what I would do to cope with the situation. First, to avoid further violence, I would continue negotiating with FULRO. Second, I would announce a series of programs that could be implemented immediately to meet some of the outstanding needs and desires that had already been expressed by highland leaders. They would include such things as restoring highland law courts, allowing indigenous languages to be taught, reestablishing courses for highlanders at the National Institute of Administration, and naming qualified highland civil servants to more responsible positions in the province and district administrations.

I also expressed my opinion that it would be better to deal with a wide spectrum of highland leaders. This could be done by calling a congress of representatives from every ethnic group and FULRO once the revolt had subsided. It could be held in Pleiku. I passed the written plan to Le Van Kim. Kim and Dinh expressed approval and telephoned Premier Khanh in Dalat to read him the plan. General Depuy and the Vietnamese officers shifted to a discussion of how to deal with the continuing revolt. It was agreed that a show of force was necessary, accompanied by a cutoff of supplies.

On 26 September a letter written in French arrived from Y Bham saying that he regretted not having communicated further about a proposed meeting, but such a meeting could only take place if the Vietnamese were removed from Ban Me Thuot. The American messenger bringing the letter noted that at Buon Sar Pa the rebel who seemed to be in charge was a "bearded Cham," whom he pointed out in a photo taken in the camp. His identity was not revealed until 1970, when, sitting in a Phnom Penh restaurant with FULRO leaders and Lt. Col. Les Kosem discussing the events of 1964, I suddenly realized that the clean-shaven Kosem looked like the "bearded Cham." I took a chance and asked him if he had a beard when he was in Buon Sar Pa. Kosem threw back his head laughing with delight. "Yes," he said, he had gone to Buon Sar Pa to direct the FULRO operations, and he had dealt with Freund. He laughed again as he said, "Please give my regards to Col. Freund."

It was pointed out previously that Lt. Col. Les Kosem, a Cambodian Cham and Muslim leader, had in the late 1950s been involved in the formation of a movement called the Front for the Liberation of Champa. Then in July 1964 Les Kosem and Col. Um Savuth of the Royal Khmer Army met in Mondulkiri province with Y Dhon Adrong, a Rhadé Bajaraka leader, to convince him to merge Bajaraka with the Front for the Liberation of Champa and the Struggle Front of the Khmer of Kampuchia Krom (Lower Cambodia). According to Ksor Kok, who had spent a long time in Cambodia with the highland dissidents, Kosem's French "adviser" (whose name he did not know) in Phnom Penh was responsible for these developments. This adviser told Kosem that the only plausible strategy for the Cham and Khmer Krom was to merge their ethnonationalist movements with the Bajaraka in order to make one concerted effort to achieve their similar goals.

Le Van Kim was called back to Dalat, and Khanh arrived in Ban Me Thuot to confer with Ton That Dinh. Unknown to the Americans, they decided that military action would have to be taken. No congress or any other concessions to the highlanders could be made until the revolt was completely resolved with the Vietnamese hostages freed unharmed. Shortly after midnight on 27 September 1964, Freund sent word to Depuy that he had just been told that Khanh had secretly given the order to attack Buon Sar Pa at 9:00 A.M. Depuy gathered his ad hoc committee in his quarters. He was angered at what he considered to be a "double cross" by the Vietnamese, who had agreed that no military action would take place. I expressed the view that perhaps it was a ploy by Khanh to goad the Americians into action. The "secret" was leaked to Freund so that Depuy would have to get the hostages released and end the dissidence.

Depuy formulated two schemes to get the hostages freed before 9:00. The first called for Freund to have rebel leader Y Tlur gather everyone at 8:00. Freund would then announce that he was going to free the Vietnamese hostages, after which he would take a crowbar and spring the lock on the prison compound. Meanwhile, helicopters dispatched from Ban Me

Thuot would arrive just as the prisoners were released (if the rebels had not restrained Freund or, worse, killed him) to pick them up. The second strategy called for sixty-eight U.S. Special Forces soldiers to attack the camp (which was defended by over three hundred well-armed highlanders). U.S. Air Force jet bombers would sweep in and bomb an uninhabited hill near the camp while helicopters would fire rockets before landing to disgorge attack troops. Depuy then consulted with Generals Lam and Dinh, asking them to refrain from any attack on the camp until the hostages were freed. They telephoned Khanh in Dalat and he agreed.

Ban Me Thuot took on the look of a war zone. Seventy army helicopters landed at the airstrip. Crews crammed into the limited space at the Grand Bungalow and some crews had to sleep in their helicopters. Jeeps raced around. At daybreak it appeared that ground fog might delay the departure of the helicopters, but by 7:45 they were able to leave. Meanwhile, at Buon Sar Pa, Y Tlur had gathered everyone in the center of the camp, and Freund made his declaration. In the tense atmosphere, he wrenched the lock, opening the prison compound just as the helicopters appeared. Y Tlur and the FULRO troops were immobile as the Vietnamese hostages ran for the helicopters. Arrangements had been made for Maj. Touprong Ya Ba, a highland officer, to go to Buon Sar Pa with General Depuy. South Vietnamese army units moved in the direction of the camp. Ya Ba explained to the FULRO leaders that the army troops were coming and that the highlanders should not open fire on them or it would set off a bloodbath. All of the Americans boarded waiting helicopters and unwittingly left Ya Ba behind. Ya Ba related afterward that he pleaded with the FULRO troops to remain calm and had very anxious moments when the Vietnamese commander entered the camp. The FULRO leaders agreed to have their men stack arms around the flagpole. After they had done so, Premier Khanh entered and, assisted by Y Tlur, lowered the FULRO flag. He announced amnesty would be granted to Y Tlur and other agitators and that the FULRO troops would be sent to Ban Me Thuot for reassignment.

At the other dissident camps Vietnamese army units moved in to assume control. With the revolts now ended, the Vietnamese government announced that new highland district chiefs would be appointed and a congress of highland leaders would be convened in Pleiku.

Y Bham Enuol and his followers, including many of the Strike Force personnel from the camps that had been in dissidence (estimates ran from

The 1974 FULRO revolt. Released hostages arrive in Ban Me Thuot.

five hundred to two thousand) moved to the old French military post at Camp Le Rolland in the neighboring Cambodian province of Mondulkiri. Y Bham's leadership attracted some young educated highlanders who subsequently went to join FULRO in Cambodia. Typical of these were Kpu Doh, the Jarai interpreter from the Special Forces camp at Bon Beng, and Ksor Kok, who later would be a FULRO leader (and eventually president of the Montagnard Foundation, Inc., in Spartanburg, South Carolina).

The FULRO revolt was disquieting for Americans in Saigon and in Washington as well. It happened at a time when American military involvement was deepening. The Tonkin Gulf bombings had taken place on 5 August, and there was a steady increase in American military personnel in Vietnam. (By the end of 1964 there were 23,000—an increase of 7,500 during the year.)

But the FULRO revolt took on added significance because of the American strategy that related the Tonkin Gulf bombing and projected future bombing of North Vietnam to attainment of political stability in South Vietnam. According to the Pentagon Papers, on 18 August 1964, Ambassador

Taylor cabled Washington recommending that "a carefully orchestrated bombing attack" on North Vietnam be undertaken on 1 January 1965 in relation to two courses of action. The first would be to use the attacks as an inducement "to persuade the regime of Gen. Nguyen Khanh to achieve some political stability." The second would be to bomb the north regardless of whatever progress Khanh had made in order to prevent a "collapse of national morale in Saigon."[2] A secret memorandum dated 5 October 1964 from Undersecretary of State George W. Ball to Secretary of State Dean Rusk, Secretary of Defense Robert McNamara, and President Johnson's Special Assistant of National Security Affairs McGeorge Bundy raised many questions about the premises of a policy of military action against North Vietnam.[3] One was, "Would action against North Viet-Nam increase political cohesiveness and improve morale in South Viet-Nam so as to strengthen the government base?" Expressing doubt that such action would have the desired effect, Ball cited the FULRO revolt in September as one of the disrupting events that took place *after* the American bombing of North Vietnamese installations following the Tonkin Gulf incidents in August. Events early in 1965 would prove that Ball's argument was rejected.

On 2 October 1964 Premier Khanh and a group of high-ranking Vietnamese officers held a large news conference at the Joint General Staff in Saigon, which I attended, wearing a white shirt and tie and writing in a little notebook as did the crowds of journalists present. In reviewing the events that had led to the FULRO uprising, Khanh stressed the role of the Americans in building the Special Forces CIDG program from the Buon Enao project, pointing out that by the end of 1963 there were twenty thousand CIDG Strike Force troops, all armed by the U.S. Special Forces. Now, he added, there was the recent revolt and "capture" of Y Bham Enuol. Going over the late September period day by day, Khanh said that there were "foreigners and Communists involved in the trouble," and he emphasized the important role of the Vietnamese army and air force in bringing the revolt to an end.

On 15 October 1964 the conference of highland leaders that the government had promised opened in Pleiku at the Phoenix Officers' Club, located under the pine trees where Jarai longhouses had stood in 1957. Along the road, banners in Vietnamese and Rhadé warned that "Vietnamese and highlanders must oppose the dark plots of the neutralists, Communists, and foreign elements." The schedule of the conference called for eighty highland delegates to meet with Gen. Nguyen Huu Co and Maj. Ngo Van Hung, chief of the Directorate for Highland Affairs, on the afternoon of the fifteenth. The following morning General Co would meet with "selected Americans," including all of the USOM representatives from the highland provinces, to discuss U.S. support for programs in the highlands. That afternoon the highland delegates would meet with Premier Khanh.

As if to remind those in Pleiku of their presence, on the morning of the fifteenth the Viet Cong attacked the Special Forces camp at Plei D'lim, south of the town. Beginning with a shelling attack, they assaulted seven villages in the vicinity, causing some two thousand Jarai to flee into the surrounding countryside.

Highland delegates included Bajaraka and FULRO sympathizers as well as politically innocuous civil servants. Among the delegates were my friends Paul Nur from Kontum, Nay Luett from Cheo Reo, and Touneh Han Tho from Dalat. The Darlac province group included Y Blieng Hmok and Philippe Drouin, who had been an interpreter at Bon Beng Special Forces camp. These delegates were dressed in tailored suits with white shirts and dark ties, but other ethnic group representatives were garbed in traditional clothes. The first morning they met with General Co and asked for a government policy that would respect the customs and traditions of the highland people and for programs that would raise the standard of living. The delegates noted that these goals were embodied in the *statut particulier* (special regulation) that had been promulgated by Emperor Bao Dai and should be adopted by the present government.

This 1951 "special regulation" called for "the free evolution" of the highlanders "in accordance with their traditions and customs," and their participation in administrative affairs in the mountain country. It also specified that highland customs courts would be continued, medical and education programs improved, and land rights recognized. The matter of land rights was of primary importance to all of the highland leaders, and it was a subject that would repeatedly be brought up. It also was a matter with which Saigon officials would play endless games because they did not want to grant the highlanders titles to any land. The Pleiku delegates also requested that a highland military force of between twenty-five thousand and fifty thousand men with its own flag be formed. Finally, they wanted foreign aid administered by highlanders directly rather than through Saigon.

On the afternoon of the second day, 16 October 1964, all of the delegates gathered while Premier Khanh addressed them, calling for unity between highland and lowland people and warning them to be on guard against Communists and colonialists. He also promised that the government would respect the highlanders' customs and traditions. Khanh then reviewed all of the requests, stating that the government would act on all of them except those concerning foreign aid and the formation of a highland military force. He also announced that before coming to Pleiku, he had signed an order placing the directorate of Highland Affairs under the prime minister, thus satisfying the desire for representation at the high levels of government. Lt. Col. Touprong Ya Ba (who had been involved in the Buon Sar Pa surrender) would be the new chief of this directorate.

During this period, opposition to Khanh increased as Buddhists and Catholics continued to mount demonstrations. Late in October 1964 Khanh was forced to turn over the reigns of government to Phan Khac Suu, who became head of state, and Tran Van Huong, who assumed the role of prime minister and minister of the armed forces. Buddhist and student groups in Hue and Danang, however, refused to accept the leadership of Huong and Khanh's Provisional Charter, so they continued to agitate. On 20 December Khanh moved again, arresting the members of the High National Council which had been provided for in the Provisional Charter. He quickly formed a new Armed Forces Council. This did not bring about any stability, and in mid February 1965 Khanh stepped down and, soon after, departed for Paris. He was replaced by Air Force Gen. Nguyen Cao Ky, chairman of the Armed Forces Council. A new cabinet was formed by Dr. Phan Huy Quat, who became the new prime minister.

In his discussion of these events while visiting Cornell University at the invitation of George Kahin in December 1973, Khanh (who now was proprietor of a restaurant in Paris) attributed his diminishing support by the Americans late in 1964 to his opposition to an expansion of the war and a continuing buildup of U.S. forces. He noted that on the occasion of the lunar new year early in 1965 he had publicly predicted that the war would be over by the end of the year. This, he said, was based on the fact that he already had made contact "with the other side" in preparation for making an accommodation with them.

Khanh related that on 7 February 1965, after being informed of the Viet Cong attack on the American military installation in Pleiku, he flew to that city to find General Westmoreland and McGeorge Bundy already there. Khanh claims they informed him of their decision to recommend bombing of North Vietnam to President Johnson. Khanh stressed that he had been *informed;* his decision had not been solicited. On 9 February President Johnson ordered reprisal attacks on North Vietnam. Soon after, according to Khanh, Ambassador Taylor telephoned him and told him to leave the country. Khanh said he realized he had either to resign and leave or to "submit to Washington's decision." On 15 February the Armed Forces Council announced that Khanh's government had ended, and on the twenty-first he left the country. On 13 February President Johnson had given the order for the sustained bombing of North Vietnam, an operation code-named Rolling Thunder.

During this period, the first use of American jet bombers in military operations began. According to Westmoreland, in mid February 1965 "after necessary clearance had been obtained from South Vietnamese officials," twenty-four B-57 Canberra bombers attacked Viet Cong positions in Phuoc Tuy (now Dong Nai) province.[4] Not long after, on 24 February, twenty-four F-100s, B-57s, and helicopters were called by Westmoreland to relieve an entrapped Special Forces unit at the Mang Yang pass (where Groupe Mobile 100 had been ambushed in 1954). It is interesting and perhaps significant that the first American bombings authorized by the South Vietnamese government were in areas inhabited by highlanders—Chrau-speaking people in the first instance and Jarai in the second. As a matter of fact, throughout the Vietnam War, American advisers pointed out that in the highlands approval of province chiefs was readily given for bombing of highland villages but rarely for assaults on Vietnamese villages.

Late in 1964 I had returned to Washington where with Phil Davison I completed my report on the adviser research.[5] Based on interviews with 320 advisers, I concluded that the success of an adviser lay not only in his professional competence but also his ability to gain "rapport" with his counterpart. I found the closest adviser-counterpart relationships at the lowest levels and noted that advisers at higher echelons rarely saw their opposites informally. Advisers at all levels appeared to be compartmentalized and had little knowledge of what others were doing. The one-year tour in general and six-month tour in operational units limited the adviser's effectiveness because, by the time he had become accustomed to his surroundings and had established a working relationship with his counterpart, his tour was ending. Lack of overlap between departing advisers and their replacements made it difficult for the advisory effort to achieve any continuity. I found that advisers felt they were being held accountable for their counterparts' mistakes. I ended the report with many recommendations, among them the need to screen adviser candidates for aptitude in foreign languages and ability to work with foreign nationals.

Now free to do research exclusively on the highlanders with a focus on leadership, I returned to Saigon on 15 February 1965 to find a more intensified wartime atmosphere. The bombings had begun and American dependents were being evacuated. French civilians were swarming to their embassy to find out if they should leave. Rumors had it that the Cholon Chinese were trying to liquidate their assets. Saigon itself began to have a neglected look with buildings in need of cleaning and painting and waste littering the streets. Refugees (an estimated 100,000) were pouring into the city, building crowded quarters on any vacant property. They spread plastic sheets on sidewalks and set up stands to sell things, turning boulevards into crowded bazaars. With the influx of American military personnel, bars were proliferating and many chic shops on rue Catinat were giving way to places with names such as "Liz Bar," "Kiss Me Bar," and "Number One Bar" with fronts protected by what looked like chicken wire. Hastily built, nondescript new buildings were immediately occupied by American military personnel. American military trucks, Jeeps, buses, and cars crowded the streets.

At this time FULRO began to receive open support from the government in Cambodia, and according to Charles Meyer this was due to Gen. Lon Nol's "grandes idées politiques," one of which was for Cambodia to lead all Mon Khmer people in a struggle against the Vietnamese.[6] This support was most graphically demonstrated late in February 1965 when the Cambodian government convened a Conference of Indochinese Peoples at Phnom Penh. In addition to the North Vietnamese and Viet Cong, a group of FULRO delegates led by Y Bham Enuol attended. Y Bham addressed the conference, beginning his speech by identifying the FULRO group as one of the "Austrien" delegation. The term Austrien had begun to appear in some of the FULRO communications to the Vietnamese government, and its meaning was not clear. I reasoned that it must have something to do with Austronesian (another designation for Malayopolynesian, the stock to which some highland languages belong). Then in 1970, Les Kosem told me

Y Bham at a ceremony
raising the FULRO flag at his
forest headquarters (1965).
*Photo by Front Unifié de Lutte des
Races Opprimées [FULRO].*

that he had devised the term from Austroasiatic (the family to which the Mon-Khmer languages belong) and Austronesian. Y Bham's address reviewed historical friendly relations among the highlanders, Cham, and Khmer and after declaring that the Austriens were now struggling with the "American imperialists" and "South Vietnamese colonialists," he lavished praise upon "Samdech Preah Norodom Sihanouk Varman." A photo taken at the conference was of a group that included Sihanouk, Les Kosem, and Y Bham.

Despite the fact that Y Bham sent periodic messages to contacts in Ban Me Thuot, the heavy overlay of Cambodian leaders, notably Les Kosem, had a stifling effect on FULRO and served to remove its leadership from the central highlands. One result was that a highland non-FULRO leadership rapidly emerged.

I realized at this time that there had been arising among younger highland leaders—both FULRO and non-FULRO—a new spirit of ethnonationalism which gave impetus to the spread of a pan-highlander ethnic identity.

For a long time the highland people had been developing a common ethnic identity. It had been a process of sociocultural change because of a number of interrelated economic, political, religious, and geographic factors, all of which are reflected in the events of Indochinese history. As a result of such a process a group of people at some point experience a "we-they" distinction and come to identify themselves, and are identified by others, as being members of an ethnic group. In the case of the highlanders there had been for a long time a growing awareness that they collectively were different from outsiders (usually lowlanders) with whom they have come into contact. It was in many respects comparable to the process of ethnicity that historically occurred among the diverse indigenous groups of Americans who came to think of themselves as "Indians." But among highlanders of Vietnam at this time there was no such generic label. Since the early 1950s the French term *montagnards* ("mountaineers" or "highlanders") had gained wide acceptance in the West but not among the highland people themselves.

Early in March 1965, Bill Beachner and I went to Kontum to see Paul Nur, a Bahnar leader I had met in 1957 and who subsequently was jailed for the Bajaraka activities. We were guided to a village where in the men's house Nur and local leaders were having a meeting. The tone was very anti-Vietnamese, particularly regarding those in the Land Development Centers, who were seen as intruders and pro-Viet Cong. "Where you have Vietnamese you have Viet Cong," Nur said. He had been organizing a Force de la Jeunesse Montagnarde (Highlander Youth Force) among villagers. (The word "youth" was used rather loosely, since some recruits were in their forties and fifties.) The function of this force was to provide village defense and also to mount operations against Viet Cong units that might come into the area. Nur said that to be more effective they needed better arms such as mortars and machine guns. (The following day when I mentioned Nur's militia to an American military adviser he simply sniffed and said they were useless because they were not well armed.)

Nur, Beachner, and I left the village and went north to the large Rengao village of Kon Trang Mone, where we were greeted by a group of village chiefs who had gathered to meet with Nur. Sitting on small carved stools, we drank from the jars and ate roasted chicken and fish while Nur talked. Several of the chiefs said that the Viet Cong had recently come into their villages. With them were Vietnamese with northern accents and they were dressed in uniforms. One chief told how some of them had said that they were "army regulars" (*chính quy*).

On the way back to Kontum, the sun began to set. The forest turned beautiful nuances of green and gold. It seemed peaceful, but as the light faded the darkness brought with it the menacing chill that is the curse of a place in the throes of insurgency.

During March the influx of U.S. military forces continued. On 8 March the 9th Marine Expeditionary Brigade arrived in Danang from Okinawa to provide security for the large airbase. The army's 716th Military Police Battalion arrived in Saigon to guard U.S. installations in the face of increased Communist terrorism.

On 30 March 1965, Mike Pearce, a RAND researcher, and I gave briefings at the Research and Development compound on the Saigon River. As we left the building, Mike offered a ride on his Honda, and just as we were going out the gate, a huge explosion jarred us and we saw a column of black smoke billow rapidly from the downtown area nearby. We sped along the quay watching the smoke, and turned into Ham Nghi Boulevard. The explosion had come from the side street in front of the American embassy, a busy, crowded area. The scene of devastation was shocking! Against a background of smashed shops and restaurants, smoke and fire, people were screaming and running about. The street was a mass of twisted bicycles, wrecked carts, and burning cars (the one that had carried the bomb was demolished). There was blood everywhere. The café across from the embassy was a popular breakfast place and it was a scene of horror. The whole front was demolished, bodies (including some paper boys) lay among the broken tables and chairs. An elderly woman holding her head, staggered amidst the bodies and, falling to her knees, wailed.

Mike and I picked our way to the embassy entrance where I tripped on a bloodied canvas shoe that had a foot in it. People were starting to stagger down the stairs, and we helped them get out. I was struck dumb by the faces which looked as though the skin had been pulled off, blood-soaked dresses, shirts, and ties. One lady whose glasses were all cracked refused help, saying there were others in greater need. The worst part was that among them were people I knew. A stunned U. Alexis Johnson, who had been at the September meeting to discuss the FULRO revolt, came down the stairs, his face badly cut. Dazed Edie Smith, the consul (who had shouted a warning when the car stopped, saving most of those in the consulate on the ground floor), had a gaping wound on the back of her neck. The consulate itself was a scene of destruction. One wall collapsed killing a Vietnamese secretary and wounding others. Edie's assistant, a Vietnamese lady, who was always very helpful getting visas, lay dead.

Sirens wailed and American military medics rushed to aid the wounded. The Vietnamese assistant's body was carried out to the sidewalk where an American medic put his fatigue jacket over her.

One never becomes insulated from the shock of war's indiscriminate violence. At military camps such as Nam Dong there always was the possibility of it, but not here in the heart of Saigon where people were enjoying breakfast under the trees, sipping coffee, and chatting or reading the newspaper.

The large plastique Viet Cong bomb had been in the back seat of a small car. It had stopped by the embassy and as one man got out to feign motor trouble the other one set off the bomb. Security guards began to shoot and the two Viet Cong fired back as they ran into the nearby busy financial district. In the embassy the sound of gunfire drew people to the windows, which, as the bomb exploded, pulverized the glass, forcing it into their eyes and faces. Air conditioners flew across rooms. In the Political Section, Jim Rosenthal (whom I visited in the hospital) was hit on the head by one of them.

The wounded were first taken to the American dispensary. My friend, Dr. Simone Truong, an American-trained ophthalmologist (who could not officially practice in Vietnam because she was not French-trained), operated for long hours on the eye injuries, saving the sight (and the lives) of many victims.

At the end of April 1965, Frank Collbohm, president of the RAND Corporation, came to Saigon. He was a very interesting man who had been one of Douglas Aircraft's test pilot engineers and in 1933 had copiloted the new DC-1 on its first flights. Later he became a senior vice president at Douglas. Collbohm had the independent and direct manner of the classical westerner. He was one of the founders of the RAND Corporation to provide the air force and subsequently other government agencies with outside evaluation of planned projects and programs. The Viet Cong Motivation and Morale Project was continuing under the direction of Leon Gouré assisted by Joe Carrier. Gouré used the interview program to study primarily the impact of aerial bombing on the morale of the combatants and civilians. I was not aware that MACV was moving to assert some kind of "editorial" control over the final drafts of RAND reports in Vietnam, so I was pleased and somewhat astonished when at ARPA and MACV briefings Collbohm stated flatly that RAND had a policy of hiring well-qualified people for its research and therefore would not accept any MACV censorship. The only review of RAND reports in draft would be by the pertinent RAND staff. This in effect reiterated the stand Collbohm had taken in 1962 when the Defense Department wanted to censor the Strategic Hamlet report that John Donnell and I had prepared. At both briefings Collbohm stated that if they would not accept RAND's independence in research and reports, he would pull all RAND personnel out of Vietnam. MACV relented. Collbohm also criticized the use of jet bombers over North Vietnam, pointing out that a jet was "one big engine" unable to defend itself so one bullet could bring it down. The bombers used in World War II and still in mothballs could do more effective bombing, defend themselves with tail and belly gunners, and limp home after taking a lot of punishment.

I accompanied Collbohm to Laos where RAND had three researchers in Vientiane. One day we flew to Long Cheng, near Sam Thong in the mountains where limestone has eroded to extreme karst forms resembling a Chinese painting. Long Cheng was headquarters of Gen. Vang Pao, commander of the Meo (later called Hmong) troops supported by the CIA. At one point the general and I were discussing in French the culture of the Meo and articles about it. He surprised me by his knowledge of all the French articles we had used in New Haven library research for *Ethnic Groups of Mainland Southeast Asia*. Suddenly he asked me to get in his Jeep and we sped up the mountainside to a Meo village where a funeral was taking place. The format of the ritual, including wailing and brushing of the corpse, was just as it had been described in the literature.

In Saigon, the shock of the March embassy attack was receding when in June, the My Canh, a floating Chinese restaurant on the Saigon River, was bombed. I was attending an interesting dinner given by the Martins of the British Embassy when the news came in and all of the journalists quickly left. A claymore mine was detonated on the bank by the restaurant so the force and shrapnel hit those dining on the deck. As survivors struggled down the gangplank to leave, a similar charge nearby was detonated. Among those killed was a popular singer and a French army officer and his wife along with three of their six Vietnamese hosts. The following morning the battered restaurant bobbed in the tide. Half-drunk glasses of beer or wine on tables were sad reminders of the previous night's horror.

Meanwhile in Saigon significant political changes were taking place. On 8 June Dr. Quat resigned as head of the government, turning over the mandate to the Armed Forces Council. On 19 June (the day after the first B-52 raid), Air Marshal Nguyen Cao Ky took over the government. He formed a directorate under the authority of the Armed Forces Council and organized a military Committee of National Leadership. Ky appointed Gen. Nguyen Van Thieu titular head of state and Gen. Nguyen Huu Co the minister of defense.

A graphic sign of the deteriorating security situation in the highlands was the crumbling Land Development Program which had been launched in 1957 by the Diem administration. Bui Van Luong, who had been in charge of the program reported that following the toppling of the Diem government, people began leaving the land development centers in large numbers. During 1964 their populations diminished by 25–30 percent. By August 1965, I found that the overwhelming majority of refugees in Pleiku province were Vietnamese who had quit land development centers.[7] Out of the ninety-four centers in the major highland provinces, twenty-six were under government control. Those leaving the land development centers usually went to the nearest town. Ban Me Thuot, Pleiku, and Cheo Reo experienced an influx of refugees who built ramshackle settlements with poor sanitation facilities.

The spreading conflict also generated larger numbers of highland refugees, although they tended to avoid the towns. Many went to other highland villages where they usually had kin. When I visited Khe Sanh in late April 1965, Félix Polin, the French planter, observed that an influx of refugees not only created a shortage of land for swidden farming but also raised the danger that much of the ground cover such as trees, brush, and fallen leaves would be removed, leaving the laterite soils exposed to sun and rain, possibly causing leaching. The district chief told me that there were four thousand Bru refugees along Route 9 outside the town. He also pointed out that of the estimated fourteen thousand Bru who had lived in villages in the Khe Sanh area, some six thousand had either moved into Laos or gone into the Viet Cong–controlled areas. In the refugee villages of Lang Troi (380 families) and Lang Van Chuoi (forty-five families) on the Laotian border, some of the Bru explained that one advantage of going to the Viet Cong–controlled zones was that there was more land for their swidden farming. They added that two hundred villagers had departed for the Viet Cong zone the previous week. The refugees were being assisted by Father Poncet of the Missions Etrangères de Paris (who was killed in 1968), Félix Polin, the Millers (Summer Institute of Linguistics linguists who lived in Khe Sanh) as well as by Special Forces personnel.

From Khe Sanh I went on to Danang. Early in 1965 there had been reports of Katu in large numbers moving westward into a Communist-controlled area. One apparent reason was revealed in May during an interview with the Vietnamese province chief. He expressed strong anti-Katu sentiment, declaring that he had ordered all of the upland interior to be a "free-strike zone" for the South Vietnamese air force. He added ominously "that will take care of our Katu problem."

At this time Nancy Costello, the SIL staff member working on the Katu language, and I had been obtaining ethnographic information on the group from Vien, a Katu boy about sixteen years old who had been wounded during a skirmish between Viet Cong and Special Forces troops. He was a High Katu, from a remote area near the Lao border. Nancy had been conducting research with the goal of devising a Katu alphabet, and Vien was giving us information about Katu society. He had surprised us by describing terraced paddy fields (a relatively sophisticated type of farming) when anyone who had visited the Katu area had found only swidden cultivation. When we asked if his people had always farmed that way, he just smiled and turned away. Later in a discussion about the men's house, he astonished us by taking the pen and writing a sentence which read, "Where is my older brother and sister?" He used the same diacritical marks as the Vietnamese to indicate vowel difference. He beamed and noted that I had written similar terms for "older brother" and "older sister" the day before (using Nancy's Katu orthography). It turned out that Vien had a complete alphabet, which Nancy judged to be well done. When we asked where he had learned to write, he just smiled and looked away. It would appear that these innovations had been introduced among the Katu by the Vietnamese Communists, the only outsiders who had been in the Katu country in twenty-five years.

Later Nancy related that one day an American Special Forces officer had accompanied her to the barracks where Vien was living. The officer threw some bullets on the bunk for Vien to play with, and while they were talking, Nancy noticed that Vien cleverly cupped a bullet and unnoticed by the officer, dropped it into his fatigue-jacket pocket. After he had done this three times, Nancy called it to the attention of the astonished officer who emptied Vien's pockets of the bullets. Not long after, the commander of the Special Forces post decided to let Vien return to his village. He was taken to the remote path where he had been captured and was released. The squad leader watched him walk down the path and just as he went out of sight there were bursts of gunfire.

The worst situation in July 1965 was in the Kontum region where by late June, security had crumbled, giving rise to conjecture in Saigon and Washington that the Communists were going to "cut the country in half"— as the Viet Minh had tried to do in 1954. On 1 July, I arrived in Kontum where American advisers said all of the roads in the highlands were subject to roadblocks and ambushes. I sought out my friends Paul Nur and Pierre Yuk who lamented that it was very reminiscent of 1954 when the Viet Minh were menacing the town from the north. The highland leaders noted that refugees were flooding into the Toumarong valley and Dak To and Viet Cong were appearing in villages near Kontum.

At Dr. Pat Smith's Minh Quy hospital there was an increased flood of sick and wounded highlanders. A tall woman with a strong face and short hair, Pat explained during a coffee break that when she first began her Kontum practice in 1959 she had encountered many problems. The most serious was the hostility of shamans who declared that her "bad medicine" would cause harm to any who used it. This had a deadly effect, because villagers were still dubious of anything alien, such as a Western hospital. As a result, Pat would get only patients who had tried traditional means to be healed, so many were ready to die when they got to her hospital. But, as an ever-increasing number of patients returned to their villages cured, word spread that the "big grandmother" had "powerful medicine." She clearly was in harmony with the spirits. Initially most of her patients were from Catholic villages near Kontum, but in time, patients, many of them carried by their kinfolk, began to make their way to the Minh Quy hospital from very remote parts of the province.

Fortunately, when the influx of patients began, Pat had moved to her new installation with two wards built around a surgical suite. She was assisted by several Bahnar nuns and laboratory technicians she had trained as well as by a young Jarai named "Scotty" who had been trained by the

Special Forces. Scotty had adopted their slang and expletives too; for example, at a birth he once said in front of some prim visitors, "Doc, that's a fuckin' good lookin' baby."

Late in June 1965 the wards had been filled and patients were being put on mats laid on the floor, which in any case many of the highlanders preferred since they were unaccustomed to the high beds and were afraid of falling out of them at night. It was curious to see elderly male patients wearing their loincloths, smoking their hand-carved pipes, and surrounded in bed by their familiar objects—water gourds, woven rattan backpacks, knives, sometimes crossbows, and food wrapped in banana leaves. The patients' kinfolk camped around the hospital. Pat provided some large army tents for them and they turned the area into a village scene with cooking fires, wash hanging on lines, and naked children scampering about.

The Summer Institute of Linguistics had just opened a new linguistic research center in Kontum for their Bible translation work. Located on the northern edge of the town, it was a collection of small simple houses around a central building that served as a meeting place and library. Staff members who had been living in places such as Dak To, Dak Pek, and Dak Sut had evacuated to Kontum, where they continued their research with informants. Like everyone else in Kontum they dug deep bunkers.

South of Kontum, near Route 14, Sister Marie Louise of the Sisters of Charity was also experiencing an influx of patients at her leprosarium. A small, wiry woman who spoke very rapid French, Marie Louise had begun her leprosarium in the mid 1950s and there now were around four hundred patients. As we sipped tea she pointed out that before it existed, lepers in the Kontum area were expelled from their villages to live alone in the forest. With help from Bishop Seitz, Marie Louise built wards on pilings in the highland fashion. Each ethnic group had its own ward. The central buildings were for therapy, and since there were many dependents, Marie Louise constructed a special pavilion where children studied and played. It was a light and airy structure with an interesting winding stairway that Marie Louise had copied from a magazine photo of a stairway at Orly Airport in Paris. She was completing a chapel that had decorative ironwork with motifs borrowed from Sedang and Bahnar weaving. It also had impressive murals depicting highlanders, which had been painted by Sister Boniface, a talented Benedictine nun, the great-granddaughter of Emperor Franz Josef, who had been trained in art and architecture in Paris and

Vienna. The leprosarium was self-sufficient in food except for bread, which they baked with USOM flour, and this was reflected in the excellent lunch Marie Louise served—steak, French-fried potatoes, bamboo shoot salad, and a dessert of avocado drizzled with a sweet syrup from a tree in the nearby forest.

In the advisers' mess at dinner I ran into Mike Benge, formerly an IVS volunteer and now assistant USOM provincial representative in Kontum. Several of the advisers were very nervous because the Vietnamese division that had been stationed in Kontum had moved to Qui Nhon, and the day before, U.S. Marines had gone to Cheo Reo to relieve some units surrounded by the Viet Cong. Kontum only had two battalions in the city. Then word came that the North Vietnamese and Viet Cong forces had captured Toumarong district town in the beautiful valley north of Kontum and launched attacks on Dak To and Dak Sut, site of a Special Forces camp. Air strikes were called in against Toumarong because the Communists captured two howitzers. Within days buses and trucks filled with refugees and their belongings crowded Route 14, and many others hurried along on foot. Mike Benge organized a relief program for them, and Paul Nur flew to Dak To to organize aid for highlanders converging on the town.

Refugees from Toumarong who brought their wounded to Pat Smith's hospital related that the Communist attack began with heavy shelling of the town and nearby villages. The highlanders fled in the night, grabbing blankets, a few cooking pots, and some rice. They ran through thick forest so fast that many tore their flesh on tree branches and brush. Some had sprains and broken ankles. One old man with a strange ailment that was affecting his flesh had carried his grandson while his own son clutched his arm, pulling him as they fled. The child and son had held the old man so tightly that their blue handprints remained on his arm. Treatment of this new flood of patients was rendered difficult by a lack of many basic medicines and other necessities. A Bahnar couple stood by with anguished looks while their little boy, who had typhoid and then developed pneumonia, breathed the last of the oxygen in the hospital and quietly died.

In Kontum, townspeople were being organized into self-defense units, sandbags were piled around houses, bunkers and trenches were being dug, and windows were taped. Gasoline was available only to officials, and some city generators had ceased to operate. There was no kerosene. Pierre Yuk shook his head, "The Vietnamese population is being depleted. The military and civil servants are getting their families out of Kontum." Tickets for Air Vietnam flights were selling on the black market at inflated prices. The dwindling food supplies were selling at prices rising by the day.

One quiet afternoon, Mike Benge and I were having a paltry lunch in a small Vietnamese restaurant on the main street, now empty of vehicles, when two trucks belonging to a Chinese transport firm in Saigon rolled to a stop in front of a Chinese general foods shop. Since all of the roads in the highlands were cut by the Communists, we were astonished to see them unloading cans of imported French peas, lichees in syrup, French wine, and Cholon brandy. The smiling drivers told us that they had come from Saigon via Dalat, Nhatrang, Ban Me Thuot, and Pleiku. What they did not say—and what everyone knew—is that they had paid the Communists to get through the road blocks.

At the SIL center, language research continued, and I worked with several of the staff and their informants collecting ethnographic data. I also met with some of the staff to discuss anthropological concepts and field methods, although our sessions were disrupted by artillery fire from the Vietnamese 22d Division headquarters, and the din of helicopters at the nearby MACV compound. On 4 July 1965 the SIL staff organized a modest celebration for Independence Day, serving lemonade, sandwiches, and cake. Mike Benge and I attended and, as we ate, American jet bombers swooped over to begin air strikes against reported Communist positions around ten kilometers north of Kontum. They were the first American bombers in operation any of us had seen.

The appearance of American jets over Kontum was a reminder of the U.S. military buildup that was taking place. In May the U.S. Army's 173d Airborne Brigade had landed at Bien Hoa, not far from Saigon, where they pitched their tents in a nearby rubber plantation. Soon after, additional marines and Seabees landed at Chu Lai in central Vietnam to develop a major base. By the end of May the U.S. forces in South Vietnam surpassed 50,000—22,500 army; 16,000 marines; 10,000 air force; and 3,000 navy.

Early in June 1965 the 1st Battalion of the Royal Australian Regiment arrived in Vung Tau while the American Seventh Fleet Task Force 77, composed of aircraft carriers, destroyers, and cruisers, took up battle stations in the South China Sea to provide air and naval gunfire support for American and allied ground forces. On 18 June (the day before Nguyen Cao Ky took over the government), B-52 bombers from the Strategic Air Command's

Third Air Division on Guam appeared in the skies over South Vietnam for the first time to strike Communist positions in War Zone D, a heavily forested area northeast of Saigon in the terrace region. On 28 June the 173d Brigade launched its first major operation against the Communists in Zone D. The following month the 2d Brigade of the 1st Infantry Division arrived and established a base camp at Di An, just outside of Saigon. On 29 July the 1st Brigade of the 101st Airborne Division landed at Cam Ranh Bay. The day before, President Johnson had ordered the U.S. forces in South Vietnam to be increased to 125,000 and stipulated that additional troops would be sent if necessary.

By mid July 1965, American interest in the highlands had increased as U.S. forces were stationed there. At this time the Political Section of the American Embassy decided to form a Montagnard Committee made up of representatives from the Political Section, MACV, CIA, USOM, and the U.S. Information Service. I was invited to be the only nongovernment member. The purpose of the committee was to exchange information on events in the highlands and formulate recommendations for the American Mission concerning ways of improving relations between the highlanders and the Vietnamese government.

Relations between the government and highlanders were at this time very uneven. On the hopeful side, in July 1965 FULRO was allowed to have a delegation installed at Ban Me Thuot where it could pass communications from Y Bham to the province chief. The FULRO delegation was led by Rhadé leader, Y Dhe Adrong, a tall man with white hair who owned a coffee estate of ten hectares. But in spite of this, clashes between FULRO units and government forces were increasing.

By September 1965, considerable concern over worsening relations between highlanders and Vietnamese was expressed at the embassy Montagnard committee. As a result, some committee members and I worked out a scheme for programs to meet the needs and desires that had been expressed by highland leaders at various meetings. We emphasized the importance of some kind of highlander political representation in Saigon. A high commission under the premier seemed to be the answer. This would give the commissioner flexibility in dealing with the numerous ministries involved in programs for the highlands. It also would give the commissioner direct access to the head of the government. The plan was presented to the embassy and it was agreed that it would be given to Ambassador Lodge, who could take up the matter with General Ky. Weeks later the committee was notified that Lodge did not consider the matter important enough to discuss with General Ky.

In early October 1965 the land question was raised by Paul Nur and a group of Bahnar, Sedang, Jarai, Jeh, Rengao, and Halang leaders before the Kontum province chief. They pointed out that some of the newly built military and administrative compounds were on land claimed by highlanders. The province chief responded that the government was giving titles in some areas. I had just witnessed a land title distribution ceremony at Dalat. After speeches by Premier Ky and Gen. Vinh Loc, the former gave out titles to fifteen villagers, ten of whom were Vietnamese. Also the titles were for squatters, allowing the government to expropriate the land at any time.

During the last half of 1965 the war worsened in the highlands and American troops became involved there for the first time. On 18 August the Communists overran a Special Forces camp at Dak Sut district in northern Kontum. Of the 250 CIDG troops there, only fifty escaped with eight of their American advisers. On 14 September the 1st Cavalry Division (Airmobile) arrived in An Khe, the first American combat unit to be assigned to the highlands. Its arrival was protected by the 1st Brigade of the 101st Airborne Division in Operation Gibraltar, which involved clearing Route 19 from Qui Nhon to An Khe, the first large-scale American military operation in the highlands.

In October 1965, the North Vietnamese army assembled three regiments in western Pleiku and in adjacent Cambodian territory. On 19 October they attacked Plei Me Special Forces camp, 45 kilometers from Pleiku. Air strikes were called in by the defending Americans while South Vietnamese army units arrived to counterattack with the 1st Cavalry Division providing support. On Westmoreland's orders, the 1st Cavalry launched a "search and destroy" operation against the North Vietnamese units in western Pleiku. This resulted in a month-long campaign known as the "battle of the Ia Drang Valley," where in 1956 my assistant Khanh and I had "hunted" in the driving rain. The peak of the fighting took place between 14 and 19 November at the base of Mount Pong. I was in Pleiku meeting with highland leaders and we were at the airstrip when helicopters brought back bodies of American soldiers. I watched in silence and sadness, finding it hard to believe that it had come to this. Some of the highlanders shook their heads, saying that it reminded them of the Indochina War.

By the end of November 1965 American military strength in South Vietnam had reached a total of 148,300.

Visits to Hong Kong provided welcome relief from the subliminal tension of war in Vietnam. On 5 November 1965 I flew on Cathay Pacific and stayed at the President Hotel with a view of Hong Kong harbor. Getting new clothes at the tailor and shopping on Cat Street and at the Shui Hing department store were therapeutic. I contacted some of the Yale-in-China folks, notably Douglas and Anne Murray whom I had known in New Haven. Jack Wolf of Caltex, whom I had met in Saigon, invited me to dinner and an afternoon at Happy Valley race track. Then, one day sitting in the President lobby and looking dazed was Robin Moore, author of the popular book *The Green Berets.* We had met in Vietnam and at the bar on the roof he explained that he was "spooked" by the deaths of his friend, photojournalist Dickie Chappelle, and three Special Forces friends in the recent Ia Drang valley battle in the Jarai country, so he packed and fled to Hong Kong. I sailed back to Saigon on the SS *Laos* (sister ship of the SS *Vietnam* on which I had sailed in December 1959). Because of the worsening situation in Vietnam it was the last voyage the *Laos* made up the Saigon River.

On 28 November 1965 I was invited to have an informal dinner with Dan Ellsberg at his Saigon villa next to the heavily guarded villa of General Westmoreland. I had met Dan in 1964 at RAND where he had the reputation of being a brilliant economist. He had joined the special liaison office which Ambassador Lodge had recently created for retired Maj. Gen. Edward Lansdale. When I was en route to Vietnam in 1956 I had read Graham Greene's *The Quiet American,* and in Saigon (where the book was not yet available) people said Pyle, the protagonist, was based on Lansdale. I could see no resemblance. In 1956 Lansdale had around him a group of young bright American army officers, but it was difficult to learn what they were doing. He seemed to work hard at creating an aura of mystery, and I eventually concluded that his mystique was more apparent than real. In 1965, at the special liaison office in the embassy Lansdale gathered about him a group of "counterinsurgency experts," with whom he had worked for many years. Included was Lucien Conein, a colleague from OSS days in

Hanoi at the end of World War II who, it was noted earlier, had been involved in the CIA's 1962 Village Defense Program in the highlands and the 1963 coup against Ngo Dinh Diem.

After arriving in Saigon, Dan had visited the RAND villa many times, but he was vague when we asked him what the special liaison office was doing. At the 28 November 1965 dinner, Dan was affable as we talked about many subjects related to Vietnam, and then he produced a packet of photos taken on trips into the countryside with John Paul Vann. In the photos he carried an automatic weapon which he said he often fired into thick foliage along the road where Viet Cong might be hiding. Talking about these trips, Dan became more excited by the bravado, the adventure, something I had seen in other such men (*combattant manqué,* the French called them) who came to Vietnam for reasons I would never understand.

On 28 November 1965, correspondent Beverly Deepe invited me to join her in a visit to the newly arrived First Infantry Division's tent encampment on a dry plain at Di An not far from Saigon. We were received by Gen. Jonathan Seaman, the commander, who had just returned from a fierce South Vietnamese–Viet Cong battle that was still raging near the Michelin rubber plantation. The general invited me back to give his staff a session on Vietnamese village society, so early in December I returned to Di An. There had been a lot of action with Viet Cong ambushes, road mining, and sniping. During dinner with General Seaman our conversation was drowned out by artillery fire. Then word came in that an American platoon was cut off near the Michelin plantation. Officers came in to receive orders (an air strike was called). When relative quiet was restored I met with the staff to discuss Vietnamese village life, and they were a very good audience, raising points and asking many questions. Younger officers wanted to continue the discussion, so we went to the "club tent." Mortar fire, artillery, and flares made sleeping difficult. The following morning I returned to Saigon and the news that the Metropole Hotel, an American bachelor officers' quarters not far from my building, had just been bombed by the Viet Cong.

While in Ban Me Thuot on 15 December 1965 I accidentally met FULRO delegation leaders Y Dhe Adrong and Y Preh Buon Krong. They invited me to the delegation house, a large frame building with a wide balcony, a style reminiscent of the old American West. Sipping coffee, the two highlanders were discouraged and angry. They pointed out that the intensification of the war had made life difficult for their people. Villages were being bombed by the Americans and Vietnamese or were getting caught in the increasing number of military operations. Communists entered villages to exact their "taxes" and force young men to go with them and the South Vietnamese military came into villages to steal. The government made many promises but did little for the highlanders. Then they informed me that talks between them and the government had broken off. The Vietnamese government representatives, Col. Thanh and Gen. Vinh Loc (an imperious portly man) claimed that they were "too busy" to see the FULRO representatives. Vinh Loc, they said, did not want the negotiations to continue. He was more interested in stamping out the FULRO than fighting Communists, and when South Vietnamese troops entered highland villages they busied themselves trying to locate FULRO sympathizers. Y Dhe warned that the present situation could lead to serious trouble.

I returned to Saigon the following day, 16 December, to notify some members of the Montagnard Committee that there was a chance that trouble might erupt in the highlands. On the morning of 17 December the second FULRO revolt began.

The first indication that another uprising was in the offing came on 16 December when a group of FULRO cadremen who were arrested at Pleiku revealed that on 17 December there would be attacks against the town and Special Forces camps. According to my friend, Y Thih Eban, it was the result of anger and frustration over what the FULRO leaders considered Vietnamese duplicity in not keeping promises made at Pleiku in 1964. They felt the Vietnamese government was indifferent to the highlanders' needs. The order to revolt came from Y Bham who had sent word to his followers in the Vietnamese armed forces and the CIDG, explicitly instructing them to avoid bloodshed. There were minor incidents at three Special Forces camps, but north of Cheo Reo FULRO forces attacked Phu Thien district, killing thirty-five Vietnamese.

The morning of the revolt (17 December) I received a telephone call in Saigon from Philip Habib asking me to meet him at the embassy. In August 1965, soon after he was named political counselor for the American Embassy, we had had a long talk about the highland leaders and what they wanted for their people. That December morning at the embassy, Habib's manner was very direct ("Gerry, what the hell can we do about this situation?") with none of the starchiness so endemic among State Department diplomats. Since American combat units were now operating in that region, he said, it was essential that the FULRO matter be resolved. I had brought the paper that Montagnard Committee members and I had prepared months before, and I gave it to him. He was clearly relieved to get something on paper, so we discussed the points in it and I departed.

On 18 December I met with General Depuy (who had conducted negotiations during the 1964 revolt) whose manner was that of a stern army officer dealing with reprehensible troopers. He brushed aside anything I said about what the FULRO delegation had to say. Depuy's face tightened as he declared that the highlanders simply had to realize they must support the government, particularly now that there was war. He drew himself up. If they rebelled, force should be used. I was more than a little surprised by his narrow attitude, and I pressed some points about highlanders' discontents that gave rise to the outbursts, but he turned a deaf ear. As I was leaving, Depuy changed the subject, perhaps to one he considered more manageable, saying that our war of attrition would defeat the Communists. They would lose so many men in the next three years they would not be able to continue the war. I expressed doubt and departed.

Gen. Vinh Loc ordered swift justice for the rebels. A military tribunal was organized in Pleiku, and late in December four of the rebels were condemned to death. They died in public executions (rumor spread that their ghosts had appeared to Y Bham demanding revenge). Fifteen others were given jail sentences.

Early in January 1966 I was meeting in Ban Me Thuot with three pro-FULRO Rhadé when word came in that Americans had bombed the village of Buon Ea Mur, northwest of the town, destroying ten longhouses and the school. The highlanders were very bitter, saying that the Vietnamese were invading the territory of the highland people with the aid of the Americans.

After returning to Saigon, I had a meeting with General Westmoreland to discuss ways in which the worsening conflict between FULRO and the government might be resolved. I pointed out that, despite disruptions of the war, there were programs promised the highlanders that could be implemented, such as instruction in indigenous languages, revival of the law courts, distribution of land titles, and political representation in Saigon. Westmoreland seemed uneasy about discussing these things. He concluded by asking if I would meet with Gen. Nguyen Huu Co who then was vice chairman of the Central Executive Committee at the prime minister's office, and I agreed.

On 7 January 1966 I was received by General Co who recalled that we had met in Ban Me Thuot during the 1964 revolt. He then lamented that the approach to the highland problem thus far had not been successful and asked what I thought could be done. I expressed the view that there was need for the government to demonstrate good faith so as to improve its image in the highlands and this could be done by implementing some of the promised programs. I outlined some of them as I had done for General Westmoreland. Co agreed and said that he would allow each ethnic group to have its own flag. The highlanders, he observed, are like "big children," adding that he could not be harsh with them. Still, he concluded, one must be firm with them or they would take advantage. After our discussion I presented General Co with a copy of *Village in Vietnam*. It turned out that his natal village was some twenty kilometers south of Khanh Hau.

By the beginning of 1966 there was little to generate optimism. Insurgency had given way to war with increased destruction in the central highlands. There was disunity cropping up within the FULRO movement, and the Vietnamese leaders were playing their usual games, blaming the Americans and not themselves for highland problems. On the American side Ambassador Lodge had refused to urge the government to make good the promises made to the highlanders because he felt American-Vietnamese relations were already very strained. Fortunately, Philip Habib's influence was very strong at the January 1966 gathering of American and Vietnamese leaders in Honolulu. One result was that on 21 February, Premier Ky announced a new war cabinet with a newly created commissioner for highland affairs, a position given to my friend, Paul Nur. This brought the first meaningful highlander presence in Saigon and it marked a new phase in the development of ethnonationalism among the highlanders.

Six

THE VIETNAM WAR

AT SOME INDETERMINATE TIME in the late 1965–early 1966 period when the "war in Vietnam" began to be felt in the United States, it became the "Vietnam War."

If American vincible ignorance of Vietnamese nationalism contributed heavily to the advent of the Vietnam War, the American failure to realize the multidimensional reality of the Vietnam situation when making military decisions boded badly for the outcome of the conflict. In a setting of war, the social, political, economic, religious, and military aspects of South Vietnamese society were intrinsically interrelated and had to be understood that way. A decision regarding one aspect had to be based on its effect, its impact, on all of the other aspects. Making military decisions without considering what effects they would have on the society as a whole resulted in ever-spreading disruption that weakened the society's order and structure and rendered its members war weary.

For the people of the central highlands, the Vietnam War was the latest phase of the conflicts that had been visited on them since 1945 by the "civilized" people from beyond the mountains—the Japanese, French, Vietnamese, and now the Americans. The highlanders could have endured very well without the "civilized" outsiders. They only wanted to be left alone. But that was not to be. With only a brief respite (1954–60) in between, the Indochina War and Vietnam War stormed across the mountain country. But of the two, the Vietnam War, with its modern, sophisticated weaponry, proved a storm of greater fury. Jet fighters appeared from nowhere all too often when innocent villagers were going about their daily business. Even worse were the B-52s which could be neither seen nor heard, unleashing destruction hitherto undreamed of by the people of the mountains. The Communists launched night assaults on villages, breaching the weak defenses within minutes with their Russian weapons and then using grenades against the women and children huddled in bunkers.

Still, the highlanders tried to go about their daily lives, responding as they always had to the rhythms of nature and scrupulously adhering to their religious beliefs and practices. Fortunately I was still able to conduct ethnographic research, but I felt it was on a world that, as the war intensified, was clearly in danger of being shattered. It therefore became imperative that I gather as much ethnographic data as I could in this race against time.

On 10 March 1966 I had the good fortune to encounter the King of Fire, the most notable shaman of the central highlands, and be able to witness the ritual he performs annually during the dry season to bring good health, prosperity, and rain to Jarai villages. In Paris and at the National Museum in Saigon I had found historical sources documenting the role of Potao Apui—the King of Fire.[1] This shaman derives his mystical powers through possession of a sacred saber which scholarly French nineteenth-century works related to the fabled Prah Khan, the palladium of the Khmer kingdom. Of ancient origin, the Prah Khan played an important role in the investiture of Khmer kings, and it had been in the care of the mysterious Baku, Brahman guardians of the royal treasure in Phnom Penh. Historical sources describe how since antiquity the King of Fire had tributary relations with the Khmer rulers, exchanging specified gifts annually until Norodom ascended the throne in 1859. Vietnamese historical annals report that at the beginning of Emperor Gia Long's reign in 1802 an ambassador of the King of Fire presented him with gifts, initiating the shamans' vassalage to the court of Hue. The exchange of gifts continued until the French conquest of Vietnam during the reign of Tu Duc (1848–83). Toward the end of the nineteenth century the French invoked these tributary relations as a rationale for them to assume, as protectors of Annam and the throne, control over the central highlands.

In Cheo Reo (fortunately not yet touched by the war), Ksor Wol, an assistant to the King of Fire, said the present king was Oi Anhot (grandfather of Anhot) of the Siu clan from which all of the kings have come. He related that the King of Fire had the blade of a sacred saber associated with a host of spirits, and his power as a shaman was derived from his role as guardian of the talisman. Wol added that the Cambodians have the hilt and the Vietnamese have the sheath.

On 9 March 1966 Robert Reed of the Christian and Missionary Alliance in Cheo Reo and I were in the village of Buon So Ama Biong, some ten kilometers northwest of the town. We were in the process of discussing marriage and residence patterns with a group of villagers. It was late in the afternoon. Suddenly some of the group became agitated when they observed men moving along Route 7 in front of the village. One woman remarked, "I hope he doesn't come into my house. It would bring us sickness." Bob Reed inquired and found that they were referring to the King of Fire. We went out to find the King of Fire standing in the road with four men and a boy. The king was an elderly man with white hair and trimmed white beard. His face was bronzed and wrinkled and he had eyes that held a somewhat mischievous glint. He, like the four men, was dressed in a loincloth and traditional Jarai ceremonial shirt—black cloth with front decorated with embroidered slim horizontal red stripes and two vertical rows of round brass buttons with the back dominated by a large embroidered red square trimmed with white. They wore tightly wound black cloth turbans. All but the King of Fire carried bundles containing clothes, cooking utensils, and some food.

At their request (the King of Fire had met Bob before), we drove them to Plei Malel farther east, where the Mai Linh Special Forces camp was located. There the King of Fire intended to perform rituals for the villages in the vicinity to bring them good health and rain for the new planting season. The Special Forces camp commander was Jarai, and he asked the King of Fire to perform a ritual to bring good fortune to his post. The King of Fire and his group installed themselves outside the village in a thick bamboo grove just above a sandy flood plain by the Ayun River. As we were departing, the King of Fire invited us to return in the morning to witness his ritual.

In the still heat of the dry season dawn, we returned to the river bank. The King of Fire's assistant and some of the villagers had spread out rubber army ponchos on the floor of the grove. They also had hung some ponchos on the bamboo branches to keep out the rays of the white sun rising in a pale blue sky. A large woven reed mat was spread out for the King of Fire. He squatted on it, smoking his pipe, and motioned for us to share the mat with him. This brought comments of approval from the group of men sitting on the slope because it was considered a great honor. I had brought some costume jewelry my sister Catherine had sent, so I gave the king a glittering peacock pin and a bronze pendant on a chain, which he immediately put on (later in some French publications about the Jarai there were photographs of the King of Fire wearing the pendant).

The King of Fire's "first and second assistants" (whom he referred to as his "soldiers") sat with him on the mat. The first assistant related that Oi Anhot had been King of Fire since 1945. He pointed out that Cambodian sovereigns used to present each king with an elephant. As he talked, men from surrounding villages began to gather in or near the bamboo grove. Women appeared, but they stayed a good distance away. It was explained that they feared the powerful spirits associated with the king. A group of men entered the grove carrying a large drum and some gongs. One of them identified himself as Ksor Na, a resident of Plei Bahrong (also called Plei Potao), the king's village. The others were from the Special Forces camp. They explained that the largest drum was the "mother gong," the middle-sized one was the "sister gong," and the smallest, the "child gong."

Another group of men approached and bowed in the direction of the King of Fire. One stepped forward and presented the first assistant with a polyethylene bag of tobacco. Another put a brass bracelet on the first assistant's wrist. The assistant passed the tobacco to the King of Fire, who did not speak but produced his large pipe fashioned from a bamboo tree root, filling it with tobacco which he then lit. Another group of villagers brought live chickens and jars of alcohol. Hacking down some bamboo, they staked the jars in place and then built a fire to cook the chicken. A large cooking pot of river water was placed before the King of Fire, who reached over and took a shirt from his bundle of clothes. Dipping a sleeve of it in the water, he passed it to the men who had been preparing the jars. They wiped their faces and hands with it. Another man passed the king a glass which he filled with the water. The man washed his face, elbows, and knees with it.

With Oi Anhot, the King of Fire, wearing his gift pendant at his Plei Malel ritual, 1966.

Around ten o'clock, gongs and drums began to sound. A new visitor approached the King of Fire, giving him money. The second assistant explained that this was an offering from the man's village. The second assistant and the boy busied themselves building a fire on the sandy flood plain to cook rice and chopping green vegetables. When the food was ready they placed it on a large banana leaf and put it near the jars, where the first assistant had placed some uncooked rice and buffalo flesh. He split the cooked chickens, put a lit candle next to them, and then put a tube into the jar. The King of Fire came forward and, squatting, took a handful of uncooked rice and cast it over the chicken and the candle. Then he held a rice bowl of water in his right hand over the jar while he chanted. Setting the bowl down, he continued to chant while he tore some flesh from the chickens, a gesture he repeated twice. The first assistant said each gesture was for a village that had made contributions to the ritual. He broke the remaining chickens into small pieces which he passed out to the villagers who had brought the offerings.

The King of Fire squatted by the alcohol jar and holding the tube with his right hand drank while the first and second assistants squatting in front of him clapped their hands. Then the first assistant began to grunt as he rose, swaying his body and moving his hands in a graceful gesture reminiscent of a Thai or Lao dance. Standing, he uttered squealing and trilling sounds before sitting again to clap his hands. He also poured water into the jar to replenish that drunk by the King of Fire.

When the King of Fire had finished his libations, the first and second assistants drank from the jar. Additional chickens were brought in, along with more jars of alcohol and bottles of Vietnamese beer, brandy, and soft drinks. I was invited to drink from the jars. Then all of the villagers began to eat and drink. Men and women approached the bamboo grove to hand in cups to obtain some of the water, with which they bathed their face, arms, and legs. The first assistant explained that when the King of Fire prayed over the water and touched it with an article of his clothing it became lustral water that would protect anyone who washed with it from evil spirits.

As the atmosphere became more festive, Bob and I made some inquiries about the King of Fire. We spoke to the first assistant because it would not have been proper to address the king himself (although he listened to our conversation while he smoked his pipe). The assistant could name nine kings who had preceded Oi Anhot (including Oi At, remembered in French literature as the King of Fire responsible for the 1904 death of a colonial officer who demanded to see the sacred saber). The assistant also told of food taboos observed by the king. Since he derives his power from the Spirit of Earth and Sky he should avoid eating beef, frogs, rats, or animal innards. He should stay out of villages for fear of causing an outbreak of smallpox. When asked about the sacred saber, he became very guarded, simply answering that it existed but it was forbidden for anyone to gaze upon it. The King of Fire listened, and, without changing expression, continued to smoke his pipe.

At 4:00 P.M., as the heat intensified and rays of sun glinted through the bamboo, men from other villages arrived, carrying large jars, chickens, and a sack of rice. They bowed before the King of Fire and presented their offerings. The jars were staked to the ground while the chickens were cooked. The ritual by the King of Fire and his assistants was repeated. At one point the king, who had drunk quite a bit, forgot the name of the village and had to be reminded. As the festivities continued, we talked with the villagers and the men from the Special Forces camp. They all knew about Y Bham and the FULRO movement and expressed strong sympathy for the goals of the movement. Then some of them began complaining about the "American airplanes" that prevented them from fishing in the river. They explained that Jarai villagers out fishing in the river had been strafed by American aircraft, so many were reluctant to venture beyond the tree-lined shore.

After I returned to Saigon from the highlands at the end of March 1966, I was informed that the Department of Defense had elected to award me the Medal for Distinguished Public Service. On 7 April at the MACV headquarters in Gen. William Westmoreland's office the citation, signed by Robert S. McNamara, was read. It mentioned my "ethnographic studies," also "contributions to the enhancement of U.S. Advisor/Vietnamese Counterpart relationships," and "presence and counsel during periods of attack by Viet Cong forces and Montagnard uprisings." Then the general pinned the medal on my lapel and shook my hand. It was a proud moment for me, but back in the United States in the 1970s I was advised not to mention the award on applications for such things as academic jobs or grants (advice I ignored).

At the beginning of May 1966, Joe Carrier, a RAND colleague with the Viet Cong Motivational and Morale Project, and I went to Dalat and then on to Danang (where Joe wanted to see a nephew stationed with the marines). I contacted Jackie Maier and Eva Burton of the SIL who were working on the language of the Cua people who lived in the mountains north of Danang in a cinnamon-producing region. I had yet to visit the Cua, and the linguists wanted to return to Tra Bong where they had lived, so I arranged with the Special Forces B Team for the four of us to get on a helicopter going to the Special Forces post at Tra Bong. We landed in the tiny post where the captain welcomed us and provided coffee. He explained that there was a battalion of Communists three kilometers to the east, interdicting the road to the coast, and a larger unit in the mountains to the west. As a result, a large shipment of valuable cinnamon intended for the Danang market was stored in the district town. The Communist units were not making any menacing moves but they were sniping, so the captain cautioned us to "stay inside the Cua houses."

Eva and Jackie had heard that the Cua in Tra Bong were experiencing a

An elderly Cua refugee from the mountains and children of Tra Bac village.

severe food shortage, but they were shocked when we entered the village to see their friends so thin, almost emaciated. Nonetheless, in typical high-lander fashion the Cua greeted us with smiles and invited us into their houses which they were sharing with refugees from the mountains. The Special Forces team was giving them rice, but the adults ate little so the children would be well fed. Joe and I took photos while Eva and Jackie visited with their friends and late in the afternoon we boarded a Caribou for Danang.

At Danang, Eva and Jackie went to stay with American nurses while Joe and I got a room at a mixed U.S. military and civilian walled compound not far from the central market and the radio station. There was a good deal of tension in Danang. Since March, Buddhists in Saigon had been holding daily demonstrations against the Ky administration, and early in May, militant Buddhist students in Hue, the heart of the "struggle move-ment," had taken control of the radio station and staged a sit-in at the university. A worse situation was emerging in Danang where the "struggle forces" had taken the radio station, municipal buildings, and the army headquarters. They in effect had control of the city. After Joe visited his nephew we met at the quiet Cham Museum, one of my favorite places, to photograph the impressive collection. Nearby on the river bank was a small restaurant, and during our dinner a middle-aged man at the next table struck up a conversation. He was a Polish army colonel with the ICC, and he became very enthusiastic when he learned I was from Chicago where he had kin. His enthusiasm was not shared by his companion, an expressionless young man with glasses, who claimed to be an interpreter. The colonel insisted we accompany him to his villa for a drink. The hulking, strange villa, a leftover from the French days, was an architectural oddity and the main room resembled the set from the film, *Sunset Boulevard*, with its high ceiling, winding stairway, and Spanish decor. Imbibing vodka, the colonel was very talkative, making veiled criticisms of the Vietnamese Communists, but his "interpreter" sat glumly, registering disapproval.

Just after midnight, 14 May, Joe and I walked through the empty, silent streets back to our compound where a young American marine guarded the gate. At 5:30 we were awakened by explosions we immediately identified as incoming mortar rounds. The marine said it was a coup d'état, which seemed unlikely because coups took place in Saigon, not Danang. After bursts of small arms fire, quiet returned so we went back to bed. At breakfast there was a report that South Vietnamese marines had landed at the airport. Joe and I borrowed a Jeep to check on Jackie and Eva at the nurses' house. They said reports indicated that General Ky had dispatched the marines to retake the city and everyone was warned that there could be heavy fighting. It would be better if Joe and I left the compound by the radio station and came to the nurses' house in a more removed area. We started back to the compound, and along the Han River, incongruously, young Vietnamese couples strolled and took photos by the flowering trees. Suddenly, grim-looking Vietnamese marines began to emerge from side streets with their weapons at the ready.

Near the compound, Vietnamese marines were running down the street and getting behind trees in preparation for an assault on the radio station. While Joe waited in the Jeep, I got the Marine guard to open the gate, rushed to our room, and threw our belongings into two suitcases. I just reached the Jeep when the marines began to open fire. Our escape was out of the question, so I jumped in the Jeep and we sped into the open compound gate. Standing inside, her arms akimbo, Bennet McDonald, a stout Red Cross lady in a Hawaiian muumuu said, "You boys oughtn't be out on a day like this." Suddenly we were surrounded by explosions and gunfire as some rounds began hitting the wall and the building. The few civilians in the compound joined us in the first-floor rooms. The American army officers staying in the compound had reported for duty, so Bennet wisely suggested we retreat into their rooms and have some of the beer they had chilled for a picnic. Beyond the wall the fighting rose and fell. By late afternoon the fighting tapered off so Joe and I carefully made our way out, past the shuttered market to the river front where a small Vietnamese restaurant was serving food. The night was eerily quiet. The following day it was clear the marines had captured the radio station, but other news was vague. One report, which fortunately proved untrue, was that dissidents had holed up in the Cham Museum and ARVN tanks were poised to attack. Joe and I decided to leave so we got a ride to the airport and returned to Saigon.

During 1966, negotiations between the Saigon government and FULRO ambled along. In mid October Gen. Vinh Loc, II Corps commander, organized a large Highland-Lowland Solidarity Conference in Pleiku to celebrate the second anniversary of the Pleiku Conference and also to welcome eight hundred FULRO troops who were going to swear loyalty to the government. On a large field below the hill where the II Corps headquarters were located, a number of tents (supplied by the U.S. Army) and a reviewing stand, flanked by shelters fashioned out of colored parachutes, were put in place. On 15 October, the eight hundred FULRO troops arrived on Air America (the CIA-funded airline), an arrangement made by USAID (as USOM was now called), and were housed in the tents. A large collection of highland leaders also arrived. These included the FULRO delegation from Ban Me Thuot, members of the new Constitutional Assembly, the staff of the Commission for Highland Affairs, all of the deputy province chiefs for highland affairs, and highlanders from the army and People's Council (a short-lived effort at having some kind of representative advisory body to the government).

Vietnamese officials and American guests began arriving on the afternoon of 15 October. Riding into Pleiku from the new jet airstrip built by the Americans, they passed under signs that proclaimed "Highland-Lowland

Solidarity," and one sign (in English and Vietnamese) announced that "Big Brother Vinh Loc is most eager about the future of the highland people." Someone must have explained to Vinh Loc the implication of "big brother" in English, for later in the day that portion of the sign was painted over. In the afternoon Vietnamese air force planes began landing with a bevy of "hostesses" who had been recruited in Saigon nightclubs to brighten the occasion. Their heavy makeup and gaudy miniskirts were reminders of the new cabaret world the war was bringing to Saigon.

That evening a large dinner was held at the Phoenix Officers' Club. Vinh Loc sipped champagne at the head table with a Vietnamese singer who was popular in Saigon (and was described as "his latest girl"). She was garbed in a modish gown cut from highland cloth. The hostesses from Saigon were seated at other tables with high-ranking Vietnamese officers and American officials from the agencies of the American Mission. Of all the highland leaders assembled in Pleiku, only Paul Nur, head of the new Special Commission for Highland Affairs, and his assistant, Col. Ya Ba, were invited to the dinner. The entertainment began with a "highlander fashion show" that consisted of Vietnamese girls in vinyl versions of highland clothes, a parody that amused everyone. Suddenly Ksor Dun, a young highland leader, appeared in a loincloth leaping about the dance floor, grimacing at the audience (particularly at Vinh Loc and Nur) and generally behaving in a simian manner. At this point I left the party. Outside I encountered Touneh Han Tho, Nay Luett, and other leaders. They were insulted at not having been invited. At their quarters they explained that the whole celebration was a fraud as far as they were concerned. Of the eight hundred "FULRO" troops, only around two hundred were actually members of the movement; the remainder were young villagers who had been offered a free trip to Pleiku. There was a good deal of unrest among them because their quarters had no water, they were not given blankets, and their food consisted of rice and watery soup. No highlanders were involved in the planning of the affair. Ksor Dun appeared and, laughing bitterly, announced, "I played the savage for them."

The following morning Premier Ky and Gen. Nguyen Van Thieu arrived (they were served a champagne breakfast en route) as did Ambassador Henry Cabot Lodge. Everyone gathered on the field before the II Corps headquarters where Vinh Loc brought some American officials' attention to the "highlander motifs" on the decorations. None bore any resemblance to anything in the highlands and looked like a Hollywood version of African designs. There was a parade of highlanders dressed in traditional clothes, after which the FULRO troops pledged loyalty to the government. Then a buffalo was slaughtered by Jarai with their spears. Lodge visibly blanched as he turned his head away from the gory scene and almost fainted dead away when they smeared some of the blood on his shiny black patent-leather shoes. Vinh Loc addressed the gathering, explaining how much the government had done for the highland people. Afterward, Nur spoke (in Vietnamese) also outlining the government's achievements. He was followed by FULRO leader, Y Dhe Adrong, whose talk (in Rhadé, which was not translated) was a plea for highlander civil rights, which he emphasized the highlanders should be granted "in exchange for the blood we have shed." That evening the Vietnamese generals retired to the Phoenix Club with the hostesses to celebrate. By this time most of the highland leaders had departed.

The year 1966 brought a vastly enlarged American presence in the highlands and a concomitant widening of the war in that region. The U.S. Special Forces increased its "border defense and surveillance" by establishing twenty-two new camps along the Laotian and Cambodian borders in the highlands. In addition, the Mobile Guerrilla Force was transformed into the Mobile Strike (MIKE) Force to be used in guerrilla operations. Company-sized groups of 150 to 200 men were taken by helicopters into Communist-controlled areas to conduct operations, after which they were extracted by the same means. By October 1966 the total CIDG was 34,800 (in October 1964 it had been 19,000) with 3,200 in the MIKE Force. At least half the personnel in these forces were highlanders. In Cheo Reo there was at this time a Jarai girl who had the reputation of being particularly adept at improvising songs (a favorite pastime of the Jarai) which usually told of current events. She sang sadly of highland boys going off in helicopters to distant places (she mentioned Cambodia when operations there were very secret) and never returning.

During the first half of January 1966 the 1st Brigade, 1st Cavalry Division, conducted Operation Matador in Pleiku and Kontum provinces. The same month the 3d Brigade of the 25th Infantry Division moved into Pleiku on operations, after which it went to the Ban Me Thuot area. Residents of Buon Ko Tam complained that they were shelled while preparing their fields for planting. In April the 1st Air Cavalry engaged in Operation

Lincoln in western Pleiku. In March the 3d Brigade, 25th Infantry moved up Route 14 repairing bridges and road beds, opening the Ban Me Thuot–Pleiku link for the first time in many months.

On 2 June the 1st Brigade of the 101st Airborne Division and some South Vietnamese units launched Operation Hawthorne in the Toumarong valley north of Kontum which had been the scene of heavy fighting a year before. Accompanying troopers of the Airborne's 42-man Tiger Force, Ward Just of the *Washington Post* (who had contacted me early in 1966 to discuss the highlanders) was wounded by a Viet Cong grenade, an event he describes lucidly in his book *To What End*.[2]

In June 1966 Kontum reflected the new American presence. On the main street were new "restaurants" such as the Honeymoon Bar and Restaurant and the more cryptically named The New Become Bar. I ran into some troopers from the 101st Airborne, which had just fought in the Toumarong operation. They said they had been six months in the highlands and were given a day's leave in Kontum. When I asked what they did for amusement, an older sergeant snorted and said, "Drink warm beer and get laid" (the young American army doctor at the MACV compound said that 98 percent of the bar girls were infected with venereal diseases, some of which defied treatment). Younger troopers read comic books and wrote letters to girlfriends. Black soldiers were singing.

By and large, until the commitment of U.S. ground troops in 1965, Vietnam was, in terms of permanent assignment of news correspondents, relatively neglected. The only one who had been reporting on Vietnam since my arrival in 1956 was my friend, French journalist, François Sully, a true "old hand" who had covered the Indochina War. In early 1964 the first journalists I met were Nick Turner, who ran the small Reuters office on rue Catinat, and Peter Grose of the *New York Times*. When the 1964 FULRO revolt began, photographer Howard Sochurek was in the Buon Brieng Special Forces camp and later in Ban Me Thuot. Malcolm Browne came to Ban Me Thuot to report on the revolt. Mert Perry of *Newsweek* was in Pleiku to cover the 1965 battle at Ea Drang. On 1 June 1966 a young freelance journalist named Frances FitzGerald came by to discuss Mekong River delta villages. On 19 August, Beverly Deepe brought television journalist Chet Huntley to my apartment, and then we went to dine at the Paprika, a very good French restaurant on a roof with a view of flares and a background of mortar and artillery fire.

In August the 2d Brigade of the U.S. Fourth Division arrived in Pleiku to establish a headquarters, and by mid October the whole division was operating in the highlands. Jarai leaders were upset that the American Fourth Infantry Division elected to build its headquarters on Hodrung Mountain which they considered sacred. The Americans called it "Dragon Mountain" because of its twin rounded peaks (a shape that earned it the name "titty mountain" for most American soldiers). The Jarai were appalled that the Americans began construction by bulldozing the top soil on the mountain, causing mud slides in the heavy rainfall. American soldiers complained, "We'll be glad when the rains end and we're rid of this damned red mud," to which I responded that "when the rains end, the red mud will become red dust." Which it did.

More than any other highland town, Pleiku was transformed by the American buildup. For the huge construction projects (military installations, air bases, and roads) private American construction firms brought in Korean, Filipino, and Vietnamese workers. Vietnamese usually brought their families with them, and combined with the large number of Vietnamese military personnel and their dependents, Pleiku's population increased to an estimated fifty thousand. A whole new large section called "New Pleiku," a dismal collection of Vietnamese shacks and flimsy shops, had spread over a hillside and was continuing to grow by the day. The main part of Pleiku had been transformed into a "G.I. town" with endless bars, snack shops, and steam baths (another designation for brothels). The Christian and Missionary Alliance compound, which in 1957 had stood alone outside the town, was now engulfed by a group of gaudy "Soul Brother" bars that catered to black American soldiers. The streets were jammed with Jeeps, military trucks, bulldozers, and seemingly endless convoys. It was curious to see files of Jarai men in their loincloths, clutching bush-scythes, followed by women with backbaskets and children, walking along the edge of the sidewalks filled with American soldiers, prostitutes, pimps, vendors, shoeshine boys, and petty thieves. The Jarai kept their eyes straight ahead as if to ignore the squalid scene around them.

Outside the town the undulating green plateau became filled with American and Vietnamese military cantonments, fire bases (artillery), airstrips, helipads, and truck parks. On some hills, large antennas swung about like strange windmills. Close to the American headquarters, Vietnamese entrepreneurs established a collection of bars and steam baths, and the soldiers dubbed this little settlement "Plei Poontang" (*poontang* is a southern American slang word for sexual intercourse). The American presence also brought another novelty to highland villagers—huge piles of garbage. Streams of trucks went daily to dump the garbage, through which bands of highlanders picked, carrying off in their backbaskets what they could use.

Gen. Vinh Loc and some of his high-ranking officers announced at this time that they were building a special "amusement area" outside Pleiku where American soldiers could enjoy such things as horseback riding and other sports. With American aid concrete, they built a collection of buildings with shops around a fountain. The shops were leased and all of them turned out to be either bars (such as The Playboy Bar and OK Bar) or steam baths. American military authorities in Pleiku, however, put the "amusement area" off limits and so it stood like a ghost town, crumbling in the rain and the heat of the dry season.

The military use of herbicides, which had begun in 1962, reached a peak in 1966 (a total of 19 million gallons of herbicide were used throughout Vietnam, most of them in the central highlands).

One of the sharpest critics of American military tactics in Vietnam was John Paul Vann, a small man with light hair and a self-confident (at times arrogant) bantam-rooster manner. Vann retained in his sharp voice something of his rural southern Virginia origin. He had arrived in Vietnam as a lieutenant colonel in 1962 and rankled his superiors, notably Gen. Paul D. Harkins, by his pessimistic reports. After the disastrous defeat of a South Vietnamese unit at Ap Bac by the Viet Cong on 2 January 1963, for example, Vann, who was an adviser to the unit gave candid interviews about the defeat to the foreign press corps. He was reassigned to the Pentagon at the end of his tour and on 31 July 1963, Vann retired from the army.

In March 1965, Vann returned to Vietnam as a provincial pacification representative for USAID, and the following year our paths crossed in the Stieng country when he landed his Cayuse helicopter near a village where Ralph Haupers and I were talking to farmers in a field. In subsequent meetings Vann and I found ourselves sharing concern over the way the American military was conducting the war. In October 1966 Vann was functioning as USAID liaison with the U.S. First Infantry Division, which had set up its headquarters on a dusty plain near Di An, not far from Saigon. Vann contacted me about giving a briefing to the division staff officers on

Vietnamese village society (as I had done in November 1965). He explained that he felt it important for the officers, who had received no orientation on Vietnamese society and history, to understand that most peasants were of necessity neutral in their allegiances. Vann wanted the First Division to treat the villagers with respect and avoid doing anything that would turn them against the Americans and South Vietnamese. Driving along the road to Di An, Vann somehow felt the need to demonstrate his bravado. He described how the Viet Cong were harassing the First Division with mortar attacks and ambushes, and then he suggested we drive around the insecure district. If we were ambushed, he said, there were grenades under the seat that I should throw out the window while he stepped on the gas to escape. I replied that it would be better if we went straight to the headquarters, adding that I already had had enough combat experience to last me the rest of my days, a reference to the Nam Dong battle. Vann laughed and changed the subject, expressing his ambition to become active in U.S. politics. With his reputation in Vietnam, he reasoned, he could become a public figure, perhaps even Secretary of the Army or of Defense. We were welcomed by younger officers of the First Division, and after the talk on Vietnamese rural society they wanted to discuss that subject and the war late into the night. Vann dealt with their observations with sensitivity and intelligence.

The American-sponsored pacification program took a new turn in November 1966 when the Office of Civil Operations was formed with Deputy Ambassador William Porter as its head. It brought together personnel from USAID and the Foreign Service of the State Department and resulted in an increased number of American civilians in the highlands.

Activities of the CIA in the highlands also increased. CIA personnel in the highlands were invariably housed in expensive villas or compounds, which they immediately surrounded with high fences, spotlights, and special guards. In 1961 the CIA had become involved in the Bureau of Highland Affairs (which subsequently evolved into the Special Commission for Highland Affairs) with a training center in Pleiku for the Mountain Scout Program. In April 1965, the Pleiku center was enlarged and renamed the Truong Son Training Center to train men from villages in gathering intelligence, spreading progovernment propaganda, and organizing community development projects in agriculture and village health. By 1966 the CIA had also become involved in the Provincial Interrogation Centers, a program under the direction of the National Police. I found that by and large the CIA people in the highlands were a strange group, very guarded about their programs, and given to playing the role of superspy. Some CIA agents overwhelmed highland leaders with their displays of money and conveniences such as use of Air America planes. On one occasion, Colonel Ya Ba observed that one of the CIA agents with whom he dealt "must be the richest man in the world." When I asked why, Ya Ba cited his suitcases full of Vietnamese money and "his private planes." I replied that neither the money nor the planes belonged to him; they belonged to the American taxpayer.

By mid 1966 the Vietnam War had become a tidal wave of death and destruction sweeping unrestrained across South Vietnam. Could the war somehow be brought to an end? This was a subject I found myself deeply probing with friends, notably Dang Duc Khoi, Ton That Tien, and Tran Nhu Trang. We agreed that the solution—the path to peace—lay within the Vietnamese cultural concept of accommodation.

While the Taoist roots of the Vietnamese value system stress individualism, at the same time there is insistence on compromise arising from the need for individuals to accommodate to one another and to nature in order to be in harmony with the universe. Tran Nhu Trang pointed out that in Vietnamese, *thõa hiệp* means "agreement" and it is used to describe something like the Geneva Agreements of 1954. Related expressions refer to the process leading to such an agreement: *mà cã* is "to bargain," *đồng nhượng bộ* is "mutual concession," and *đồng lợi* is "mutual benefit." In Vietnamese life accommodation is an integral part of social relations and everyone knows the rules. The concept is captured in the popular Vietnamese saying, "A man proffers a chicken, a woman proffers a cruet of wine." A man is apt to relish the wine more than the chicken and the woman the chicken more than the wine, so the best bargain is for them to share a chicken dinner washed down with wine.

Since the war essentially was a political conflict, there would have to be a process of political accommodation by the Saigon leaders with the existing political parties and movements in South Vietnam drawing them into a pro-peace coalition government that would include the National Liberation Front. Its goal would be to declare a cease-fire and to rely on international pressure to force the North Vietnamese and Americans to remove their troops from South Vietnam.

We did not know at the time that attempted implementation of the accommodation-coalition approach had caused the downfall of the Ngo Dinh Diem administration as well as the administrations of Gen. Big Minh and Gen. Nguyen Khanh. Nor did we know that despite this, the Diem, Minh, and Khanh attempts at accommodation-coalition had succeeded in establishing working relationships with leaders of the National Liberation Front.

Historically there had been in Vietnam coalitions such as the Congress of National Unity and Peace, formed in September 1953 when it was clear that the Indochina War was drawing to a close. Among the organizers were Ngo Dinh Nhu, Madame Huyen Cong Bo (mother of Huynh Phu So, founder of the Hoa Hao sect), and Cao Daist leader Pham Cong Tac.

In 1966 there were two promising accommodations made by the Nguyen Cao Ky government. It was announced that the hierarchical factions of the Hoa Hao drew together and made an accommodation with the government of Nguyen Cao Ky, so the Hoa Hao–controlled area of the Mekong River delta became "secure." Then in 1966 Ky made accommodations to the highland leaders by forming the Special Commission for Highland Affairs, reestablishing highlander law courts in some provinces, appointing more highlanders to provincial posts, and providing scholarships and funds for highland secondary schools.

Why wouldn't it be possible for the Ky government to make accommodations with the other political parties and political movements (including the National Liberation Front)?

In 1966 there were in South Vietnam a host of older nationalist political parties such as the Viet Nam Quoc Dan Dang, Revolutionary Dai Viets, and Southern Dai Viets. There also were political movements among the Buddhists, Catholics, and Cao Daists. Then there were political movements among the highlanders, the Cham and Khmer. The Chinese had no formal political party but their *bang* or congregations were a significant force in the urban milieu. My premise was that in such a complex setting, there is the potential for a kind of solidarity to arise out of recognized need to cooperate in order for the society to continue to function.[3] Solidarity of this genre was an element in the 1966 formation of a Constitutional Assembly in Saigon which provided the first real open forum for political, religious, and ethnic representatives in South Vietnam. Of the 117 seats, 104 were filled by ethnic Vietnamese, six were occupied by highlanders (two of whom were active FULRO members), four were Khmer, and one Cham. Among the delegates were thirty-four Buddhists, thirty-five Catholics, five Cao Daists, and ten Hoa Hao. Although political party affiliation was not declared, among assemblymen were Southern Dai Viets, Revolutionary Dai Viets, and Viet Nam Quoc Dan Dang.

Since in 1966 political power was in the hands of the military, the accommodation process would entail the military sharing of power with civilian leaders, leading to a new political arrangement, a coalition. The next step would be to invite the National Liberation Front as a southern political party to participate. The National Liberation Front had been a tool of the North Vietnamese but its leadership and membership were southern-ers. There had long been deep antagonism between southerners for north-erners and it still pertained in 1966. It would be in the southern leaders' interest (as well as in the interest of the other groups) that northern Com-munists be prevented from taking over the South. Also, it would be in the interests of all parties to maintain the balance of power in a coalition since the reward for everyone would be peace.

In December 1966 I returned to the RAND headquarters in Santa Moni-ca where I was scheduled to give a briefing on the sixteenth. Everyone in attendance expected a briefing on the highlanders, but I elected to present my ideas on accommodation. Very lively discussion ensued and some social science staff members made useful suggestions for improving the concept so that it might receive a favorable reception in Washington. The RAND office in Washington invited members of the State Department, Department of Defense, USAID, U.S. Information Agency, and the CIA to the 5 January 1967 briefing. The first to raise his hand at the conclusion of my presentation was Richard Holbrooke, whom I had known in Vietnam as one of the young bright lights at the American embassy. "What you're say-ing, Gerry, is that we're not going to win a military victory in Vietnam." I responded that he could draw his own conclusions. My major premise was that the war in Vietnam was a political struggle that could only be resolved in political terms.

Unfortunately the accommodation idea was viewed around Washington as heresy. Nonetheless, RAND in October 1967 published it in a report, *Accommodation in South Vietnam: The Key to Sociopolitical Solidarity*.[4] The published version did not circulate in Washington and Saigon until late December. (It was well received by some Vietnamese and journalists.)

I realized that by late 1966, negotiations between FULRO and the government were not going anywhere. Still, there was reason to be optimistic because ethnonationalism was intensifying among highland leaders and a pan-highlander ethnic identity was spreading. The highlanders had the potential of becoming a force to deal with in a war where Saigon badly needed support in the rural areas, particularly the strategic mountain country. It was significant that at this time some young leaders began to favor as an ethnic label for all highland people the indigenous Jarai term *Ana Chu* (or a cognate thereof) meaning "Sons of the Mountains," found in the Austronesian languages of the most populous groups—from which the leaders came. It was an appropriate term, capturing the almost mystical relationship that exists between highlanders and their mountains, which for them is the world where they know they will survive or die out as a people.

Furthermore, my study of highland leadership was revealing that many of the most active of the FULRO and non-FULRO leaders were related through blood and marriage. Among highlanders, as among the Vietnamese, kin ties provide the basis for very strong interpersonal relationships, and kin groups are to be reckoned with at any level or in any segment of the society. The highland kin networks came about in the early 1950s when the French established the Collège Sabatier in Ban Me Thuot and Bao Dai granted young highlanders scholarships to the prestigious Lycée Yersin in Dalat. Most of those who benefited were sons of the upland elite composed of traditional chiefs and the first civil servants in the French administration. Strong bonds of friendship were formed among highlanders at both schools. Although intermarriage among elite families already was taking place, these new friendships resulted in a vastly increased number of intermarriages. The genealogies I was gathering among the ethnic groups continually expanded, and it was inevitable that they would link together. The result was one vast kin network extending over a wide territory and incorporating elite families of the Bahnar, Sedang, Rengao, Jarai, Rhadé, Mnong Rlam, Sre, Lat, Chru, and Bru. Included in the network were older leaders such as Nay Moul and Pierre Yuk as well as Paul Nur and Nay Luett, both of whom would be named Minister for Development of Ethnic Minorities; Touneh Han Tho (who studied at the Louvain University in Belgium) and Toplui Pierre K'briuh (who had an American bachelor's degree); and Y Jut Buon To, a young leader in the CIA's Truong Son Program. Others were Y Thih Eban (a founder of the Bajaraka Movement), Nay Alep (graduate of the National Institute of Administration), National Assembly members Rcom Anhot and Nay Blim, the controversial young leader Philippe Drouin, Ksor Kok a FULRO leader (in Cambodia), and Bun Sur who studied in Paris and became a province chief in Cambodia.

Unfortunately, while leaders in the elite network were prime movers in the emergence of ethnonationalism and the spread of a pan-highlander ethnic identity, by early 1967 they had yet to become a presence in Vietnamese national politics. Although the FULRO and non-FULRO leaders shared the same ideals and maintained communication, the division weakened the highlander cause at a time when concerted efforts and manifest solidarity were important. Vietnamese officials would only negotiate seriously with anyone who clearly had a mandate and the Americans were uneasy in situations where the locus of power was not well defined.

I felt there was at this time a pressing need for some kind of strong definition of the highlanders' place in the national framework. So, based on what highland leaders declared they wanted of the government, I prepared a report drawing together social and economic programs into a comprehensive blueprint. In addition to defining the highlanders' place in South Vietnam, it would give highland leaders something on which to focus their ethnonationalistic sentiments, thereby generating badly needed unity. The blueprint also would give the Saigon government a picture of interrelated programs highland leaders had requested at the 1964 Pleiku conference. Finally, it would provide a guideline for American-aid programs in the highlands.

This report took the position that, while assuming a place in the state of South Vietnam wherein they would contribute socially and economically, the highlanders would retain their ethnic identity. It would be important, therefore, that they preserve certain cultural institutions, such as their languages (which would be taught in the first years of primary school), their own law courts, and special land-tenure laws that would accommodate to their varied forms of agriculture (particularly to slash-and-burn farming). The report pointed out (with examples) that economic development already was taking place in some highland areas, so it advocated special programs geared to augment such development. This would include such things as organizing a wide range of education programs to train young highlanders to assume roles in improved pedagogy, agriculture, health, commerce, and civil service. Young qualified highlanders would be encouraged to pursue higher education in preparation for leadership roles. Included in the report were population estimates of highland ethnic groups. Since beginning this research project early in 1965, I had been gathering population data in collaboration with missionaries and SIL staff members. We estimated a total of 900,000 to 1 million highlanders and had specific population figures for each ethnic group.

In January 1967, while in Washington to present my accommodation approach at RAND, I also gave at RAND a seminar for State Department and USAID guests outlining my social-economic blueprint for the highlanders. After I returned to Saigon on 3 February 1967, a copy of the draft was distributed to those in the American Embassy and USAID concerned with highland affairs. When visiting the embassy to see Robert Oakley he introduced me to Political Counselor John Calhoun, who simply said, "Yes, I met Mr. Hickey. I attended your little lecture in Washington."

In 1967 the NLF announced its political program, declaring in Article 10 its intention to "implement the agrarian policy with regard to peasants of the national minorities. To encourage and help them to settle down to sedentary life, improve their lands, develop economy and culture."[5] It also granted the minorities the right to use their own spoken and written languages and "maintain or change their customs and habits." Finally it stated that "in the areas where national minorities live concentrated and where the required conditions prevail, autonomous zones will be established within independent and free Vietnam."

On 15 February 1967 at a lively party in the Eden Building apartment of François Sully, Bernard Fall, who had just arrived, and I were discussing the situation in the central highlands. Since I was leaving for Kontum the following day and Bernard was going to Hue, we agreed to get together when we returned to Saigon. On 22 February SIL linguists in Kontum said they had just heard on the radio that on 21 February, Bernard Fall had been killed when he accompanied a U.S. Marine patrol and stepped on a land mine. It had happened north of Hue on the coastal plain the French military had called the "Street Without Joy" which ironically had been the title for Bernard's 1961 work on the Indochina War. I had lost a real friend who had supported me in the dark days of the late 1950s when my views on the highlanders had isolated me.

Around this time I was contacted by Martha Gellhorn, the war correspondent, writer, and former wife of Ernest Hemingway, who had been given my name by Gloria Emerson. She came by for a drink. With her record of covering wars, beginning with the Spanish Civil War in 1937, she had interesting observations about the Vietnam War, some of which I agreed with. But Martha Gellhorn conveyed a bitterness that was disturbing. And at the small restaurant she was annoyed by the street sounds, referred to the chopsticks as "these things" as she called for a fork, and sniffed at the tasty Vietnamese cuisine. But on the roof of the Hotel Caravelle for coffee, she relaxed and, watching the distant flares, expressed a feeling of resignation to the inevitability of war in the world.

On 18 March 1967, upon returning from a field trip to the Stieng country (and still covered with dry-season red dust), I was greeted with a summons from General Westmoreland's office to see the general right away. He wanted to discuss the draft of the social–economic blueprint report, and we spent an hour talking about it in the context of highland affairs. In conclusion the general said he was coming away with ideas to take to an upcoming meeting in Guam with President Johnson, Secretary of Defense Robert McNamara, Gen. Nguyen Van Thieu, and Gen. Nguyen Cao Ky. His favorable response was echoed by Maj. Gen. Richard M. Lee, deputy senior adviser of II Corps. In September 1967, RAND made the final version of the report available.[6]

Meanwhile, the Vietnam War was steadily intensifying. In February 1967 the U.S. 3d Marine Division launched Operation Prairie Fire III along the Demilitarized Zone in the Dia country around Khe Sanh. North Vietnamese infiltration from Laos increased in May, and their forces occupied hills dominating the airfield and Special Forces post at Khe Sanh. The U.S. Marines dispatched two battalions and there was heavy fighting in the area. Late in June, reconnaissance revealed the presence of four North Vietnamese regiments in the vicinity of Dak To north of Kontum in the Sedang country. Special Forces elements accompanied by units of the 4th Infantry Division and a South Vietnamese battalion went into the area. They soon were joined by units of the U.S. 1st Cavalry, the 173d Airborne Brigade, and six South Vietnamese battalions in Operation Paul Revere IV. Massive air strikes were provided by jet fighters and B-52 bombers.

In April 1967 I had an opportunity to see the varied effects of the war in central Vietnam. After doing research in the Jarai country near Cheo Reo, I went to Qui Nhon to join Joe Carrier from the RAND Viet Cong Motivation and Morale Project who was giving John Harbut, a new employee, an orientation tour of contacts for interviews. Qui Nhon is located in a spectacular setting on a flat, sandy peninsula that juts into the South China Sea from a backdrop of lofty green mountains. I had not visited the town since 1957 when it was being rebuilt after its destruction in the Indochina War. Now Qui Nhon had become a tawdry wartime boomtown, crowded and dirty with endless bars and shoddy cafés. We met at the Peace Hotel and it soon became clear why the American soldiers called it the "Piece Hotel." Lounging in the lobby and surrounded by soldiers was a group of very floozy American girls whose dress and hair identified them as hookers. Added to this was a steady stream of Vietnamese hookers arriving and leaving on noisy Honda motorcycles which served as taxis in Qui Nhon. Despite the fact that we were given rooms on the top floor (from where, incongruously I could see an enduring Cham tower on a peak to the north) it was impossible to sleep. As evening descended the place filled with soldiers who seemed to enjoy shouting at one another and at the hookers. Mixed with this was the roar of Honda taxi drivers revving their motors and the clatter of beer cans being thrown at them from the rooms.

Joe had made contact with Korean army staff and they invited us to the Tiger Division Headquarters which was a spotless post with whitewashed rocks and a Korean-style house for the commander. The troops were all tall and husky, and looked ready to use their martial-art training. After meeting with the commander we were served a delicious Korean lunch.

From Qui Nhon we went to Danang. Joe had informed the U.S. Marines in the Communist Defector Program, and they sent a Jeep to take us to their post on the Han River across from downtown Danang (which was off limits). I got in touch with the Reverend McGonigal, a Protestant chaplain who had looked me up at RAND in Saigon to obtain information on Vietnamese village society to use in training marines for Combined Action Platoons (CAP) composed of integrated teams of marines (all volunteers) and Vietnamese Popular Forces. Each team was assigned to a village where the men would live and work with the villagers, thereby gaining their support. Afterward, General Owens, the commander, invited us to have drinks and dinner with the staff.

At breakfast in the mess (where they served excellent SOS) I talked with some young marines who where involved in the fighting at Hill 881 near the Special Forces post at Khe Sanh. They said the North Vietnamese troops were very well equipped and very tough. Then, shaking their heads, the marines said they could not understand why, when they were fighting the enemy, the Viet Cong flag was honored in New York while the American flag was burned.

The marines arranged for us to fly to the Hue airport where Lieutenant Mattingly met us with a Jeep to visit villages between the marine base at Phu Bai and Hue where CAP teams were operating. The first village was relatively small and most of the marines had been there a year and had extended. The village chief told me that the team members did not bother anyone and were well behaved. Their presence, he said, provided security. The chief complained, however, that the marines had backed their truck into the masonry council house gate, demolishing it. The second village's CAP had an impressive sergeant named Brown who had been there nine months. Some women told how team members had helped the villagers in many ways. In a village shop we had some beer with marines who said they could not understand why the people at home did not support them.

Lieutenant Mattingly drove us into Hue (which was off limits for the marines) to a hotel on the Perfume River. Unlike Saigon or Qui Nhon, Hue was deadly quiet and I felt as though I had been transported to the late 1950s. We walked through the tranquil streets and went into a small restaurant where they served the delicious Hue cuisine which can only be found in that city. The following morning we visited the Citadel and found ourselves the only ones in the Palace of Supreme Harmony, the Dynastic Temple of Emperor Gia Long, and the exquisite gardens. But despite the timelessness of Hue I had a strange foreboding, a feeling that this world of Vietnam's past could not remain untouched. Perhaps this was due to fears expressed by Vietnamese at the hotel because North Vietnamese units were close to the city and attacks on Quang Tri presaged similar attacks on Hue. The hotel manager confided that he would like to take his family away but he had to remain and work to support them. The following day we returned to visit more CAP teams. The CAP teams were reassuring, but at the Hue airport my forebodings about the city were stirred again when some marines told us that there were three battalions of crack North Vietnamese troops in the vicinity.

By mid June 1967, American military strength in South Vietnam reached 450,000. Intelligence estimates placed the Communist forces at 260,000 including 50,000 North Vietnamese.

With the chief of a Vietnamese village near Hue and Sergeant Brown of the U.S. Marines'
Combined Action Platoon (1967). Soon afterward, the chief was killed in a
Communist ambush.

As the Vietnam War intensified it concomitantly was increasingly
Americanized. To press the war effort more efficiently, in May 1967 the
entire American pacification effort was placed under MACV control. An
agency called the Civil Operations and Revolutionary Development Support (CORDS) was formed to direct civil affairs. In each corps area a
brigadier general or a top civilian was responsible for pacification. The former Office of Civil Operations people reported through him to Deputy
Ambassador Robert Komer (an intense hard-driving figure whose ruthless
manner earned him the nickname "the Blowtorch"), who was directly
responsible to General Westmoreland. A graduate of the Harvard Business
School, Komer brought to bear his managerial skills as if the pacification
program was a large corporation instead of an ill-defined effort with a history of failure under various names (such as the 1962 Strategic Hamlet
Program, 1963 Rural Life Program, and 1966 Rural Construction) before

becoming the Revolutionary Development Program. In corporation fashion, Komer launched a computerized system called the hamlet evaluation
system to measure rural security. American pacification advisers were
required to fill out monthly questionnaires asking such questions as, "Are
the children of the hamlet friendly?" and "Does the hamlet chief sleep in
the hamlet?"

I found the whole approach appalling, and in an interview with the *New
Republic*'s Zalin Grant I expressed my view that "if you have a pacification
program, you obviously want it well managed, but that shouldn't become
the all-pervading end. The US pacification program is largely monolithic. It
is not attuned to the variations in the society and thus has not been effective." As for the hamlet evaluation system I observed, "You just can't
devise a set of indicators that are applicable to the whole of Vietnamese
society."[7]

In August 1967 the MACV headquarters moved from the former
MSUG office building on rue Pasteur to a massive new heavily guarded
building on the edge of Tan Son Nhut airport. In many respects it symbolized the bigness of the whole American effort and it signaled the further
removal of this effort from the realities of Vietnam and its people.

The work ethic was brought to bear as everyone was ordered to be in the
office seven days a week. With the American fondness for surveys, CORDS
personnel were assigned to research (one eager young foreign service officer said how easy it was to design a survey. "All you do is think up some
questions and slap them together."). Also, the number of research contractors increased. Most of those conducting the research were ill-
prepared with little or no knowledge of Vietnam, its history, and culture.
This resulted in such inappropriate projects as administering psychological
tests devised for Americans to Vietnamese Regional Forces personnel.

By October 1967 CORDS had become an ever-burgeoning bureaucracy
in a constant state of flux. Floods of new civilian personnel swelled its
offices in Saigon and in the provinces as well. At Ban Me Thuot there were
fifteen CORDS civilians along four IVS volunteers and a growing number
of CIA people. A team of American military medical personnel was running the province hospital while military teams engaged in civic action
were fanning out into surrounding villages doing such things as digging
latrines and other projects the villagers were perfectly capable of doing
themselves. American aid was building the new Normal School. During

one visit to Ban Me Thuot the Vietnamese province chief shook his head, looked up at the ceiling and sighed, "So many Americans here . . . "

In the midst of these developments the September appearance of the final version of my blueprint for highland social and economic programs was largely ignored (Komer remarked to a RAND visitor that the highland people were not a significant group in the overall population). I was never contacted by anyone from the CORDS headquarters (whether anyone there even read it was doubtful) and I had yet to set foot inside the new building which everyone called "Pentagon East."

I did have a favorable response to the RAND report from Ambassador Ellsworth Bunker who took a lively interest in the highlanders (one result of his study of anthropology at Yale University in 1916). In September 1967, Eva Kim, Mr. Bunker's secretary, telephoned to invite me to his house for dinner. She explained that Mr. Bunker's son, Samuel, who was with the Ford Foundation in India, was visiting. I gladly accepted. The ambassador's residence stood on a street that was closed to traffic and so it had the quiet, leafy charm that because of the war had vanished in other Saigon streets. The other guests were Barry Zorthian (head of JUSPAO), Donald MacDonald (director of USAID), and Don Luce (director of IVS). Mr. Bunker, an intelligent, courtly gentleman, introduced his son, Samuel, who he explained faced a great deal of criticism in India about American involvement in Vietnam. So the ambassador thought it would be useful to discuss this involvement, focusing on such things as the pacification effort. During dinner Mr. Bunker expressed concern that Americans were doing more and more while the Vietnamese did less and less. He said it was due to pressure from Washington for results, so when for whatever reasons Vietnamese counterparts failed to act, the American advisers ended up doing the job. After dinner, in the study the ambassador opened the discussion asking Mr. Zorthian his opinion on the pacification program. Characteristically, Zorthian gave a balanced negative-positive answer. Then MacDonald spoke with great praise for the pacification program. I replied that the basic flaw in the pacification program was that it was conceived by Americans with no Vietnamese contribution and so it had little chance of success. I cited "an intelligent Vietnamese friend" (it was Ton That Thien) who asked me in all frankness, "Do the Americans have an overall plan for Vietnam that we, the Vietnamese, somehow fail to understand, or is there no plan at all?" I replied that as far as I could determine there was no overall plan, only reactions to poorly perceived situations. Don Luce had nothing to say, but on 19 September 1967 there appeared an open letter addressed to President Johnson signed by him and forty-eight other IVS volunteers documenting how the ordinary Vietnamese were "suffering by today's American presence." The letter recommended de-escalating the war, allowing Vietnamese self-determination, recognizing the National Liberation Front in peace talks, and halting use of herbicides.

Highland villagers, already suffering because of fighting and bombing, were at this time subjected to another source of disruption—forced relocation. In a war without front lines, American and Vietnamese military commanders sought to create them with "free strike zones" for shelling and bombing

When in January 1966, the 3d Brigade of the U.S. 25th Division arrived in Pleiku, its commander and Gen. Vinh Loc envisaged a scheme for resettling almost all of the Jarai villages (with an estimated population of ten thousand) west of Pleiku city in order to provide a "free strike zone." The program was discussed through 1966, and early in 1967 the U.S. 4th Infantry Division, commanded by Gen. William Peers, began implementation in conjunction with Gen. Vinh Loc and the South Vietnamese army. This marked the first organized large-scale relocation of highlanders since the 1957 scheme of the Diem government. The plan called for relocating some eight thousand highlanders from forty-eight villages to a large settlement called Edap Enang (which in Rhadé means "peace and prosperity" but planners thought it was a Jarai term).

I gained information on Edap Enang from visits to the centers as well as from Americans familiar with the project (one of the most critical report on the project had been prepared by a U.S. Army Civil Affairs officer). Edap Enang was a masterpiece of bad planning. It was decided to move the villagers in April, just after they had planted their new crops. The South Vietnamese army was supposed to have informed the villagers involved, but most had not been told about it when the Chinook cargo helicopters landed to take them away. Nonetheless, they were forced to go, leaving most of their belongings (including their precious jars and gongs), their cattle, and their newly sown fields. The villages were burned, and one American civilian was furious, reporting that an American officer had boasted, "We set the houses on fire before the villagers were taken away to show them we meant business."

A Vietnamese contractor was hired to build frames and roofs (the settlers would provide their own walls). He obtained poor wood from a nearby forest and tin roofing from USAID. The wily contractor, in effect, only had to purchase nails. To make matters worse, the settlers were charged a large portion of their five thousand piaster resettlement compensation for house construction materials. The dumpy houses, built on the ground, were a far cry from the sturdy traditional Jarai houses built on pilings with thickly thatched roofs. Visiting Edap Enang I had the impression that the entire settlement resembled an extensive rural slum. In May 1967, 7,200 Jarai were moved into the Edap Enang center. By August the situation was becoming dire. Food rations were delayed (for two weeks at one point), forcing the inhabitants to subsist on bamboo shoots and leaves. Pigs were shipped from Saigon for the settlers, but they were very small, and the Jarai had nothing to feed them. Many of the pigs were eaten by the hungry villagers, or, since the pigs were not used to highland conditions, died. Banana trees had been planted in the dry season and soon withered. The wells dried up, and when the rains began both the spillways and fish ponds overflowed. Security was very poor and Viet Cong propaganda teams entered the settlement at will during the night.

Farming at Edap Enang was unsuccessful because of the planners' ignorance of highland agriculture. When I asked the American officer taking me around the settlement if the settlers had selected their own farming sites, he replied, "Oh, the montagnards will farm anywhere." Containing my rising anger I explained that they examined soils and inspected existing flora to assess fertility. Not so at Edap Enang. An area near the settlement had been arbitrarily set aside for farming, after which, in November 1967 bulldozers cleared trees, brush, and top soil. By January, 1968 some two thousand acres had been cleared, so the laterite soil had been exposed to the sun for two months, causing diminished fertility because of leaching.

Finally, it was deemed necessary to allow the villagers to return to their old fields and harvest what was left of the crops that had been planted before the resettlement. This precipitated an exodus, and by early 1968 only about 2,700 remained in Edap Enang. The others had gone back to the "free strike zone." All the while, Viet Cong propaganda teams were active in and around Edap Enang playing on Jarai villagers' discontents.

Despite these failures, during its implementation, Edap Enang was hailed as a success. Visitors from Saigon were paraded through the settlement and special welcoming ceremonies were held. These demanded the presence of at least two thousand villagers who were told to appear early in the morning for rehearsals of "spontaneous" welcomes and then wait around under the rains or hot sun until mid afternoon for the important guests to arrive. The speeches were invariably in Vietnamese, a language few of the villagers understood. By March 1968, Edap Enang had cost the U.S. Mission $900,000.

I reported in detail to the U.S. Embassy's Montagnard Committee and also passed some of my findings to journalists who contacted me about Edap Enang. My friend Nay Luett was now the representative of the Special Commission for Highland Affairs in Ban Me Thuot, but unfortunately his protests about Edap Enang were ignored by the Vietnamese officials.

Meanwhile, highlanders in other areas were experiencing the horrors of being "a people in between" during the Vietnam War. Late in 1967 my friend Touneh Han Tho related that a helicopter landed at the Chru village of Proh Tom Lan, dropping off a group of twelve American Special Forces men accompanied by some Vietnamese officers and Rhadé soldiers. They forced the residents to come out of their houses with their hands behind their heads. Among them was Han Tho's elderly kinswoman, Yolong Ma, who was pushed to the ground by one of the Rhadé. When her grandson Ya Loan objected, telling the intruders that there were no Viet Cong in the village, an American threw him to the ground and put an M-16 to his head. Then while the villagers huddled under the hot afternoon sun, soldiers killed pigs and chickens and ransacked all of the houses. Yolong Ma lost ivory and an ancient Cham saber. Photographs of her family were torn up. The villagers protested to the district chief, but nothing came of it.

Beginning in June 1967 there was a rash of North Vietnamese Army attacks on highland villages. The pattern was for the attackers to strike during the night, penetrate defenses to enter the village, killing as many of the defenders as possible, and throw grenades into the bunkers sheltering the elderly, women, and children. I visited the Bahnar village of Kon Sitiu, close to Kontum, after one such attack and villagers described what had happened. Also, information on similar attacks was gotten from victims who had been taken to Pat Smith's hospital. The worst North Vietnamese attack occurred on 5 December 1967 at Dak Son, a Stieng refugee village near Song Be. According to Ralph Haupers, the SIL staff member working on the Stieng language, the Communists had been sending warning notes to the camp, ordering the villagers to join them on the Cambodian border with the threat of "punishment" if they did not. Undoubtedly the Stieng were to be used as bearers in the movement of arms and supplies through the area. Few villagers obeyed, so the North Vietnamese assaulted the camp. The men rallied to the defense with their spears, crossbows, and the few rifles some possessed while women and children hurried to the bunkers. The Stieng defenders were no match for the Communists with their sophisticated Russian weapons. Once inside, the attackers used grenades and flame throwers against the Stieng, killing more than two hundred of them. Haupers visited the village the following day to find charred bodies of adults, children, and tiny infants in the scorched earth of the bunkers. Their metal wrist and ankle decorations were melted into grotesque shapes. Survivors, many of them wounded and burned, picked through the ruins and ashes in the hope of finding some of their missing family members still alive.

During 1967, a WRAIR team headed by Capt. Andrew Cottingham, M.D., gathered thick blood samples of Vietnamese, Khmer, Cham, Rhadé, Sedang, and Stieng. Between 24 June and 4 July, 1967, the team conducted thick blood film examination for malaria and filariasis in the Stieng village of Bu Kroi near Song Be. Since 1966 I had been visiting this village where with the help of SIL linguist Ralph Haupers I had been gathering ethnographic data, which included a kin-network survey of eight households embracing seventy-one people. The WRAIR team asked Haupers and me to assist them in gathering the sample. The villagers agreed to be examined, but they objected to having any children in the sample "because they're too small and don't have much blood." Of the fifty-three villagers examined, the *Plasmodium vivax* was found in seventeen (32.08 prevalence ratio), *Plasmodium falciparum* was diagnosed in one (1.89), a mixture of the two was found in one (1.89), and *Microfilaria* was detected in ten (18.87). Among the highland samples in the broader survey the highest frequencies of hemoglobin E were found in the Stieng (0.365) followed by the Rhadé (0.212) and the Sedang (0.029).[8]

In 1967 the wartime changes in and around Saigon rendered it difficult to remember how charming, small, and quiet the city had been when I arrived in March 1956. My street, Huynh Thuc Khang, had become a thriving black market with stands displaying American PX goods including expensive hi-fi sets and tape recorders along with canned food, detergents,

Gathering ethnographic data (including a kin-network survey) with Ralph Haupers and Stieng of Bu Kroi village, 1967.

and alcohol. The stands were operated by cheeky, hardy Vietnamese women who, chewing quids of areca nut and betel leaf, lounged in beach chairs and quickly offered catalogues for the prospective buyer to place an order. The influx of refugees and country people seeking employment in the burgeoning urban economy brought jerry-built slums everywhere, even in sections where new, costly villas had been built. And the city had expanded well past Tan Son Nhut airport. An April trip to Long Binh to obtain maps revealed some startling changes. Traffic sped along the new, modern Bien Hoa road which had attracted large textile plants and other industries. But most of the area between Saigon and Bien Hoa was given over to American cantonments, particularly Long Binh (which included a military jail the GIs fondly called the "LBJ"), a bleak expanse on dry high ground where military convoys and helicopters kicked up dust storms blotting out the sun.

Late in October 1967 in the company of Bui Quang Da who had been my assistant in the village study and Nguyen Van Thuan who had assisted

Jim Hendry, I returned to Khanh Hau for my first visit since 1964. Changes were readily apparent as we drove southward out of Cholon along Route 4. In 1964, just beyond the big market the city ended and paddy fields stretched in all directions. Now paddy fields along the road had been replaced by a mixture of commercial buildings, including some manufacturing plants, garages, gas stations, and three- or four-story structures with shops on the main floor and apartments above. Route 4 itself had the usual number of large trucks and buses jammed with passengers and goods. There were, however, more Lambretta carriers, Vietnamese army and U.S. Army trucks and Jeeps. Also, now there were masses of Japanese-made motorcycles careening wildly along the road.

At the first large bridge a sign in English warned, "No Stopping on the Bridge," obviously intended for American military drivers. Close to Binh Chanh district town was a U.S. Army post, a jumble of sandbags and barbed wire with snouts of howitzers barely visible and a collection of vehicles parked in front. Standing by a stream filled with high-tide water an American soldier fished with a pole. Da, Thuan, and I lapsed into silence. Farther along by the Ben Luc bridge was a similar post, and another stood at the entrance to Tan An. On the southern edge of Tan An was a fortified American helicopter pad.

Many people dressed in their best clothes walked along the main road in Ap Dinh A and Ap Dinh B (now fused into one administrative unit named Ap Nguyen Huynh Duc, for the eighteenth-century military hero whose tomb was in the village). They were going to the primary school to vote in the Lower House elections. There were signs of prosperity—new masonry buildings including a council house, residences, and shops. As was our habit during the study, our first stop was the council house to pay respects to the village chief, a man in his early forties (who was serving as a sergeant in the army when we did our study). He greeted us warmly and when I presented him with a cloth copy of *Village in Vietnam,* he smiled and said he had heard it existed. Then he and others in the office quickly turned pages to find photos and identify those in them. The chief explained that American army officers (mostly colonels and majors) had visited the village to take photographs. Some U.S. Army doctors came to have sick call at the school (and healed the chief's eye infection). The chief related that security in Ap Nguyen Huynh Duc was good so villagers had moved there. Some fifty-five refugees from other villages had moved in with kin in the hamlet. Security in other hamlets was "50-50."

The chief reported that because of ample rains the crops this year would be good, although a blight had affected some of the better varieties of paddy. Much glutinous rice was being farmed. Villagers had profited from the increased demand and prices for pigs and cattle.

Out on the road some of the children greeted us with "hello," "OK," and a few said "number one," all expressions that had diffused with the American military build-up. We were glad that none of the children begged.

The ex-village chief who had held office when we were doing our study was visiting in a house near the primary school so we went to have tea with him. Other villagers we had known crowded in to greet us. The ex-chief invited us to have lunch at his own traditional wood-thatched house with its high main roof and ancestral altar in the rear. New additions were a large concrete barn with tin roof for pigs and a similar smaller structure for chickens.

It was incredible that our host and his wife could muster such a wonderful meal on so short a notice. Our friends gathered and everyone drank beer or pop in a convivial atmosphere. The ex-chief toasted with rice alcohol and said he and the villagers had great admiration for our research team. Villagers always commented on how "correctly" we had always behaved. Then he added, "If those running this election would behave like that instead of shouting from trucks, they would understand the people more." We took photos and departed late in the afternoon. It was my last visit to Khanh Hau.

Elections for a president and vice president and for the Upper House of the National Assembly were set for 3 September 1967. In order to rally votes among the highlanders, presidential candidates Nguyen Van Thieu and his running mate, Nguyen Cao Ky, flew to Ban Me Thuot where Thieu signed a decree. One article created the Ethnic Minorities Council. Another article on land rights stated that "highlanders will be given ownership of lands they are farming in rotation," but the Vietnamese expression for "farming in rotation" means rotation on the same field, implying permanent cultivation. The Vietnamese term for "swidden farming" did not appear in the law. Senator Ksor Rot rightly called this a "jeu de mots Vietnamien."

The elections brought in a new national assembly and Nguyen Van Thieu as president, Nguyen Van Loc as premier, and Nguyen Cao Ky as vice president. When the new government was formed in November, a cabinet post (to which Paul Nur was named) for the minister of Development of Ethnic Minorities was created for the highlanders, northern highland refugees, and the Cham (the Khmer Krom were not included). I knew from my MSUG administrative studies that the highlanders needed flexibility in dealing with other ministries for programs such as those concerned with agriculture, education, and health. A high commission in the presidency would have given this flexibility whereas a ministry, especially one with vague functions, would only box the highlanders in.

By the end of 1967, Taoist Vietnamese mystical skepticism about government swept Saigon where it seemed everyone from my Vietnamese friends to cyclo drivers I talked with was fed up with the political posturing, empty promises, and rampant corruption. Mixed with this was a deepening weariness as the war worsened and became more Americanized. And a new mobilization law sent shock waves among the youths who would be affected. The mood of skepticism and disillusion seemed to reach a peak on Christmas Eve when masses of people descended on downtown Saigon, packing sidewalks, pushing and shoving. Streets filled with motorcycles, motorbikes, and every other kind of vehicle, careening madly without regard for stoplights or policemen (there were reported to be 270 accidents). From the mob there arose waves of noise that did not have the ring of holiday joy but rather the hard edge of anger and revolt.

Seven

THE TET OFFENSIVE

THERE WAS SOMETHING MOMENTOUS about the arrival of the year 1968. Perhaps this was because the Vietnam War, as is the case with many wars, took several years to reach its full fury. Following the arrival of American combat units in 1965 and the increase in North Vietnamese forces at the same time, the conflict had steadily intensified, bringing the death and destruction already described. The U.S. troop commitment in late 1967 had reached almost 500,000. The year 1968 *had* to bring decisive events, dramatic turns in the war. And it did, sooner than expected. At the end of January on the eve of Tet Nguyen Dan, the lunar new year, marking the advent of the Year of the Monkey, the Vietnam War reached its real peak of violence with Communist attacks on urban areas throughout South Vietnam. This fateful event is known in history as the Tet Offensive.

Despite the madness of central Saigon on Christmas Eve 1967, the foreign community celebrated the holidays, a welcome respite from wartime grimness, with joy. Everett Martin, bureau chief of *Newsweek* and his wife, Linda, invited me and my friend from UNICEF, Virginia Callahan, cousin of John McAlister, a Yale colleague, to a Christmas dinner. Shortly after, the Martins had to leave Vietnam because Everett had written a piece urging the South Vietnamese army to be integrated into the U.S. forces under a U.S. command. After Christmas, Peter Arnett of the Associated Press and his wife, Nina (a charming Vietnamese lady I had known in 1958 when she worked as librarian at the National Institute of Administration), gave a brunch that drew many of the press corps in Saigon. George McArthur, George Esper, and photographer Horst Faas were present as was Raymond Coffee of the *Chicago Daily News,* where he worked with my boyhood friend Tom Gavagan.

The year 1968 was ushered in by a group of journalists and young foreign service officers who billed themselves as "The Flower People of Saigon." They invited their guests "To See the Light at the End of the Tunnel" a joke on a recent optimistic statement about the end of the war being in view made by General Westmoreland at the National Press Club in Washington on 21 November 1967. I joined friends Steve Cummings and Jay McNaughton at their small house near the Independence Palace, and since the party was "masked," a young Vietnamese artist, Nguyen Quyen (who later became well-known), painted our faces. He said I was a scholar of Vietnamese and highland cultures so he would do an appropriate depiction. The result was a striking rendition of a dragon flying over the mountain (my nose). The party at the large French villa occupied by young Foreign Service Officers was very gala. After being greeted by H. D. S. "David" Greenway of *Time* and David Sulzberger, I wandered into the garden. While chatting with Tom Buckley of the *New York Times* and his wife, Barbara, we were approached by Robert Komer (wearing a baseball hat with BOSS across the front). Tom introduced me and with the noise of the crowd and the band, Komer made a remark I could not hear. After Komer walked away, Tom said it was a "put down," which was no surprise because I was not popular at Pentagon East.

On 7 January many of the journalists also attended a lively farewell party for R. W. "Johnny" Apple, the bright bureau chief of the *New York Times.* There was at one point a curious scene when everyone gathered around a bed where Dan Ellsberg lay, claiming that his "hepatitis" had suddenly wearied him.

Peter Braestrup who was in the *Washington Post* bureau (and later a colleague at the Woodrow Wilson International Center for Scholars at the Smithsonian Institution) reports that as of 19 January 1968 there were 464 journalists (179 of them American) accredited under the local rules of both the South Vietnamese government and to the Office of Information of MACV. The media build-up spawned what Braestrup calls the Mission's "own mini-ministry of information" headed by Barry Zorthian at the Joint U.S. Public Affairs Office (JUSPAO) which provided civilian media with a "Vietnam Roundup." The MACV Office of Information prepared for the civilian media daily communiques from operational reports which were taken to JUSPAO next to the downtown Rex Cinema for the military portion of the daily briefings (which the journalists called "the Five-O'Clock Follies").

By early January 1968, copies of my RAND report, *Accommodation in South Vietnam: The Key to Sociopolitical Solidarity,* had circulated in Saigon and reactions were mixed. Vietnamese friends expressed agreement with the idea and were having it translated. Some journalists wrote articles about it. Raymond Coffey's appeared in the *Chicago Daily News.*[1] Robert Shaplen included my accommodation idea in a 20 January 1968 article in the *New Yorker* which later was incorporated in his book, *The Road from War: Vietnam, 1965–1970.*[2]

There was no reaction to the report from either the embassy or Pentagon East.

American political figures descended on Vietnam in the late 1967–early 1968 period. On 27 December 1967 I, along with two other social science researchers, were invited to a dawn patrol 7:00 A.M breakfast with Governor George Romney of Michigan at the Hotel Caravelle. While we covered a range of subjects about Vietnam, the focus was on pacification. On 11 January 1968 I had dinner at L'Amiral with Senator Edward Kennedy and some of his staff. The senator was very impressive and asked good questions as did his staff members. It was a most interesting evening and I presented them a copy of the accommodation report.

I noticed an interesting pattern with VIP visitors from Washington. When they were guests of the American military they were issued the loose-fitting fatigues (which disguises paunches) with a name tag, and they were taken to the mess where they stood in line to get their "chow." A VIP in effect became "one of the boys," and those with wartime service reverted in their minds to the days when they were indeed one of the boys.

Early in January I was invited by Professor Aaron Wildaysky of the University of California, Berkeley's Political Science Department to deliver a lecture at a Vietnam War conference. I was ready to accept when I was approached by my friends, Dang Duc Khoi and Tran Nhu Trang who had become valuable assistants to Nguyen Cao Ky who, now as vice president, had been moving ahead on programs within his delegated area of responsibility. Khoi and Trang were busy organizing an Ethnic Minorities Council provided for in the new constitution. They already were making use of my RAND report on highland social and economic development and since I had the only solid information on highlander leadership they wanted my help in selecting members of the council. They envisaged a council with a strong advisory role to the presidency and to the Ministry for Development of Ethnic Minorities (MDEM), which was floundering badly.

It clearly was important for me to remain in Vietnam to assist Khoi and Trang in organizing the new Ethnic Minorities Council. I drew up lists of highland leaders which I gave them. I needed additional information on leaders in the Kontum area so in mid January 1968 I went to Kontum after a brief stop in Nhatrang where a Special Forces captain told me the situation in Kontum was grave: Viet Cong forces ringed the town in spite of several battalions of the U.S. 173d Airborne in the vicinity. In Kontum the MACV compound was filled with additional military personnel and a group of American civilians who had been evacuated from their own quarters. The SIL linguists kindly offered me use of a small house in their compound located next to a U.S. Special Forces camp. The compound was nearly empty because a week before, the ten-year-old son of Halang-language specialists Jim and Nancy Cooper had awakened in the night and while getting a glass of water heard explosions. He hurried to rouse his parents saying, "In-coming mortar fire, get in the bunker." They did, just as rounds began to fall around the house. The next day all of those with families moved into Kontum.

Pat Smith's hospital was filled with wounded highlanders. Some were from nearby villages the Communists had attacked at night, throwing grenades all around, even into the bunkers. The Bahnar warned Pat that the Communists were going to raid the hospital to kidnap her and the nurses. I suggested she move into town, but she refused, pointing out that with the nocturnal attacks she had to be available to tend the wounded brought to the hospital. I went about my work but sleeping in the SIL house was difficult because of periodic blasts of artillery from the military compounds.

The threatening situation around Kontum in January 1968 was rendered more unsettling by dire news of a potentially explosive situation at Khe

Sanh in the Bru country of northern South Vietnam. The North Vietnamese 304th Division had infiltrated across the Laotian border to join the 325C Division in the vicinity of Khe Sanh, while the 320th Division appeared to be getting into position along the Demilitarized Zone to attack Route 9 east of Khe Sanh in the vicinity of Camp Carroll, where U.S. Army 175-mm guns provided artillery support for Khe Sanh. At Khe Sanh itself, two battalions of the 26th U.S. Marine Regiment held the position and on 16 January 1968 a third battalion was flown into the area as part of Operation Niagara II.

Later, John Miller, the SIL linguist working on the Bru language, related that as it became apparent a major battle was in the offing, the Americans ordered all of the Vietnamese population (around 1,500) in Khe Sanh to evacuate to the base where they were airlifted to Danang. John described how his Vietnamese neighbors in the town quickly packed their belongings and boarded up their houses. At the same time, Anha, the Bru leader, led a large group of Bru villagers inside the defense perimeter of the base. Busy packing his linguistic materials, Miller was the last one to leave the empty town. No sooner had he departed when North Vietnamese troops began to infiltrate abandoned buildings. On 21 January this prompted the marines to call in massive air bombardment that completely leveled Khe Sanh. The Bru at the base were airlifted to Cam Lo on the coastal plain. Miller reported that some three thousand Bru villagers began to make their way down the Rao Long valley on foot to Cam Lo where large numbers of Vietnamese from the Demilitarized Zone were converging. Also on 21 January, marine positions on Hill 861 came under heavy attack. The marine battalion and a reinforced company occupying that hill, and hills 558, 881 South, and 950, faced two Communist divisions numbering between fifteen thousand and twenty thousand men with one more division within striking distance. These events marked the beginning of the Khe Sanh siege that lasted seventy-seven days.

As Tet Nguyen Dan, lunar new year marking the Year of the Monkey, approached on 29 January, the Saigon central market near my building filled with festoons, vendors, bursts of firecrackers, and stands selling flowers. But, typical of Saigon, the holiday color was mixed with jarring reminders of war. On the morning of 25 January there was heavy artillery fire close to the city and convoys of American combat units moved along boulevards. One convoy with trucks filled with dusty American soldiers in battle gear—helmets and flak-jackets—included tanks and large artillery pieces (on one cannon barrel was stenciled in large letters BIRTH CONTROL). The Vietnamese just stared.

I met with Trang and Khoi to review the list of highland leaders who might be included in the new Ethnic Minorities Council. Then I decided a trip to Ban Me Thuot was in order. First of all it would enable me to gather additional names of Rhadé leaders as possible candidates. Also, while the November decree #003/67 provided land titles for highlanders, I knew from past experience that the Vietnamese government was not happy with the idea of granting titles to highlanders and would therefore drag its feet. One excuse for inaction no doubt would be the shortage of available personnel to conduct cadastral surveys. So I had consulted an American adviser to the land reform program among the Hoa Hao and he explained that the survey could be done through a combination of aerial photos (which existed for all of South Vietnam) and minimal ground research. One objective of this trip would be to determine if Route 21B running southeast from Ban Me Thuot to Lac Thien would lend itself to an experimental survey for obtaining cadastral data needed to grant land titles for highlanders practicing permanent cultivation and swidden (slash-and-burn) farming. Finally, Tet near the Saigon central market would be very noisy whereas Ban Me Thuot, I thought, would be tranquil.

On the bright, clear Saturday morning of 27 January 1968, Guido (Yogi) Ianiero, who ably managed the RAND office, drove me to the Air America terminal at Tan Son Nhut Airport. It was jammed with Vietnamese going home for the Tet holiday. Vangie Blood (whose husband Hank, an SIL linguist, was working on Cham) and her children were returning to Ban Me Thuot. Marie Millar from the British Embassy, carrying her tennis racket, was en route to Danang to visit her friend, Daisy Lim. Major McCarthy from the Special Forces MIKE Force in Pleiku was accompanied by a tough-looking sergeant.

Mike Benge, as usual, offered hospitality at the USAID house, located near the center of town, across the street from the Catholic church known locally as the "cathedral." Mike shared the house with Dick Spurgin, a foreign service officer I knew from the 1950s. It was reassuring that the government and Viet Cong had announced cease-fires due to start with the beginning of Tet on 29 January. But there was a disturbing report that a Communist sapper squad was going to penetrate the town that evening. At

BAN ME THUOT
~ 1968 ~

1 Paradise Bar
2 USAID House
3 CIA Compound
4 Dorlac Hotel
5 Military Intelligence Compound
6 Truong Son Advisors' House
7 Truong Son Compound
8 La Souris Blanche Restaurant
9 Kinh Do Hotel
10 International Bar
11 Benedictine Highland Girls' School
12 Dorlac II Night club
13 Buddhist Pagoda
14 American Nurses House
15 Catholic Cathedral

16 Jane Ford's Apartment
17 Ministry for Development of Ethnic
    Minorities' Office
18 MACY Compound (Bao Dai's Grand
    Bungalow)
19 U.S. Special Forces B-Team
20 Stadium (site of the loyalty oath
    ceremonies)
21 Bao Dai's Hunting Lodge ("Le Palais")
22 ARVN 8th Armored Headquarters
23 Nguyen Du School (former Groupe
    Scholaire Antomarchi)
24 Y Ut Technical School
25 Province Hospital
26 23rd Division Headquarters
27 Provincial Administration
28 Highland Law Court
29 USAID Office
30 Province Chief's Headquarters/Residence
31 Highland Handicraft Center
32 Christian and Missionary Alliance
    Evangelical Mission
33 Highland Solidarity Party Headquarters
34 FULRO Delegation Headquarters
35 Highland Normal School
36 Police Interrogation Center
37 Provincial Prison

Ban Me Thuot, 1968

the house, the Rhadé guards were piling sandbags around the balcony on the second floor. Mike had the barbed wire on the front wall charged with 200 volts of electricity. There was a heavily guarded CIA compound behind the house and nearby was the Darlac Hotel, an air force billet with Nung guards.

Mike and I went to the Special Forces B Team behind the MACV Grand Bungalow to meet Colonel Reed, the new commander, and discuss the FULRO. I went on to Buon Ale-A to talk with Y Dhe Adrong about possible local candidates for the new council.

On Sunday, 28 January Mike and I went to Buon Kram a village some twenty kilometers from Ban Me Thuot on Route 21B to visit his adoptive parents, village chief Y Bham Nie and his wife. We were warmly welcomed. In the January dry season the harvest is ended and clearing of new fields has not yet begun. It is the time to celebrate and feel carefree. At Buon Kram celebrations were in full swing at several longhouses, with groups gathered around jars drinking while gongs sounded. We were invited to these longhouses and as we drank from the jars we discussed the situation in the area and the possibility of doing the survey of fields along the road. Everyone agreed the Route 21B area would provide a range of agricultural patterns and they would be very happy to have titles to their lands. The general consensus about security was that it was not good. Y Bham invited us to dine at his longhouse where we talked about crops and he showed us his full granary.

The following hot and still day, 29 January, we drove back to Buon Kram past dried fields and dusty woods. But upon entering the village it was immediately clear that the atmosphere had changed. There was no gong music and villagers wore anxious looks as we made our way to Y Bham's longhouse. He emerged looking harried and explained that the night before, the Communists had savagely attacked the post at Lac Thien to the south, leaving many of the defenders and villagers dead. Among them were some Buon Kram men, and Y Bham was organizing a dog sacrifice, an offering for those killed in battle. "Don't go farther south on Route 21B," he warned, adding, "All of the villages are filled with North Vietnamese troops, and they're taking the villagers' rice and killing all of their animals for food." He explained that his FULRO troopers who survived the attack said the Communist troops were well armed with AK-47s and had many rockets and mortars. FULRO men in loincloths so they would pass as ordinary villagers heard the North Vietnamese discussing a planned attack on Ban Me Thuot the following day, 30 January 1968.

I greeted the news with a sense of dread similar to what I had experienced before the Nam Dong attack. Having survived one violent battle I had no taste for another, but it was too late to leave. At this point all I could do was hope against hope that the Communist attack somehow would not take place.

Mike and I decided to return to Ban Me Thuot. He wanted to stop at Buon Ale-A, and when we arrived it was evident that the news of the Lac Thien attack and a Communist assault on the town had not reached here. A group of pretty Rhadé girls dressed in traditional clothes were going from longhouse to longhouse inviting everyone to a celebration at the house of Y Wik Buon Ya, a member of the Lower House in the National Assembly. We had just arrived at the house of some FULRO people when a young man came with the news of the impending attack. They quickly dispersed to alert their own armed groups. Mike and I went over to the Grand Bungalow, where in a calm atmosphere some of the American military officers said they felt the Communists would honor the truce. We encountered a group of American missionaries coming out of the mess hall. Among them were Bob and Marie Ziemer, whom I had not seen since the 1950s, and youth-worker Carolyn Griswold (smartly dressed in a white gown and wearing red pumps), who was accompanied by her father Leon, a genial man. He was retired and had come to Vietnam to assist the mission in any way he could. Bob Ziemer and Mr. Griswold expressed their concern over the deteriorating security situation in the area, and we told them what the Rhadé had said about a possible attack. I was somewhat surprised when Bob said they had no bunkers near their houses in Buon Ale-A, but they would begin digging them right away.

At the Special Forces B Team behind the Grand Bungalow, there was feverish activity. The CIDG militia troops were digging trenches and bunkers and filling sandbags. Men were sitting about cleaning weapons. An American sergeant invited us into the bar. "We have intelligence they're going to hit Ban Me Thuot tonight, coming from two directions—a full regiment." He suggested we evacuate the USAID house and move to the Special Forces compound. We thanked him and departed.

Driving through the streets of Ban Me Thuot, I had a sinking feeling as I looked at shops displaying festive Tet decorations. Crowds of smiling people, many of them holding the hands of small children, milled along the streets and filled the central market buying new clothes (a lunar new year requirement) and Tet food specialties, all wrapped gaily in red and gold paper. Music blared from loudspeakers. The restaurants were jammed. At a small sidewalk café, some Rhadé we knew were drinking beer, and they waved for us to stop. When Mike told them the news, their smiles vanished, and they quickly paid their bill to leave.

At the USAID house, Mike gathered the other Americans and the Rhadé guards to work out a defense of the compound. Weapons were distributed. More sandbags were piled up on the balcony and the front door. Cans were filled with water, and we checked the food supplies, candles, and other essentials. We prepared some dinner while everyone became curiously silent. Tanks and armored personnel carriers from the ARVN 8th Armored detachment rumbled by in front of the house, the first sign that there might be trouble. Mike telephoned the three American public health nurses attached to CORDS who said they would stay in their apartment. The sight of our Rhadé guards around the house and on the garage roof with weapons at the ready was very reassuring.

As the sun went down and darkness fell, Ban Me Thuot became very quiet. Only military vehicles sped through the streets. At midnight, in spite of the province chief's order not to fire weapons to celebrate the arrival of the new year (and chase way evil spirits) there was a great deal of shooting of weapons mixed with firecrackers. By 12:30, the noise began to subside quickly and within a half hour tapered off. The night was warm with no stirring of air. Feeling exhausted I fell into a deep sleep.

Around 1:30, in a jarring reminder of Nam Dong, the still, black night was shattered by a rapid succession of explosions as mortar rounds and rockets began to rain down on the military installations and the center of the town. Quickly there was the sound of small arms and then machine guns beginning to sound from every direction. Tracers zoomed and flares lit the sky. Automatic weapons fire burst from the Darlac Hotel and the nearby CIA compound. Flames shot up from burning buildings in the Ban Me Thuot market area and the crowded Vietnamese quarters. Clutching our weapons we huddled behind the sandbags on the balcony as the house shook from explosions all around. South Vietnamese tanks positioned themselves in front of the gate, and we could hear the high-pitched voices of the soldiers shouting on their radios. Armored personnel carriers moved into the traffic circle in front of the cathedral and began opening fire. Helicopter gunships swept up from the American 155th Assault Helicopter unit at the nearby city airstrip to fire rockets in the vicinity of Buon Kosier and Buon Ale A.

Ban Me Thuot was fast becoming a battle ground, but unlike the tiny Nam Dong camp which became immediately inundated, the unrestrained violence was coming in waves that seemed to be getting closer. The clatter and staccato of automatic weapons mixed with the explosions in a strange counterpoint steadily mounting to a staggering crescendo that fell and then rose again. To the west an enormous explosion sent shock waves over the roof tops as a fuel dump blew up. Then, around 3:30, there was an unusually resounding blast from the direction of Buon Ale-A to the south. Mike miraculously reached the nurses by telephone and they assured him they were alright.

Suddenly the house was engulfed in violence (we found out later that a Communist unit was coming up the road behind us). Explosions all around, and tanks began to spray gunfire in every direction. Windows splintered when some of the tanks' 50-caliber rounds came crashing into the living room of the house. Tracer bullets streaked overhead. In an instant, gunships began swooping over the roof, firing rockets that spewed sparks before exploding. Flares descended directly overhead with their bright orange light that caused shadows to distend. The garden, filled with acrid smoke and lit by flares and explosions, seemed unbelievably tranquil.

Finally there came the first signs of dawn, and, as at Nam Dong, the morning light seemed to have a soothing effect, bringing the fighting to a halt. Calm, broken by occasional bursts of gunfire and the thud of mortars, descended when the sky began to brighten on what normally would have been a sultry day.

The tanks began to move away, still sporadically firing their guns. We began to take stock of the house and locate everyone. Fortunately, no one was injured. The front of the house was peppered with bullet holes and one of the vehicles was smashed. The telephone was dead and there was no electricity or water. As the sun rose there was a stirring on the street with military vehicles, some of them ambulances, passing the house. Several young Vietnamese sped by on motorcycles. People began opening their shutters to gingerly peer out and some women held handkerchiefs to their eyes. There were several bodies on the circle in front of the cathedral. Great clouds of black smoke rose from several parts of the town. There still was the sound of gunfire in the southern part of Ban Me Thuot.

While we stood in front of the house, Mike Benge suddenly roared out of the front gate in a vehicle, obviously on his way to Buon Ale-A on the southern edge of the town to assess the situation there. I walked down the road behind the house. People stood in their doorways looking dazed. Further along was the Benedictine sisters' girls school with its beautiful chapel. The chapel had been the work of Sister Boniface, the talented Benedictine nun. Built of locally available hardwoods, the structure had been designed along the lines of a Rhadé longhouse. The priest was looking at the roof damaged by mortar rounds while the nuns swept broken glass. The priest told me that during the night many Communist troops had moved down the road and the tanks had fired on them. I entered the chapel and sat for a moment to reflect on how the war had escalated since the Nam Dong battle, and how sad it was that it had come to this.

Back at the house Dick suggested that in the absence of any cooking wherewithal we get some breakfast at the MACV Grand Bungalow. It was not far and we drove along a debris-strewn main street on which carcasses of dead cattle lay. MACV soldiers were still in their bunkers wearing steel helmets and brandishing weapons. We went into the mess, washed some dishes and utensils, and served ourselves breakfast. Around 10:00 A.M. under clouds of black smoke, Vietnamese refugees from sections of the town that were burning began to appear on the streets, making their way to the cathedral. They hurried along the edge of the roads, clinging to what belongings they could salvage. The bewildered children were wearing their new Tet clothes. Frightened and confused, the refugees reported that fires were spreading and that Communist troops were still in the southern part of the city. Black smoke billowed from a quarter east of Bao Dai's hunting lodge and one refugee with his wife and six children said their house located there had burned. At noon, American fighter-bombers began to dive on the Buon Ale-A area and the exploding bombs rocked the downtown. Some of the refugee women fell to the ground wailing and crying. Vietnamese air force Sky Raiders swooped overhead to drop bombs southeast of the town. Walking by the Kinh Do Hotel, Corvassi, the Italian owner, insisted I come in and have a beer. He said we should stay off the streets because his Vietnamese wife had learned from her relatives that Communist troops were still in the nearby market area. They were trying to organize demonstra-

First afternoon of the Tet offensive. Reinforcements pour into Ban Me Thuot in anticipation
of renewed fighting, 1968.

tions and warned there would be trouble again when darkness fell. It was becoming clear that the fighting was not over.

By this time the cathedral was filling with people streaming down the streets from the south. I went over to talk with some of them. Since they had fled in a great rush they had little with them. I gave them what money I could spare suggesting they try to buy food at the market if it was open. I also suggested that they organize themselves and begin recording names of family members so we could get relief for them. They found some paper and began. I sought the American refugee adviser among the CORDS personnel who had gathered at the USAID house, but he reported that the warehouse holding refugee goods was in an area where fighting was breaking out anew. By late afternoon the sounds of battle in the southern part of Ban Me Thuot began to grow louder and the tanks began to fire down some of the streets. Nonetheless, refugees continued hurrying to the cathedral. The bombing increased, and an American jet flew low over the USAID house, unloading a napalm bomb that burst with a huge mass of fire on the grotto behind the cathedral now jammed with refugees. (We learned later that the Communist troops were reported to be hiding in a church—the one in Buon Ale-A—but the pilot picked the cathedral by mistake.) Fortunately no one was hurt badly.

The Americans in the house decided to evacuate, so we made our way through the center of Ban Me Thuot, past the shuttered shops, through the sports field to the Grand Bungalow. I elected to go to the Special Force B-Team Detachment behind the Bungalow. Just as I arrived a French planter brought in a truck loaded with badly wounded Rhadé from Buon Kosier near the airstrip. The French planter explained that the Communists had forced the villagers to march toward Ban Me Thuot for a demonstration. As they approached the police checkpoint, someone threw a grenade into the group. Most of the Rhadé were elderly, women and children. An elderly man whose legs were mangled and a woman with serious head wounds died while being lifted from the truck, but Captain Cohen, the Special Forces doctor, assisted by the three American public health nurses saved the rest.

Colonel Reed, commander of the B-Team, gave me a carbine and I went to a bunker on the edge of the inner perimeter facing west. The Special Forces troopers manning the bunker were from A-Teams and in salty language they expressed anger about thatched housing built up to the perimeter wire. Two Rhadé strike force men joined us. The bunker was supplied with ammunition and flares, and the senior sergeant gave me a blanket with the advice that if things remained quiet I should roll up and get some sleep. Things did not remain quiet. About 8:30 P.M. shooting began all around as mortar rounds exploded. The nearby MACV compound came alive with machine gun and automatic weapons fire. The troopers in the bunker were in contact with the B-Team command post which, somewhat to their annoyance, told them to hold fire until they had a real target. The Special Forces troopers were very good at determining how close the shooting was and identifying the weaponry, notably the Communists' AK-47s.

Flares lit up the whole area revealing in front of the bunker a depression filled with thatched houses and an array of banana and coconut palm trees. On the rim of the depression in the orange light a Buddhist pagoda took on an aura of mystery.

The fighting broke out in sporadic bursts. A cold wind had picked up, and feeling exhausted I rolled up in the blanket. But just as I dozed the shooting began again, forcing me to grab my glasses and carbine and take a position either in the bunker or, if it was crowded, next to it behind sandbags. Around 2:00 A.M. I went into the dispensary to get water. Captain Cohen and the nurses were busy tending the wounded Rhadé villagers and casualties from the fighting.

At 4:00 the fighting increased with angry volleys and in-coming mortar rounds. Heavy fighting was taking place around the headquarters of the 23d Division and in the vicinity of Bao Dai's lodge. Rockets exploded nearby. I suddenly smelled something strange just as one of the troopers shouted, "Gas!" The men in the bunker began to put on gas masks and one threw me a sealed box which one of the Rhadé CIDG quickly opened with his sharp knife. I slipped on the mask as I was trained to do at Camp Roberts, California, in 1944. Soon after, the senior sergeant removed his mask saying the gas was gone, adding it probably was in one of the rockets.

With sunrise, fighting subsided, but mortar rounds continued to fall near Bao Dai's lodge and the province chief's house. Finally when quiet descended, there was movement around the B-Team compound. We took turns going to the mess for some breakfast. I went to one of the latrines to wash and shave, and then fell into one of the empty bunks for some badly needed sleep. At Colonel Reed's office the news came in that there had been attacks on urban areas throughout South Vietnam and that fighting in Saigon was very intense. Word also came in that a helicopter at the city airstrip was being repaired and would go to Nhatrang. Since there was no reason to remain in Ban Me Thuot and I worried about what might be happening in Saigon, I secured a seat on it.

The truck leaving for the airstrip was packed. When I asked the driver to stop at the USAID house in the hope of getting news of Mike Benge he gruffly replied that with the continued fighting we'd be lucky to make it to the airstrip. Lined with smashed buildings, streets were filled with broken masonry, telephone wires, and animal carcasses. Tanks moved southward where sounds of battle steadily rose. In front of the cathedral a crowd of refugees looked skyward toward the south where Sky Raiders were dropping bombs. More refugees surged along the side of the road.

The airstrip was alive with men from the 155th Helicopter Assault Group digging bunkers and repairing choppers hit during operations and in the mortar/rocket bombardments. When we reached the Chinook helicopter the pilot said they needed a crucial pin which was being brought from the Cam Ranh Bay base by helicopter. He said the chopper would not leave until at least 2:00 P.M. I decided to return to the USAID house which was not far away. None of the 155th people would go back into town because of renewed fighting, so I walked to the main gate to hitch a ride. A South Vietnamese Jeep with a colonel from the 23d Division accompanied by an armed escort stopped and I explained my mission. The colonel kindly said I could borrow the vehicle if I had it back in ten minutes. With air strikes sending shock waves down the streets we sped to the USAID house where Dick Spurgin (who had spent the night at the CIA compound) was standing at the front door. He said the only news they had was that Mike had gone to Buon Ale-A, the scene of heavy fighting.

Back at the Chinook I ran into two American NBC television reporters who were very worried about their wives because news from Saigon indicated that the Rex Officers' billet near their apartments had been hit. They did not want to wait for the helicopter and left to find an Air America flight. Inside the steamy chopper cabin the Special Forces troopers going to Nhatrang were sound asleep. I lay on the floor to do the same when shooting began. Everyone outside began running and as we got under the chopper someone shouted that the Communists were attacking the back entrance to the airstrip. Relative calm, however, was soon restored. I looked at the great clouds of black smoke rising from Ban Me Thuot, and then jet bombers swooped over the field to release charges in the nearby rubber plantation, sending white smoke billowed up from the pastoral, peaceful-looking trees. At 4:30 the helicopter from Cam Ranh arrived and while we were boarding, shooting started all around the airstrip. The crew quickly shut the door and the chopper swung away from the ground. I looked out the window to see areas of Ban Me Thuot burning. Buon Ale-A was in flames and I worried about Mike, the American missionaries, Vangie Blood and her family, and the many Rhadé leaders who lived there. From miles away I could still see the smoke from the burning city. Other puffs of smoke below were no doubt the result of Rhadé farmers burning in preparation for the new planting season, a reminder that away from the Tet violence, ordinary life went on.

We arrived in Nhatrang around 5:30, and the Special Forces men got a Jeep to take us to the 5th Special Forces Headquarters. My friend, Col. Fred Ladd, the commander, was in the United States and his deputy, Colonel Kelly, was in charge. We drank coffee and Kelly suggested I accompany him to see General Quang, head of the Vietnamese Special Forces. On the eve of Tet the Communists had attacked Nhatrang with squads moving through the streets and they still occupied parts of the city. There had been very heavy fighting around the enormous statue of Buddha on a hill overlooking the city, and also around the province headquarters and the radio station. General Quang and his staff were just ending a meeting, and they seemed very calm and quite in control. They had intelligence that a force of some three hundred Communist troops was moving into the northern part of Nhatrang in the direction of the U.S. military and CORDS at the old Grand Hotel on the beach. Driving by the empty beach (where there had been snipers the day before) I was reminded of the beautiful days of 1956 when Nhatrang was a blissful place.

We returned to the Special Forces headquarters where I had a shower (I was grimy with red dust), some food, and a drink before falling into bed and deep sleep. But at 1:30 A.M. I was jolted by loud explosions, gunfire, and the orange glare of flares as the Communists attacked the Special Forces headquarters and the nearby U.S. Army First Field Force. I went to the solidly built concrete command bunker. While the fury of battle swirled around I was impressed by the professional way the Special Forces officers quickly appraised the situation and gave orders. The attack turned out to be very severe with heavy casualties at the First Field Force compound.

The following morning while typing notes, Capt. Carl McCarden, whom I had met on a previous visit to Nhatrang, came in looking very tired. He had spent the last two days involved in the fighting. Leading a company of Rhadé MIKE Force militiamen, Carl deployed them around the hill on which the Communists forces had dug in below the great Buddha statue. At his signal the Rhadé threw grenades and then advanced with weapons at the ready. They retook the hill with few casualties, leaving most of the Communist troops dead or wounded. Then his force helped recapture the radio station. Carl was going to visit the radio station so I accompanied him. Surrounded by Vietnamese Rangers (all of whom wanted to be photographed as they ate handfuls of sticky rice), the station was a scene of devastation—the building had been smashed and even the palm trees were blasted to shreds. Nonetheless, in a studio with a missing wall the Vietnamese were broadcasting a program denouncing "the Communist dark plot which had been thwarted" and they followed that with music.

Upon returning to the Special Forces compound we learned that a U.S.

Army pilot had landed at Ban Me Thuot and found forty-seven Vietnamese orphans huddled at the end of the airstrip. Their orphanage had been caught in the fighting, and the frightened children had no place to go. The pilot got them on board the aircraft and took them to the base at Cam Ranh.

Although reports told of continued fighting in Saigon with Tan Son Nhut airport still closed, I was able to get a seat on a Caribou going there on the morning of 3 February 1968. The airport was a confusion of contrasts. The airport itself was eerily quiet. A lone transport plane was parked in front of the silent commercial terminal, and the Air America terminal, which a week before had been jammed with people, stood empty. Yet, Jeeps filled with armed American soldiers wearing steel helmets and flak-jackets sped by, Sky Raiders flew overhead, smoke rose from areas near the field, and there were large explosions. I walked to the road where American military vehicles raced past and fortunately an army ambulance stopped. The young driver said he was going to the 17th Field Hospital on Tran Hung Dao Boulevard so he could drop me off at the central market. He said there was continued fighting in Cholon. Driving into Saigon the streets were strangely empty, save for military vehicles. Shops and places of business were closed and there were piles of garbage everywhere. Troops blocked all streets around the Independence Palace and the Cercle Sportif was shuttered as was the central market. At the central market a cyclo driver looked at me sadly saying he had no customers, so I threw my bag and typewriter into the cyclo for the short ride to my street by the Saigon hospital. Vietnamese Rangers held back a crowd of people in front of the hospital, and as I made my way through them I was shocked to see Huynh Thuc Khang Street filled with rows of dead bodies! The Rangers let me through and I carefully stepped over the bodies to reach my building. The elevator was broken, and the concierge said Hoa, my cook, has just left.

I breathed a sigh of relief at being home and finding everything as I had left it. Hoa had filled the tub with water and there was electricity because my building was next to the hospital. One of the first tasks one faces in a crisis is to account for friends. I tried telephoning the USAID office but got no response, but I did reach the UNICEF office to learn, despite a very bad connection, that my friend, Virginia Callahan, was home sick with a fever but she had no telephone. Since she lived nearby I walked over to her apartment where she assured me she was feeling better and would rest. I decided to go to the RAND villa on rue Pasteur, so Sau, one of my cyclo drivers, peddled through the filthy streets to Boulevard Le Loi where Vietnamese soldiers blocked Pasteur Street. American tanks roared past as I walked up the street and then I ran into François Pelou of Agence France Presse picking his way through the barbed wire. He said that there was a serious food and water shortage, and high prices might trigger food riots. It occurred to me how difficult it would be for the ordinary Vietnamese who had spent their savings on Tet, to buy any food.

The RAND villa seemed normal with blond Kay O'Bligh, the secretary, typing and sipping coffee. I was greeted with shouts of joy because I had been reported "missing." Yogi said the only casualty was John Harbut who had been badly wounded and was now in the 3d Field Hospital. A manuscript I had left to be typed had not been touched. This turned out to be fortunate because the Communists occupied the COFAT compound (a former cigarette factory) in Cholon where the Army Post Office (APO) post office was located and American jets bombed it.

I walked over to the small house Steve Cummings and Jay McNaughton occupied near the heavily guarded Independence Palace. Peter Glick of the Asia Foundation was there and everyone had stories about friends being caught in tight situations. Peter and Jay were shot at by one of the many Communist snipers around the city. The American embassy had declared a 24-hour curfew but searching for food necessitated going out. Since all stores and markets were closed we drove over to USAID to get some C-rations and gasoline. All of the male American civilians there seemed to be armed. We stopped at the Summer Institute of Linguistics compound which was locked, but David Standing came to the gate. The linguists in Kontum had been evacuated to MACV and then to Nhatrang, but their research center had been destroyed in the fighting. Five of the six American missionaries at Buon Ale-A on the southern edge of Ban Me Thuot had been killed when the Communists attacked their center. Caroline Griswold and her father, Leon, were told to go to the second floor of their villa and then the Communists blew it up (it probably was the huge explosion we had heard in the USAID house). Ruth Wilting, the mission nurse, and the Reverend Ziemer were gunned down while Ed Thompson died when the Communists threw grenades into the bunker which he shared with Marie Ziemer who survived but lost her hearing. The Communists had carefully booby-trapped the bodies. There was no news of the Blood family or Mike Benge. Night brought silence to the downtown streets, a contrast to distant explosions and fires. Sunday morning, 4 February 1968 I ran into Lily Chiang and her brother, Jean, both of whom lived in my building. Like everyone else, they exclaimed how scarce and expensive food was, and then invited me to join them shopping at a Chinese place they knew. The Chinese shop was small and unmarked, surreptitious because most of the shelves were filled with food from the American Post Exchange (PX) selling at vastly inflated prices. The customers were Chinese and French (who, with their pushing and grabbing, had the look of Saigon "old hands"). Lily calmly made her purchases and handed me some American powdered eggs, jam, and a jar of Nescafé. I was glad to find my cook Hoa at the apartment. Since he lived near the airport I knew it was very difficult for him to make his way downtown on a bicycle. He said he had to take his brother somewhere so he departed. Peter came by with news that public executions would begin this morning in front of the Ministry of Communications across the street. I prepared breakfast and as we tried to enjoy our eggs, jam, and coffee the crackle of nearby gunfire sounded from the direction of the ministry.

After breakfast, Peter and I drove along quiet but garbage-strewn streets to the American 3d Field Hospital near the airport to visit John Harbut. I remembered the compound when it was the American School for Dependents' Children and it was strange to see the transformation. Military ambulatory patients in hospital robes were on the lawn carrying weapons, obviously on guard duty. At the rear entrance where we parked, ambulances raced in and out. Stretchers with wounded soldiers were being carried in. The corridors were busy, and at one point a nurse opened double doors of what had been the gym. It was now a large ward and I had the fleeting picture of bloody bandages and stumps where legs had been. In a crowded ward, John, who was already very thin, seemed to have shrunk. He had been at the house of Thuyet, his Vietnamese girlfriend, near the airport when Communist soldiers came through the street looking for Americans. He hid on a ledge, hugging the wall, but a mortar round hit the wall. Thuyet braved street fighting to ride her bicycle for help which she found at a Catholic church. John underwent surgery to remove the small finger of his right hand and close a large hole in his lower abdomen. A soldier next to John had lost a hand, another had his eyes patched, and a strapping black soldier had lost a leg. When we shook hands with him he laughed, "And one of those dudes said to me, 'Hey buddy, you won't be playin' golf for awhile.' I said, 'Shit man, folks like me *never* play golf ever.'"

Back in town the word was that anyone on the streets after 7:00 P.M. would be shot. I returned to my apartment and soon after, Virginia and two colleagues from UNICEF came by for a drink. Virginia was still shaken up from fighting near her apartment building when Communist troops attacked a police station. We lit all the lights, fixed some food, and I played some soothing classical music on the phonograph. Virginia and her friends departed as the sun went down.

Monday morning, 5 February 1968, brought some people out of their houses despite the snipers around the city. Most gas stations were closed so I rode my Vespa to USAID where a grumpy American dispensing gasoline hesitated about giving me any because the scooter might not be "issue" (i.e., issued by the government). The important thing right now was to find out what was happening in the highlands. With this in mind I rode over to the American Embassy in the hope that David Brown who was on the Montagnard Affairs Committee would have news. The embassy chancery had been sieged by Communist sappers and the garden, surrounded by a high wall, had been the scene of heavy fighting. There was a large hole in the chancery wall, another hole in the hardwood entrance door, and the protective cement grill had been damaged by B-40 rockets. The lobby was a mess. Over coffee David expressed regret that the embassy had no contact with the highlands. I stopped to chat with Eva Kim, Ambassador Bunker's secretary, who pointed out that the embassy attack had been well planned and there were strong indications that the invading sappers had been under the influence of drugs.

I continued on to the house of Paul Nur, the minister for MDEM but he was at the ministry. I went there to find Nur and the guards the only ones in the building. Nur was nervous. He said he had been sleeping on the roof of his house and since there was no contact with the highlands, he was worried about his kinfolk in Kontum.

Peter and I returned to the 3d Field Hospital to visit John and at the rear entrance there was the grisly scene of dead American soldiers, all blood and mud, being taken out of an ambulance. John was depressed by the doctor's news that mending the broken nerves controlling muscles in the left leg would be a long process. At the small PX Peter and I bought some candy to give Vietnamese children in another ward. I returned home to find cold chicken and some cheese left in the refrigerator by my cook, bless him.

Tuesday morning, 6 February, I was pleasantly surprised to emerge from my bedroom to find Hoa had breakfast waiting on the balcony table. "Where," I asked him, "did you find French bread?" He replied that the Chinese were producing bread and since shops and markets were closed they set up sidewalk stands. Hoa also displayed fresh vegetables which women using shoulder boards were walking from country truck gardens to sell on the city streets. As I left my building I saw diners at Fat Number Three's sidewalk restaurant eating bowls of his beef-noodle soup. When I expressed surprise, Fat Number Three laughed and explained that Chinese had sold him beef bones, liver, and some meat with which he made his stock. On nearby boulevards small stands vending other essentials such as toilet articles and oil lamps had cropped up overnight. It struck me that, while the "great economy" had come to a halt, the "little economy" was providing city dwellers with essentials.

Hoping to get a picture of what was happening in the highlands I returned to the MDEM to find Paul Nur and some of his staff without any information and without any kind of contingency plan to get relief to the region. And they could only work until 1:00 P.M. when a curfew for Vietnamese went into effect. Perhaps, I thought, USAID might have some information. Getting to the USAID office on my Vespa proved challenging. Many streets were closed, and seemingly endless military convoys were moving through the city. At one intersection I found myself caught in a hopeless traffic jam. Suddenly, sniper fire rang out and American soldiers in flak-jackets jumped from trucks brandishing their weapons. In the confusion I managed to edge the Vespa between trucks to a sidewalk where I made good my escape.

Back in my apartment the telephone rang. It was Arnaud de Borchgrave, senior editor of *Newsweek,* who wanted to know if any of the RAND staff could meet with him. He was particularly interested in how the Vietnamese were reacting to the Tet Offensive. As it turned out, Dave and Mai Elliott had been conducting some interviews with Vietnamese, so I arranged for Arnaud to meet with them at the RAND villa. David Elliott reviewed a paper he had just prepared on reactions of RAND Vietnamese researchers and South Vietnamese army officers. Most of them believed a rampant rumor that the United States had collaborated with the Viet Cong to force the Saigon government into a coalition. When the Tet fighting began in Saigon, many educated Vietnamese were convinced it was an attempted coup d'état by Vice President Nguyen Cao Ky to topple his rival,

President Nguyen Van Thieu. David rightly pointed out that there is a tendency among the Vietnamese to see dark plots in every event. David and Mai also found that by and large the Vietnamese were not reacting to the Tet Offensive with any community spirit; most were only concerned with the safety of their own families so they stayed home and played gambling games.

The next day at lunch, my friend Tran Nhu Trang said that Ky had been trying to alter the constitution to fuse the positions of vice president and premier (thus getting rid of Nguyen Van Loc) and expand his own power base. Trang also reported that despite the dire situation there was a disturbing disunity among government ministries because of personal jealousies. Our friend Dang Duc Khoi fortunately organized an effective Relief Committee to work with the dedicated Minister of Social Welfare and Refugee Problems. Other ministries, however, refused to cooperate and used the curfew as an excuse to close early every day. Trang expressed the view that the recently formed National Salvation Front which included most sociopolitical groups should be given the real power to run the government. He felt that the front had the potential of bringing together the diverse sociopolitical elements into a body in which solidarity would arise from the recognized need for unity in the present crisis. Trang favored a decentralization of power to give greater authority to worthwhile leaders in regions and provinces. He advocated, for example, giving FULRO a more formal role in planning and implementing programs for the highlands. I found Trang's views particularly interesting because in many respects they echoed the accommodation theme we had been advocating. But it soon became clear that the National Salvation Front's promise would never be realized. Writing about the National Salvation Front on 23 March 1968, Robert Shaplen, an astute observer of the Vietnamese political scene, pointed out that while it held the promise of political unity, this never materialized because such groups as the militant Buddhists and Catholics along with the Cao Daists and Hoa Hao stayed out. "All in all," Shaplen lamented, "it seems impossible even under conditions of the gravest urgency, for the Vietnamese to get together."[3]

Still seeking information on the situation in the highlands, I stopped by the *New York Times* office but Tom Buckley said the only news they had was that relative quiet had returned to Kontum. The last resort was to go to Pentagon East where MACV had radio contact with the highland posts. I was relieved that Yogi offered to accompany me because it was my first visit and he knew his way around that huge, complicated building. He left me with some American army officers who had the information I wanted. They said that of the highland towns attacked, Ban Me Thuot was the worst with about one-third of the town in ruins. The center of Kontum had been reduced to rubble. In Kontum Pat Smith had continued to work, caring for the wounded, but on 1 February she and the SIL linguists and their families were evacuated. There had been intense fighting in Pleiku and Dalat. It had been reported on Radio Hanoi that Mike Benge had been captured. The officers also reported that fighting in Hue continued and I worried about my friend Ton That Thien who had gone there to spend the lunar new year with his family. Back in town I went to the MDEM but it was closed.

By Monday, 12 February 1968, two weeks after the assault opened on Ban Me Thuot, South Vietnam was still feeling effects of the Tet Offensive. In Saigon, government rice was being sold in school yards, some restaurants were open for lunch with small portions and high prices, and the Cercle Sportif offered tennis and swimming from 9:00 to 1:00 but no food. Keyes Beech of the *Chicago Daily News* telephoned to have lunch at the American airbase mess where we discussed the failure of the Communists to organize any demonstrations in Ban Me Thuot.[4] Although the Saigon postal service was still shut down, the APO mail service was restored (and Yogi was livid when a friend in New Jersey sent a letter that only said "Keep your head down!"). My friend Bob McDonald sent money, which I passed on to Father Olivier, who operated a farm for abandoned women and children. My niece Judy Walsh sent food, which, along with PX Spam, canned chicken, and sardines, I shared with the poor on my street and my cook (who now had in his small house three large refugee families). Fighting continued in Cholon and the suburbs near Tan Son Nhut airport (where there had been no commercial flights for more than two weeks).

By the end of February an uneasy calm descended on Saigon for brief periods broken by Red Alerts, meaning "anticipated attacks." No one thought the Tet Offensive ended and so preparations for more attacks were being made. Americans were advised to lay in supplies of food, water, and other essentials. The ARPA Research and Development Unit supporting RAND issued weapons to all civilians. I asked for a carbine because in 1944 I was awarded a sharpshooter medal for the carbine during basic training at Camp Roberts. The city began to take on the aura of an armed camp. With the government's new civil defense program, all men between the ages of eighteen and forty-five, and all civil servants (including university faculty members), began receiving training in weapons. With the 7:00 P.M. curfew, restaurants only served lunch, cinemas and night clubs were closed. Everyone talked of kin and friends missing, wounded, or dead. It was confirmed that Mike Benge had been captured along with Betty Olsen and Hank Blood. I wrote to Mike's mother and sister in Oregon, and they replied that the State Department had not informed them and had made no arrangement to have Mike's personal effects sent home.

Ton That Thien returned from Hue where he had been detained by Communist troops but they released him. Sadly, however, his mother was killed by artillery bombardment and they feared his brother was dead. Thien said that Hue was in ruins. In a November 1972 lunch with the elderly mandarin, Ton That Hoi, he told how his friend, Emperor Bao Dai's mother, had stayed in Hue during the fighting to protect the Palace of the Ancestors and carry on the cult. But Communist troops entered the palace and the Americans called in naval gunfire which destroyed it. At MACV I overheard a Vietnamese cleaning lady tearfully telling how her sister and six children were killed in the fighting. At the Vietnamese barber shop all they talked about was friends who had been wounded or killed. While reporters were flooding in the newly reopened airport, dependents were leaving.

The irrepressible social life of Saigon, however, was rapidly reviving. Westerners began having "sleep-ins" with guests arriving at 6.00 P.M. to help prepare dinner and then remain until the end of curfew in the morning. I never graced a "sleep-in," but I did attend a welcome curry lunch with imported lager given for a British member of the Chartered Bank who was leaving. And the "bottle gang" had returned to their favorite spot in front of the altar of the Five Goddesses on my street.

On 28 March 1968 I flew up to Nhatrang where I stayed in the guest room of Col. Fred Ladd, commander of the Special Forces. U.S. Navy destroyers were deployed off the coast to fire at the Communist positions on the hills west of the city. The swoosh of shells overhead and then the explosions punctuated the night calm. At Colonel Ladd's request I gave a briefing on the highlanders which they taped. Afterwards, Carl McCardin drove me around Nhatrang which sadly reflected wartime change. The charming French villas along the beach had been turned into military establishments and the beach itself was filled with warehouses and barbed wire. In the hope of seeing something of old Nhatrang I suggested lunch at Hotel la Frégate. At first that hope seemed dashed. There had been heavy fighting around the nearby military compound which was in ruins as was the elegant old school across the street. The hotel had been riddled with bullets which left holes in the bar and the large refrigerator. But hope revived when the Vietnamese woman running the hotel smiled broadly as she recalled meeting me the first time in 1956 when her aunt ran the place for her French husband. She set a table on the terrace where Carl and I enjoyed a fine lunch of cold langouste and chilled wine.

Whole sections of Ban Me Thuot were charred ruins and every standing building appeared to have been damaged. An estimated 18,823 in the town were homeless. Bao Dai's hunting lodge bore gapping holes. The administrative buildings built by the French on Route 14 were rubble, and Y Dhuat Nie Kdam, a Rhadé leader who lived in one of the buildings, lost his right arm. The American missionaries' houses were smashed or flattened and the bodies of those the Communists had murdered were buried in the garden. Even the Jeeps I rode in had bullet holes in the windows. The USAID office had burned so the house had become the new office. I stayed in the Kinh Do Hotel where the ceiling in my room had a hole from a mortar round that hit during a Communist shelling the day before. La Souris Blanche, the little French restaurant, also had been hit, wounding FiFi, the owner's lady friend, and a young Vietnamese girl who waited on tables. Some four thousand Rhadé villagers whose rice and animals had been taken by the Communist forces had converged on the highlander boarding school seeking food.

About one-third of Buon Ale-A was completely destroyed in the fighting. Sipping coffee in his battered house, FULRO leader Y Dhe Adrong told how Mike Benge had been captured along with Hank Blood and Betty Olsen. The FULRO network reported that they were being held in a jungle prison. (After he was released in March 1973, Mike told a harrowing story of watching Hank and Betty die after being denied food and medicine by their captors.) Vangie Blood and the children had been allowed to walk to MACV.

According to Y Dhe, when the attack began, thirty FULRO troops were stationed at the delegation headquarters in Buon Ale-A. Communist forces came through villages south of Buon Kram where we had visited Y Bham, and for two days and two nights the FULRO fought back. Y Dhe claimed that the movement suffered seven dead and four wounded, while they killed eighty-five Communists. The Communists captured some forty-five residents including two FULRO leaders, Y Ngo Buon Ya and Y Wik Buon Ya who also was a member of the Lower House in the National Assembly, and Benge reported that both were executed. Y Dhe described how the FULRO troops fought bravely but as American bombing became more intense they realized that they would have to evacuate. He, along with other FULRO leaders and their families, fled across fields to Buon Kosier. But Y Preh Buon Krong wept as he told how he and his family tried to flee just as an American air strike began. Several of his children were killed by a napalm bomb. Y Preh said, "My youngest son was hit by the bomb and we could not even find any remains."[5]

Back in Saigon, more details of the siege of Khe Sanh were reported. While the Tet Offensive was going on, North Vietnamese troops along the demilitarized zone were moving into positions to surround the marine base and airstrip at Khe Sanh. On 6 February a North Vietnamese regiment assaulted Lang Vei Special Forces camp southwest of Khe Sanh, using flamethrowers, artillery, and nine Soviet PT-76 tanks—the first time tanks were used by the Communists during the war. During an air strike some bombs were dropped by mistake on Bru CIDG men, killing many of them (and also Co Cuc, the Vietnamese nurse who had been at Nam Dong). For the next eleven weeks the Khe Sanh base underwent heavy daily shelling (on 23 February, for example, some 1,307 rounds landed on the airstrip). Nonetheless cargo planes continued to resupply the garrison, although some were hit by shells and blew up. One victim was Félix Polin, the young French coffee planter, who was arriving on a C-130 that crash landed.

The conflict continued through March and April when the 1st Cavalry Division, the 1st Marine Regiment, and some ARVN airborne units combined to launch Operation Pegasus/Lam Son 207 to open Route 9 and allow ground communications with Khe Sanh. On 10 April they reached the base, and for the first time in forty-eight days no shells fell in the area. There were indications that the North Vietnamese were beginning to withdraw.

In Saigon there continued to be nightly reminders of Tet with circling helicopters and flares, then outbursts of gunfire and explosions lending credence to endless rumors of imminent Communist assaults on the city. Amidst all of this, the British ambassador, Murray MacLehose and his lovely wife, Margaret, elected to celebrate the birthday of Queen Elizabeth II. It was for everyone a real tonic, a chance to be reminded of the civilized world that still existed beyond the sounds of battle. I got out my white suit and wore a gold tie to join the festive gathering that filled the ambassador's residence and large garden on Phan Thanh Gian Street. The ladies were elegantly gowned and military officers in their dress uniforms added a splash of gold braid and medals. We toasted the English ruler with champagne. The din of the celebration drowned out the sound of American military convoys rumbling down Phan Thanh Gian Street. But as I walked around the garden savoring the splendid tropical foliage, I was jarred by the sudden sight by the wall of fierce-looking Gurkhas, half-hidden by banana trees, brandishing their weapons to provide security.

One April morning, I received a most welcome telephone call from Carl Mydans, the *Life* magazine war correspondent and photographer. He had come to Vietnam to report on the plight of people who had been rendered homeless by the war. Over coffee in my living room we talked about the Tet Offensive and the vast numbers of refugees. I expressed my view that most refugees had become demoralized by what had happened to them. They had become beggars, a totally alien condition for the independent and tough kind of people who make up the nation of Vietnam. While some in the American mission saw refugees as government assets, they failed to realize that in the name of military expediency we were producing a rootless proletariat, desperate and disoriented.[6] Mydans made the interesting comment that he had been in Shanghai just before the city fell to the Communists and his Chinese friends expressed the view that after years of wrenching war, if a Communist victory would end the long night, so be it. They were exhausted, Mydans said, and he asked if I felt the Vietnamese might be reaching the same stage. I replied that the Vietnamese were already very war-weary and now with the Tet Offensive, they were exhausted and dreamed of one thing—peace. Then Mydans said that on the advice of his son, a student at Harvard, he had read *Village in Vietnam,* which he found fascinating. He was very complimentary about descriptions of rituals such as weddings and offerings to the Guardian Spirit of the Village, saying that in his mind's eye he could visualize the scenes that he would have liked to have been present to photograph. I was somewhat overwhelmed and thanked him for his kind words. After he departed I realized that the words of Carl Mydans, a talented and intelligent man, were more than kind—they held a deep message of encouragement, something I badly needed in the discouraging days I had known since the Tet Offensive began.

Eight

AFTERMATH

WITH THE TET OFFENSIVE, urban centers which thus far had been spared any battles were drawn into the vortex of the Vietnam War. The war in effect had now engulfed all of South Vietnamese society. This had dire effects in Saigon and Cholon which had remained relatively unscathed during the Indochina War. The Tet Offensive ushered in a long nightmare of street fighting, bombings, and rocket attacks that set off huge fires in thatched poor sections. Bunkers and trenches were dug in parks and gardens. Sandbags were piled in front of public buildings and houses, in living rooms, and on apartment building balconies. Barbed wire was ubiquitous. All glass windows were taped. Strict curfews were enforced. Still, given the Vietnamese ingrained belief in destiny, no one complained. After a night of rocket bombardment they would just shake their heads and go about their business.

And the war began to intensify. Westmoreland received approval for a manpower authorization of 549,500 military forces in South Vietnam. New units, such as the 27th Marine Regimental Landing Team and the 3d Brigade of the 82d Airborne Division, began to arrive.

Outside of Vietnam, two important events occurred at this time. On 31

248

March 1968, President Johnson announced that he would not run as a presidential candidate in the November elections. He also called for a partial halt in the bombing of North Vietnam to induce the North Vietnamese to agree to negotiations. On 3 April, the North Vietnamese accepted President Johnson's invitation to establish direct negotiations. This led to the beginning of the Paris Peace Talks on 13 May 1968.

On 5 April in Ban Me Thuot, highland leaders expressed anxiety because the Tet Offensive had demonstrated the force of Communist military power throughout South Vietnam. Combined with this was the unsettling news of Johnson's intention not to run for president and his invitation to the North Vietnamese, both of which suggested a possible American withdrawal from South Vietnam. FULRO leader Y Dhe Adrong said he had just received a letter from Y Bham Enuol in which he stated his determination to return to the highlands to lead his "liberation armed forces." I also was informed that Paul Nur, minister for MDEM, and Nay Luett had met with Gen. Lu Lan, the new II Corps commander, to present him with a scheme for a "highland force" to cope with the problem of defending the highlands in the face of increased Communist aggression.

FULRO leaders in Ban Me Thuot were also concerned about reports that the government was considering moving large numbers of Vietnamese into the highlands. They were equally upset at the forced relocations of highland villagers, explicitly mentioning the Edap Enang project.

When I returned to Saigon I brought these matters before the embassy Montagnard Committee. I also prepared a memorandum reporting the views of the FULRO leaders.[1] In it I recommended that resettlement of highland villagers be suspended. I had by this time learned that such recommendations must be couched in terms of highland security and so I stressed that such unpopular projects only worsened the already strained government-FULRO relations, lessening support for the government in the highlands. The memorandum was sent to Generals Westmoreland and Abrams and also to Ambassador Bunker and William Colby, assistant chief of staff for CORDS.

The Montagnard Committee prepared a formal recommendation that further forced movement of highlanders into Edap Enang be stopped. The committee also recommended that for all future resettlement schemes, approval of appropriate Vietnamese government ministries (notably the MDEM) and the embassy Montagnard Committee be obtained. Gen.

William Peers, commander of the U.S. 4th Infantry Division, was furious at attempts to halt relocations into Edap Enang (I was told Peers blamed me and at hearing my name he removed his cigar and denounced "that damned sociologist" as he stomped on the stogie). On 5 May 1968 there were reported to be 4,800 highlanders in Edap Enang, and a CORDS report indicated that around 1,200 highlanders had been "picked up and brought to the camp."[2] Most of these were elderly men and women along with some children. By 7 May around half of them had "drifted away from Edap Enang and possibly returned to their home areas."

Nonetheless, on 11 May 1968 General Peers called a meeting of his staff and II Corps MACV/CORDS personnel, and they agreed that a "proscribed area" southwest of Thanh An district in Pleiku province would be completely cleared of population. This plan would be implemented without consulting any Vietnamese government agencies.

Sunday morning, 5 May 1968, was a morning I shall long remember. At 3:00 A.M. I was struck by violent intestinal cramps combined with vomiting and diarrhea. Then at 4:00 A.M. with great explosions by the port and toward the airport, a new series of Communist attacks, popularly called the "Mini Tet," began. The explosions were followed by flares, mortar and artillery fire, and air strikes. Just as my malaise reached its peak, rockets, the first to hit Saigon, rained into the downtown and along Boulevard Le Loi. Rockets swooshed over my building exuding showers of sparks before exploding by the central market. These were the same 120-mm and 140-mm Russian rockets the Communists had fired into Nhatrang and Ban Me Thuot. (Special Forces men had explained that they were antitank weapons with shaped charges making them capable of penetrating thick armor.) Experiencing sheer physical misery I went back to bed not caring if a rocket plowed through my window. I dozed off, but around 6:00 A.M. a huge explosion shook the building.

I was scheduled to attend a noon brunch for Kay O'Bligh, the RAND secretary, who was leaving. Joan Allen, her replacement, had served as a secretary in the American embassy Political Section (after serving in Casablanca, Rangoon, and Kuala Lumpur). She had married Duong Thieu Cuong, a young Vietnamese Air Force captain. On an assignment to Air Vietnam, he had piloted a passenger airliner which in September 1965 had crashed at Quang Ngai, killing everyone on board. (Among the victims was my friend, the talented Jerry Rose.) I had agreed to give Virginia Callahan a lift to the brunch on my Vespa. Around 11:00 A.M. I felt well enough to drive the scooter through streets that seemed normal. After the night of explosions, Virginia was glad to see a friendly face, but she was too dazed to even consider going to a brunch. She poured tea and said I probably had salmonella and would do well to remain in bed all day. As we were chatting there suddenly was shooting behind her building in what clearly was a fire-fight. When it subsided I slipped out and returned home. As the day wore on, sounds of battle increased and great columns of smoke arose from Cholon and Phu Tho. By 7:00 P.M. the streets were empty. Fortunately, nightfall brought quiet and I slept well.

On Monday 6 May 1968, despite battle sounds of air strikes and artillery explosions toward Cholon and the airport, the streets downtown were crowded. At the RAND villa Leon Gouré was supposed to leave for the United States, but Yogi had learned from the embassy that Tan Son Nhut airport was closed due to a Red Alert. There were reports that the Communists would fire more mortars and rockets into Saigon in an attempt to knock out police stations. By noon, shops began to close, and when I went to my barber I found everyone in a panic, grabbing coats while the lady who owned the shop screamed, "The Viet Cong are coming!" From the circle in front of the central market I could see great clouds of black smoke rising from several directions, and suddenly sounds of gunfire and mortars erupted from the port area not far away.

The following morning downtown of Saigon seemed relatively normal. In mid morning I took a break to swim at the Cercle Sportif. Early in the afternoon, while typing in my small office, there suddenly were fire engines roaring down Boulevard Ham Nghi which I could see from my balcony. Then there were loud explosions and noise of gunfire rising from the Khanh Hoi port area behind the boulevard. I knew that since the new offen-sive began there had been fighting in Khanh Hoi, and everyone said it involved a "very tough" North Vietnamese battalion. But the noise was get-ting very close so I went down to the entrance of the building where all of the servants were in a state of excitement. I was shocked to see the street full of people rushing along carrying belongings. The servants said there was heavy fighting in Khanh Hoi and everyone was getting out. I returned to my apartment just as the telephone rang. It was Bernard Klausner, Vir-ginia's boss at the UNICEF office. In a frightened voice he said Virginia was home with a fever and he had been told that a battle had broken out not

May 1968. A quarter in Saigon where heavy fighting had raged for days.

far from her house. Would I get her out? On my faithful Vespa I slowly made my way through the refugees out to Pasteur Street with the intention of crossing Boulevard Ham Nghi to enter Bac Si Yersin Street where Virginia lived. But the boulevard had become a madhouse with mobs of rushing people mixed with horse carts, trucks, automobiles, and taxis jammed with people and belongings all fleeing Khanh Hoi. I got off my scooter to guide it slowly through the stream of humanity and I was struck by the sad scene of children and old people being buffeted by the pushing mob.

Worry over the helpless people in the mob quickly faded when the crackle of gunfire and exploding mortars coming closer jolted me into the realization that I has heading into a battle zone. At Bac Si Yersin Street, South Vietnamese soldiers were positioning themselves behind trees and some began to open fire down the street leading to Khanh Hoi. The police station was cordoned off, so I had to stop. Behind their barricades the police were firing down the street. I heard one of them shout, "They're at the Salt Bridge!" a reference to the Salt Market bridge over a small channel nearby. With automatic-weapon fire very close I considered hitting the ground behind a tree and then decided to make a run for it, so I got on the scooter and gunned it down the sidewalk. At Virginia's third-floor apartment I found her packing while her cook screamed in terror with every burst of gunfire and mortar explosions.

We three could not fit on the scooter so we walked to nearby Boulevard Tran Hung Dao in the hope of finding a taxi, but chaos reigned. I hailed a Jeep containing two American officers sweating in battle gear. As they helped Virginia and her maid into the Jeep, the officers said they had just come from Khanh Hoi where the fighting was very intense. I gave them directions to the RAND villa and drove there on the scooter. Joan Allen, RAND's new secretary, had just moved into an apartment on Boulevard Ham Nghi very close to my building, and she asked me to take her there to get some clothes to move into the RAND villa. By this time the mobs of refugees had invaded the downtown, huddling in arcades and in schools. As we made our way through pedicabs and taxis bringing wounded to the Saigon hospital, I stopped the scooter for two men carrying a stretcher on which lay a little girl covered with blood.

When we reached Joan's apartment, American helicopters were swooping over rooftops in Khanh Hoi strafing and firing rockets. I watched them from the terrace while Joan got her things together. She brought iced gin and tonics which we sipped, a calming moment. Yogi, who hurried up the stairs to take Joan back to the villa, was dumbfounded to see us on the terrace with cocktails. Better, we retorted, than running about in a panic! At the RAND villa, everyone said I should join them, which, when American F-105 jets began to dive over Khanh Hoi to bomb and strafe, I elected to do. As I rode home to gather some things I would need, I reflected how little I thought as I sat typing in the morning and swimming at the Cercle Sportif that such turmoil would engulf me that same afternoon.

On 11 May, Marie Millar from the British Embassy invited me to have a pre-curfew drink at her apartment atop the Hong Kong Bank on the Arroyo Chinoise facing Khanh Hoi. She laughed and said, "You can watch the war!" From her terrace you could indeed "watch the war" with smoke rising from Khanh Hoi and Cholon to muffled sounds of fighting. Marie related that on 9 May she had a small luncheon and when the fighting began she and her guests went out to the terrace to watch the flood of refugees. They saw the French lady who ran the Guillaume Tell restaurant at the port flag down an American Jeep to flee. Then, suddenly the battle sounds came closer and Marie was shocked to see American soldiers in combat gear retreating back over the bridge in front of the bank. Marie quickly packed a bag and joined her friends in a hasty departure. USAID offices and businesses in the financial district were rapidly evacuating.

When fighting flared between Saigon and Cholon along Boulevard Tran Hung Dao (where Diem's forces defeated the Binh Xuyen in 1955), watching the war from rooftops became a Saigon pastime. People gathered on roofs of hotels to drink and point at the jets diving to discharge bombs. I joined a group of friends on the roof of the Hotel President, a newly built, architecturally nondescript place with cracks in the walls. A creaking elevator brought us to the roof which was packed with beer-drinking Westerners engrossed in the battle nearby. Tanks were firing down streets lined with smashed and burning shops and houses. Choppers were sweeping in firing machine guns and rockets. Jets seemed to come from nowhere to drop bombs that shook the hotel.

We heard laughter from downstairs and went down to find a surreal scene. The large gaudy bar and restaurant was jammed with noisy Vietnamese bar girls in extreme miniskirts and American soldiers in dirty, torn, baggy fatigues drinking beer from bottles as they gyrated around the dance floor to loud music. Barely audible were machine-gun fire and blasts from tanks. The merrymakers were totally oblivious of the nearby battle, even the shaking caused by bombs.

Symptoms of my malaise persisted, so on 18 May 1968 I went to the WRAIR lab for tests, but my friends there advised going to the 8th Field Hospital at Nhatrang. They began to make arrangements. That evening, in the company of Joan Allen and Virginia Callahan, I attended a reception for Monsignor Swanstrom, director of Catholic Relief Welfare in New York at the villa of Father Robert Charlebois, head of the Saigon office. As was the case with the Queen's birthday, everyone was happy to dress up and enjoy the respite, but since General Westmoreland and Ambassador Bunker were among the guests, security was provided by American troopers in battle dress around the garden and even on the roofs of neighboring houses.

Around 1:00 A.M. Sunday 19 May, I was rudely awakened by a great explosion near my building. I had fallen asleep without closing my heavy drapes and the room was lit by a bright flame and sparks, signs of rockets landing. I quickly closed the drapes and peeked out the bathroom window to hear a sound like a jet plane going overhead as another rocket exploded by the market. There followed a series of rocket explosions at the railroad station and down Boulevard Tran Hung Dao sending shock waves right through the apartment. A fire roared at the railroad station and soon fire engines raced down Boulevard Ham Nghi. The 2:00 A.M. news on the radio reported that rockets and mortars were falling in the vicinity of the central market and the Independence Palace.

The next morning as I rode my scooter to the Cercle Sportif (where I found out later that rockets has landed on the tennis courts), I realized with a shock how damaging the rocket attack had been in my neighborhood. On Boulevard Le Loi near the market where the first rocket had hit, visibly shaken people gathered around a gaping hole in the street. Nearby, a new hotel and shops were badly smashed. The crowd was talking about where rockets had landed and they pointed to a fire that had already consumed much of a small quarter of houses near the railroad station. The burning ruins were very close to Virginia Callahan's apartment building so I went there. Bac Si Yersin Street was filled with debris and a curiously quiet crowd. For a frightening instant it appeared her building had taken a direct hit, but as I edged closer I breathed a sigh of relief that the demolished building was two doors down. Several cars parked in front were still burning. There was not much left of three soldiers who had been sleeping at the entrance to the ground floor shop. Even their web belts were in shreds. Virginia's landlord and his wife stood by their battered entrance too dazed to speak. I hurried up the stairs to find Virginia badly shaken. She had awakened at the whooshing sound and saw the spray of sparks, after which the explosion knocked her out of bed against a wall. She was not injured but she felt exhausted. We had tea and she agreed to go out for an early dinner at (we hoped) some quiet restaurant. I arrived at the 8th Field Hospital in Nhatrang on 20 May 1968 for tests. I brought along the draft of a paper I was scheduled to present on 21 June in the Pacification Panel of the Army Science Conference to be held at West Point, and in the small hospital library I was able to make revisions. The tests revealed salmonella and hepatitis A, so I remained in the hospital for ten days to begin treatment.

The stay provided a needed rest, although the war was never far away. The hospital was located next to the military airfield and early one evening while I was typing, mortar rounds began exploding on the airstrip, and from the window I saw one round land next to a parked aircraft. As a siren sounded nurses helped bed patients onto the floor to put mattresses over them.

On the lighter (and more ethnographic) side, a group of new patients included a young Roglai from a remote Special Forces camp who had a head wound that had been badly treated by an ARVN doctor. After his surgery the nurses asked me to translate for them, but it soon became apparent that he spoke very little Vietnamese. It also became clear that he had never been out of the mountains and now found himself in a very strange place. I tried to reassure him that he was with friends, and he mustered up a smile. When he was able to sit up and eat, the American soldiers in beds around him went out of their way to help him. I was fascinated at how well he adapted by watching the way the soldiers held forks, knives, and spoons and repeating words they and the nurses said to him. When he expressed horror at ice cream, the soldiers laughed, licking their lips to indicate how delicious it was. Within days the Roglai was latching into the food and ice cream like the soldiers. And, while at first he was somewhat frightened by the television, he soon was sitting up imitating the reactions of the soldiers to sports events and sitcoms. By the time I was discharged from the hospital, the Roglai was on the mend, in good spirits, and very much one of the boys.

Back in Saigon the recent attacks had sent prices skyward, making life extremely difficult for the ordinary Vietnamese.

I got in touch with Paul Nur at the MDEM and also with Dang Duc Khoi and Tran Nhu Trang to discuss the situation in the highlands in the aftermath of the Tet Offensive. I also prepared to depart for leave in the United States. Fighting continued in Gia Dinh near Saigon and my airline tickets got fouled up when there was an air strike next to the villa where the travel office was located. At a bon voyage gathering everyone talked about the latest attacks. On 1 June 1968 as the Pan Am jet taxied to the runway I could see through the window columns of smoke from the direction of Gia Dinh.

Being away from the almost ceaseless strife that had begun on 29 January 1968 gave me the chance to reflect on what the war was doing to Vietnamese society. Since the Nam Dong battle in July 1964 I had been caught up in a conflict that had continually escalated and spread throughout South Vietnam affecting every aspect of the lowland and upland societies. Looking down on the blue South China Sea I realized that the world I had seen through the window in 1956 was gone forever.

It was then that I decided to focus the paper I was scheduled to present at West Point on my ever-deepening concerns about American military strategy in Vietnam and on the failure to recognize that the war was political, rooted in Vietnamese nationalism, so it could only be resolved by political means.

American military planners and decisionmakers failed to understand that the political, economic, religious, and military aspects of wartime South Vietnamese society were intrinsically interrelated as a whole and they had to be understood that way. The strategy of making military decisions without considering what effects they would have on the society as a whole had resulted in ever-spreading disruption of Vietnamese society that was weakening its order and structure and rendering the people war-weary.

As to ending the war I would emphasize that as a political struggle rooted in Vietnamese nationalism, it could only be resolved through a process of political accommodation by the Saigon government with all of the nationalist parties and other political movements including the National Liberation Front to draw them into a coalition government. This would be the first time I would present my accommodation-coalition approach in a public forum.

On 12 June 1968, at the RAND office in Santa Monica I presented the paper at a staff seminar. It was well received and stimulated interesting discussion. Alice Hsieh, a very bright lady who had proven a friend at RAND, on 19 June wrote to William F. Bundy, assistant secretary for East Asian and Pacific Affairs at the State Department, saying that I was "in the process of developing further some very interesting ideas on political 'accommodation' which people in State may find of interest insofar as they might have at least an indirect bearing on the U.S. negotiating position."[3] Alice noted that since Bundy was in Paris for the peace talks his secretary might direct me to the appropriate person to contact. Perhaps Alice should not have added that I was "an extremely modest individual who is not inclined to promote his ideas aggressively," because no contact with anyone at the State Department took place.

At West Point, members of the Pacification Panel gathered at the huge conference hall on the afternoon before the presentation to work out a format. It became readily apparent that the military officers on the panel were relying very much on visual aids—slides with colors. I suddenly remembered that all military briefings made use of such aids and without them, the audience would have nothing visual on which to focus. So I hurried over to the visual aids office where a young artist kindly worked out a colored slide depicting the social-political makeup of South Vietnam. The next morning, 21 June 1968, I presented the paper. The session ended with panel members seated at a long table to answer questions. My paper brought several inquiries and the only notes of disagreement (one bordering on hostility) were sounded by civilians from Washington bureaus.

As it turned out, my friend Ton That Thien who now was serving as minister of the Ministry of Information and also was vice dean at Van Hanh University in Saigon, had been making public statements critical of the American conduct of the Vietnam War. One statement, "A Martyr Nation," was published in the March 1968 issue of *Asia* magazine and another statement was in a paper, "Vietnam's Reaction to Western Impact: The Search for a New Identity," presented on 13 June at the East-West Center in Hawaii. Both were quoted extensively in an article by Bernard Weinraub who interviewed Thien on 10 June in Saigon.[4] Thien's stand was that Vietnamese continued "to be horrified and embittered at the way the Americans fight their wars." He explained that "our peasants will remember their cratered rice fields and defoliated forests, devastated by an alien air force that seems at war with the very land of Vietnam," and "villagers will remember their hamlets uprooted from the earth, all to no purpose." Thien observed that "until the Americans find a way of allying themselves with Vietnamese nationalists, there is little hope of achieving an early peace, or bringing Communism in Vietnam under our control. As long as America persists in its present course, Vietnamese nationalists can do nothing but wait and pray—realizing that the hour is late, that Vietnamese society may soon be past saving and that Communists and Americans may wind up contending for sterile victory over a wasteland." Weinraub commented that "Mr. Thien's views appeared to reflect the opinions of a number of Vietnamese intellectuals, teachers, students, and government officials."

At the invitation of Norton Ginsburg, who had been on my dissertation committee at the University of Chicago, on 9 August 1968 I presented a paper on urban development in South Vietnam at the Urban Development Seminar of the Southeast Asia Development Group at Asia House in New York. Afterwards I met my friends Lee and Roy MacLaren at the U.N. headquarters where Roy was with the Canadian delegation. While we were having a cocktail in the delegates' lounge there was a flurry of excitement when Che Guevara, dressed in what looked like army fatigues, entered the room. Soon after, excitement gave way to panic as people began running out of the lounge. Roy rose rapidly to find out what was going on and soon returned to the table with news that anti-Che activists were firing mortar rounds at the U.N. building from across the East River. "Is there no escape from mortar bombardment?" I said, adding, "Even on the east side of Manhattan?" And so we had another sip.

On 7 November 1968, Alice Hsieh, who was visiting Vietnam, accompanied me to see Ton That Thien at the Ministry of Information. He was very bitter over what he considered American presumption in dealing with the Vietnamese government. According to him the Vietnamese were not informed that President Johnson was going to announce in the 1 November address the bombing halt and enlarged peace talks in Paris. Thien said that pressure was being brought on the government to send a delegation to Paris, but President Thieu was holding fast and even tore up the letter from President Johnson in the presence of Ambassador Bunker who delivered it to him. Thien felt that Thieu's stand had generated a new spirit of pride and unity among the Vietnamese the little guy standing up to the big guy. In a resolute tone, Thien said the Vietnamese ability to cope with the war is increasing while the need for the physical presence of the Americans is concomitantly decreasing. Just because the Americans want to quit the war is no reason to assume that the Vietnamese do too.

On the evening of 8 November I had dinner at the residence of Ambassador Bunker. The only other guest was Father Robert Charlebois, director of Catholic Relief Service in Vietnam. Mr. Bunker said he wanted to discuss frankly several topics with non-government people familiar with the situation in Vietnam. The topic about which he was very concerned was the matter of getting President Thieu to agree to have a delegation participate in the Paris Peace Talks. What, Mr. Bunker asked, would we suggest he do? Father Charlebois talked at length about various strategies the ambassador might employ to convince Thieu of the need to send a delegation. Mr. Bunker then looked at me. I simply said that I thought it best for him not to do anything. He and Thieu had been in contact and Thieu knew that despite what he said in public, he would have to send a delegation. I pointed out that the Vietnamese can be tough and stubborn (as they had demonstrated for the past twenty years), and they react to what they consider excessive pressure by becoming difficult. Mr. Bunker thanked us. By the end of 1968, Nguyen Cao Ky led a South Vietnamese delegation to Paris.

One hopeful development on the American side at this time was the emergence of the Long Range Planning Project ordered by Gen. Creighton Abrams who, in mid 1968, had replaced Westmoreland as commander. The project was placed under Col. Don Marshall, a bright anthropologist graduated from Harvard whom I had met when he was serving earlier in Vietnam. Marshall's Long Range Planning Project involved a comprehensive examination of American strategy in Vietnam. It called for a depth "Appraisal of Current Strategy" and it projected future strategy based on geographical, historical, economic, socio-psychological, and political (including "Montagnards and the FULRO Context") perspectives.

It struck me that Marshall's broad conceptual framework (which reflected the anthropological "total culture" approach) was badly needed to lend a multidimensional perspective to American strategy. Marshall had recruited from RAND Brian Jenkins, a promising UCLA doctoral candidate in history who had served as a captain in the U.S. Special Forces in Vietnam. Marshall also enlisted some very capable young American military officers of varied backgrounds. The "Marshall Group" began their research with gusto and wisely contacted some Vietnamese officers with long experience dating back to the Indochina War. I agreed to do the "Montagnards and the FULRO Context" for the project.

Meanwhile in November and early December I made field trips to Nhatrang, Ban Me Thuot, and Cheo Reo. In Nhatrang and Ban Me Thuot reminders of the continuing war were nightly shellings of military compounds and airstrips. The FULRO delegation in Ban Me Thuot expressed disappointment that a recent meeting with government representatives had gone nowhere. Highland leaders still harbored hopes of being allowed to form their own defense force, despite the government's insistence that such a force be integrated into the Regional Forces, which FULRO rejected. The leaders also were very concerned about lack of implementation of Thieu's 29 August 1967 decree providing land titles for highland villagers. This concern was heightened by government plans to move Vietnamese

refugees into the highlands and the continued forced relocation of highlanders. Back in Saigon I was told by Minister Paul Nur that in a letter to
the prime minister dated 12 October 1968, Gen. Lu Lan, the II Corps commander, declared that it would be pointless to grant land titles to highland
people because they were migratory. To have titles they would have to settle
in "permanent villages." I found his ignorance discouraging because I had
sent him a copy of my RAND study, "The Highland People of South Vietnam: Social and Economic Development," which pointed out clearly that
the highland people were sedentary, that is, neither "migratory" nor
"nomadic." (And on 30 April 1968 I had received a letter of acknowledgment from the general.) I was well aware that the myth of highlander
nomadism was for some unknown reason very difficult (perhaps impossible) to dispel among the Vietnamese and the Americans as well. The
revised *Hamlet Evaluation System Handbook* published by CORDS in
November 1968, for example, stated that "in the central highlands, Montagnard settlements are often not fixed locations. These people practice
slash-and-burn farming, moving to different locations within a tribal area
every four or five years."[5]

In the hope of enlightening some folks at CORDS, I prepared a memorandum pointing out that none of the highland groups was migratory:
although many villagers practice swidden (slash-and-burn) farming, villages remained in place for years and, in many cases, for generations.[6]
Also, in the highlands where topography and water availability were
amenable, there was paddy farming.

I sent a copy of the memorandum to William Colby at MACV headquarters. He responded: "Your short paper 'Myths Concerning the Highlanders' raises an important point often overlooked. Thanks for the good
advice. I'll see that your paper gets proper distribution as a CORDS
notice."[7]

At least I ended the banner year of 1968 on a bright note. On 5 December I was honored with the MDEM's Medal of Merit, First Class with its
silver elephant's head. Minister Paul Nur read a very nice citation. Friends
gathered at the lovely villa of my friend Nguyen Hong-Nhan to raise a toast
with excellent champagne.

But the year 1969 opened under the shadow of new ill-conceived
forced relocations of highlanders. Paul Nur and Nay Luett were particularly troubled at reports that early in 1969 the government planned to move

between four thousand and seven thousand Vietnamese from insecure areas along the coast to the Nam Phuong plantation (a Bao Dai property named for the empress) in the country of the Maa people. The local regional forces, the U.S. 1st Battalion, 173d Light Infantry Brigade, and the U.S. 116th Engineer Battalion were to secure the area. There were Maa living and farming land in the plantation and the government planned to move them to make way for Vietnamese. Father Grison of the Kontum Mission and Father Quang, a local Vietnamese priest, actively opposed the project but to no avail. In February 1969, some six thousand Vietnamese were brought to the Nam Phuong Plantation after the Maa villagers had been moved.

Then we learned that the forced relocation of Jarai villagers that Gen. William Peers, commander of the U.S. 4th Infantry Division, and the MACV/CORDS staff had agreed to in May 1968 was implemented by early 1969 with the movement of 817 Jarai. Nay Luett reported that each family was given 7,000 piasters, but since there was no wood in the area for house construction a province official arranged with a local Vietnamese contractor (without consulting the villagers) to provide a standard package of building materials at a cost of 5,200 piasters per family. The contractor delivered bamboo and other flimsy materials that would only permit construction of lean-tos. During the month of February 1969 some 117 Jarai departed.

At the Montagnard Committee meeting in the U.S. Embassy on 28 January 1969, several members (including myself) reported there was growing anger among highland leaders at these relocations. It was decided to formulate a statement concerning the U.S. Mission policy regarding resettlement of highlanders. A subcommittee (of which I was a member) prepared a statement declaring that "no U.S. civilian agency or military command shall initiate or support any population relocation within or into the Central Highlands of South Vietnam until the project for relocation has been thoroughly examined by the interested U.S. agencies and until final approval has been received by the Mission Council."[8] The statement also specified that, since there would be situations where immediate military necessity "dictates the rapid evacuation and relocation of small groups of civilians," the local military commander could initiate such relocation but would be responsible for providing logistical support to those relocated and returning them to their homes as soon as it was practicable. We noted in the statement that this policy was in conformity with President Thieu's 1969 Pacification Plan which stated that "the object is to bring security to the people and not the people to security."

A copy of this statement was sent to Gen. Creighton W. Abrams, commander of MACV. Nicholas Thorne, chairman of the Montagnard Committee (a retired marine colonel who also had worked as assistant to Ambassador William Sullivan in Laos), delivered copies to Ambassador Bunker and William Colby, head of CORDS. Initial reaction from Abrams and the military was negative. General Peers, now commander of the First Field Force in Nhatrang, saw a copy of the statement and immediately went to confer with Abrams for three hours. Peers clearly saw the statement as a criticism of his resettlement projects while commander of the U.S. Fourth Infantry Division. The Montagnard Committee also learned that both military and civilian personnel at CORDS felt that if the statement was accepted it would put undue restraints on their new pacification efforts. At CORDS there were ambitious young men who were determined "to make pacification work." They had set a goal of bringing 90 percent (Abrams is reported to have said "Why not 100 percent?") of the population under government control by the end of 1969. There were strong suggestions that the CORDS people saw relocation schemes as a means of attaining their goals in the central highlands.

Also, as a result of the increasing pacification efforts, a conflict between CORDS and the Political Section of the U.S. Embassy had developed. Since the Political Section sponsored the Montagnard Committee, the statement was seen as an effort to assert the embassy's authority in the area of pacification.

To support acceptance of the statement, on 20 March 1969 I distributed copies of a report I had prepared concerning the negative effects of population relocation in the highlands.[9] In this report I reviewed the resettlement policies and programs since the Diem era, pointing out the disruptive effects on highland societies and the resentment they had generated among the highland people. I concluded that the statement issued by the Montagnard Committee provided the best guidelines in the matter of population relocation. Ironically, at the same time, a comprehensive postwar plan for Vietnam compiled by a Vietnamese-American research team was gaining great attention.[10] Like other economic development schemes in the past, it ignored the role of the highland people in developing their own region and recommended that Vietnamese be brought into the highlands to provide labor and skills for the new projects. On 21 March Thorne informed me that the Montagnard Committee's statement had been rejected. As it turned out, the Montagnard Committee was never to meet again. The statement was something badly needed to inject some sense into our highland strategy. I felt deeply disappointed but not surprised that it died because of power struggles and personal ambitions.

Hoping that it might have some positive effect, I put the finishing touches on the final version of "The Highlanders and FULRO Context" for Don Marshall's Long Range Planning Project which I submitted late in March 1969.

Meanwhile I had begun an updated revision of my October 1967 accommodation RAND publication. Late in 1968 with the Paris Peace Talks moving ahead there was the increasing possibility that a political solution to the war might become a central subject of discussion. In the hope that my ideas on ending the war might be weighed more reflectively than they had been in Washington or in the American Mission in Vietnam, on 19 November 1968 I had presented them to the Marshall Group. As I expected the discussion was very useful and interesting. This was encouraging, but then early in December, officials in the American Mission told Marshall that they were lukewarm about the accommodation idea because the word carried the connotation of "giving in." In a similar vein, at lunch on 8 December 1968, Bob Shaplen of *The New Yorker* had related that his article on accommodation which had appeared in *Foreign Affairs* a year earlier had been "laughed at" in Washington. He said there was less criticism of my RAND report because "it had a strong sociological basis," but nonetheless they were not buying it. Bob and I agreed that Washington and Pentagon East believed the Saigon government did not have to make any political accommodations because it could expand its support in the rural areas through the current Accelerated Pacification Campaign. It was the old story of giving a failed strategy or program a new name and expecting success.

In March 1969 I welcomed the opportunity to test my accommodation-coalition approach on two visiting eminent journalists—Marquis Childs and C. L. Sulzberger.

The question of whether, given the political disarray in South Vietnam, the United States could, as a result of the Paris Peace Talks, withdraw its forces was on the mind of the syndicated columnist Marquis Childs when I had lunch with him on 23 March 1969. In a subsequent article, Childs wrote about the various factors affecting any possible American troop withdrawal, such as "military progress with air striking power once directed against the North now concentrated in the South and on the Ho Chi Minh Trail," and "progress in the tough task of pacification with new techniques." He added, "But the challenge in the view of one of the most knowledgeable men, Gerald C. Hickey, who has spent eight years in Vietnam with the RAND Corporation, is for a government that can reach an accommodation with the multiple factions so long at odds." Childs ended his article saying, "According to Hickey, that accommodation in any meaningful sense had not yet begun. Until it is achieved, a peace settlement is an illusion to be dispelled sooner or later—sooner rather than later—by a Communist takeover."[11]

Around the same time I had an interesting discussion with C. L. Sulzberger of the *New York Times* about the current political picture in South Vietnam in the light of the Paris Peace Talks. The matter of a possible coalition came up, and I expressed the view that having the NLF in the political arena could have the effect of drawing the other political groups together. In Sulzberger's piece on the subject I was quoted as saying, "It will be in the interest of all the other groups that the Vietcong do not assume a predominant place and, as solidarity is generated through accommodation, their means of preventing any Vietcong takeover are improved constantly. It cannot be assured that the Vietcong, once they are in the Government will act in concert. Not all of them are Communists."[12] Sulzberger found the approach "venturesome," adding, "Nevertheless, it seems the Thieu Government now feels both strong and self-confident enough to offer some such audacious plan."

By mid August 1969 I had the revised version of "Accommodation and Coalition in South Vietnam" completed and sent it to RAND in Santa Monica for review. In September I had a discussion about it with Maynard Parker, Saigon Bureau Chief for Newsweek. He was working on an article dealing with the new strategy of "Vietnamization" launched by the Nixon administration which called for a systematic withdrawal of U.S. forces while turning over more and more of the fighting to an ever stronger South Vietnamese government and army. Parker noted that Vietnamization "provides neither a method of reconciliation nor a means for the total withdrawal of foreign troops."[13] It is a program that promises continued fighting,

much of it by Americans. As an alternative, accommodation at the local
and national level entails risk but sooner or later such risk will have to be
taken. "As anthropologist Gerald Hickey has warned, 'If an effort is not
made at accommodation, people in the U.S. had better be prepared for
many years of fighting.'"

In September 1969 a strange incident related to my accommodation-
coalition idea occurred. It involved Tran Ngoc Chau, a nationalist who had
been elected to the National Assembly in 1967. In 1968, Chau, a man with
strong convictions about free elections and social justice, advocated a
peace settlement that would have involved allowing the Communists to run
for office. Chau sought to establish contact with Hanoi through his brother,
a senior Communist intelligence officer, and he was denounced as a Communist sympathizer. Then in September 1969, while accompanying some
RAND visitors, I was in Can Tho where John Paul Vann was the senior
adviser to the IV Corps, which included most of the Mekong River delta.
At our meeting in his office Vann was highly critical of the way the U.S.
Ninth Infantry Division was using airpower without adequate intelligence
on the ground, and he claimed that the "kill figures" being released were
almost fictional. Then, while the RAND visitors went to meet with the military, Vann drove me to a house where much to my surprise in an upstairs
room was Tran Ngoc Chau. Vann explained that Chau was in danger of
being arrested, so Vann had provided this refuge. Since I was advocating an
accommodation-coalition solution, Vann thought that Chau and I should
meet. Vann left Chau and me to talk for at least an hour. After we left Chau,
Vann outlined a daring scheme that he had devised for Chau's escape from
Vietnam. Vann would land his small helicopter on the roof of the house and
fly Chau across the Cambodian border to the seaside resort of Kep. From
there Chau would make his way to Phnom Penh and then to Bangkok. As it
turned out, Chau left the house and in February 1970 was ordered arrested
by President Thieu. (He remained in jail until the fall of Saigon in 1975
after which he was again jailed by the Communists.)

In January 1970, RAND published the new report "Accommodation
and Coalition in South Vietnam."[14] On the Vietnamese side I realized all
too well that the ruling Saigon regime would not respond favorably to the
notion of political accommodations leading to a coalition government. The
military leaders were not nationalists: they were people only interested in
retaining power. One of the journalists who read the report was Daniel

Southerland, and in February he wrote in the *Christian Science Monitor* that "the palace position is that each of the sociopolitical groups wants too much power, that they are politically unsophisticated and incapable of working together, that some of them are too divided within their own ranks to be effective, and that many of their leaders are incapable or unwilling to cast aside personal interests and work in a meaningful way with the government."[15] Southerland added, "The Vietnamese Communists are not the compromising sort, palace sources contend. They are not like the European Communists, goes the palace view. They are single-minded fanatics who will not go in for an accommodation unless it guarantees a Communist triumph." Southerland ended the article drawing on my view that the matter of accommodation rested with relatively small groups of people on both sides who know that accommodation and coalition offers a compromise course where both parties sacrifice something for the goal of ending the war and building the Vietnamese nation in a peaceful and independent setting. And he quoted my conclusion that "to expect them to put aside personal and group ambitions for the good of society is, perhaps, unrealistic. One way or the other the time has come for them to make the decision." If they are willing to compromise, I said, they can end the war, but if they are unwilling to do so, the war will go on and on.

I turned my attention back to field research for my RAND study of highlander leaders which was yielding very good information on the interrelated kin network of elite families that spread across the major highland ethnic groups. One was centered in the Dak To-Kontum Pleiku area, another two in Cheo Reo, a fourth in the Danhim-Dalat-Djring area, and a fifth in Ban Me Thuot. As inter-group marriages continued during the Vietnam War, the five genealogies linked, forming one vast kin network extending over a wide territory and incorporating elite families of the Bahnar, Sedang, Rengao, Jarai, Rhadé, Mnong Rlam, Sre, Lat, Chru, and Bru.

In the course of traveling throughout the highlands during my years of research, I collected examples of village-level economic innovations, some of which were included in the 1967 RAND report outlining a socialeconomic blueprint for highland development.[16] In 1970, notwithstanding disruptions caused by the war, there were some impressive additional examples of economic innovation among the highland people. When the French developed coffee estates in Darlac province during the 1920s and 1930s, they hired numerous Rhadé as laborers. Although it went unnoticed, in the course of time some of these laborers began to grow their own coffee trees in villages and eventually in small estates. By 1970 there were 326 registered highlanders with coffee estates. They totaled 531 hectares and the medium holding was 1.0 hectare. These planters had their own association. Their robusta and arabica coffee was purchased by Chinese who transported it to the Saigon market.

In many highland villages near towns, there was an increase in cash cropping. This was the case in the vicinity of Cheo Reo, where kitchen gardening was developing into truck gardening. This began to happen in 1962 when Phu Bon became a province with Cheo Reo (Hau Bon), its capital with an influx of Vietnamese civil servants and military. Jarai villagers saw Vietnamese planting gardens containing tomatoes, cabbage, onions, and chili peppers, all of which sold at the Cheo Reo market for high prices, which prompted some Jarai to plant more vegetables in their swiddens to sell in the market. By 1970 many swiddens had become sizable truck gardens and women were making daily trips at dawn to bring their produce to the Cheo Reo market. Dominating the open-air section of the market, these Jarai women were selling (the Vietnamese complained that they had a fixed price and refused to bargain) a wide range of fruits and vegetables and also tobacco and animals (chickens, ducks, pigs, and sometimes cattle). They even vended live river fish in polyethylene bags filled with water.

In the 1950s , when the Vietnamese began moving into the Danhim valley between Dalat and Phan Rang (the heart of the Chru country), they farmed using their traditional method of transplanting paddy from seed beds into the fields. Many also used chemical fertilizers. According to my friend, Touneh Han Tho (son of the Chru chief, Touneh Han Dang), his kinsman Touneh Ton was one of the first Chru to adopt the Vietnamese farming methods. Han Tho's uncle, Touprong Hiou, followed suit. He had the reputation of being an adept farmer, and over the years he had expanded his landholdings, cultivating a wide range of cash crops. In 1966 he and some Vietnamese farmers imported seed potatoes from Holland and he began to transport potatoes along with other produce in rented trucks to markets in Saigon, Nhatrang, Dalat, and Phan Rang. Having accumulated considerable capital, Hiou joined two Chinese friends in opening the first rural bank in the highlands. He insisted that the architecture be based on traditional Chru house lines "so the villagers would feel at home in the bank."

There also was an increase in the number of highlanders involved in nonfarming enterprises. Many were engaged in petty commerce, usually operating village shops. These shops, like those of the Vietnamese, were small and built of locally available materials, most often wood, bamboo, and thatching. The stock included a wide variety of manufactured goods likely to be in demand by villagers. A number of those running such shops had been in the Special Forces CIDG program and had accumulated enough capital for the initial investment. Some of them pointed out that they had a problem with kinsmen and fellow villagers purchasing items on credit. Since among highlanders, it is more important to maintain good social relations than it is to make money, they could not force payment of these bills, and in most instances it was unlikely they would ever receive the money.

In 1967 some Rhadé in the vicinity of Ban Me Thuot began to engage in the transport business, using tri-wheel Lambrettas. By early 1968 six men in Buon Ale-A were operating carriers. They made constant runs between villages and the Ban Me Thuot market. In January 1968, Y Hue Buon Krong, a resident of Buon Kram, purchased a Lambretta, paying cash he had saved in the Special Forces. He operated his carrier between Ban Me Thuot and Buon Ea Khit (south of Buon Kram), making four round trips a day. The service was interrupted only during the planting season when Y Hue worked in his fields to clear, sow, and harvest. He explained that he did not follow the usual Rhadé pattern of buying cattle. To begin with, the transport business had become very lucrative, and secondly, security in Darlac had gotten bad during 1967. Y Hue reasoned that if he and his family had to evacuate their village in a hurry—a contingency most highlanders considered very real—they would have to leave many things such as cattle behind. But with the Lambretta they could load all of the family and many of their personal belongings to flee into Ban Me Thuot. If they should need money, they could always sell the Lambretta. Ironically, I interviewed him in Buon Kram the day before the Tet Offensive began. While Buon Kram was untouched, large sections of Ban Me Thuot were scenes of fighting.

With the goal of making the Vietnamese government and the American Mission more aware of the potential role of the highlanders in any future economic development I wrote up my findings which were presented in a report that RAND (after a delay of many months) published in 1971.[17]

The matter of land titles for highlanders was a subject with which the Vietnamese government had played endless games and in 1970 it continued to do so. A law granting such titles had been signed in August 1967 and a decree dated 15 July 1969, issued by the Ministry of Land Reform, provided a scheme for identifying lands being farmed by highlanders. In March 1970 the MDEM had proposed legislation that would provide each highland village with title to a delimited territory (this had been one of the recommendations in my 1967 report).[18] This would be in addition to lands already claimed by individuals and families. The Ethnic Minorities' Council, provided for in the 1967 constitution, did not convene until 4 November 1970 with a special session to discuss land titles for highlanders. At this meeting it was decided that every village would have a "main living area" (i.e., a village-owned territory), determined on the basis of ten hectares for each family. On 9 November 1970 the prime minister signed this into law. But implementation was not forthcoming because as some USAID officials pointed out, the provincial authorities were "indifferent" to any program geared to giving land titles to highland people.

One reason the highland leaders at this time were anxious to have the land title program implemented was because of increasing land-grabbing by Vietnamese. The most blatant example of an attempt took place early in 1970, when Vice President Ky's wife applied for a concession of 1,500 hectares within the boundaries of Tu Tra, a Chru village in the Danhim valley. According to Touneh Han Tho, she had flown over the area in Ky's special helicopter and decided that the land would be good for a farm and ranch. When it was made public that she had bid for the land, the residents were outraged. They immediately wrote to their deputy in the National Assembly. Touneh Han Tho and other Chru leaders marched to the district headquarters to protest. Finally Mrs. Ky withdrew her bid.

Early in 1970 I decided to try to visit Phnom Penh to interview FULRO members there and perhaps even see Y Bham. I applied for a visa and some American journalists (who were denied entry) laughed, saying the Cambodians no doubt considered me a "CIA agent." Much to their surprise (and in some cases, chagrin) I was given a visa. But in March, Norodom Sihanouk was deposed as head of the Cambodian government by a military junta led by Gen. Lon Nol. I waited a month to let things settle down and then went to Phnom Penh.

I was met at the airport by Pat Hughes, the ambassador's secretary, who in the late 1950s had been in the Political Section of the Saigon embassy. Pat had reserved a bungalow at the Hotel Le Royal and as we drove into town she filled me in about the situation in Phnom Penh (now attracting reporters and hippies) and the newly reopened American Embassy with its "wavering electricity, packing-crate desks, jugs of water carried from home, bizarre visitors and equally bizarre in-coming cables." One such cable simply signed "Coolidge" (no doubt Harold Jefferson Coolidge, the primatologist who led expeditions in Indochina) called for American pilots to desist from targeting koupreys, a type of rare forest ox.

I found the city much the same as it had been in May 1969 when I had visited en route to Angkor Wat. Phnom Penh was one of the most attractive cities in Southeast Asia, with a French colonial charm that Saigon had lost during the Vietnam War. There were shaded streets, quiet squares, pastel colored buildings, beautiful wats (temples), and by the river, a glittering royal palace. There was little street traffic, and in the still heat between noon and three o'clock Phnom Penh closed its shutters and slept.

The deposal of Sihanouk had been brought about by a disgruntled urban military-civilian group led by Lon Nol. Sihanouk and his wife, Monique, were decried as corrupt (one Cambodian lady remarked, "When the new government took over the coffers were empty"). Everywhere there were posters denouncing Sihanouk as a dupe of the Communists, such as one depicting him dressed in a natty continental style suit with a herring-bone twill pattern composed of conical hats, each containing the yellow Viet Cong star. Other posters decried the Viet Cong as "eaters of Cambodi-an territory," or warned that the Viet Cong "are worse than cholera." The name of the port of Sihanoukville had been changed to its original designa-tion, Kampong Som, and Avenue Sihanouk was now Avenue March 18, 1970 (the day of the deposal). The word "royal" was deleted from buildings and names, for example, the Royal Khmer Army became the National Khmer Army. But general criticism of Sihanouk was quite guarded. When an American at the Hotel Le Royal offered to buy the portrait of Sihanouk that the manager had removed from the lobby, the manager declined, saying he would store the portrait because they might need it again.

Slogans written on walls and pamphlets blowing down the streets called for support of the Salvation Government of Lon Nol. Signs of the new war between National Forces and the Communists were just beginning to appear. Sandbags were being placed in front of public buildings. The bags were large rice gunnysacks or woven reed bags similar to those used in Vietnam before the United States provided more efficient bags of slick, dark green nylon. Trenches were being dug in front of ministries and along the Mekong River.

Despite grim reminders of conflict, the city had taken on a kind of "Oh What a Lovely War" atmosphere with dull work-a-day routines relieved by the inevitable excitement a new war brings. Mixed with this was a new spirit of nationalism. Students and civil servants were rushing to join the army. All civil servants were receiving daily training in the city parks. The government asked them to wear military clothes, and while many wore military shirts issued to them, they still retained their own trousers. University and secondary-school students sported khaki berets for training on the school grounds. Sneakers were the most common footwear. Instead of weapons, the trainees carried sticks. Everyone seemed to have a knife.

Even at the serene Buddhist Institute the staff wore military shirts and trained in the dusty park during the afternoon. They expressed anti-Vietnamese sentiments reflected in opinions of other Cambodians in Phnom Penh: "The crafty, scheming Vietnamese who have long lived in Cambodia retain their culture, and it is the aggressive Vietnamese who are invading Khmer territory." They were determined to drive the Vietnamese out.

I found it curious that people in Phnom Penh knew so little about the war in Vietnam. They had only vague information about the Tet Offensive. They asked if the Vietnamese had any troops to defend Saigon as they were going to defend Phnom Penh, and they thought the Communist rockets were only a foot long.

I went to the Australian Embassy to see Mack Williams, whom I had known when he was posted in Saigon, and he gave me a picture of current events in Cambodia. At the Hotel Le Royal the group of journalists from Saigon included Kevin Buckley (*Newsweek*), Keyes Beech (*Chicago Daily News*), Larry Stern (*Washington Post*), George McArthur (*Los Angeles Times*), Bernard Kalb (CBS), Lou Jaffe (NBC), David Sulzberger (on an assignment for *Time*), and Larry Burrows (*Life* photographer killed in February 1971 when the South Vietnamese helicopter in which he was riding was shot down). The "Friends of Sean Flynn and Dana Stone," photographers who had recently disappeared in the countryside, were converging on a bungalow behind the hotel. They were led by affable John Steinbeck, Jr., replete with love beads, carrying his Indian flutes, and accompanied by an ex-IVS girl, Crystal, dressed in an Indian outfit. They were very friendly and insisted I come to the bungalow for a drink. Ironically, it was the same bungalow I had stayed in while visiting Phnom Penh for the 1957 Fête des

Eaux. Now, however, the prosaic bungalow had been transformed into a "pad."

Then I contacted the FULRO young-Turks. I had first known Kpa Doh when he was an interpreter the Americans called "Pardo" at the Bon Beng Special Forces camp near Cheo Reo in 1964. With him were other young Jarai—Ksor Dhuat and Ksor Kok (who was in my elite genealogy)—and Y Bhan Kpuor, a Rhadé. All of them had commissions in the Khmer Army and were living with their families in apartments on Boulevard Monivong across from a military compound where Col. Les Kosem had a house. Y Bham Enuol was still in the villa of Col. Um Savuth near Pochentong Airport. Kpa Doh indicated that it was necessary to arrest Y Bham to prevent his "selling out" FULRO in Saigon.

By April 1970 fighting was breaking out in parts of the rural areas, some of them close to Phnom Penh. Laughing soldiers rode out of the city in buses as well as in beer and Pepsi Cola trucks to battle areas south and east of the capital. To accommodate the foreign media crowd, every morning a news briefing was held by army officers in the tea room (which had a large bar) above the Magasin d'Etat (which still was selling East European goods). The colonel giving the briefing had an amiable manner and used French expressions such as "mort au champ d'honneur" in reference to the military dead, drawing scowls and moans from the longhaired young French journalists. After the briefing, the journalists would scramble to their rented white air-conditioned Mercedes to go to the scenes of new fighting. Unlike Vietnam, Cambodia offered little protection for journalists near battles and a number of newsmen and photographers were killed or wounded.

One morning at the lobby of the Hotel Le Royal there was a scene that somehow captured the moment in Phnom Penh. A large contingent of French planters and their families packed around the check-in desk to get rooms. A bus in front unloaded a collection of tourists, the last to leave Angkor Wat and, seeking rooms, they mingled with the planter group. Then, excited journalists fresh from the briefing pushed into the lobby which by this time was something of a noisy madhouse of linguistic confusion, angry faces and waving arms. Suddenly, the front doors opened to admit four imperious Air France stewardesses who, ignoring the chaos, fended their way to the desk where the clerk smiled and handed them room keys. They turned on their heels and briskly departed.

Rumors were rampant as foreigners gathered at Le Cyrene or La Tav-

erne for lunch. They discussed such things as how the defenses of Phnom
Penh were feeble (at the airport, for example, there were a few scattered
outposts). These conversations fed tensions arising as the foreigners realized that they could suddenly find themselves trapped in the capital city
with little to protect them.

By the end of April all Australian dependents and an increasing number
of Russian technicians and their families were departing. The Cambodians
were reporting dire signs, such as the appearance of a white crocodile in the
Mekong River and the flash of a comet over Phnom Penh. My old friend,
the French reporter, François Sully and I went to have tea with Charles
Meyer, a Frenchman who had been close to Sihanouk and who was then
packing (books, Khmer heads, statues, and scrolls) to leave for France. He
confirmed a story that soon after Sihanouk had been deposed, the Queen
Mother had the *baku* (Brahman priests who are guardians of the royal
treasure) bring her the Preah Khan, the sacred saber. She performed a ritual, partially removing the saber from its sheath (to remove it entirely would
precipitate a calamity for the kingdom). The blade was reported to have
been rusted and dark in color, a sign of great trouble for Cambodia (at the
end of the sixteenth century, a turbulent time, a similar ritual had revealed
that the saber was rusted).

On 30 April 1970, the American–South Vietnamese invasion of Cambodia began with the goal of destroying "Communist sanctuaries" to prevent
further infiltration into the Saigon area and the Mekong River delta.
Despite nervousness over traveling in rural areas, some journalists drove
over to the border area where the invasion was taking place.

Months later when I returned to Phnom Penh in July 1970 the war had
intensified in the countryside as the government forces concentrated on
defending population centers while the Communists took control of more
rural areas. Southeast of Phnom Penh, the Khmer Krom were doing much
of the fighting. I had a discussion with Thach Chia, a Khmer Krom teacher
in the Lycée Sisowath, who had been with the Khmer Krom delegation in
an August 1968 Ban Me Thuot meeting between Y Bham Enuol and Vietnamese government officials. He admitted that Khmer Special Forces
CIDG militiamen from Vietnam were doing most of the fighting. (Thach
Chia later was killed in a student demonstration.) Another Khmer Krom
leader was the flamboyant Kim Khet, who, dressed in a "tiger suit," and sitting in the garden of the Hotel Le Royal drinking Bloody Marys, described

how his "force" of sixty Khmer Krom had just warded off Communist attacks on Takeo. He claimed to have been the bodyguard of Ba Cut, the Hoa Hao leader who had been guillotined in 1956. Kim Khet related that he had fled to Phnom Penh, where he hoodwinked Sihanouk into thinking he was a hopeless playboy by frequenting nightclubs such as Maxim's while he secretly was organizing the Khmer Krom.

I saw more of the FULRO leaders on this visit. Kpa Doh told me that when the American–South Vietnamese invasion had begun at the end of April, Communist forces had moved westward. The Communists moved in trucks at night over back roads. Doh claimed that FULRO forces backed by American artillery in the Ratanakiri-Pleiku border area had on 24 June mounted an operation against Communist forces.

Bun Sur, a Mnong Rlam who had left Vietnam, had just arrived from Paris where he had been studying in Paris and working as an assistant to Georges Condominas, the French ethnographer who had done research among the Mnong. Kpa Doh, Ksor Kok, and I gathered at Les Kosem's house to greet Bun Sur. From there we went to a popular Cambodian restaurant. It was on this occasion when a conversation with Les Kosem I described in Chapter 5 revealed that he had been the "bearded Cham," who had mysteriously appeared at the Buon Sar Pa Special Forces camp during the FULRO revolt in September 1964. Bun Sur was given a commission in the Khmer Army and named chief of Mondulkiri province. Soon after, Bun Sur, Kpa Doh, and the other FULRO leaders began making frequent visits to Vietnam to recruit highlanders to go to Cambodia (some American military officers were involved in this effort). They had little success. Privately, Kpa Doh also began to complain about Les Kosem's treatment of the FULRO people in Phnom Penh, saying that the Cham leader (who persisted in referring to the highlanders as "nos petit frères, les montagnards") was "too authoritarian."

François Sully had in the past spent much time in Cambodia and he knew many people in Phnom Penh. In his Hotel Le Royal bungalow he had photos of a condominium he had just bought in the Aga Khan's Sardinia development on the Costa Smeralda. It was an impressive with a large terrace and splendid view of the sea. François was planning to retire there to write a book about his close friend Bernard Fall. François, Arthur Domen (a scholarly journalist with the *Los Angeles Times*), and I were intrigued with the Khmer Rouge's success in recruiting in the rural areas where Buddhism was deeply rooted and outside ideologies were viewed with suspicion. After talking with some Cambodian officials we concluded that the Khmer Rouge had its initial recruitment success in fringe rural populations, particularly in the northeast where there was little Buddhist influence. In the course of our interviews one official related that he had heard from several sources that after Sean Flynn and Dana Stone disappeared, there were reports of villagers having seen the Khmer Rouge leading two Westerners (one tall with blond hair) into an isolated area where they staked them out in the blazing sun to die.

Anti-Vietnamese feeling was running high in Phnom Penh and it took an ugly turn when Cambodians attacked Vietnamese homes and businesses, particularly in Roussey-Keo, a Vietnamese enclave on the Tonle Sap. François and I went there to find the Vietnamese residents barricaded in the Catholic church yard. They were living in a state of fear and lamented having abandoned their houses and shops. The following day a South Vietnamese navy destroyer docked to evacuate all of them to Saigon. It was an orderly departure with the evacuees given loaves of bread as they were piped on board the ship.

In early November 1970, I was interviewed by Dan Southerland about the situation in Cambodia. Discussing why the Vietnamese Communists failed to gain any substantial support among Cambodian peasants away from the border area, I drew on some of the ideas that François, Arthur, and I had worked out as a result of our interviews and also articles by some French experts such as Jean Delvert.[19] The outstanding factors militating against peasant cooperation with the Vietnamese were such things as virulent anti-Vietnamese sentiment, the strong role of Theravada Buddhism in Cambodian peasant society, and past aloofness of Cambodian villagers toward dissident movements.[20]

By this time the effects of the war were being felt in Phnom Penh. Rains had washed away the anti-Sihanouk posters, and bunkers were everywhere as were coils of barbed wire. An artillery unit had been moved to the river bank close to the shuttered gambling casino and troops with their dependents had occupied the partially completed Hotel Cambodiana (that Sihanouk had been building for the tourist trade). Civilian hospitals were now forced to accept wounded soldiers because the military hospitals were overcrowded. Newspapers carried many photos of Communist dead and charred ruins of such towns as Kampong Speu and Skoun. Nonetheless,

Phnom Penh, 1970. Wedding of the National Bank assistant director's daughter
to a Khmer army officer.

Phnom Penh restaurants and bars were doing a lively business and Madame
Choup's elegant establishment where one could get food, drink, pot, opium
("o"), and girls drew crowds, including many of the foreign media people.
François Sully and I were invited to the very grand wedding of a Khmer-
Chinese army officer and a daughter of the assistant director of the National Bank. The reception was held in a mansion and guests, proffering expensive gifts, were dressed in traditional Khmer clothes. The ladies, many
chewing betel-areca quids, filled the large reception room to inspect the
gifts displayed on marble tables. The wedding dinner, catered by a Chinese
restaurant, was served in the tropical garden.

But the war was moving closer to Phnom Penh. On 2 August 1970 a
bus, several taxis, and a beer truck were hit with B-40 rockets on the road
from Kampong Som, leaving eleven dead. This was the first such ambush
in the vicinity of Phnom Penh. River traffic on the Mekong had ceased, and
the city was slowly being isolated. At the beginning of August, in the quiet
of early evening, Pat and I were riding cyclos to La Taverne for dinner

when we heard the thumping sounds of mortars and explosions of artillery for the first time in Phnom Penh.[21]

Returning to Saigon I was struck how, after Phnom Penh, the city had the look of a place that had long been at war. Rocket attacks were still plaguing the city (Joan Allen had been sleeping in her enclosed small bathroom for months). With the war dragging on there was little to perk up the Vietnamese in Saigon, but I was happy to see that their ironic sense of humor had not abandoned them. One night a Russian 140-mm rocket hit the Rex Cinema. Fortunately it happened just after the cinema closed, for if it had struck sooner, it would have been disastrous. The following day the Saigonese shook their heads and laughed because the film playing at the time was the James Bond thriller, *From Russia With Love.*

On the evening of 26 September 1970, a young Canadian publisher from Toronto named Conrad Black (who was said to be very well-to-do) came by for a drink. He was very articulate and asked penetrating questions about the war and events in Cambodia. He was leaving the next day and complained that he had some 30,000 piasters (about $200 at the official rate) which he was unable to convert to dollars. Since I had just given Father Olivier 10,000 piasters for his farm for abandoned women and children, I suggested Black give the money to a local charity. He expressed horror that I would suggest such a thing. The following day he telephoned, still worried about his 30,000 piasters and he asked about a "raincoat" he had left in my apartment. When I asked Hoa about it he replied that he had found a "dirty plastic sheet" which he threw away.

In November 1970 I was contacted by an editor at *Encyclopaedia Britannica* about doing two articles, one on North Vietnam and another on South Vietnam. Because of my crowded schedule I was only able to accept the offer for South Vietnam. Gathering data and analyzing it for the article provided an interesting overview of South Vietnam in 1970. The war had disrupted the society badly with such things as the vast increase of refugees. But the war also generated a great deal of capital within South Vietnam, and it produced more skilled and semiskilled workers. Since 1960, foreign aid and foreign investments had been increasing production of textiles, glass, ceramics, ethyl alcohol, sugar cane, pulp and paper, vegetable oils, natural silk, and coal. But when the war, notably the Tet Offensive, began to affect urban areas, manufacturing decreased. With the urban influx of population and the allied military presence, the production and sales in beer, soft drinks, tobacco, and canned foods increased (but it was clear that American withdrawal would affect demand for some of these products). The needs generated by the enormous American military presence had brought vastly improved facilities, such as ports, jet airstrips, and roads as well as a number of buildings.

Between 1964 and 1970 the fishing industry grew 29 percent and there was a 33 percent growth in transportation, a 26 percent increase in trade and banking, and a 21 percent increase in services. By the beginning of 1971 there were twenty-eight commercial banks in South Vietnam, not including rural banks. Despite the war, capitalism was on the move in South Vietnam.[22]

Nine

AMERICAN WITHDRAWAL

IN SEPTEMBER 1970 I was most pleasantly surprised and honored to receive a letter written to me in August by President Nixon. Ward Just had passed along to him a copy of *Village in Vietnam,* and the letter expressed Mr. Nixon's thanks. In it he said, "Our understanding of the Vietnamese people, their customs and way of life, has never been what it should be. Hopefully your study of that country, in the microcosm of a single village, will do something to correct that."[1]

I found it very interesting but not very encouraging that Mr. Nixon, president of the United States, would, in August 1970, observe frankly that we, the Americans, lacked understanding of the Vietnamese, their customs and way of life. The pall of vincible ignorance had yet to be dispelled by knowledge, however rudimentary.

But then I had become acutely aware during my Vietnam years that pursuit of knowledge was sadly lacking among Americans dealing with the war. I had no illusions that the letters, reports, "think pieces," and other written analyses I had made available to the American Mission in Saigon and officials in Washington had serious readers who might consider the information one way or another in formulating ideas for dealing with the situation in South Vietnam. Nor did I have any illusions that by and large, with few exceptions, the RAND staff in Santa Monica and Washington would behave any differently.

I had at first naively expected reflection to be intrinsic to decision-making in Saigon, Washington, and Santa Monica. But in time I became aware that Washington was an incredibly unreflective place. It was (and still is) a swamp of mediocrity made worse by having an excessive number of mediocre people with power fantasies. One result is that nothing stirs them into thinking, into a mode of reflection. When in 1962 John Donnell and I briefed in Washington on the misdirection of the Strategic Hamlet Program the reaction was to pressure RAND into changing our findings rather than heeding the warning. I concluded that Washington was like a ten-ton marshmallow; if one gave it a good kick, nothing happened. It just sat there, mushy and immutable.

And while there were reflective people at RAND they were scarce among the physicists, political scientists, and economists who held sway in Santa Monica.

By 1970 the only information on Vietnam that excited people in Saigon, Washington, and Santa Monica was statistical. The American Mission relied on the Hamlet Evaluation System to give it a picture of the situation in rural South Vietnam while RAND and the Department of Defense had unshakable faith in systems analysis. Both approaches yielded fictional versions of what was really taking place in Vietnam: they were effective forms of self-delusion.

By this time I thought it was patently clear that the statistical approach was yielding few encouraging results in pacification efforts. I was mistaken. While there was an awareness that pacification was not going as well as everyone would have liked, the statistically-minded simply said that the problem lay in lack of statistics about such things as "what was happening in the villages," a reference to whether administrative changes legislated since 1965 had affected village government and society. Subsumed were questions of peasants' attitudes toward village leaders and the Saigon government.

By mid 1970, as Vietnamization proceeded with the withdrawal of U.S. forces, it was imperative that pacification be moving along smoothly, a sure sign of successful Vietnamese performance in assuming responsibility for conducting the war.

The pace of American troop withdrawals was measurable. On 8 June 1969 Presidents Nixon and Thieu had ended a one-day summit meeting on Midway Island to discuss Vietnamization and announced that by the end of August 25,000 American military force would be withdrawn from South Vietnam. As of the end of 1969 there were 321,600 American military personnel remaining in Vietnam (and by the end of 1970 this figure would drop to 250,342). Among the units that departed was the U.S. Fourth Infantry, which closed its Pleiku headquarters in March. By mid 1970, some Bachelor Enlisted Quarters on Boulevard Tran Hung Dao had closed. The Rex Bachelor Officers' Quarters in downtown Saigon had shut its doors. The closure of the dreary International Club on Boulevard Nguyen Hue signaled the cutback in the civilian contractors who frequented it.

Success of a turnover to the South Vietnamese military of responsibility for fighting the war was, however, not measurable. While American officials paid high praise to Vietnamization and the improved performance of Saigon leaders such as President Thieu, Vietnamese and knowledgeable Americans outside the Mission had different views. They characterized Vietnamization as Americanization, a program to saddle the Vietnamese with the huge, costly war machine that thus far had not worked well for the Americans. On 3 April 1970 I had a discussion about it with Mr. Duyet, director of the Post, Telephone, and Telegraph (PTT) who lamented that the Americans wanted the Vietnamese to take over the complicated and costly communications system they had set up in South Vietnam. "Why do we need 2,000 circuits to Danang?" Then there were the support facilities. A Vietnamese major related that MACV coerced the South Vietnamese Army into taking over the U.S. 1st Division base at Lai Khe by promising to pay Pacific Architects and Engineers, a costly contractor, to maintain the facility. The major shook his head when he pointed out that the U.S. 1st Division needed two battalions to secure the base, something the South Vietnamese Army could ill afford. Some of the young American military advisers expressed concern that we had generated among the Vietnamese commanders too much dependence on American air support. This was graphically demonstrated in the Tet Offensive. An adviser to General Giai, commander of an ARVN division in Quang Tri province, said that the general had asked that the Americans provide B-52s over the DMZ on a twenty-four hour basis so if his units made contact they could call for air strikes by the big bombers.

In late April 1970, Pham Kim Ngoc, a friend from the late 1950s and now minister of the economy, expressed his frustration in trying to increase revenues at a time of soaring prices and rising unemployment as American forces withdrew. Poor Ngoc stumbled when he sought to tax newsprint which precipitated a newspaper strike. Without any support from President Thieu, Ngoc had to abolish the new tax. Then, he said, everyone at the American Mission was optimistically predicting that by the end of 1970 South Vietnam would be self-sufficient in rice when in truth, some 500,000 metric tons would have to be imported. Also, the Vietnamese had become dependent on American-imported commodities such as gasoline, white sugar (preferred to the local brown cane sugar), and cooking oil (that had replaced the practice of larding).

I had not anticipated that by mid 1970, Vietnamization would put me in a position where I had to reiterate to RAND the importance of completing my research on highland leadership in order to resist getting involved in research on Vietnamese village society that would "benefit" the pacification effort. Robert Komer, who had left CORDS and returned to Washington, was hired by RAND Santa Monica, and in June 1970 he replaced Jim Digby as program manager for defense studies, making him responsible for the contracts with ARPA/AGILE which included those for the RAND projects in Vietnam. This was not good news because I knew all too well that Komer considered the highlanders a relatively unimportant segment of the South Vietnamese population, so research on them by someone who already had done field work in Vietnamese villages was a waste.

I realized also that an underlying problem was the change that had taken place at the RAND Corporation since the 1967 retirement of Frank Collbohm who had preserved a spirit of independent research. He had been replaced by Harry Rowen from the Department of Defense and RAND's spirit of independent research began to give way to a posture of pleasing the client.

In July 1970 Komer (who was billing himself as "Ambassador Komer") and Digby visited Saigon, and one afternoon they met with the small RAND staff (Joan Allen, Chuck Benoit, Andy Sweetland, Ted Serong, and I). Komer began his presentation with the threatening news that budgets for research were being cut. He followed that with his view that nonetheless there were possibilities for expanded research. For RAND, this meant we should play a more important role in research focused at the Vietnamese village level. He cited a recent village survey done by another contract group as the kind of thing that was needed. Discussion on current RAND research followed and Komer suggested that RAND could contribute more than it had thus far. I raised my hand to point out to Komer and Digby that we made distributions of our reports and memoranda (some of which I cited) to the American decision-makers but they did not read them. I was surprised to hear Komer admit that was true. Then I was even more surprised at his admission that when he was at CORDS he did not make use of the expertise and valuable reports of research groups in Vietnam such as RAND.

A dinner at Colby's barnlike villa drew a large VIP group of all the high-ranking Vietnamese generals and American CORDS officials. Digby and I were the only RAND people invited and we were seated at a fringe table (where Digby sniffed at the "middling cuisine" and rosé wine which he whispered tasted like "something that should be served with ham sandwiches at a picnic"). In response to a toast, Komer stood up and held forth on his achievements in Vietnam (such as successful pacification, containing the American military, and getting on with the Vietnamese officials).

Soon after the Komer-Digby visit I prepared a 20 July 1970 memorandum emphasizing the importance of resolving highland land claims as a means of rallying greater pro-government sentiment among the highlanders. Owning land would also serve to motivate highland villagers to participate in economic development programs. I had learned from American journalists in Saigon that it was advisable to have a lead line and/or short paragraph that would capture the reader's attention. My lead paragraph was also intended to underline the strategic role of the highlands in 1970. It read: "As U.S. military forces continue to withdraw from South Vietnam it is inevitable that increased Communist pressure will be brought to bear in the central highlands. This would be a continuing pattern, for the most intense military activity of the present war has been in the highlands. Significantly, the 1965 Communist attempt at cutting South Vietnam in half—an attempt which prompted the decision to send in U.S. combat units—was concentrated in the uplands. It is not beyond the realm of possibility that such an attempt will be made again in the same area."[2]

I had also learned that, while Eva Kim handed my memos to Ambassador Bunker and John Kirk, the MACV science adviser, passed them on to General Abrams, it was good to deliver most of them myself. When I delivered this memo to Colby's office, he asked me to step inside for a chat. He pointed out that the U.S. Mission lacked information on the current situation with village government, and he asked whether I thought it would be possible to find this out through research, particularly in the Mekong River delta. I replied that I thought it would, whereupon he asked whether RAND might be interested in doing it. I said perhaps David Elliott, who was coming back to Vietnam for RAND to do research in the Mekong River delta, might be of assistance.

I wrote to Komer in Santa Monica describing this meeting. Komer replied that he had suggested such research to Colby and they both agreed that I would be the one to do it. After emphasizing "real budget cuts," he said, "I have striven hard to save a full man-year to cover your continued useful participation out there. But it goes without saying that the more immediately useful work you have under way, *in response to specific field requests,* the better we can defend your cause."[3]

And so the handwriting was on the wall. I was in Cambodia when Komer's letter arrived. Returning to Vietnam I was determined to immerse myself in field work to complete my study of highland leadership and record more ethnography.

By this time I also had become the official collector of ethnographic materials from Vietnam for the Smithsonian Institution. During visits to Washington I often contacted Eugene Knez, associate curator for Asia at the Smithsonian Institution whom I had long known. On several occasions we had discussed the possibility of starting a Vietnam ethnographic collection. In February 1970, Eugene had written that the Department of Anthropology at the Museum of Natural History and the Smithsonian Institution agreed to fund such a collection and Eugene recommended me to do it.[4] On 24 March 1970 I had written to Fred Iklé in Santa Monica to obtain RAND approval. In the letter I emphasized the importance, given the war's destruction, of preserving ethnographic materials from Vietnam. I noted that collecting Cham art was particularly pressing because of the black market in what were supposed to be Cham carvings. A 1970 scandal had revealed that a Vietnamese member of the lower house had Cham carvings he claimed villagers outside of Hue had sold him, and he intended sending them to the United States. But the villagers, who venerated the statues (they usually do) protested to the district chief, and the culprit was arrested. Peter Arnett had recently told me that two Frenchmen were caught trying to force their way into the Cham Museum in Danang to steal pieces they intended to sell in Saigon. On the day I wrote the letter to Iklé, Sean Flynn, a photographer (and son of actor Errol Flynn), had shown me a "Cham" figure, one of several that two South Vietnamese army officers were selling. Iklé's response was that RAND had no objection to my collecting materials for the Smithsonian as long as I did it on my own time.

The first week of September 1970 I went to Nhatrang where highlander refugees were located on the edge of the city. With the help of Ernie Lee, the SIL linguist studying the Roglai language, we gathered data on an impoverished camp, and I wrote a memorandum describing the situation and suggesting some remedies.[5] Nhatrang, which in the late 1950s had been an idyllic place, was now very crowded and squalid. Hotels built during the war were very tacky and gangs of teen-age Vietnamese crowded around the entrances to surround and attack foreigners, picking their pockets and ripping off watches.

I went on to Kontum where I was invited by Dominic d'Antonio, a former Special Forces captain, to stay at the USAID house in a small compound on the bank of the Bla River with a pleasant view of Bahnar rice fields and majestic stands of bamboo. There were meetings with highland leaders and visits to villages where, among other things, I gathered for the Smithsonian artifacts such as backbaskets and crossbows, which Jim Cooper, the SIL linguist working on the Halang language, agreed to store in his house. Dr. Pat Smith had gone on leave to the United States, and Dr. Hoffman, her young replacement, was somewhat overwhelmed at the inundation of patients in the hospital which since the 1968 Tet Offensive had been located in a former school. I was shocked at the MACV compound which in the past had been an orderly post. Now it had an air of neglect; bunker sandbags were falling apart, the grounds were strewn with litter, and the officers' latrine was marred with graffiti. One evening we went to the Enlisted Men's Club to watch a film. The men in the club were behaving strangely, wobbling and giggling as they tried to get the movie going. The corporal tending bar laughed as he pointed out that "they are too high on pot to get the film into the projector."

On the weekend of 1 November 1970 a full alert was declared in Kontum. The Vietnamese military had intelligence of two North Vietnamese battalions massing south of the city for an assault. At the USAID compound, brakes screeched as an American army major in full combat gear rushed in to order Dominic and me (as he had just ordered Pat Smith's staff) to evacuate to the MACV compound. He sped away in a cloud of dust. We had twenty-five former CIDG Bahnar to guard the USAID compound so, given the sorry state of the MACV compound, Dominic and I decided to remain. By 8:00 P.M. Kontum was a dark, silent town. Dominic suggested we visit the Special Forces B-24 detachment, and we entered to find a bizarre scene. The troopers were having a party with lots of food and drink. Their guests —"The Girls"— a group of Vietnamese bar hustlers, were led by Helen, a skinny little madam dressed in a bushy sweater and miniskirt, her dyed hair piled high, clicking around in high heels. The American troopers did not believe the alert and they were right. There was no assault, but the Communists did fire rockets into Kontum, none of which, thank heaven, landed near Cooper's house.

From Kontum I went to Cheo Reo, and Dr Hoffman, who was interested in establishing a hospital there, accompanied me. Nay Luett informed me that Oi Anhot, the King of Fire, was ill and had been brought to the town. We went to see him, and Dr. Hoffman diagnosed a stroke and began treatment.

Back in Saigon, on 12 November 1970 I wrote to Eugene at the Smithsonian with news that I had obtained materials (including women's skirts, loincloths, carved pipes, fish traps, winnowing baskets, and knives) which I documented (photos, provenance, use, and location of ethnic group on a map). The American Research and Development compound where RAND now had a small office agreed to transport the collection from the highlands on their aircraft and mail the smaller items to Washington.

A vacation, late in November 1970 on Penang island off the coast of Malaysia provided a needed rest. It also provided time to reflect. One result was that I decided to leave Vietnam around June 1971. A year or two writing at an American university would be ideal. I decided to write to Professor Fred Eggan under whom I had studied at the Anthropology Department of the University of Chicago. It would be nice to return to Chicago, be close to my family, and savor the scholarly atmosphere of the university. It would be bliss to be away from the Vietnam War.

Back in Vietnam my cook fixed a Christmas turkey dinner for my guests, Joan Allen, Pat Hughes, Arthur Dommen (of the *Los Angeles Times*), Jorgen Skakke (a Danish journalist), and Charley Tuoi (publisher of the *Vietnam Guardian*).

With 1971 and the changing American military presence in Vietnam there was a flurry of interest in the new role of the adviser. At the invitation of John Kirk, the science adviser, I spent New Year's Eve at Cu Chi with the U.S. Advisory Team for the ARVN 25th Infantry Division. The team had just moved into the huge facility recently abandoned by the U.S. 25th Division. It was strange, almost startling, to see the normally bustling facility standing like a ghost town with silent streets and roads, and empty clubs, PX, and office buildings. GI huts were beginning to get a run-down look and bunkers were crumbling. With eleven kilometers of perimeter requiring a full battalion to secure, I wondered how the Vietnamese could maintain such a facility. Then the advisers described how Communist troops had the night before entered a village only four kilometers away, killing nineteen of the defenders. It sounded like Cu Chi in 1962 when John Donnell and I had visited it.

One result of Vietnamization I had not anticipated was new, harsh forced relocations in the highlands by the Vietnamese military. With the American troops withdrawing and the Vietnamese assuming greater responsibility for conduct of the war, in mid 1970 Gen. Ngo Dzu, the new commander of II Corps, issued an order stating that by 31 October 1970 there would be no more "D or C hamlets" (in the Hamlet Evaluation System, D and C hamlets were not under government control) in the region. His method of attaining this goal was to launch a massive resettlement of highland villages in areas that were supposed to be "insecure." The first phase of this effort took place in the northwestern portion of Buon Ho district, north of Ban Me Thuot, where, General Dzu claimed, the Jarai Krung population was lending support to the Communists by supplying them with rice and recruits. The 23d Division made a "sweep" of the area, and Regional and Popular Forces were sent in to move the villagers. By early 1971 large numbers of Jarai Krung were being relocated. At a January conference in Nhatrang at this time, the American senior advisers in Darlac province reported that "all of the villagers are happy to move." Kurt Sawatzky, a volunteer for the Vietnam Christian Service in Darlac, however, informed me that he had visited the relocated highlanders and found an appalling situation. The villagers had to leave most of their possessions behind, the Vietnamese soldiers looted, and the resettlement center lacked tents and water.

On 5 February 1971, Y Puk Buon Ya, a young Rhadé leader, and I went to the Buon Kli resettlement center. One group of villagers reported that in the vicinity of their former village there had been some Viet Cong activity since 1964 and they had asked the district chief to "improve security," but nothing was done. They requested permission to move but nothing was forthcoming. The Viet Cong entered their villages twice a month to engage in propaganda and to "tax" each longhouse a 250-gram can of rice. This forced the villagers to purchase rice in Buon Ho town. Y Puk and I found that what Sawatzky had reported was all too accurate. The villagers had been given a three-day notice that they would be moved, and they left most of their possessions, including valuable gongs and jars, which were then looted by Vietnamese soldiers. Two villages were burned to the ground. The new settlement was located on a barren, windy hill devoid of trees and water. Villagers were only given tin roofing, so they scoured nearby forests for building materials. The result was an assortment of shabby structures of gnarled logs and weathered deadwood.

I wrote a memorandum concerning the situation and managed to get a copy to Hoang Duc Nha, kinsman of Thieu and an eminence grise in the Independence Palace.[6] He in turn brought it to the attention of Thieu, who advised General Dzu to discuss it with me. The general and I did discuss it, but it was futile. Dzu went ahead with relocations, and by April 1971 an estimated 40,000 from 100 to 150 villages had been relocated. There were reports of Viet Cong moving into some of the abandoned villages to begin farming the paddy fields. In the resettlement centers there was an increase in sickness and deaths. Nay Luett visited a large group of Jarai who had been forced from their villages and found them living in the open with no shelters and poor drinking water. Many were sick and dying. The doctors from the Vietnam Christian Service Hospital in Pleiku found a deplorable situation in two settlements where three hundred villagers had died since being moved. Those involved in Pat Smith's Village Health Worker program reported that between 1 and 5 May 1971 some seventy-five children died of a cholera-like ailment in a relocated Bahnar village. Then, the Communists attacked the village on 19 May, prompting a South Vietnamese Army reaction that resulted in thirty-seven dead, many wounded and twenty-nine houses destroyed.

Some American journalists investigated the relocation situation. My views were reported by *New York Times* writer Gloria Emerson and by *Washington Post* correspondent Peter Osnos.[7] Early in April 1971 I had a long discussion about the relocations with William Colby, head of

CORDS, and since he had been in Vietnam in the late 1950s, I recalled the trouble resulting from forced relocations at that time. We were joined by John Paul Vann. I continued to outline the reasons why the resettlements would best be halted. En route back to Saigon, Vann told me that he soon would be named senior adviser in II Corps and he would do what he could for the highland people. On assuming this position, he immediately organized an Office for Highland Affairs to deal with programs for the highlanders. By May it was evident that Colby and Vann had decided to bring pressure to end the relocations. Early in June, General Dzu let it be known that he wanted to resettle ten thousand more highland villagers but that "American sensitivity prevented it."

A bright ray of hope at this time was the emergence of my friend Nay Luett as the most dynamic and dedicated highland leader. He had held various administrative posts and had received considerable formal training (Lycée Yersin, the National Institute of Administration, and the International Rice Research Institute in the Philippines). He spoke Jarai, Rhadé, Bahnar, Vietnamese, French, and English. Luett also had become adept at dealing with American and Vietnamese officials. At the same time, Nay Luett had retained his ties with highland traditions, and whenever possible he returned to his wife's village near Cheo Reo to work in the fields and enjoy "the rousseauean ambience of village life."

Nay Luett also was very concerned about preserving the ways of the highlanders while still organizing social and economic programs to raise their standards of living and prepare them to compete economically with the Vietnamese. Early in 1970 we had visited Plei Bahrong (also known as Plei Potao), the home of the King of Fire, a figure Luett viewed as representative of Jarai tradition. First we stopped to pick up Siu Choi, son of the King of Fire's sister and likely successor to the king. (An elderly man in the village was excited to meet Nay Luett, about whom he had heard so much, but he was disappointed that the leader, a slight, wiry, dark-skinned man was not "big and light like an American.") With fifteen longhouses, the village was tranquil and had none of the modern touches (such as metal roofs) found in many other villages. We spent the day with the King of Fire, who, like an ordinary villager, had been preparing his fields for planting. Luett treated him with great deference.

During 1970 and early 1971, Nay Luett and a small group composed of Touneh Han Tho (of the Chru elite) and Pierre K'briuh (of the Sre elite),

Minister Nay Luett and Director General Toplui Pierre K'briuh at a
highland refugee camp, 1971.

both of whom had been fellow students with Luett at the Lycée Yersin, met
frequently to discuss the fate of the highland people in the face of continuing war and disastrous relocation programs, such as the one taking place on
orders from Gen. Ngo Dzu. On 13 June 1971, President Thieu announced
changes in his cabinet and Nay Luett was named the new minister of the
MDEM. Luett appointed Touneh Han Tho as secretary general and Pierre
K'briuh as director general. One of those instrumental in Nay Luett's
appointment was Hoang Duc Nha, Thieu's kinsman, who had gone to the
Lycée Yersin with Luett and the other highlanders and had played together
with them on the soccer team. Soon there was talk around Saigon of the
"Lycée Yersin mafia."

Nay Luett and his group immediately began to formulate strategies for
coping with highland problems such as land-grabbing by Vietnamese. (One
elderly Bahnar said to Pat Smith, "We were here long before anyone else
came. We now may be the first to disappear and even then, the soil that cov-
ers our graves will be taken.") Another pressing problem was the swelling
number of refugees, particularly in I Corps where security was rapidly

crumbling following the Lam Son 719 campaign mounted by the Vietnamese army early in 1971. In January the North Vietnamese began moving thirty-one thousand new soldiers southward along the Ho Chi Minh trail. This prompted Operation Lam Son 719 with the goal of invading Laos to cut the Ho Chi Minh trail with sixteen thousand troops (including the elite Ranger and Airborne elements) and heavy U.S. military support. The operation began on 8 February along Route 9. The South Vietnamese forces rolled through the Ai Lao pass and in Laos captured Tchepone, where they were savagely assaulted by the North Vietnamese using Russian and Chinese rockets, 130-mm artillery, and effective antiaircraft weapons that took a heavy toll on Vietnamese and American helicopters. Although Thieu proclaimed it a great success, Lam Son 719 was generally conceded to have been a debacle for the government forces which suffered heavy losses. In a chilling comment on Vietnamization, an American army officer who was in Khe Sanh at the time later told me that he and other advisers reported to their superiors that Lam Son 719 convinced them that the South Vietnamese forces were no match for the North Vietnamese.

When in Saigon, the late afternoon was a good time to walk to Tu Do (former Catinat) Street where I usually ran into someone I knew at Café Givral, Café Brodard, La Pagode, or the terrace of the Hotel Continental Palace. One of those I often met was Pham Xuan An who was an assistant to Bob Shaplen of the *New Yorker* and to Kevin Buckley, bureau chief for *Newsweek*. An was a southerner who was experienced in journalism and politics, and, over coffee, we had very interesting discussions about current events. Often he would come to my apartment for Vietnamese food. When Bob Shaplen was in Saigon, An and I would go to his room (overlooking the square in front of the National Assembly) at the Hotel Continental Palace where a variety of people gathered. They included journalists, among them Jean Claude Pomonti of *Le Monde,* George McArthur of the *Los Angeles Times,* Keyes Beech of the *Chicago Daily News,* and old Vietnam hands such as Lou Conein. From time to time, Vietnamese officials, including Gen. Tran Van Don, would appear.

I also would stop to chat with Gloria Emerson at the *New York Times* office. We often recalled the Vietnam of the late 1950s and compared notes on the current situation. Gloria went into the field to get her stories, staying with the troops and contacting some of their families when she returned to Saigon. Craig Whitney was bureau chief and favored all of us one day with a beautiful organ concert featuring Handel's *Messiah* at the Cathedral of Our Lady. At the *Washington Post* office next door, the impressive staff included Don Oberdorfer, Peter Osnos, and Robert Kaiser (who with his bright wife, Hannah, gave very interesting dinner parties). The secretary was Jolynne d'Ornano, an attractive lady who had been a research assistant of Wesley Fishel at Michigan State University and had married Pierre d'Ornano, a charming French businessman of Corsican birth. I often met Jolynne at the National Museum where she and Toby Pyle (wife of Associated Press reporter Dick Pyle) were doing an admirable job of restoring the collection of porcelains.

All of us were shocked at the 23 February 1971 news of François Sully's death with Gen. Do Cao Tri in a helicopter crash. Kevin Buckley and I attended his funeral in the small chapel of the Grall Hospital, where the French chaplain gave the eulogy. We joined the other mourners in the cortege that moved slowly through the streets to the Mac Dinh Chi cemetery (where Joan Allen's husband was buried).

A very interesting visitor at this time was Arthur T. Hadley, a well-known journalist who also had written books and plays. Arthur had been a senior editor at *Newsweek* and his expertise on the American military brought him to Vietnam. Kevin introduced us, and I was happy to offer Arthur Vietnamese meals during which we discussed the condition of the U.S. forces at this time of American disengagement.

In April 1971 Bob Shaplen and I received invitations from Senator William Fulbright to appear as witnesses before his U.S. Senate Committee on Foreign Relations on 13 May regarding a McGovern-Hatfield bill (Vietnam Disengagement Act of 1971) which called for a "safe and systematic withdrawal of remaining American Armed Forces by December 31, 1971." The other witness was Don Luce, former head of IVS in Vietnam and now with the World Council of Churches. We accepted and began working on statements.

On 1 May 1971, Nguyen Van Bong, rector of the National Institute of Administration and head of the southern, intellectual National Progressivist Movement Party, came to see me. I had long known Bong, a very intelligent and capable nationalist whose popularity was well deserved. He had heard that Bob and I were going to testify before the Fulbright committee, and he was interested in what I was going to say. He already had read both versions of the accommodation-coalition RAND reports, and I indicated that my statement would be a brief reiteration of the more recent version. I added that the accommodation-coalition approach's success depended on Thieu and the military loosening their monopoly on political power to make way for the NLF to participate. Bong agreed and explained that his party intended to support Thieu in the coming presidential elections because he promised to share political power with civilians after his victory. Bong clearly hoped to be named to a high position (such as prime minister). When I asked Bong what would happen if Thieu failed to make good his promise, he replied, "There would be trouble by the end of the year."

On 3 May 1971, Kevin Buckley came to my small, book-lined apartment for an interview (I had been expecting to leave Vietnam in June). I pointed out that the old French books and journals told us about strategies considered new by American planners in 1971.[8] One journal, for example, had French General Leclerc saying that he was building a new Vietnamese army to take over from the French. "The French had pacification programs and we have pacification programs," I observed. "Through the years the same strategies have been used with different names but the same old mistakes have been made." One cause was lack of institutional memory in the American organization because of the short tours of duty. Another factor was the American determination to emphasize the positive no matter how bad the news. The ubiquitous progress reports did just that, always reporting progress no matter what. Kevin asked about Vietnamization and I responded, "We will not know if it (Vietnamization) can work until the Vietnamese military looks over his shoulder and sees no American there. When there are no Americans here, then we will know if Vietnamization can work."

As the date of the Fulbright hearings approached I had a recurring dream where I was seated in a leather chair surrounded by an imposing large room with columns, facing a semicircular row of august men with the look of those sitting in judgment. My feeling was one of being overpowered. In Washington, Lynn and Jim Hendry offered me warm hospitality for which I was particularly grateful because, since my statement was based on my accommodation-coalition approach to end the Vietnam War, the atmosphere at the RAND office was, to say the least, cool. Nonetheless, Dotty Manning, a no-nonsense former journalist whom RAND had hired because she knew "the hill" extremely well, offered excellent advice. First of all, she was sure that Mr. Fulbright would welcome my views, but she warned, he had a way of putting words in witnesses' mouths. Then, she pointed out that, with a clerk recording the proceedings, it is important to compose responses so as to avoid half-sentences in the Congressional Record. Before responding, she said, draw a deep breath and take a sip of the ice water (this may seem an eternity) and then respond. Finally, pointing out that Fulbright would be wearing his sun-visor to shield him from the glaring klieg lights for the television cameras, Dotty recommended wearing very light clothes.

After a good night's rest, at 9:00 A.M. I arrived at Room 4221, New Senate Office building for the 10:00 A.M. meeting. I walked into the almost empty room to find it exactly as it had been in the recurring dream. A feeling of dread was stirring when Bob Shaplen came in and we were taken to Senator Fulbright's office where a secretary informed us that Don Luce, who was suffering from fever, would be late. Back in the imposing room which was coming alive with people, cameras, and klieg lights, we were seated in leather chairs. Senators Fulbright (wearing his sun-visor), Symington, Pell, McGee, Muskie, Spong, Aiken, Case, and Pearson took their places in the semicircular row. I thanked heaven that Bob was there to divert my attention from the dream scene. When Senator Fulbright called on me to proceed, I took a deep breath and calmly read my statement, looking up for effect at the faces of the august senators. In conclusion I pointed out that in the accommodation process leading to a coalition, the important thing is for all of the parties concerned to make compromises. "If they do so the conflict will end, but if, for whatever reasons, they are unwilling to do so, the war, like a dismal low-pressure monsoon rain, will go on and on."[9]

Bob (who was suffering in heavy clothes under the hot klieg lights) presented a longer statement that viewed our role in Vietnam in the broader Asian context, and touched on the possibility of political accommodations as a way of permitting the United States to disengage. Luce had no prepared statement, submitting instead three letters written by Vietnamese anti-Thieu dissidents (which Senator Fulbright pointed out did not really address the matter at hand).

Mr. Fulbright asked me how accommodations are "carried on." I responded that it is a process of bargaining between two parties with mutual compromises to arrive at an agreement from which both sides benefit.

Basically it has to do with the rules of politics such as were demonstrated by Nguyen Cao Ky when in 1966 he made a deal with the Hoa Hao religious sect and rallied their support, bringing a large part of the western Mekong River delta to the government's side. I noted that the political accommodation process in Vietnam "is not some kind of mysterious oriental puzzle that somehow the Western mind cannot grasp." Bringing it closer to home I said it involves the kind of accommodations that I had seen taking place as I grew up in the old 14th ward on Chicago's south side. "It's sort of basic ward politics with an oriental hue." I added that surely such quid pro quo arrangements take place here in Washington, which drew a smile from Fulbright who simply said, "Sometimes."

The Fulbright hearings were the last time I publicly advocated accommodation-coalition as a means of ending the Vietnam War.

While in Washington for the Fulbright hearings, I was contacted by Philip Ross, staff officer at the National Research Council, asking if I could meet with him and Dr. Anton Lang concerning a study on the use of defoliants in Vietnam. I knew that the American Anthropological Association and many academics had been strongly criticizing the use of herbicides in Vietnam. In 1970 I had been contacted by Harvard biologist Dr. Matthew Meselson, who was in Vietnam on an inspection of highland areas where the spraying had been done. We met several times, and I gave him information on the ethnic groups located in these areas. I met in Washington with Ross and Lang to discuss their proposed study, and they expressed interest in my being part of it. I declined because of my crowded schedule and also because at that time I considered forced relocation of highlanders a more damaging program.

Dark days lay ahead for me, not in Vietnam but back in Chicago. For, if my accommodation-coalition approach earned me the reputation in some American political circles of being a heretic, my being in Vietnam with the RAND corporation earned me pariah status among my academic colleagues.

While vacationing on the island of Penang early in December 1970, I had written to Fred Eggan, my professor at the Anthropology Department in the University of Chicago. I had kept in touch with Fred and sent copies of my RAND reports and memos. In the letter I said I felt I had done all I could to bring my training and experience to bear in trying to help the highlanders. I reminded Fred that I had advocated ending the war through a process of political accommodations leading to a coalition government (I had sent him copies of my RAND reports on this subject). I was worn out, and I would like to return to the United States to write up my ethnographic materials in the quiet atmosphere of a university.

On 17 December 1970 Fred responded with news that he had consulted Norton Ginsburg, a professor in the Geography Department under whom I had functioned as editor for the 1955 *Area Handbook on Laos*. I also had studied economic geography of Southeast Asia with Norton. Both Fred and Norton had served on my doctoral committee. They were "delighted" with the prospect of my returning, and began arranging for a research associate appointment, but funds, which were low because of budget cuts, would have to be found outside of the university. The Ford Foundation was a possibility if RAND did not provide funding. Fred also warned, "There is also a strong feeling on the part of some students and a few of the faculty about research for the government and an even stronger feeling about classified research." He added, "I tell you these things not to discourage you but to let you know the situation. (The AAA [American Anthropological Association] has had a big blowup about research in Thailand.)" Fred ended the letter with, "I think you've done a great job for the Montagnards, and I hope that we can get you here, one way or another."[10]

Norton wrote on 3 March 1971, "At long last, a letter concerning developments about your coming here. The main thing is that the news is good."[11] Norton mentioned several funding possibilities (through the Committee on Southern Asian Studies and the Center for International Studies) and pointed out that the appointment would undoubtedly be a research associate, but that "it mattered little, and we'll work it out in the end." I wrote back to Fred and Norton to express my deep appreciation for their help. Norton wrote again on 22 March to say that Fred was dealing with the Department of Anthropology concerning an appointment. He observed, "People seem to be singularly up tight these days about research carried on in Southeast Asia. Be that as it may, however, there is money for you to stay here and the point of attachment is a minor issue."[12]

A memorandum dated 11 March 1971 from Fred Eggan to Bernard S. Cohn, chairman of the Department of Anthropology, proposed that the department "appoint Dr. Gerald C. Hickey as a Research Associate for the year 1971–72, to facilitate the writing up of his ethnographic materials on the Montagnards of the Vietnamese Highlands. His research complements my own on the Mountain Province, Philippines, and he would be working in the Philippine Studies Program of the Committee of South and Southeast Asia."[13] Fred made it explicit that "the Department will be under no obligation to provide funds or working space, nor are there any commitments beyond one year." Fred pointed out that I was "distantly related to the Lichtstern family" (my mother's sister Cecille had married Edward Sickle, son of Gertrude Lichtstern), which had contributed generously to the University of Chicago. He attached a curriculum vitae and a complete bibliography of my writings, which, along with our correspondence, he made available to the faculty, and he included my Vietnam address should any of the faculty wish to contact me personally. Fred stated, "I am personally convinced that Hickey has acted throughout as an anthropologist and I find no evidence of any violation of ethnic standards, as I have practiced them and as I have tried to teach them to graduate students."

Fred wrote on 15 March that the Policy Committee on South Asia tentatively approved the appointment subject to assurances that the "fellowship" was not to write a report for RAND, subject to RAND or Defense Department censorship. He also reported that in view of the students becoming more radical as the war expands rather than contracts, a few members of the Anthropology Department "are worried at what 'secret' research you may have been doing for the army." He added that if the department is badly split on that issue, it "may be difficult."[14]

On 21 March 1971 I wrote to Fred expressing regret that my affiliation with the RAND Corporation was causing him problems at the University of Chicago. I emphasized the spirit of independent research that had guided RAND when I joined the staff in 1964, a spirit that continued to guide me, pointing out that RAND had not had any of its research reports subject to censorship by the funding agencies. Completed reports were only reviewed by RAND staff. Often, reports question the efficacy of clients' programs causing some ruffled feathers, but the evaluations and recommendations were never changed. I cited the critical 1962 study of the Strategic Hamlet Program that John Donnell and I had done and my recent "Accommodation and Coalition in Vietnam" report which was not popular with some people in Washington and at RAND. Neither report was altered. Any parts of reports that had been classified were, by 1971, declassified. There never was any "secret research."

*   *   *

On 27 March 1971, Arthur Hadley wrote from his Martha's Vineyard home to say that he was in touch with Fred Eggan about obtaining funds. Funds were not available from a New Haven foundation, but Arthur was prepared to make a non-tax gift of $3,500 from profits of a new book. *Playboy* magazine had accepted the article on the American military that he had researched in Vietnam.[15]

On 5 April 1971 Fred wrote, "The department met today and voted against an appointment for you next year. Needless to say I am very sorry since I was hoping to have you here this coming year. But since you wrote the new escalations in Laos and Cambodia, and the activities of the AAA Ethics Committee in regard to Thailand have stirred everybody up and all decisions are emotional rather than intellectual."[16] Of the fifteen faculty members present only three voted in favor of me. Two of them were Fred and Lloyd Fallers.

The bad news was rendered worse when later Fred told me that no one came to his office to look at the materials he had made available. Nor had any of the faculty contacted me in Vietnam. And so the pall of vincible ignorance that long had hung over Vietnam now cast its shadow on the groves of academe.

I responded to Fred on 12 April to say how disappointed I was in the rejection which I felt was made worse by the fact that emotions rather than reason ruled the decision. It was, I felt, a malaise that would have a damaging effect on scholarly research in Southeast Asia. I reminded Fred that none of my research had been funded as a grant. I always had jobs. It was ironic that some professors lamented the lack of American scholarship in Indochina when foundations that they had the wherewithal to influence had not supported any research in Indochina for the past fifteen years.

On that same day (12 April) I also wrote to Norton Ginsburg expressing my disappointment. I wondered what the emotionalism in the academic milieu and the polarization on campuses would do to the intellectual tradition in American society. In this environment, I said, it was courageous of Fred and Norton to submit the proposal and voice faith in my integrity.

Meanwhile I had been occupied by the Fulbright hearings and when I returned to Vietnam I continued my work. In June 1971 a field trip took me to Dak To, north of Kontum town, where I stayed at the Vietnam Christian Service house. The atmosphere of Dak To was very strange with sudden outbursts of gunfire: at dinner one night a firefight broke out only two hundred yards from the house. Sleeping was difficult with periodic bursts of artillery and more gunfire all night. I joined Ron Ackerman, the agricultural volunteer who was driving his battered Land Rover to Pleiku. The town, which was dirty, muddy, and piled with garbage, seemed on the brink of anarchy. From the peak of some thirty-six thousand American forces, only three thousand remained. South Vietnamese soldiers were everywhere and we were told that equipment the Americans had given them during the withdrawal was available in the black market. At the CORDS club, sloppy American soldiers sat about drinking beer making blunt remarks about taking "stuff to mama-san" to sell. One laughed as he told how the U.S. Army Military Police's Criminal Investigation Division (CID which he called "El Cid") was on his "tail" because he had stolen a Jeep.

Ron wanted to buy some carp fingerlings at the government fishery in a beautiful valley near Tan An, southwest of Pleiku. When we reached the valley, Jarai villagers told us it was full of Communist troops so the main road was mined, but we could enter the fishery via a back road that passed through a village. The fishery had a strange air, to say the least. The house of the director had been empty since 1965 and the whole place was overgrown. Still, workers were there and they efficiently used nets to gather fingerlings, pouring them into polyethylene bags into which they shot oxygen. One worker told me there were North Vietnamese troops on the hill behind the fishery, and another told Ron they were in the Jarai village. We drove out with no difficulty and breathed a sigh of relief when we reached Pleiku.

Back in the United States the controversy over anthropologists in Thailand, which had long been brewing, became a cause for deep concern in the American Anthropological Association. On 15 June 1971 in response to a request for information, I wrote to Margaret Mead, chairperson of the Association's Ad Hoc Committee to Evaluate the Thailand Controversy. I simply outlined my contact with anthropologists, notably my friends Clark Cunningham, Charles Keyes, Peter Kunstadter, Bob Kickert, and David and True Marlowe during visits to Thailand. They all were engaged in field research which we discussed and there was nothing to indicate that any of them was involved in anything other than straightforward ethnographic work. Although Bob Kickert worked for the Defense Department I was not aware of any "secret research" he might have been doing. According to Israel Shenker in the *New York Times,* Dr. Mead's committee sent letters of inquiry to 188 anthropologists (fifty-seven replied) and studied six thousand pages of documents.[17]

On 19 November 1971 at the annual meeting of the American Anthropological Association in New York, the council rejected the committee's report which "warned that anthropological data should be safeguarded to prevent its use in warfare, but it exonerated civilian anthropologists of involvement in counterinsurgency." Shenker observed, "An overwhelming majority of the 700 anthropologists at the Meeting at the Statler-Hilton Hotel were clearly unhappy with the language of the report and many felt the counterinsurgency allegations were justified."

In the midst of this turbulent period, on 18 November 1971, the *Wall Street Journal* published an article by my friend Everett G. Martin concerning "McCarthyism of the Left." Two themes in the article were my rejection by the Anthropology Department of the University of Chicago, and also the MIT refusal of his old post teaching economics to Walt W. Rostow, who had served as an assistant for security affairs to President Johnson. The article also reviewed the train of events in the Thailand controversy.

Ev's article began, "To the primitive Montagnard tribes that roam and farm the rolling central highlands of South Vietnam, a Chicago anthropologist named Gerald C. Hickey has been a special friend." Noting that I had tried to protect the highlanders' lands, Ev quoted Samuel Popkin, a Harvard political scientist who had done research in Vietnam—"Gerry's the main reason why there are any Montagnards left at all." Ev added, "One might think this defense of threatened native tribesmen would make Mr. Hickey a hero to American leftists. Not so. In many left-wing circles, Mr. Hickey is, in fact, a pariah."

Ev noted that in my attempt to spend a year at the University of Chicago to write up field research materials, the faculty members in the department "refused to have him." The department, he wrote, "would not discuss the decision, but sources say the professors considered Mr. Hickey's association with Rand reason enough to refuse the request." An "East Coast professor who has observed the Hickey affair" was quoted as saying, "It's the same old Joe McCarthy thing, guilt by association, conviction without trial. Only this time it's being practiced by the kind of people McCarthy made his victims."

"Ironically," Ev pointed out, "Mr. Hickey is himself a 'dove.' He has even testified before the Senate Foreign Relations Committee against the war. To him it would have been immoral to leave the Montagnards without his protection and he felt he could protect them best from inside Rand." Regarding any involvement by anthropologists to use their research findings for the betterment of the people they study, Professor David Schneider was quoted as observing, "If applied anthropologists do good or harm, it's by luck."

While researching for the 18 November 1971 article, Ev Martin had written to me on 20 October to outline his approach.[18] He had interviewed key figures (including the accused anthropologists) in the Thailand controversy, and at the University of Chicago he talked to Bernard Cohn and David Schneider of the Anthropology Department. "Neither Cohn nor Schneider would say anything about you specifically, although Schneider was quite expansive on the general topic of working for the Pentagon no matter what the motives or the job that was done. They both said that the matter had been confined entirely to the Anthropology Department." Ev pointed out that the matter had been treated in an editorial by the *Maroon,* the University of Chicago student newspaper, and it was mentioned by some of the other academics he had interviewed.

I responded to Ev on 29 October 1971, giving him a summary of my correspondence with Fred Eggan and Norton Ginsburg and a run-down on the subsequent events. I pointed out that those who condemn any government support, direct or indirect, scream when Fulbright, National Science Foundation, and other government-funded research agencies have their budgets trimmed. It was disquieting, I said, how few people expressed any real sympathy for my plight. Encouragingly, however, outrage was voiced by some of my journalist friends, including Tom Buckley, Gloria Emerson, Bob Shaplen, Arthur Hadley, and Flora Lewis.

If Ev's article on 18 November caused disquiet, my old friend Nicholas Von Hoffman sent out shock waves with his 3 December broadcast on the CBS radio network's "Spectrum." In it, Nick said that he had known me for over twenty years and advised me not to pay any attention to the "fashionably left professors" who did not want me, whom they considered a "war collaborator," around to write a book. The shock waves obviously penetrated the campus sanctuary of Edward Levi, president of the University of Chicago, who issued a statement contesting both the *Wall Street Journal* article and Nick's CBS broadcast. Reported in the *Chicago Sun-Times* on 8 December 1971, Edward Levi's public statement declared, "I am informed that the question of the appointment for the scholar as a research associate, which is an academic appointment, was raised in the anthropology department where it was deliberated upon, and the decision was made on academic grounds not to recommend the appointment."[19] On 13 December the University of Chicago Alumni Association sent out to all alumni Mr. Levi's statement with a cover letter that explained this was a response to the *Wall Street Journal* article and the Nicholas Von Hoffman CBS broadcast. The cover letter stated, "In its assessment of quality in graduate education in 1966, and again in 1971, the American Council on Education rated the Department of Anthropology first in the nation. We hope this reputation will not be impinged by these misleading reports."[20] As an alumnus I received a copy in Vietnam, the only communication on the whole affair from the University of Chicago that I ever received.

Other voices at the University of Chicago campus also joined the chorus. In a letter to William F. Kirby, president of the *Wall Street Journal,* dated 6 December 1971, Joseph A. Morris, chairman of Students for Capitalism and Freedom at the University of Chicago, stated that he was "shaken by the JOURNAL'S charge," so he contacted the student newspaper, *Rap,* and they investigated the story. "It may be that the Department declined to talk to the JOURNAL; however, Department members spoke freely with RAP and me." Morris found that "the article's information is wrong. He asked the University support of his full-time research with an academic appointment and salary." He concluded that "the request for academic position was turned down, surprising as it may seem in this politicized age, on academic grounds."[21]

Ev Martin wrote in an 8 December letter about an exchange between the *Wall Street Journal* managing editor and the University of Chicago. "They've written us an angry letter and the managing editor is writing back today standing by the story and offering to print a letter from the university spelling out the grounds on which they rejected you."[22]

On 12 December 1971 the *New York Times* published an article by Andrew H. Malcolm (complete with the same photo of me used in Gloria Emerson's 25 April 1971 article) reviewing the affair and quoting Mr. Levi's statement. In Malcolm's interview with Bernard F. Cohn, chairman of the Department of Anthropology, he mentioned "teaching" and a "stipend," neither of which were part of the proposed appointment. There was mention of my doctoral dissertation being "a study of a Vietnamese village," which was not true (it was on "Social Systems of Northern Vietnam"). Malcolm then reported that "Dr. Cohn said that copies of Dr. Hickey's available published work had been distributed among department members before the vote last spring and that the department's 'decision was based solely on this.'"[23] This disingenuous statement was the last one issued by the Department of Anthropology at the University of Chicago.

Throughout, letters from Fred and Norton reiterated their support of me. Norton, who was now at the Center for the Study of Democratic Institutions in Santa Barbara wrote in the February 1972 issue of the *Center Report,* "Hickey had the bad judgment, in the opinion of his peers, to work for several years for the RAND Corporation. As a result it has become extremely difficult for him to obtain a job in an American university, even through most of his work was strictly anthropological and constructive, both in terms of its contributions to knowledge and its effect on human affairs. Clearly, there is confusion between ends and means here."[24]

Harry Holloway, a psychiatrist and friend from Vietnam, wrote on 8 December 1971 offering to have me as guest scientist at the Walter Reed Army Institute of Research in Washington. He added that "Joe Sharp, Dave Marlowe, and I deeply respect your work and commitment."[25]

In his excellent 1978 work *Certain Victory: How Hanoi Won the War,* Australian Vietnam correspondent Denis Warner discussed the harmful effects of guilt by association regarding the Vietnam War. "Even those opposed to the war, who were nonetheless identified with it, suffered. Gerald Hickey of the RAND Corporation was a notable example of this. Hickey, whose important book, *Village in Vietnam,* was followed by the most scholarly and important work ever attempted among the montagnards, found himself unable to get a billet in an American university simply because he was associated with Vietnam."[26]

My status as a pariah was mentioned by my colleague Charles Keyes in a 1984 review article of my 1982 books, *Sons of the Mountains* and *Free in the Forest.* "While Hickey's commitment to carry out research in the highlands of Vietnam between 1963 and 1973 had many personally tragic repercussions for him, as he saw highlander and other friends killed and came to be viewed as something of a pariah by many American anthropologists, it did lead to his writing a unique chronicle of the efforts made by highlanders to ensure their survival as distinctive peoples during the Vietnam War."[27]

On 15 January 1972 I wrote to Fred saying, "I have remained silent, but one day I shall make my version of the whole thing public. I prefer to do that when emotions have cooled, and you are well out of it." (Fred Eggan died on 7 May 1991.)

Meanwhile, Philip Ross and Anton Lang had formed a Herbicide Study Group with the goal of recruiting interested scientists to participate in an unbiased depth study of the effects of defoliation on the population and physical environment in Vietnam. The National Academy of Sciences, which guaranteed that data and reports would not be classified, sponsored it. But since the study was funded in part by ARPA, the same Department of Defense agency funding RAND projects in Vietnam, five American anthropologists invited to Washington to discuss participation refused to cooperate in any way. Early in January 1972 I met several times with Ross and Lang in Vietnam on visits to organize the study. They were disappointed and somewhat chagrined that no anthropologists would participate. I was not free at the time to join the study, so I suggested my friend, Joe Carrier, who had been part of RAND's Viet Cong Motivation and Morale Study and had just received his Ph.D. in anthropology.

While these unpleasant events were unfolding in the United States, I continued my work in Vietnam. The Vietnamese presidential elections were set for 4 October 1971 and stirred up the political pot months in advance. This election and Nixon's idea of leaving a residual American force brought Washington visitors to Saigon. In mid August 1971, David Elliott and I had lunch with Senator Adlai Stevenson and John Lewis, a Stanford professor, at the Hotel Royal to discuss the political situation and mood of the Vietnamese. The same topics were talked about during a mid September dinner with Senator George McGovern at the Hotel Caravelle.

In late September I was invited to have a drink at the villa of Charles Cooper, former RAND economist now with the American Mission. Others present were Robert Sansom, Steven Young, and Arthur Smithies, a Harvard economist who was said to be the mentor of Cooper and Daniel Ellsberg. They were familiar with my accommodation-coalition paper and when one of them brought it up they expressed opposition to any kind of accommodation leading to a coalition. Thieu, they said, was very popular and Vietnamization was rolling along so eventually the war would wind down and end. I took issue with them but realized all too well they considered my views to be unbridled pessimism. Cooper and his group served to substantiate my Vietnamese friends' conviction that the Americans' unqualified support of Thieu reflected fear of a coalition. The Vietnamese fatalistically reasoned that the only alternative for Washington was to continue the war. I left Cooper's villa in that same fatalistic mood.

Dang Duc Khoi returned to Vietnam to act as Ky's adviser in his election campaign and his positive influence was immediately apparent in the way Ky handled the media. Khoi told me that he was present when Ky met with Henry Kissinger who warned Ky not to mount any coups to get elected. Khoi also was present when Ambassador Bunker offered Ky "financial support," which everyone saw as a bribe. Ky turned the money down, and Khoi expressed disgust at the blatant way the Americans were interfering with the election. Thieu won the election with some 95 percent of the vote. In his room at the Continental on 6 October, Bob Shaplen related that Nguyen Ngoc Tho (former vice president under Diem) told him that since Thieu had total support of the Americans, anti-Thieu people in the administration could not prevent his winning, so they got their revenge by overwhelming him with a ridiculous victory. Just after the election I had an interesting conversation with Tran Van Tuyen, a well-known lawyer (who was favored to become speaker of the Lower House). He shook his head as he observed that the Americans did not understand Vietnamese nationalism, so in their unqualified support of Thieu they were trampling Vietnamese nationalists underfoot.

One of the nationalist leaders who had supported Thieu's election was Nguyen Van Bong, who on the previous 1 May had told me he would support Thieu because he had promised to share power with civilians. I felt Bong would be a remarkable and hopeful presence in the Thieu government, and he had the potential of emerging as a really effective leader in South Vietnam.

But that was not to be. On 11 November 1971 around noon when Bong was driving from the National Institute of Administration to have lunch at home, an explosion destroyed his automobile. Bong was taken to the Saigon Hospital next to my apartment building where he died.

With the 1:00 A.M. curfew the city was completely still, save for the barking of dogs. At around 1:45 A.M. I awoke suddenly with a deep feeling, not of fright but rather of calm realization that there was something taking place nearby. I went out on my balcony and for some reason the scene below on Huynh Thuc Khang Street came as no surprise. There were lights, flickering candles, and people standing silently in the street where a small building behind the hospital was used for funerals. For the Vietnamese, one must die in one's own house in order to have the funeral there. Death in a hospital means that the funeral must be held at the hospital (so a dying person usually is rushed home). Most of the hospital funerals I had seen thus far were for poor people. Suddenly it occurred to me that this funeral was for Nguyen Van Bong.

The street began to fill with people. Then came cars, some Saigon police on motorcycles with red lights, and a somber French-style black hearse. The only sounds came from the funeral building. As everyone gathered around, men dressed in black lifted the wooden coffin into the hearse. The policemen revved their motors and then let them idle. Men and women dressed in white gauzy mourning clothes stood behind the hearse. With dogs barking in the background, the cortege moved slowly down the street and disappeared from view.

The cortege carried Bong's body to his party headquarters. The following morning I went there to pay my respects. The coffin was set amidst green plants, national flags, candles, burning joss, and offerings. The mourners were a mixed group—older people in traditional clothes, young people in Western dress, men in uniforms, Buddhist monks who chanted, and some French Catholic nuns. Kevin Buckley was there so we joined the cortege to Mac Dinh Chi cemetery. It occurred to Kevin and me that Bong had delivered one of the orations at the funeral in February for François Sully whose grave was in a corner of the cemetery with few tombs. We were shocked to find that corner now filled with new graves, on which photos identified most of dead as young Vietnamese military officers, a grim reminder of the cost of the war to the Vietnamese. So now with a remarkable nationalist like Bong murdered and the post-election power structure no different than it had been before the election, the war would go on.

Collecting for the Smithsonian was a fascinating, if sometimes anxious task. It also was satisfying in that results were readily apparent and people were willing to help. On 26 November 1971 Joan Allen and I sent boxes of Rhadé and Rengao artifacts to Eugene at the Smithsonian. On 6 December Eugene wrote saying he had just received the ethnographic items. "There is absolutely nothing like them in the national collections of the Smithsonian. You, sir, have achieved a first." Eugene added, "They will be accessioned and catalogued for the exhibit and research collections as the Dr. Gerald C. Hickey Collection, which I hope, will give you some personal satisfaction."[28]

With the help of Nay Luett and other highland leaders as well as SIL staff members I continued to collect items in the highlands (the final collection included materials from the Rhadé, Jeh, Rengao, Halang, Bahnar Jolong, Bahnar Golar, Bahnar Kon Kodeh, Jarai Cheo Reo, Jarai Krung, Jarai Arap, and Cil). Mai Elliott, whose husband David was doing research for RAND in the delta, collected some Vietnamese materials commonly found in villages. Joan Allen and I also made trips to kilns at Lai Thieu and Thu Dau Mot outside of Saigon to make purchases of hand-painted kitchenware. Mai then catalogued the Vietnamese items.

Thanks to Eva Kim and Ambassador Bunker, I was put in touch with Ambassador Samuel Berger who arranged through Col. Arthur Cates of the Mission Coordinator's Office to see about shipping the entire collection to Washington. The collection was now stored in a warehouse at the Research and Development compound, and Constantine Sioris, supervisory procurement and supply officer at the U.S. Embassy, supervised packing. As luck would have it, Ambassador Bunker was flying to Washington for consultation, and he gave orders to have the ethnographic collection shipped on his aircraft. On 25 January 1972 I wrote to Eugene with the good news, advising him to contact Col. Robert Storey at the office of the director of the Vietnam Working Group at the State Department. Colonel Storey arranged for Eugene to meet the Ambassador's plane at Andrews Air Force Base near Washington.

On 16 February 1972 Eugene wrote, "Your shipment came through fine and in style aboard the Ambassador's plane."[29] An acknowledgment of my "gift of seventy-nine specimens of native handicrafts from the peoples of South Vietnam" was contained in a 6 September 1972 letter from Clifford Evans, chairman of the Department of Anthropology at the Smithsonian's National Museum of Natural History.[30] I have often wondered what ever became of the Dr. Gerald C. Hickey Collection. As far as I know it has never been displayed.

As trying as 1971 had been, it ended on a happy note thanks to Kevin Buckley who, as bureau chief for *Newsweek,* had a very charming old French villa where he gave a Christmas party. The guests included Frances FitzGerald, Gloria Emerson, Nick Profitt, Barbara Gluck, Joe Treaster,

Hannah and Bob Kaiser, and Larry Green. Guests brought things so there were two turkeys, a Chinese-style roasted suckling pig along with shrimps, lots of salad, cooked vegetables, strawberries, and a bûche de Noël. Gloria thoughtfully gave everyone presents. Everyone had such a good time the curfew and the war were forgotten.

Ten

LAST DAYS

BY 1972, ordinary people in South Vietnam lived from day to day, numbed by the terrible events that were touching everyone. They only wanted one thing—*hòa bình* (peace). But despite the continuing Peace Talks in Paris and the continuing withdrawal of U.S. Forces, the year 1972 held little promise for an end to the Vietnam War. Incredibly, it held an escalation of the war with a new and deadly Communist offensive.

As the year dawned it seemed the war was everywhere, an almost inescapable presence. While the 1968 Tet Offensive had transformed Saigon into a city under attack, four years later it had become a crowded chaotic slum. Streets were filthy. (My street had piles of bloody bandages from the hospital and when I pointed it out to a doctor he simply replied, "There's garbage on every street everywhere in the city.") Rue Catinat was a skid row of neglected buildings (housing tawdry bars and squalid shops where illegal documents could be easily obtained for a price). American soldiers wearing beads and headbands slouching along in dirty fatigues mixed with beggars and hostile wounded Vietnamese veterans. The dope problem among American troops had become epidemic (fixes could be bought at the street stalls selling bad art and cheap souvenirs) as had racial conflicts (most graphically manifest in the "fragging" incidents). Herbicides that had blown into Saigon destroyed the lovely tamarind trees on downtown streets, adding to the bleakness. Even the bar girls had a dispirited air.

One place I found an island of civilization and tranquility was the library of the National Museum in the Botanical Garden at the end of Boulevard Thong Nhut. Built during the colonial French era as the Musée Blanchard de la Brosse, the museum had interesting architecture of mixed Chinese and Vietnamese inspiration. The roof was of cool green glazed tile and in the middle rose a well-proportioned imperial hexagonal cupola around which wound a simple balcony. On either side of the main entrance (guarded by carved stone dragons) extended terraces with high arbors supporting cascades of brilliant bougainvillea in shades of raspberry red, white, yellow, and muscatel orange. Entering, to the right was an unexpected atrium garden with a dancing fountain set in a small pool surrounded by potted tropical plants.

Sun pierced the interior through tall windows at either end of the building and around the cupola. The collection held impressive Cham and Khmer stone carvings and cases containing stone tools from archaeological sites. There were displays of elegant blue and white porcelains (particularly the "Bleues de Hue" made in nineteenth-century China for the royal court of Hue) and antique dark wood furniture, some of it inlaid with superb Vietnamese five-color mother-of-pearl.

I was not surprised that the museum attracted many country people visiting the capital city. In small groups they moved through the halls, gazing and musing at the traces of their traditions. Most seemed to be elderly men with fine faces and wispy goatees, dressed in the loose-fitting white garb so common in the villages. I was sure it was they who respectfully burned joss before carvings and statues, leaving throughout the museum an exquisite and exotic fragrance.

At the rear of the museum, the library, reached through a wrought-iron door, served as the seat of the Société des Etudes Indochinoises. It consisted of one very large room made impressive by stacks soaring to the high ceiling. Most of the collection was old venerable books with titles of faded gold lettering. In the middle of the library was a long dark hardwood table, the territory of the society's members who marked their places with piles of books. Usually one or two members sat in bentwood cane chairs reading. In the corner was the card catalogue, of dark hardwood, containing entries written in curlicue script. Nearby was the desk of the librarians, an elderly Vietnamese man and younger woman. They knew members by name, and when a book was checked out, they made the entry in a solid ledger using the same curlicue script.

What apparently had been at one time the museum's rear entrance now served as a sizeable window looking on to a small terrace and a corner of the botanical garden completely vacant save for tall, still hardwood trees. The view never changed and lent a timeless air well suited to the scholarly feeling of the library, an island of tranquility.

New Year's Eve 1972 was unreal. The group of Americans who shared a large villa on Phan Thanh Gian Street gave a party with the "best band in Saigon." After midnight, Ambassador Bunker departed. Marine guards at the gate left, allowing hordes of Vietnamese "hippies" to flood in. The band began to produce more noise than music to set a tone for the boys in their tight bell-bottom trousers and girls dressed in gold miniskirts, strap dresses, and boots, who devoured the buffet in minutes before creating a frenzy on the dance floor.

On 6 January 1972 I accompanied Nay Luett, Touneh Han Tho, and Dorohim (the Cham Director for Highland Reconstruction) to Quang Tri on Air Vietnam's new jet service to visit Bru refugee camps. We also went to Hue where the extensive damage was a grim reminder of the heavy fighting that had taken place during the 1968 Tet Offensive. We drove past stone tombs and then boarded boats to move up the Perfume River to the vicinity of the imperial tomb of Emperor Minh Mang around which Bru and Pacoh refugees had built shacks among weathered tombs of mandarin families. In 1964 and 1965 I had visited the beautiful Bru villages (which had been completely demolished in the 1968 bombing) near Khe Sanh and it was very sad to see the Bru in this muddy rural slum made even more dismal by cold misty rain. Still, the refugees, dressed in their best clothes, came forward with smiles and bows to greet Nay Luett who had gifts for the children.

According to Father Aimé Mauvais, the French priest living with the Bru and Pacoh in the large refugee center at Cua, of the original seven thousand who had settled in Cua, some six thousand remained. Lack of security prevented the Bru from gathering wood and farming in the nearby hills. Father Mauvais lamented the rise in theft among the refugees, a departure from their normal pattern. Nonetheless, in spite of hardships, the Catholic mission had established a school with two Vietnamese nuns and two Bru giving instruction to between 120 and 170 children. Back in Hue, at a candlelight dinner given by the province chief in an elegant nineteenth-century house, Nay Luett expressed his determination to move all of the Bru and Pacoh farther south.

Crumbling security in the northern provinces and the ever-worsening refugee problem had prompted Nay Luett and Han Tho to devise a plan to regroup all of the surviving highlanders in seven provinces. Another reason was growing fear that the government might abandon the highlands. Han Tho himself had become convinced of this when in 1971 he had spent a year at the National War College in Saigon. One of the lecturers, retired Australian colonel Francis P. Serong, strongly advocated a strategy of withdrawing government forces from the highlands in order to concentrate them along the coastal plain.

By the beginning of February 1972, Saigon was abuzz with talk of a new Communist offensive in the offing. I had been told in Hue that there was a build-up of North Vietnamese troops along the demilitarized zone and another in the Achau Valley. Communists with armored units were massing in the border area west of Kontum, a possible threat to the American firebases at Dak To. An offensive at this time might discredit Vietnamization and shake confidence in the South Vietnamese armed forces.

I was in the last stages of a long report for RAND on my highland leadership research when I was suddenly faced with the possibility that RAND support for my work would soon end. Late in 1971 I had asked for more time to complete my research and write up the results, but response from RAND had not been encouraging. Now, with American forces withdrawing from the highlands there was rapidly diminishing interest in the region. My resistance to working on pacification in Vietnamese villages had not put me in good stead with RAND. With December 1971 budget cuts at the Pentagon, RAND was shifting with the Washington winds to "longer-range problems of tactical, limited war and deterrence under the Nixon Doctrine." A letter dated 20 January 1972 from a friend at RAND contained the observation that "RAND gives you little or no credit for the direct advice and consulting you give to the Embassy and Vietnamese government." The letter pointed out that RAND was only interested in reports and "they simply don't count the other things you do." This letter had been received just two days after an 18 January letter from Social Science head Fred Iklé (with whom I had never managed to attain any rapport whatsoever) stating bluntly that I would receive support from RAND until 30 March 1972. This was a far cry from the letter of 24 May 1968 that I had received from Harry Rowen, president of RAND, which said, "As an early 'settler' in Vietnam, and one who has made an outstanding contribution to our work there, we owe you a larger debt of appreciation than I can express. So I'll just say thanks."[1]

But all was not lost. My friend Arthur Hadley, who in March 1971 had very kindly offered a gift of money to help support my research associate appointment at the University of Chicago, again in November 1971 offered financial help to allow me to complete my highland research in Vietnam. Arthur's gift plus my own savings would permit me to continue my research.

On 2 February 1972 I accompanied Nay Luett and other highland leaders to Kontum where we found a great deal of tension at the approaching Tet holiday and rumors of a new Communist offensive. The airport was filled with civilians leaving the city, and, as in 1965, the townspeople were piling sandbags in front of their houses and digging ditches and bunkers. Chinese merchants on the main street were closing their shops and taking their families to Saigon. Men and women of all ages were being armed. After the Tet Offensive Pat Smith had moved her hospital to an old school in Kontum. It resembled a temporary hospital in the American Civil War (her surgery was a dank storeroom). There were more than the usual number of patients because, Pat explained, the Communists were attacking villages at night, burning the houses. They also had begun to fire on people working in their fields. She reported that Bishop Seitz (who obtained a great deal of information from his priests in the villages) was expecting an attack on Kontum. Villagers west of the city were warned by the Communists to stay indoors, turn weapons over to them, and not get in the way "when we come through."

On 31 March 1972 the Communists launched an offensive that was to have devastating effects in the highlands. It began with heavy shelling along the Demilitarized Zone. The population in the area, including the Bru and Pacoh refugees, began to flee southward as North Vietnamese troops, using tanks, moved rapidly to capture the former American bases at Cam Lo and Gio Linh and the naval base at Cua Viet, north of the town of

Dr. Pat Smith in her temporary hospital in Kontum, 1972.
Photo by Barbara Gluck.

Dong Ha. By 3 April refugees were streaming out of Dong Ha and Quang Tri along Route 1 into the city of Hue. Nay Luett became furious at the news (his planned resettlement of Bru and Pacoh had been scheduled to end on 31 March but was delayed) and began formulating a new plan to move the refugees quickly. He dispatched Binh, a young Bru leader, to Hue while Luett and a group from the ministry flew to Ban Me Thuot to arrange for settling the refugees there. He selected a site at Buon Jat, east of Ban Me Thuot, but John Vann, the CORDS senior adviser for II Corps, objected to it, insisting that the refugees be resettled in more remote Quang Duc province. Luett refused to change his plan, and this set off a conflict between him and Vann. Han Tho and Luett went to Hue to find that around one thousand highlanders had gathered. Most of those at Cua had been caught in the Communist sweep (Bru leader Anha's four wives and their children were reported to have been killed). Anha was with the Hue group and he had performed a divination ritual, using a chicken, eggs, and rice. Since the signs were unfavorable, he advised the refugees not to go south. Luett and Binh, however, convinced them it would be better, pointing out that the situation north of Hue was becoming very serious. The highlanders agreed to leave and began to board the Air America cargo planes arranged by CORDS.

No sooner had most of the Bru been airlifted from Hue than the defense lines north of Quang Tri city collapsed, sending ARVN troops and civilians flooding down Route 1 in panic. Practically all of the population of Dong Ha fled. As the mass of refugees reached Hue, residents of the city also panicked and began pouring down Route 1 to seek refuge south of the Hai Van pass in Danang. Later, my friend Nguyen Van Mung related that his mother and younger sister fled Hue to stay with another sister in Danang. A rocket hit the house, killing both sisters. As the situation worsened, reserve troops were hurriedly sent from Saigon to the northern zone. On 6 April, however, North Vietnamese troops captured Loc Ninh and attacked An Loc, north of Saigon. What reserves still remained in the city (including the Ranger battalion guarding the Independence Palace) were rushed up Route 13 to meet this new threat. With these developments, the American Armed Force Radio in Saigon announced that a squadron of bombers was being sent from Kansas to Vietnam.

When the attack in the An Loc–Loc Ninh area began, many Stieng villagers were caught in the fighting and large numbers of them went south into An Loc to seek refuge. As the fighting continued, An Loc was surrounded by North Vietnamese forces who subjected the city to constant shelling, assaulting it with tanks. The Stieng, like the An Loc residents, were unable to get out. Later, Huynh, a Stieng Protestant pastor, described to me how he and his kinfolk huddled in bunkers during the two-month siege, only going out to try to get some of the food that was being dropped from aircraft. The stench of decaying corpses lay heavy over the town which daily was being reduced to rubble. Huynh sadly told how many of his relatives died in the stricken city.

According to Ron Ackerman, a Vietnam Christian Service volunteer who had an agricultural project among the refugees at Dak To north of Kontum, during March the villagers had been busy preparing their fields in the valley for planting. On 2 April they paused when they heard explosions marking the beginning of rocket attacks by the North Vietnamese against the strategic ARVN fire bases (Charlie, Yankee, and Delta) that had been established by the American army on the ridge dominating the valley and Route 14. As these attacks became more intense by 7 April, the highlanders, whose past experiences with war had prepared them to sense the beginning of a battle, left their fields and retreated into their houses. Later, Jarai Arap villagers from Plei Kleng, west of Kontum, related that in March, North Vietnamese troops entered their village, shot some people, destroyed houses, and slaughtered cattle to feed themselves. The villagers fled to Kontum, and Plei Kleng was demolished by American bombers.

Meanwhile, farther south, North Vietnamese forces captured some posts at An Khe, cutting Route 19 between Pleiku and the coast. On 17 April a North Vietnamese unit attacked what was now called "rocket ridge," overrunning Firebase Charlie and scattering its five hundred defenders. Firebases Yankee and Delta were immediately abandoned. Two days later, on 19 April, Communist units attacked the former Special Forces camp at Dak Pek. At a press conference held in Pleiku on 22 April 1972, John Vann reported that the Communists had committed two divisions—the 2d and 320th—in addition to two independent regiments of infantrymen, an artillery regiment, and a sapper regiment to an offensive that would focus on the towns of Kontum and Pleiku.

Suddenly on the morning of 24 April North Vietnamese tanks rolled into the compound of the forward headquarters of the ARVN 22d Division at Tan Canh as other units attacked nearby Dak To. The ARVN troops made no attempt to defend the post and fled at the sight of the tanks. Not long after, American bombers began to swoop over the Dak To valley as helicopters attempted to evacuate the advisers. (One helicopter with six advisers was shot down.) Soldiers from the 22d Division, mixed with civilians, began heading southward on Route 14 in an attempt to reach Kontum. As Communist units moved down Route 14, B-52 bombings rocked the Dak To valley, sending highlanders either into the surrounding forests or down Route 14 with the swelling tide of refugees. Later, refugees told how when they saw Vietnamese soldiers rushing down Route 14 they prepared to leave. When North Vietnamese tanks caught up with them the Communist soldiers forced some highland refugees to move in front of the tanks and many were killed by American bombing. Meanwhile in Kontum, people with automobiles began packing them to go south to Pleiku, but the flow ceased abruptly when the North Vietnamese 95 B Regiment occupied the Mount Pao pass, cutting the only means of escape south from the city on Route 14.

Busy trying to evacuate his seminarians, Bishop Seitz ordered Pat

Smith to close her hospital. She objected, pointing out that most of the patients could not be moved. Dominic d'Antonio, the able CORDS representative, radioed Nhatrang for an aircraft to take some of the patients out. He called for a helicopter for Pat, her two adopted Bahnar sons (whose parents had been killed in a Communist attack on their village), and her American staff. It was decided to leave the hospital in the hands of the Bahnar nuns, Sister Gabrielle and Sister Vincent, and Pat's Jarai assistant, Scotty, all of whom insisted on remaining. By this time the Communists had begun to shell Kontum and the airstrip from the surrounding hills. When Pat and her group arrived at the airstrip, the scene was chaotic. Civilians of all descriptions and soldiers were trying to force their way onto every aircraft landing. There were lumbering C-130s and C-123s filled with troop replacements, ammunition, and other cargo; helicopters bringing troops; and even Air Vietnam DC-3s (the province chief's wife was selling tickets at vastly inflated prices). As they taxied to a halt, the mob rushed forward, pushing the elderly and children to the ground. VNAF chopper pilots were trying to charge those getting on board, and VNAF door gunners pushed soldiers to the tarmac so that they could haul their motorcycles (probably stolen) on instead. Pat and her group scrambled on a helicopter along with some soldiers who forced their way on board—and sometime during the flight stole her bag containing the boys' adoption papers. Shells fell on the field, and two C-130s filled with ammunition were struck, killing many of the refugees (including some seminarians). The Air America C-47 sent to pick up Pat's patients quickly filled up, but when it arrived at Nhatrang the pilot found that most of his passengers were soldiers who had stripped off their uniforms.

As B-52 raids increased north of Kontum, whole ethnic groups abandoned their traditional territories. Kek, a young Sedang from Kon Horing, a large village on Route 14 north of Kontum, related that most villagers packed what they could in their backbaskets and went into the forest when the B-52s began bombing in the vicinity. As he was leaving he encountered a large group of Vietnamese civilians from Dak To coming into the village. They told Kek that they had been on Route 14 going to Kontum but North Vietnamese tanks blocked the road. They were frightened and tired, so they were going to remain in Kon Horing. Kek went into the forest as the Vietnamese men, women, and children moved into the abandoned houses. That evening the Sedang refugees heard ear-splitting explosions of B-52 bombs

Sedang and Bahnar refugees from Kontum arrive in Pleiku during the 1972 offensive.

from the direction of Kon Horing. The following day Kek and some of the men went back into the village to find it completely demolished, and everywhere were the mangled bodies of the Vietnamese refugees. No one appeared to have survived.

In Kontum, the confusion continued as evacuation helicopters began to land in a sports stadium near the center of the town. When it became apparent, however, that the Communist forces were not going to attack the city at that time, the panic began to subside. Townspeople returned to their houses as great masses of refugees—most of them highlanders—continued to flood into Kontum. Schools and churches were now jammed with Jarai Arap, Bahnar, Sedang, Jeh, Rengao, and Halang refugees. The Kontum Mission was rapidly depleting its stores of rice to feed them.

At the beginning of May the situation worsened as shells and rockets began to rain down on the center of Kontum with a new intensity, immediately raising fears of a Communist assault on the town. Then, according to Dominic d'Antonio, when news spread that the American military advisers were evacuating the MACV compound on the northern edge of Kontum close to Route 14, panic seized everyone. People bolted from their houses and headed for the airport and sports stadium. At the province hospital, the few remaining staff fled, leaving patients on their beds (their kinfolk tried to drag them to the airstrip). Again chaos reigned at the airstrip and in the sports stadium as both soldiers and civilians mobbed the few aircraft that landed. A Buddhist leader told d'Antonio that he was ready to lead a group of ten thousand desperate followers down Route 14 on foot carrying their religious flags.

Vietnamese soldiers burst into the MACV compound before the last Americans boarded their helicopters. (They had to brandish their weapons to complete their evacuation.) The soldiers ran around the abandoned buildings looting hi-fi sets and other possessions left behind. They drank all of the alcohol in the abandoned clubs, then vomited and defecated everywhere as they went on a rampage of destruction, smashing everything in sight. After the last of Kontum's officials and police left, soldiers began looting the downtown and shuttered houses. Later, Hiu, a Bahnar leader, described how the soldiers came to his village of Kon Rohai, as they did all of the neighboring Bahnar villages, and pushed their way into his house, taking all of the family belongings and money. They killed fifteen head of cattle.

Later I found a handful of Kontum residents who had not left during those chaotic days. They explained that they were poor people with no money and they had no kinfolk or friends in Nhatrang where most refugees went. "We are poor, and no one would take care of us," one elderly man said. He added, "Here in Kontum we have houses and small gardens." He and others described how they stayed in their bunkers, and when a semblance of order returned they sold some of their vegetables to the soldiers.

Meanwhile the panic spread to Pleiku, sending an estimated 90 percent of the population down Route 19 to Qui Nhon or down Route 21 to Nhatrang. They moved out in every kind of vehicle, including many army trucks the drivers of which charged a high fee. Chinese merchants were hiring these trucks to carry all of their merchandise and household goods down to the coast. It was reported that 50 percent of the Vietnamese Regional Forces abandoned their weapons to flee with their families. Most of the civil servants and police left, and only one doctor remained at the province hospital.

While these events were unfolding in the highlands I remained in

Saigon dividing my time between the MDEM and home, where I worked on the final phase of my report on highland leadership. The 30 March deadline came, so I sent the almost-completed manuscript to Iklé in Santa Monica. I also sent a copy to George Tanham at the RAND Washington office. George, an intelligent scholar who had spent considerable time in Southeast Asia, had been a very good friend at RAND. In the cover letter I wrote, "Sad to say that in the long run my peers were quite correct—it was bad judgment on my part to have come to Vietnam to do research for the RAND Corporation. The bad judgment was in my believing that the RAND Corporation was serious about doing depth research." The response this elicited was a 25 April 1972 letter from John P. White, vice president of RAND, who offered to enter into a letter of agreement with me for a period of support which would allow me to complete my highland leadership report.[2] When the letter of agreement arrived in June, I signed and returned it. But my involvement in the events of that period prevented me from devoting full time to the report. In Saigon by early May there was deepening gloom and sense of unease at the flow of bad news from Kontum, Quang Tri, and An Loc. In Quang Tri the ARVN 3d Infantry and the elite Ranger and marine units had fled after burning the city when North Vietnamese units with PT 76 tanks began to enter. Almost the entire population had fled to Hue and then to Danang, which was now jammed with refugees. But the attention of the Saigonese was focused more intently on An Loc, where new fighting was erupting along Route 13 within fifty kilometers of the capital. Saigon was swept with rumors that Communist forces were preparing to attack the city or subject it to massive rocket and artillery barrages. Everyone was talking about a large force of U.S. Marines standing by on Seventh Fleet ships off the coast preparing to land in Vietnam. This was not true. In fact, the American military withdrawal was continuing at an unabated pace. (The 30 April 1972 figure of 44,748 remaining American military diminished to 37,129 by the end of May.)

Thieu proclaimed martial law and asked the National Assembly for emergency powers. A stringent curfew was set for Saigon as the university and other institutions of higher learning closed. The draft age was changed to make men between the ages of seventeen and forty-three subject to call. Prices were rising, and there was a rush for basic foods. All bars, nightclubs, and other places of amusement were darkened. Nonetheless, the American Women's Association announced that it would hold a fashion show (with a "Far East" theme) in the Champs Elysée Room on the top of the Hotel Caravelle, and at the Saigon city hall there was an exhibition of Dada art.

Even my island of tranquility, the library in the National Museum, was rudely jolted out of its tranquility. As Communist forces edged closer to Saigon, ARVN troops were bivouacked in the otherwise quiet corner of the Botanical Garden. Some of them elected to sleep on the small terrace behind the library, spreading their gear and weapons about. In the daytime they stared listlessly through the wrought iron grill, making the librarians uneasy. The scholars stayed away and the number of visitors to the museum tapered off to a trickle. Then, one afternoon, a huge explosion in an ammunition dump not far away shattered cupola windows, cracked glass in the cases, and sent some porcelains tumbling from their shelves, breaking into pieces (much to the distress of Jolynne d'Ornano who as a volunteer was reorganizing and cataloguing the porcelain collection). The only thing that remained unchanged was a pervading scent of joss—the fragrance of forgotten offerings.

At the MDEM, the staff worked feverishly on plans to remove the growing number (now estimated at around fifteen thousand) of highlanders caught in the city of Kontum. Young leader Nay Alep reported that he was unable to obtain any aircraft to take them out, prompting Minister Nay Luett on 14 May to consult with John Vann in Pleiku. Vann informed him that he had already taken twenty thousand Vietnamese out of Kontum and could do nothing for the highlanders because the American senior province adviser (a colonel) and the Vietnamese province chief claimed that the highlanders did not want to leave Kontum. The province chief was going to organize them to defend the city against an expected Communist assault. Furious at this, Luett went to Kontum where he was greeted by highlander refugees who told him they were anxious to leave because of the heavy fighting and shelling. Luett returned to Pleiku for a confrontation with Vann. Luett related to me that he had told Vann that he, Luett, was not afraid of Vann, Abrams, Bunker, or Nixon. He said to Vann, "I will praise you for the good you do and condemn you for the bad." Afterward Vann and Gen. Nguyen Van Toan, the II Corps commanding officer (whose role in a cinnamon scandal in central Vietnam had earned him the name "the Cinnamon General") arranged for aircraft to take the highlanders to Pleiku. Unlike the Vietnamese (who stormed the planes and helicopters), the highlanders lined up in orderly fashion, putting the elderly and children on the aircraft first. By 17 May some eight thousand highlanders had been airlifted from Kontum to Pleiku.

The following day I went to Pleiku with Nay Luett, Pierre K'briuh, and some USAID officials. Chinook cargo helicopters were shuttling between Kontum and Pleiku and the streams of highlanders were being moved into old military compounds and schools. Since there was the possibility of a Communist assault on Pleiku, Luett told the CORDS officials that he wanted the refugees moved to Ban Me Thuot. The Americans responded that there were no aircraft because the Communists had blown up a large ammunition dump near the airstrip and all of the planes were needed to fly in new supplies. We visited the refugee centers and it was clear that they soon would be inadequate. The buildings were already filled and there was not much space for more tents. Lack of water was a problem because the rains had not yet begun, Pleiku city water trucks had gone to the coast with the exodus of the population, and ARVN water trucks would only serve the army. Fortunately the ethnic groups tended to remain together as did village groups, so there was cohesion and leadership, both of which made it easier to organize refugee relief.

At the first refugee center, a dilapidated former munitions dump, I met Kek, the Sedang leader (who related the story of the bombing of Kon Horing). In the second center in a school I encountered Bahnar leader Hiu and his family. They had just arrived from Kontum with what few belongings they had left after the soldiers' looting. They seemed dazed, and Hiu was very bitter. Normally bustling Pleiku was strangely quiet with most houses and shops shuttered. Soldiers and civilians who remained in Pleiku were breaking into houses to squat in them. There were soldiers wandering around the center of the town, which we were advised to avoid because of lack of order and rampant thievery. (On three different occasions one CORDS worker had his watch pulled from his wrist while driving with the window open.) Another CORDS worker related that when panic stuck Pleiku and the flight began, prices soared. In the market a woman quoting a vastly inflated price for a sack of rice was shot in the head by an angry soldier.

Pat Smith had been given a new wing of the Pleiku province hospital, where she was setting up her medical practice. Some of her patients were being airlifted from Kontum and she already was treating refugees.

At the urging of Nay Luett I went to see Vann about trying to obtain some cargo planes to fly highland refugees south to Ban Me Thuot. His wood-paneled office on the hill where the II Corps headquarters was located was a world away from the dismal refugee camps and the disorder of the town. He was agitated and very defensive about his position concerning the highlanders in Kontum city. He claimed to have received fifteen reports from the Vietnamese province chief saying that highland refugees preferred to remain in Kontum. Furthermore, because of an impending attack on Kontum, he could not be bothered with the refugees (he had not visited any of the highland refugee sites). I replied that as senior adviser in II Corps, he was responsible for them. Then I could not resist adding that many of them were refugees because of the B-52 bombings which he, Vann, had ordered. He bristled and replied that there were no available aircraft but there was a convoy of trucks going to Ban Me Thuot in the morning and the refugees could go on the convoy.

Vann then went into an explanation of his use of B-52s. The Communists, he said, had lost the war at Tet. Now they were resorting to using tanks, and the B-52s (which he called "Arc Lights," their code name) were the only means to deal with such a strategy. He stated that "Kontum will break the back of the North Vietnamese army," adding that "in six months there will be no more North Vietnamese army left." Vann asserted that he intended achieving his goal through the B-52s, and when I objected, noting that he had no intelligence on the ground north of Kontum, he retorted that he gained the information on Communist positions by sending helicopter gunships into the area. At night the gunships had spotlights to "draw fire" from the North Vietnamese troops, thus revealing their positions. Vann would then quickly plot a "box" (a one-by-two kilometer zone) that the B-52s would saturate with bombs. As he paced around the office, his voice rose to a high pitch and his eyes took on a strange look. He claimed to have seen North Vietnamese troops dead and wounded among the craters following some of the raids—so he called in napalm "to put them out of their misery." Cringing inwardly, I sat back. All of this was necessary, he continued, because Vietnamese ground forces in the highlands were insufficient and inadequate to cope with the situation. I pointed out that highland leaders had repeatedly asked for their own force to defend the uplands, because the lowland Vietnamese would never fight for what they considered an alien region. Vann, however, reflected the view common to the American leaders in Vietnam that it was hopeless to expect the Vietnamese to ever agree to such a plan.

Since refugees in the ammunition dump were living under the worst conditions, it was agreed that they would be the ones to leave on the convoy. The following morning, 19 May 1972, as we made preparations, it was clear that a major problem was lack of water. (Pat pointed out that highlanders dehydrate rapidly, causing death.) Early in the morning, Nay Alep, Tracy Atwood (the IVS volunteer at Buon Sar Par during the FULRO revolt and now with CORDS), and I went to Lake Tenneung—in the waters of which, according to Jarai legend, a Cham army had once been drowned— north of Pleiku, but we found that the only city pump was not working. Many of the highland refugees were there fetching water, but they were afraid to bathe in the sacred lake. There were, however, army tank trucks loading up on water. We returned to the compound where the refugees reluctantly were preparing to leave (they feared going farther from their villages) and some of the Catholics knelt to say their rosaries. Nay Luett came to assure them that when the situation improved, the ministry would transport them back to their villages. The convoy was due soon. Still no water and the 950 refugees, most of them elderly, women, and children would be on the road for at least seven hours. Suddenly I remembered the army trucks, so I hurried out to the road where two of the water trucks were approaching. Holding a fistful of piasters, I flagged them down and offered the drivers money if they would deliver water to the refugees. The drivers agreed and just as the convoy arrived, the water trucks careened into the compound to fill all of the drums, canteens, gourds, and other containers. The refugees crammed all they could on the trucks, reluctantly leaving firewood.

Atwood went with the convoy. To make preparations in Ban Me Thuot, Nay Alep and I took a helicopter (we flew over the convoy and children waved at us). None of the panic in Kontum and Pleiku had affected Ban Me Thuot, which seemed surprisingly normal. We alerted the province chief Y Jut Buon To, the ministry representative; the Catholic sisters; and the Protestant Mission. The province chief ordered the Dam San camp east of Ban Me Thuot (near a clear stream and a thick forest) to be prepared. (Upon seeing the thick trees and foliage, Vietnamese refugees from Pleiku had refused to stay in the camp because they feared "forest spirits.") When the convoy arrived, the dusty and sick (from the jiggling over the bad road bed) refugees got off the trucks to receive hot food, water, and relief goods from the province chief and his family, the Boy Scouts, the Catholic sisters, the Vietnam Christian Service, and Betty Mitchell of the Christian and Missionary Alliance. Y Jut had rounded up some young highlanders who were there to help the refugees get settled in the buildings. The refugees spread mats, poncho liners, and rain capes on the floor for the children to sleep. Some of the refugees immediately went to bathe in the stream, while many of the women gathered wild greens and men began to chop wood for fires and fish traps. The different ethnic groups separated into the various buildings. That afternoon another convoy with one thousand refugees arrived and the highlanders already in the camp helped them get settled.

When Atwood and I returned early the following morning, the refugees were busy. Some were roasting fish they had caught in the stream, and others were foraging in the nearby woods. One man was cutting hair. Kek said they were happy to be away from the bombs and shooting ("We know we're away from the war"). There had been some grumbling, however, about having the Halang in the camp because they had the reputation of possessing powerful sorcery and witchcraft. Several Bahnar claimed that they had seen a disembodied head floating through the night. I suggested to Kek that he organize a ritual to cope with such a phenomenon because there was no possibility of moving the Halang out of the camp. As we walked through the camp, we came upon an elderly woman with sagging breasts, cataracts in both eyes, wearing a dusty skirt. She looked up and smiled as she churned the earth with a hoe to plant kernels of corn. She, bless her, embodied the highlanders' spirit of survival.

On 25 May 1972 the North Vietnamese attack on the city of Kontum began as four regiments of infantry, reinforced with sappers, antiaircraft machine gunners, and ten T-54 tanks moved into the east side. The defense of the city was in the hands of some elements of the 23d Division. In addition there were two thousand highlanders who on 22 May had been organized into a defense force as a result of an agreement between Nay Luett and the prime minister. The Vietnamese military, however, would only issue each of them a carbine and eighty rounds of ammunition. The attack began with heavy artillery shelling followed by sapper ground assaults not far from Pat Smith's hospital and the Kontum Mission headquarters. Highland refugees still in Kontum huddled in church compounds and schools while the fighting raged around them. Sister Gabrielle related to me later that North Vietnamese troops dug trenches in front of the hospital. Some of them came into the hospital looking for Americans, but she told them there were only poor, sick people in the wards and asked them to leave. They did leave, but soon thereafter helicopter gunships began to swoop over the building firing rockets. Artillery shells burst nearby as the nuns and Scotty got all of the patients under their beds. Heavy fighting took place all around the hospital. Sister Gabrielle worked in the surgery, operating on wounded civilians and soldiers who were carried into the hospital. When the fighting reached its peak, she and the others remained on the floor. "We all prayed very hard," she said, "and God heard us." While every building in the vicinity was either badly damaged (such as the Mission seminary) or totally demolished (such as the bishop's residence), the hospital was almost untouched.

On 27 May 1972 I accompanied Nay Luett and Touneh Han Tho to Ban Me Thuot where we were met by Rhadé leaders. We visited the refugee camps which still lacked basic things. All of us then went to Buon Pan Lam to pay our respects to Y Blieng Hmok whose son had been killed by Vietnamese soldiers. That evening all of the highland leaders gathered in the village to discuss the organization of a highland military force. The leaders were very concerned about the failure of ARVN to mount an effective defense of the mountain country, resulting in vast disruption and destruction because of reliance on B-52s. Luett was also angry at the conversion of the CIDG camps into ARVN Ranger posts and what he considered the misuse of highland troops. Earlier in May highland troops at Ben Het, northwest of Kontum, had revolted against their Vietnamese officers just as a North Vietnamese assault on the post was about to begin. (They nonetheless fought well, withstanding two ground attacks and knocking out two tanks.) Also, as the siege of Kontum developed, Gen. Nguyen Van Toan, the II Corps commander, ordered highlanders to be sent from some of the border (former CIDG) camps to open Route 14 between Pleiku and Kontum. The North Vietnamese were well installed at the Mount Pao pass with artillery, and the highlanders were sent up the road without any armored protection or air support. Some of their units lost as many as 50 percent of the men, and many began to desert. One senior American adviser in Pleiku described it as a "meat-grinder operation."

On 1 June 1972 Vann met with the press in Pleiku and announced that

the North Vietnamese, who still held two military compounds on the northern edge of Kontum, had lost "phase one" of their campaign. He emphasized the importance of American air support in turning the tide of battle.
In addition to B-52s there were navy planes that dropped "smart bombs"
(with television nose cameras for accuracy). Vann was making daily trips to
Kontum in his helicopter to direct operations. On 9 June the helicopter
crashed and everyone on board was killed. Vann's body was found in a
grove of high trees amidst highland tombs with carved depictions of squatting men in contemplative poses, their hands framing faces and elbows
resting on knees. Soon after, North Vietnamese units began to withdraw
from Kontum.[3]

On 5 June, people in central Saigon on their way home to lunch were
startled by the sight of a large group of half-naked, dark-skinned men,
women, and children fending their way through the tangle of motorcycles,
pedicabs, and cars. They were Stieng, and for five days they had walked
seventy miles from the vicinity of An Loc over fields, avoiding embattled
Route 13, to the capital city. Tired and without money, but clutching their
bush scythes (essential in the jungles of the highlands as well as the jungle
of Saigon), they were looking for the MDEM to seek help. I was on my
scooter en route to the ministry when I encountered them, so I guided
them. Touneh Han Tho quickly got them food and drink. They were probably the first highland refugees to enter Saigon on foot.[4]

Given the pressing needs of the highland refugees, I dropped my own
work to assist with the relief efforts. I got in touch with Mildred Colantonio
and Marilyn Tank of the American Women's Association, and they immediately made plans for refugee relief for the highlanders. They were told by
an official at the Ministry for Social Welfare that the minister would be
happy to have them provide relief for the highlanders because he intended
devoting the ministry's efforts to Vietnamese refugees in Danang and Hue.
The two ladies efficiently collected clothes, mats, plastic buckets, canned
milk, dried fish, and rice, booking Air America cargo planes to deliver all
of it to the highlands.

On 12 June 1972 I accompanied the first flight to Pleiku on a C-123
loaded with five hundred plastic buckets; five hundred cooking pots; and
odds and ends of heavy clothing, blankets, and drapes for making clothes
(the rains had begun and it was chilly in the highlands). Atwood had notified the young FULRO highlanders working with the refugees. As the air-

craft taxied to a stop I was disappointed that none of the highlanders was there to meet it. There was, however, a stuffy young Foreign Service type (assigned to CORDS), who approached with a Vietnamese. "Well done, Dr. Hickey," he said, adding, "We'll take it from here, and my counterpart will see that the government goods are delivered to the province warehouse."

"There must be some mistake," I responded, "These goods don't belong to the government, they belong to me." His jaw dropped as I produced the manifest made out to me. "I'm signing for them." Then, knowing that highland refugee goods would be sold out the back door of the province warehouse, I made it clear that "none of these goods go to the province warehouse, they go directly to the refugees in the camps."

Fortunately at that moment a truck with the FULRO highlanders wheeled onto the airstrip, and we proceeded to unload the cargo. I let them handle the distribution. The highland refugees lined up to receive goods, and they worked out their own equitable distribution sharing needed goods.

Pat Hughes had given me dollars to buy goods for the refugees, and I added money. Atwood and I went down to the Pleiku market where some tough older market ladies had stayed during the flight from the city. We needed large mats, so I began to bargain with one vendor, and since there were few buyers in the market, the others gathered around. I said that there was danger of a Communist attack on Pleiku, in which case they would have to flee and leave the mats. The cynical ladies all burst into laughter, but they agreed it was a possibility. Then they all began to chide the vendor into lowering her prices. As a result we purchased two hundred large mats at quite a good price.

Vann's death had caused quite a stir because he had assumed almost mythical status. Atwood and I attended the memorial service for him in Pleiku. There we ran into Vann's replacement, Gen. Mike Healy, who had been the last commander of the Special Forces in Vietnam, and his assistant, Col. Bob Kingston. They invited us back to the senior adviser's office on the hill where we discussed the highlander refugee problem. Mike, who had worked with the highlanders in the Special Forces, promised to help them.

Such help was soon needed because Atwood and I faced a dire situation with the inundation of new refugees from Kontum where they had been for a month after fleeing their villages north of the city. They were uncharacteristically dirty because of lack of water and some had been wounded in the fighting but received no medical attention. We helped them off the army trucks and most only had their backbaskets, knives, and bush scythes. One poor woman carried her son, a deformed boy of about twelve, wrapped in an old rain poncho. Caked with dirt, he suffered with a lot of fragment wounds on his body. We said we would take him to Pat's hospital, but the woman burst into tears at the thought that she and her son would be away from her relatives and fellow villagers. Her niece, a little girl with a huge backbasket filled with clothes and pots, agreed to go along. The woman, her son, and the niece were much relieved at the hospital to find themselves in the hands of highland nurses who took care of them. The following day we found them clean and tended, and their smiles attested to the good treatment they had received.

The rains were lashing the Pleiku plateau, and buildings such as the dismal ammunition dump with its high roof and open sides provided little shelter. I went over to rouse the province chief, Col. Ya Ba, a highlander, from his sleep, insisting he come to see the plight of the refugees. The worst of it was that the abandoned prisoner-of-war camp could accommodate four thousand, but the Vietnamese bureaucracy refused to open it for highland refugees. Several of the refugees in the ammo dump died, one of them a pretty girl of about three, who, her mother said, got chilled in the rain waiting for the helicopter and then got soaked on the army truck. She began shivering and suddenly died. That night a storm swept Pleiku, and the following morning Nay Alep and I went to the ammunition dump with some relief clothes to find the refugees with fires burning to dry out their blankets and mats. A weathered Sedang village chief approached me saying in English, "Cold, cold." His village apparently had been close to a Special Forces camp where he had learned the expressions, "Cut bamboo" and "Fill sandbags," which he said with appropriate gestures. Among the relief clothes I found a tuxedo jacket which I gave him, and it transformed him into a figure of authority. From there I went to see Mike Healy, and he agreed to visit the ammunition dump. Shocked at the squalid conditions, he promised to take it up with General Abrams.

Dan Southerland of the *Christian Science Monitor* was in Pleiku and we discussed the current situation in the light of past events. Dan interviewed highlanders and remaining American advisers, and then interviewed Nay Luett in Saigon. His article, published on 19 July 1972 was particularly comprehensive, putting the plight of the highlanders in perspective.[5] I expressed my view that the Americans got the highlanders committed to the government side and were now abandoning them. "We've used them just like we used the poor Meo up in Laos."

I accompanied most of the subsequent flights (by 1 September 1972 there had been five of them). The second shipment to Pleiku on 23 July 1972 required two C-123s, and I went on the first one. When the second aircraft arrived, and the cargo door was dropped I was astonished to see a trim lady dressed in slacks jump down to the tarmac. She turned out to be a French baroness, Marguerite de Gunzbourg (of the de Gramont family), a volunteer with the French Red Cross. She had supplies for Pat Smith's hospital and she had gotten them on the second aircraft. Marguerite, who was a friend of Bob Shaplen, was a great help and Atwood arranged for a helicopter to take her and the supplies to Kontum, where the airstrip was not officially opened. Mike Healy was not in Pleiku, but his deputy Bob Kingston invited all of us, including Marguerite, to dinner where discussion of World War II brought out the fact that she had been in the French resistance.

Nay Luett went along on one flight to Ban Me Thuot and another to Cheo Reo on 15 July where Ed Sprague, the CORDS representative, and his assistant, Rcom Ali, saw to the distribution of goods and made sure that refugees in more outlying areas received some of the supplies. I stayed in Cheo Reo to collect more data for the final version of my highland leadership report for RAND. From Cheo Reo I stopped at Nhatrang in the hope of a few days rest, but I found the city worse than it was when last I visited in September 1970. Most of the American military were gone, but the few that remained were unkempt. With the military withdrawal there were many unemployed Vietnamese who set up food stands all along the beach which attracted grubby customers who wolfed down food, spitting bones and seeds on the sand. There was an inordinate number of Vietnamese males urinating against trees and walls. Masses of wounded vets hobbled along the beach and in one section they built a crowded shantytown. On the beach were groups of bar girls with fat, foul-mouthed American civilian contractors guzzling beer out of cans they crushed with one hand after emptying. I took a cyclo to a quiet spot next to the Korean military section of the beach, but the cyclo driver warned that anything left on the beach would be stolen. So I entered the Korean beach where they welcomed me and even offered a can of Korean beer.

At the end of July 1972, the Kontum airstrip was opened although with warnings of snipers in the vicinity and Communist artillery in the surrounding hills. I met with Mildred Colantonio and Marilyn Tank to put together a shipment for the refugees and Pat Smith's hospital (which was experiencing severe shortages of just about everything). Joe Carrier, who was back in Vietnam with the American Academy of Sciences herbicide study, and Peter Kunstadter, a fellow anthropologist with the same study, accompanied the flight. I was annoyed at Tan Son Nhut airport to find that Air America had given us a camouflaged C-123 that could easily be mistaken for an military resupply aircraft, a good target. The crew members were Chinese civilians. As we approached Kontum I looked down through the rain clouds with some apprehension. When we landed, as the Chinese cabin crew began running around the cabin, the plane touched the tarmac but did not slow down very much. I saw the waiting trucks shoot by as we went off the end of the airstrip and bounced violently. All of us breathed sighs of relief when the aircraft came to a halt. (An American Air America pilot told me the Chinese crew was unfamiliar with the C-123 and in September the same crew and aircraft hit a mountain in Pleiku, killing everyone, including Touneh Han Tho's younger brother.) A truck was brought out to haul the aircraft back on to the runway and fortunately a rain squall obscured everything. Dominic d'Antonio and a group of young highlanders lost no time unloading the plane. Ruins marked the terminal and other buildings, and all around were burned-out hulks of cargo planes that had been struck with artillery shells and rockets. It set a tone for the dismal rainy drive into Kontum with smashed cars and trucks by the road and damage to almost every house and public building.

The CORDS compound on the bank of the Bla River fortunately was intact, and we went to deliver goods to the refugee centers, which like those in Pleiku were jammed and grim. We took truckloads to Pat's hospital. She was in the United States, but the hospital was being run by Sisters Gabrielle and Vincent, two American nurses (one of them, Hilary Smith wrote a fascinating account, *Lighting Candles,* of her experiences) and Tom Coles, an ex-Special Forces medic who ran a village health program. Everyone was excited about the shipment of goods and they set about emptying the trucks. It was then that Sister Gabrielle related the events of the battle around the hospital. The hospital, a former school, was packed with patients of all descriptions. I asked why they had not moved back to Pat's hospital outside of Kontum, which she had to vacate after the Tet Offensive. When that facility was almost completed, Pat had taken me to visit it, proudly showing me her new surgical suite, kitchen, and a thriving garden tended by highlanders. She also had a fine stock of cattle and pigs and masses of chickens. The hospital soon would be almost self-sufficient in food. Sister Vincent told how during the fighting in Kontum the ARVN 23d Division set up a command post in the hospital. Claiming that Pat was anti-Vietnamese (because she insisted the province chief's wife await her turn for treatment like the other patients), the ARVN officers encouraged their troops to loot the hospital buildings and smash what they could not take, such as the x-ray machines and surgical lamps. They killed all of the animals and destroyed the gardens, after which they put mines in them.

The whole northwestern portion of Kontum (including Jim Cooper's house) was charred ruins. The Communists had their cannons in the nearby hills, and they would fire volleys of shells into the town. Everyone could hear the guns fire and would wait to hear where the shells were landing before falling to the ground (if the explosions were near) or going about their business (if they were far away). At the Bach Dang, the only restaurant, people paused in the midst of their meal when a volley was heard. Later, Pat Smith admitted that when she was in surgery the sounds of the guns firing made her a bit nervous (many of the shells fell in the vicinity of the hospital). Joe and I walked around to take photos. An elderly Vietnamese man came out of his half-wrecked house to tell us how soldiers had looted every house not demolished. There was nothing left in the man's house except his small shrine to the Blessed Virgin in the living room. On one street a girl had set up a stand and was selling cans of Budweiser beer. Joe was taking to a young highland refugee girl who, using English she obviously had learned from GIs, said, "'mericans go and fuckin' VC come. Ver' bad!"

For most of the highlanders the refugee camps were a new and somewhat bewildering experience. In normal times the highlanders are self-sufficient people who satisfy all of their own basic needs. With only a few exceptions, in the camps they had no land to farm, no streams to fish, and no forests to supply them with wood, bamboo, and rattan for artifacts. They were forced to depend on outside agencies for everything from rice to plastic mats for sleeping. Nonetheless, whenever possible they planted small gardens among the barbed wire surrounding the camps. They also walked long distances for firewood and wild fruits and vegetables. The Jarai Arap women had carried their shuttles in their backbaskets when they fled their homes, and they kept busy weaving. They wove particularly interesting textiles with mixtures of traditional and innovative motifs. The latter were based on the contemporary situation. As one woman put it, "We weave what we see around us." Their textiles, in effect, were chronicles, and in mid 1972 they were depicting various kinds of helicopters (Chinooks, Huey gunships, and the bubblelike Cayuse), jet fighters, army trucks, bombs, M-16 rifles, strange people the women identified as "Americans," and a scene they said was "a group of Jarai waiting to go on helicopters" (they used a variation of the Vietnamese word for helicopter). One woman found a U.S. Navy mail order catalogue from which she reproduced a row of Japanese watches. Another woman wove the names "Judy" and "U.S. Army" without having any idea what they meant, but she explained that she "likes the shape."

During this time the siege at An Loc continued. Early in June 1972 word spread through the ruined town that Route 13 was open. Around ten thousand desperate Vietnamese and Stieng civilians emerged from their bunkers and, picking their way through the rubble and burned vehicles, moved in a mass down the road. Some were elderly, and there were many women with small children and babies. Some young boys and girls whose parents had been killed carried their small siblings strapped to their backs. All of them were caked with red dirt. Ignoring the continuing fighting, they walked to Tan Khai, eleven kilometers to the south, where they were stopped temporarily by North Vietnamese troops. Tired and hungry, they pushed on to refugee centers in Phu Cuong.

Some ten thousand Stieng refugees from An Loc had been moved near the huge American base at Long Thanh where they were jammed in tents. Back in Saigon I met with Mildred Colantonio and Marilyn Tank. They were running out of money and volunteers. I went around to the offices of *Newsweek, Time,* NBC, CBS, the *New York Times,* and the *Washington Post* to solicit cash contributions. The American Women's Association also sought contributions and the largest one was given by the U.S. Seventh Fleet. The new funding allowed the ladies to purchase badly needed relief goods.

Joe Carrier went with me to Long Thanh on one of the two trucks filled with relief goods. The center was on a hill not far from the American base which had been hit by Communist rockets the night before, and columns of black smoke rose from it. Huynh, the Stieng pastor, greeted us. There also were cars and buses that brought out members of the American Women's Association to witness the delivery of their relief goods. With them were strapping U.S. Marine guards from the embassy dressed in full battle gear. "They came to protect the American ladies," Mildred explained. The ladies were shocked at a group of newly arrived refugees still caked with red dirt and looking very much in need of food and clothing. Stieng chiefs organized the refugees for the initial distribution, which was very orderly. A group of Vietnamese Catholic nuns accompanied by my friend, Martine Piat, the linguist working on Mon Khmer languages arrived. They had a feeding program and had been working in the center every day. Since Joe and I were helping with the unloading in the relentless heat, the nuns provided us with cold soda pop.

In mid August 1972 I had a long discussion with Nay Luett about the situation. He reported that there were estimated to be around 150,000 highlanders in refugee camps, and he figured that since 1965, some 200,000 highland people (both civilians and military personnel) had died because of the war. At least 85 percent of highland villages had, for one reason or another, been displaced. Whole ethnic groups had been forced to abandon their traditional territories. The Bru well illustrated the effect of the war on one group; whereas in 1965 there were an estimated forty thousand Bru, only some seven thousand could now be accounted for. Not one Bru village remained in place.

Completing the final version of my report on highland leadership was no easy task because only one typist, an American army corporal swamped with work, was left at the Research and Development compound. I sent the report off on 13 October 1972 (and received payment two months later).

Late in September 1972, Joe and I went to Phnom Penh at the invitation of my friend from the late 1950s, Don Sohlin, who was serving as assistant economic counselor at the American Embassy. Don's villa, on rue de Tchécoslovaquie, built by a well-to-do Chinese entrepreneur, was very elegant. We went around the city with Silvana Foa, the bright, charming *Newsweek* correspondent in Phnom Penh. There were more refugees and heavier traffic, but the city had not changed much since my last visit in 1970. At the terrace of La Taverne we ran into Martine Piat who thought I might be

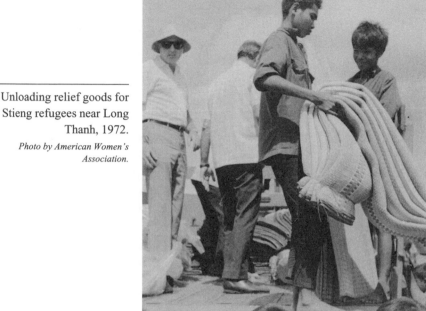

Unloading relief goods for
Stieng refugees near Long
Thanh, 1972.
*Photo by American Women's
Association.*

interested in some historical documents concerning tributary relations
between the Khmer rulers and the Jarai King of Fire she had found at the
nearby archives of the Commission des Moeurs et Coutumes du Cambodge
in the Buddhist Institute. She gave me the name of Madame Pich Sal who
had translated them from Khmer into French. In the still heat of the following morning I went to the Buddhist Institute, a traditional Cambodian
building in a quiet compound with lots of greenery and coconut palms.
Moving silently around the compound, young Buddhist monks in saffron-
yellow robes shaded by matching parasols set a mystical mood. I was taken
to Madame Pich Sal, a charming woman, who brought the documents to
the empty library where I copied them. I worked slowly so as to savor the
wonderful timeless feeling of the place, an island of tranquility.[6]

In October 1972 I agreed to participate in the study being conducted by
the National Academy of Sciences on the effects of herbicides in Vietnam.
During the chaotic movement of refugees as a result of the offensive, I had
encountered some from areas that had been sprayed. The method I selected

was to locate villagers who had witnessed the spraying and have them relate their perceptions to me. Since they live close to nature, the highlanders readily detect any changes in the surrounding physical environment. Normally, such changes are much discussed among the villagers in the light of their past experiences. The cause of a given change in the physical environment may be defined as physical (they can identify numerous kinds of blights) or occult (such as the wrath of the spirits). In the latter case, the judgment is usually left to the older, wiser members of the group. The observations of these individuals normally becomes knowledge shared with all members of the community.

Interviews were conducted in a variety of refugee camps holding Sedang, Halang, Jarai Arap, Jarai Tu-Buan, and Rengao villagers. Given the situation in late 1972, my herbicide interviews usually were interspersed with involvement in other aspects of the continuing war. The first interviews, for example, were conducted in mid November at the Dam San camp near Ban Me Thuot when I accompanied two plane loads of refugee goods. With 5,500 in the camp the goods I delivered proved insufficient (I gave older men the shirts I had brought with me). The refugees related that when the North Vietnamese swept into Dak To, they forced most of the younger men to stay behind. And so practically all of the refugees in Dam San were elderly, children, and women who had no idea if their husbands were alive or dead. Father Wolf, the French priest living in the camp, had it well organized with a school and medical service. The refugees also were weaving textiles and producing baskets and mats, some of which they sold. Father Wolf said the crowded conditions and disruption of their traditional ways gave rise to conflicts and stealing, signs of strain on the social order that had previously characterized village society.

After the herbicide interviews at Dam San I contacted my Rhadé friends who expressed fear that, with the Americans withdrawing, there would be no one to protect them. "Who," two FULRO leaders asked, "will be our mother and father when the Americans leave?" They described how Vietnamese were land-grabbing which precipitated fights between them and Rhadé villagers. They were also concerned about the illegal logging that was destroying much of the forests and the unexploded shells and mines causing deaths and injuries.

The town of Ban Me Thuot seemed normal and French planters still gathered at La Souris Blanche, but some were uneasy about the future of

South Vietnam and were selling their plantations. Only nine American military advisers remained, and civilian contractors (most were former soldiers who returned to be with their Vietnamese "wives") had taken over their mess which they transformed into a strange night club with psychedelic posters on the walls and candles on the tables and bar. The former sergeant running the mess made trips to Nhatrang where his military buddies supplied him with food and beer.

I returned to Saigon to write up notes before continuing herbicide interviews in Kontum and Pleiku. A welcome respite took place when we celebrated the twenty-fifth wedding anniversary of Hugh Mulligan and his charming Irish wife, Brigid. Hugh was with Associated Press, and in addition to being a first-class journalist, he brought badly need wit to the grim Vietnam scene. At the Hotel Miramar a group including Denby Fawcett (*Honolulu Advertiser*), Jolynne d'Ornano, Barbara Gluck (a photographer), Toby Pyle, Father Bob Crawford, and Dr. Tom Durant had a Vietnamese feast. Shortly after, Hugh did an interview with me in the garden of the Hotel Continental Palace. It was one of the longest "print interviews" I had ever done in Vietnam and we covered the whole spectrum of events from my arrival in 1956 to my imminent departure in 1973, including my problems with the Diem government over highland policies and the battle of Nam Dong. Reviewing some of the current problems inflicted by the war I emphasized our responsibility as a nation to help both North and South restore social order. I ended the interview asking myself whether in 50 years time anyone would be around to recall the American presence. And what would they tell their grandchildren?[7]

Meanwhile good fortune struck with an offer by Cornell University's Southeast Asia Program for me to spend the academic year 1973–74 as visiting associate professor. This had come about as the result of two visits to Vietnam by Professor George Kahin, an eminent Southeast Asia scholar who had been critical of the American position in Vietnam. George had contacted me through Tom Fox of the IVS, and I had invited him and his wife, Audry, to my apartment to discuss the war. I also sent him copies of the RAND reports, notably the one on accommodation and coalition. He and Professor Thomas Kirsch, an anthropologist who had done extensive ethnographic research in Thailand, made the decision to invite me, and on 18 December 1972 Tom had sent a letter with the offer. On 8 January 1973 I wrote a letter accepting. I shall be ever grateful to George and Tom, for now I could complete my research without worry and look forward to a university setting where I could write up my findings.

The coming cease-fire dominated Saigon conversation and thoughts. When I returned to Saigon on 20 January 1973, there was a message to telephone Ernie Colantonio (husband of Mildred Colantonio of the American Women's Association). Ernie said Senator Ernest Hollings of South Carolina was visiting Saigon and wanted to get together. The senator wanted to discuss the refugee problem, and it was inevitable that the cease-fire would come up. He asked if it held the promise of peace, and I replied that I felt that the possibility for peace arising from the Paris talks and the cease-fire was very slim.

On Sunday morning 28 January 1973 at 8 o'clock the cease-fire agreed on in Paris (Agreement on Ending the War and Restoring Peace in Vietnam) went into effect. I was in Kontum conducting herbicide interviews and I also had accompanied another shipment of relief goods for Pat's hospital. Pat's hospital was very busy. She was getting highlanders who had been forced to go with the North Vietnamese during the offensive. They had been kept in a remote part of the mountains east of Dak To and many had malaria as well as being seriously undernourished. I accompanied Sister Vincent and Sister Gabrielle to the hospital that ARVN had looted. We were pleased to find the buildings battered but intact. The garden area was still mined, but nevertheless it was apparent that the facilities could be refurbished.

North Vietnamese troops were camped on Route 14 just north of the city (they could be seen washing their clothes in a stream.) My Halhnar assistant and I were doing interviews in the Mary Lou Refugee Center, a former American firebase south of Kontum within sight of the Mount Pao pass where fighting continued. ARVN had launched an operation to retake the pass, and highland refugees were swarming out of villages in the area. In the small Vietnamese settlement near the pass we encountered a group of Jarai Arap who were escaping North Vietnamese troops who the previous day had come into their villages and tried to force the Jarai to go with them. When the villagers refused, the Communists shot a young man in the head. He was still alive, and the refugees were carrying him in a blanket. We put him in a Lambretta transport and told the driver to take him to the Ming Quy (Pat's) hospital. He was treated immediately. A week later, in spite of having the bullet still lodged in his skull, he was sitting up, smiling, and smoking his pipe.

I went to see Bishop Paul Seitz. The pale dry-season sun shone through the French windows, illuminating the faded antique gold lettering on the books lining the shelves of the study in the Kontum Mission building. Bishop Seitz leaned forward over his desk, bringing his hands together in a gesture of finality. "The future of the highland people, Monsieur, is dark." Then he added in an even tone, "They are between zero and infinity." The meaning was all too clear. We had been discussing the history that had swept the highlands since the relatively tranquil day in 1957 when I first saw the bishop coming down the stairs of the rambling building. It was just before a storm broke, a symbolic event in retrospect, for the storm of war in all its fury had ravaged the highlands since that day.

The bishop felt that the cease-fire was part of a Communist strategy. One must remember, he pointed out, that the NLF and North Vietnamese were one and shared the goal of a Communist victory in the south. The North Vietnamese were strong and dedicated, but they were tired and needed a respite, so they agreed to the cease-fire. This also afforded the Americans an opportunity to leave South Vietnam without a disaster. President Thieu was too timid and hesitant to rally any effective force to oppose the Communists successfully. The situation was bound to deteriorate and, since the Communists' strategy called for taking the highlands first, in a matter of time Kontum, Pleiku, and Ban Me Thuot would fall. Standing by the window, the bishop pointed to the hills north of Kontum saying, "Look Monsieur, all that you see to the north, where many of the American battles were fought, is in the hands of the Communists."

Kontum, which before the war had been a very charming town, now had a dispirited air. Sounds of fighting to the south and west could be heard. Much of the city still was in ruins. Most of the surviving shops in the market area were closed, but two restaurants were open and charging very high prices for indifferent Vietnamese food. There was no electricity and in the evening ARVN soldiers wandered around the main street, some of them eating roasted corn being sold by women near the market. Most of those who had fled had not returned, and many of those who did return were preparing to leave.

Before leaving Kontum I went back to Pat's hospital where the nuns and nurses had organized a "jar party" for me with rows of rice-alcohol jars and tables of food in a setting of typical Bahnar decorations. In this festive setting they presented me with hand-woven Bahnar textiles, including a splendid tablecloth and napkins.

The following day I went to Pleiku to conduct the final interviews for the herbicide study. Pleiku was filled with ARVN troops and their dependents. There was more of a feeling of life here than in Kontum, but the town had a squalid air. Most of the bars and steam baths were closed, their gaudy façades now faded. Gone were the heavily made-up girls with their miniskirts (prostitutes who catered to ARVN did not bother with such frills) and the petty thieves (there was nothing to steal). The refugees were now housed in a former prisoner-of-war camp near Route 14 and in Camp Enari, the former U.S. Fourth Infantry Division base on the side of the sacred Hodrung Mountain. Tracy Atwood and his Jarai assistant accompanied me there to conduct interviews. Having seen Camp Enari when it was newly built, I found the scene depressing. ARVN had looted such things as doors and window frames, and dusty wind whistled through the buildings. ARVN also had shot holes in the pipes of the water system so water wastefully spouted into the air. The refugees were jammed in the small rooms, where smoke from cooking fires blackened signs still announcing "Mail Call at 0900" and "Movie Tonite at 2000." Looking at the squalor of the refugees I thought, "Well, the U.S. Fourth Infantry Division came to save them from Communism, and look at them now."

After the interviews I went to see Mike Healy, the last American senior adviser, in the highlands at his quarters on the hill. The building had been built around a beautiful tropical garden that now was overgrown and neglected. With most of the rooms empty, doors banged in the wind. Mike pulled two chairs on to the corridor facing the garden and produced two cans of beer from the last refrigerator in the building. We lamented the situation in the highlands, and Mike asked, "Gerry, who's going to win the war?" I sat back and replied, "The Communists." Mike's views were very similar to those of Bishop Seitz. While I agreed with them, I still felt I should do what I could to help keep Pat's hospital going. Mike agreed to take American hospital equipment and supplies left in Pleiku installations to Pat before the ARVN got them (and would no doubt sell them). Since he was going to Saigon for a meeting with General Weyand, Mike offered me a seat on his plane which I accepted. On 19 February 1973 I left Pleiku and watched the mountain country pass beneath.

Back in Saigon I went to check mail at the Research and Development compound and was surprised to find the few American personnel gone. The

Fuselage hulks of two helicopter gunships stand silent in a grassy field as a storm passes, 1973.

Vietnamese staff seemed incredulous as they told how Sergeant Booker was fixing his usual lunch when a telephone call informed the Americans that a vehicle was coming to take them to the airport. They already had their bags packed, so when the vehicle arrived, Booker turned off the gas under the pots of food and they all departed. I went into the kitchen and since I had not eaten all day, I enjoyed some of the excellent soul food Booker had prepared.

At home I worked on my final report for the Herbicide Study Group. In most of the interviews the informants claimed to have seen the actual spraying. Most aircraft were C-123s but in two instances they were helicopters. Some informants were very explicit about seeing the spray leaving the aircraft. An elderly Sedang lady said "it looked like smoke," and it came from both sides of the aircraft, and this observation was repeated by other Sedang villagers. Jarai Arap informants said that "it looked like rain," and some said they could smell it while others said that when it reached the ground it looked black. Halang from Dak Siang even noticed that protruding from the helicopter was a tube which turned and began to spew a liquid. In only one of the interviews did it appear that there was a deliberate attempt to spray the settlements themselves, although in some instances the villagers' swiddens appear to have been targets. In most cases, however, the spray drifted into the settlements.

There was a definite pattern in perceptions regarding the effects of the herbicides on those residing in the sprayed areas. The most common symptoms reported were abdominal pains and diarrhea. In addition, at the Sedang village of Long Djon many experienced a stinging sensation in their nasal passages, and many developed coughs that lasted more than a month. Sedang of Dak Rosa who went into swiddens following the spraying broke out with skin rashes that lasted for weeks. Halang from Dak Tang Plun reported widespread skin rashes, cramps, diarrhea, and fevers. Jarai Arap described how at Plei Ro-O villagers had the same symptoms, noting that some villagers coughed blood. Jarai Arap from Polei Krong villagers suffered these same ailments and specified that the skin rashes looked "like they had been burned, with small blisters all over the red areas." Halang from Dak Siang noted that after some of the villagers drank from the stream that was in the sprayed area they became ill with abdominal pains and diarrhea that lasted for days. They also reported that some villagers had eaten bamboo shoots from the sprayed area, after which they became dizzy "like you feel when you have drunk too much from the alcohol jar," and later started to vomit. Jarai Arap from Plei Kleng and Plei Jar Tum fell ill with abdominal pains, diarrhea, vomiting, and fever.

During all of the interviews, the revelation of these symptoms was very disturbing, but when the highlanders told of fatal effects, I experienced shock.

At the Sedang village of Long Djon "many children died." Dak Rosa Sedang informants said some women carried their small children on their backs in fields where "medicine" had been sprayed and the children subsequently developed rashes that looked "like insect bites" all over their bodies and died. Several children died after developing abdominal cramps, diarrhea, and skin rashes that resembled burns with small blisters. One Dak Rosa woman knew of three such deaths. At Dak Rosa there also were an "unusual number" of stillbirths among mothers exposed to the herbicides. One woman reported knowing of five stillbirths after the mothers, during pregnancy, had worked in the sprayed fields. Villagers from the Halang village of Dak Tang Plun said that many children became ill and thirty died, while at Dak Siang some children died after drinking water from a sprayed area. In the Jarai To-Buan village of Plei Ngol-Drong, two days after the spraying, some people developed rashes that resembled chicken pox and died. At the Jarai Arap village of Plei Jar Tum, four children and one adult died, and in Plei Kleng about forty adults and children died, while at Polei Krong, a higher than usual number of children died after the spraying. In the village of Plei Ro-O, thirty-eight Jarai Arap children died as a result of eating sprayed crops. One Rengao village chief said that in the week after the spraying "two children died one day and two died the next day."

Most of the informants interviewed reported widespread deaths among domestic animals following the spraying. The Sedang of Long Djon noted that since they were refugees they had few animals, but most of their chickens and pigs died shortly after the spraying. Dak Tang Plun and Plei Ro-O Halang said the same thing and added that some of their cattle died. Polei Krong Jarai Arap information said that in addition to cattle, their dogs died, while Jarai To-Buan of Plei Ngol-Drong reported that they also lost goats (and they noted that goats are "very strong"), and one man also said that the villagers found dead deer and wild boar in the nearby forests. A Plei Ro-O informant noted that villagers found a number of dead wild animals, particularly wild boar, in the nearby forests. Rengao and Jarai Arap informants from Polei Krong also pointed out they found dead wild boar in the forest.

Highland villages normally are located near steams or rivers from which the residents draw water for drinking and cooking. They also wash clothes and bathe, and water their domestic animals in the nearby watercourses, which also provide fish, an important part of the highlanders' diet. Responses concerning perceived effects on the aquatic life in the streams varied more than did those regarding effects on humans and animals. Sedang from Long Djon were not sure whether the dead fish floating on the surface of the neighboring stream were the result of spraying. Since many soldiers in the area commonly threw grenades in the stream to get fish, an abundance of dead fish was not an unusual sight. Dak Rosa Sedang said they did not perceive any changes in the nearby stream. One Plei Ro-O Jarai Arap, however, reported that there were a great many dead fish seen in the streams close to the settlement following the spraying. Most of the fish appeared to be swollen, and villagers who ate them became ill with abdominal pains and diarrhea. Rengao informants from Polei Krong reported that after the spraying they noticed a large number of dead and dying fish floating on the surface of the Bla River, and they specifically noted that the gills of some dead fish were blackened or reddish in color. Some villagers ate fresh or dying fish, and most of them became ill with swollen abdomens and diarrhea. Jarai Arap from Plei Jar Tum said the aircraft sprayed the banks of the Bla River near the village, and afterward a very large number of fish began to float to the surface. They noticed blood and reddish discoloration around the gills, and when some villagers cut into them there was a strange explosive effect which they likened to striking a match. This frightened them, and they did not eat the fish.

Responses regarding the perceived effects on plant life were highly patterned. All of the highland groups in the study farm upland rain-fed rice in their swiddens along with secondary crops. In their settlements they have kitchen gardens and groves of fruit trees next to their houses. Dak Rosa Sedang informants reported that some of the spraying occurred over their swiddens, and very soon afterward the banana plant leaves wilted and the plants died. This also happened to the manioc plants and eggplant. Some villagers dug up the manioc roots, which seemed to be unaffected, but when they cut into them, they were "rotten." Some villagers gathered manioc leaves that had not wilted and boiled and ate them, but they became ill with abdominal pains and diarrhea. Rice plants that had not died continued to grow, but did not produce buds. Dak Tang Plun and Dak Siang Sedang, Jarai Arap from Plei Ro O, and Plei Jar Tum and Rengao ot Plei Krong noted that there was spraying over some of the swiddens in which they cultivated rice and secondary crops (maize, manioc, eggplants, pumpkins, sugar cane, yams, pineapples, cabbage, tobacco, chili peppers, papaya, and orange trees) and all died. On 23 November 1972 at the Dam San refugee camp near Ban Me Thuot a group of five men and two women from the Halang village of New Dak Tang Plun described how they had farmed rain-fed rice and vegetables in swiddens. In 1968, just as the plants were maturing, an American C-123 sprayed the area. Describing the spray as "medicine" the group said, "We didn't know what was happening. We didn't know what to do." Plants began to wilt: leaves on trees dried up and fell. Sickness and death followed and the Halang villagers were reduced to foraging in order to survive.

It was evident that the herbicides had had what could only be called deadly effects on the highlanders and their physical surroundings. Since all of those interviewed were located in areas where Agent Orange was the herbicide sprayed, it clearly was the toxic ingredient dioxin that caused the deadly effects. Of this I had no doubt, but in the report I simply presented the results of my interviews.

When I submitted my report, some members of the committee were surprised at the dire findings and suggested that perhaps the highlanders were not telling the truth. I replied that the highland people by and large were quite honest and frank. Furthermore, those interviewed were from different ethnic groups and villages and their responses were highly patterned. When asked if I would agree to make some changes, I said no.

The comprehensive report prepared by the Committee on the Effects of Herbicides in Vietnam was submitted to the president of the Senate, the Speaker of the House of Representatives, and the secretary of defense on 15 February 1974. In his introductory letter to the report, National Academy of Sciences President Philip Handler stated that "the Committee was unable to gather any definitive indication of direct damage by herbicides to human health. However, to a greater extent than in other areas, there were consistent, albeit largely 'secondhand' reports from Montagnards of acute and occasionally fatal respiratory distress, particularly of children. The inability of the Committee to visit the Montagnards in their own locales so as to verify these tales is greatly regretted."[8]

There was not the slightest effort made by this committee or the National Academy of Sciences to visit the highlands to determine if there was any truth to the highlanders' "tales," as Dr. Handler called them. Nor were any of the researchers of the study group ever consulted by any subsequent agencies examining the effects of herbicide on Vietnamese or Americans exposed to them in Vietnam.

While getting ready to depart, I did some interviews with Jim Wallace of *U.S. News and World Report* concerning prospects for post cease-fire South Vietnam. I pointed out that the fighting was not over because the conflict has been and continues to be political, something which was not resolved by the truce agreements. The cease-fire, I said, created Communist and non-Communist zones, but I felt they would not last. "There simply must be some more general resolution of the over-all problem." I also emphasized that we were leaving a society badly disrupted by the death and destruction of the war with urban populations swollen with refugees and rural people who sought jobs during the American presence (and were now unemployed). These interviews were supplemented with a meeting with the *U.S. News and World Report* staff in Washington, and the results were published in August 1973.[9]

Nay Luett gave a large dinner at a Chinese restaurant with highlander and American friends. Pierre and Jolynne d'Ornano also had a bon voyage dinner (guests included Martine Piat and Nghiem Tham) as did Barbara Gluck and Joe Treaster whose guest list included down-to-earth author James Jones, a welcome addition to the gathering. On the morning of 31 March 1973 (the day the last American military personnel departed) I boarded the States Lines SS *Idaho* (and one of the sergeants at customs had been a MSUG driver, so he got his troopers to carry the luggage). That evening friends came on board for cocktails and then we all went to the nearby Tour d'Argent restaurant for cracked crab and other Vietnamese specialties.

The following morning, 1 April 1973, I left Vietnam, perhaps never to return. There was, as the ship moved silently away from the quay into the receding tide, a sudden feeling of finality—a mingling of sadness with a curious sense of relief. I stood on the deck as the buildings of Saigon passed out of view. Life along the Saigon River seemed normal until we reached the Rung Sat mangrove swamp, now desiccated by herbicides, a reminder of the continuing Vietnam War.

As the SS *Idaho* sailed in a northeastern course within sight of coastal central Vietnam, the setting sun fell on two peaks the French called "La Mère et l'Enfant" in the Rhadé country. I watched them fade into the darkness, my last glimpse of Vietnam and the highland world.

EPILOGUE

WHEN, IN TIMES PAST, doctors recommended a sea voyage for replenishing the wellsprings of those suffering from maladies of the spirit, they were right. My spirit had been battered by the war years in Vietnam, and I badly needed the tonic of a voyage on the sea with its blue waters, wide horizons, and fresh winds to sort things out and put the Vietnam years in perspective.

As the SS *Idaho* made its way across the Pacific Ocean, I pondered my years in Vietnam and what I had seen through the window. The years from 1956 to 1973 had been for me an ethnographic odyssey, and like all odysseys it was a journey full of adventures, changing fortunes, and varying quests.

One absorbing quest was into the mysterious depths of "Vietnameseness," that is, the heart, the veiled essence of Vietnamese culture and character. Another equally absorbing quest was into the formation of a highlander leadership that would fuel ethnonationalism in the mountain country. As it turned out, these two quests became intertwined when they took me down unexpected ethnographic paths, from the high Vietnamese culture of Hue through urban quarters to the village of Khanh Hau and beyond, into the world of the highlanders. And they carried me into the realm of history from the recent to the primordial.

With the ethnographic study of Khanh Hau and visits to Hue, I came to realize that while most scholars of Vietnamese history and culture emphasize the importance of Buddhism and Confucianism, the religious ideology most intertwined with life in the village and in the high culture world of Hue was Taoism mixed with the Spirit Cult. Taoism was part of Vietnam's Chinese heritage, but what was the origin of the Spirit Cult? This is not an easy question, as the syncretic Vietnamese have a long his-tory of borrowing cults, rituals, and deities. Then, as my ethnographic odyssey took me to the central highlands, I found among the northern-most Mon Khmer–speaking Bru, Pacoh, Katu, Hre, and Cua, certain cul-tural elements, notably veneration of spirits associated with nature and with rice farming, similar to those in the very early Lac culture of north-ern Vietnam. Since linguists have concluded that the Vietnamese lan-guage belongs to the Austroasiatic stock and very likely of the Mon Khmer family, these links strongly suggested that the Spirit Cult of the Vietnamese has its roots in their primordial Mon Khmer past. Most Viet-namese with whom I discussed this balked at the idea that they shared ancestral roots with highlanders. I nonetheless clung to my hypothesis. Looking at the endless rolling waves of the Pacific Ocean, I felt deep down that while it no doubt could never be proven, my hypothesis had validity.

My thoughts also turned to the setting—the Vietnam in which my odyssey had taken place—and the changing scenes between 1956 and 1973. During that period my anthropologist's eye observed the initial peri-od of peace between 1956 and 1960, then the insurgency of the early 1960s, and finally the Vietnam War.

In 1956 I had felt strongly that American economic support of the new Ngo Dinh Diem government was justified because South Vietnam showed promise of becoming a viable state within the new post-colonial order of Southeast Asia. In Saigon, the enthusiasm and sense of hope were palpable, and seeing thousands of northern refugees arriving in Cai San to escape Communism and begin a new life was a reminder that South Vietnam was a haven. Traveling throughout the rural areas, I marveled at the way the Viet-namese were repairing large bridges blown up during the Indochina War and building new roads. American aid was contributing to construction of new institutions of education from primary schools to universities, and medical facilities were being improved and expanded. Everywhere were signs that capitalism was on the rise.

At the same time, I was beginning to experience a loss of innocence concerning American leadership. Initially I had an image of American leaders in Saigon seriously engaged in efforts to understand the Vietnamese, their history, and particularly their intense nationalism. I soon found that this was not true. By and large, American leaders were suffering from vincible ignorance about Vietnamese nationalism because it was something they did not care about. They ethnocentrically projected their own values when judging the conduct of leaders such as Ngo Dinh Diem and his brother, Ngo Dinh Nhu. Consequently, American officials never gained any understanding of these Vietnamese leaders with whom they would have to deal in the perilous times ahead.

When my odyssey took me to the central highlands, I found a region of South Vietnam ripe for trouble that could have far-reaching effects on the stability of the new nation. I sympathized with the highlanders' discontent with President Diem's policy of forcibly integrating them into the Vietnamese cultural sphere. My concern led to a quest into ways of establishing communication between highlanders and leaders in Saigon and in the American mission. I was in effect becoming an intermediary, something I did not anticipate.

The June 1957 reports Price Gittinger and I wrote (the only ones on the highlands based on field research) contained pertinent ethnographic information and suggested an accommodation by the Saigon government to the wants and desires of highland leaders. Price's report was suppressed and mine was ignored. I was discouraged from further work in the central highlands.

It occurred to me that perhaps the American mission in Saigon ignored our findings because Price and I were making recommendations that would have delayed implementation of the Highlands Land Development Program that President Diem wanted and the American aid mission was eager to finance. After all, in 1957 I was a graduate student and Price was not a high-ranking member of the aid mission. We were not people to contend with. Or perhaps American decisionmakers simply were not concerned because they viewed the central highlands as a peripheral area with a numerically insignificant population.

In 1957 I believed that American decisionmakers in Saigon and Washington would heed the results of research that spoke to a situation with which they should be very concerned. Their refusal, for whatever reasons, shook my faith in the American presence in Vietnam.

On the Vietnamese side, I understood that with no experience at administering the highlands, President Diem lacked knowledge of its people and their desire to retain a highlander ethnic identity. It was very possible that President Diem was prevented from learning anything about the reality of the highlands situation by some of his advisers, notably the self-serving Wolf Ladejinski, the most vocal critic of our reports. Or, perhaps President Diem did not want to be exposed to the reality of the highlands situation. I soon was to learn that those in positions of high leadership often surround themselves with a cordon of "advisers" to prevent the intrusion of any realities that might raise disturbing questions about decisions or strategies. I came to realize that, by and large, Vietnamese leaders did not want to learn anything about the highland people.

By 1959, the golden afternoon of peace and hope in South Vietnam was fading. In Khanh Hau we witnessed the advent and initial spread of Communist insurgency in the Mekong River delta. At the end of the decade it was apparent that social and economic gains made by the South Vietnamese since 1956 were, because of the Communists, being slowed and in danger of being reversed.

In January 1961, the official founding of the NLF (to create the fiction that the emerging insurgency was an independent southern movement) prompted Washington's response with the Counterinsurgency Plan, which increased American military involvement.

In January 1962, in a setting of insurgency, John Donnell and I embarked on a study of the newly launched Strategic Hamlet Program. This turned out to be an experience that sorely tested my already wavering feelings that American involvement in South Vietnam was justified. Since the Khanh Hau study had given me great respect for South Vietnamese villagers, I bristled at the extreme examples of disruption and disregard we found in some of the Strategic Hamlets. The theatrical ceremony marking the official opening of the Cu Chi Strategic Hamlet, with its abundance of tanks, troops, and American military and civilian officials, and total absence of ordinary villagers, embodied the faults of the whole program.

In our Saigon and Washington debriefings, it was apparent that the generals and Pentagon officials wanted to believe that all Vietnamese villagers feared and opposed the Viet Cong and would therefore welcome the Strategic Hamlets. They had convinced themselves that the program was succeeding. Our assessment of the program questioned this, and the Pentagon's attempt to rebut our findings jolted me into the realization that decisionmakers in Saigon and Washington were less interested in seeking the truth than in doggedly defending programs they had conceived and formulated in American terms. As it turned out, the Strategic Hamlet Program proved to be a failure.

I came out of this experience with enhanced respect for Frank Collbohm, president of RAND, who in the name of independent research successfully defended our report.

In 1963 I had no idea that the rising tide of anti-Diem reporting in the American media and the brutality of the Diem government in coping with protesting Buddhists were playing into the hands of American and Vietnamese plotters out to overthrow the Saigon regime. They had uncovered the well-guarded secret that Diem and Nhu were making an accommodation to the NLF in the hope of avoiding a destructive war in South Vietnam. Diem and Nhu were murdered. Had they lived, the Vietnam War might well have been averted.

The question remaining unanswered is, "Who on the American side decided that because they were making an accommodation to the NLF, Diem and Nhu had to be removed?" Lucien Conein acted as CIA liaison with the Vietnamese generals involved in the plot, and Ambassador Lodge had a role. Washington gave the green light for the coup, but who made the decision? It has never been revealed.

Drawing on their belief in fate and destiny, Vietnamese friends immediately pointed out that on 1 November in a moving vehicle President Diem was shot in the head and on 22 November President Kennedy died the same way.

In 1957 the central highlands had been adjudged peripheral; by 1964, with Communist infiltration and American military build-up, the region had become "strategic." It was all too clear that the worsening conflict would threaten the highlanders' way of life, so gathering ethnographic data was imperative. In the highlands I was not surprised to find leaders I had known, now very involved in ethnonationalistic activities expressed in movements such as Bajaraka. Then the September FULRO revolt brought to the highlands a new era of armed dissidence, and at the same time it made highlander ethnonationalism a force to be reckoned with. With this it was inevitable that my role as intermediary would deepen and highland leaders would become close friends. This led to my interest in their pattern of interethnic group marriages among the elite, a conscious effort to produce a kin network effective in the spread of ethnonationalism and a pan-highlander ethnic identity.

Conducting the American military adviser study in 1964 made me aware of the very professional caliber of many army and navy men serving in Vietnam. Those at low levels working closely with Vietnamese counterparts understood the nature of insurgency. As I spent time with the U.S. Special Forces A-Teams throughout the highlands, I increasingly felt that their operations were well suited to insurgency. Their program drew men who wanted to be soldiers and face the dangers that rural South Vietnam held. This was dramatically demonstrated when my odyssey took me to the Nam Dong Special Forces camp, where on 6 July 1964 a large force of crack Communist troops attacked. Facing overwhelming odds, members of A-Team 726 displayed professionalism, discipline, and courage, delivering a victory. Despite this, some American generals in Saigon regarded the Special Forces with unease and sometimes downright suspicion (the adjective "unconventional" was officially used in describing their style of warfare). If more conventional warfare was what the American generals wanted, they no doubt were pleased when American forces—army, navy, marine, and air force—intervened in South Vietnam. With this, and the presence of North Vietnamese forces, insurgency became the Vietnam War.

American military strategy was drawn from experiences in World War II and the Korean War, but the very different Vietnam War called for a new approach. This never happened. Military decisions to dispatch combat units, unleash firepower with bombers and artillery, and use herbicides were made without regard for their impact on the social, political, economic, or religious dimensions of South Vietnamese society. To anyone like me on the ground, witnessing the results was appalling. Our military strategy in response to increased Communist aggression was contributing unduly to widespread death and destruction that were tearing apart the fabric of the society and rendering the Vietnamese people warweary.

Such blind strategy was inevitable, given that American leaders were making decisions far removed from the ground and its grim realities. They were comfy in wood-paneled offices surrounded by "advisers." Together they used the latest systems-analysis tricks to construct models that were fictions, far removed from reality. They wanted to hear positive results, so the models were geared to show "progress." It was an elaborate and convincing form of self-deception. In response to criticism of his destructive strategy, Robert McNamara cried, "I didn't know," but everything indicated that he didn't want to know.

Had I known that Ngo Dinh Diem and his brother Nhu were murdered in 1963 because of their accommodation-coalition idea to prevent escalation from insurgency to war, I might have hesitated to advocate the same idea. But by 1966 the Vietnam War was wreaking havoc and so I spoke out. It was to no avail because American leaders did not understand that the war was a political struggle that could only be resolved by political means and they firmly believed that their military strategy was succeeding.

And so the Vietnam War raged on and reached a peak of violence with the 1968 Tet Offensive, which drew the urban areas into the vortex. Now the war enveloped all of South Vietnam: willingly or unwillingly everyone participated.

The shock of the 1968 Tet Offensive and the opening to the Paris Peace Talks on 18 May raised the possibility that a political solution might be considered, so I prepared an updated version of accommodation-coalition. It still was to no avail. American leaders had deluded themselves into believing that pacification and the firm leadership of President Thieu would deliver a successful end to the war.

By the beginning of 1971 American interest in the central highlands had faded, and I realized the time was coming when I would best return to the United States to write up my field materials. My quest to find an amenable American academic setting, like most of my quests since 1956, brought mixed results. In an April 1971 decision ("emotional rather than intellectual") the anthropology faculty at the University of Chicago rejected me. But on 18 December 1972 Cornell University professors George Kahin and Thomas Kirsch offered me a visiting associate professor slot.

The 1972 Communist offensive that began on 31 March and lasted for months was deadly, causing incredible disruption and shattering most of the social and economic programs that I had helped my friends at the MDEM devise and implement.

When by October relative calm returned, my last quest in Vietnam was to determine the effect of herbicides on the highlanders. I was stunned and saddened by the harmful effects of Agent Orange on the villagers. The comprehensive report prepared by the Committee on the Effects of Herbicides in Vietnam (dated 15 February 1974) was submitted to the president of the Senate, the Speaker of the House of Representatives, and the secretary of defense. The National Academy of Sciences president Philip Handler's introductory letter carried a disclaimer, calling reports by the highlanders "secondhand" and "tales." The Academy of Sciences' disclaimer was an attempt to discount any possibility that Agent Orange might have had deadly effects. Experience should by now have prepared me for such denial, but I found it shocking that such a supposedly august institution would stoop so low.

There was no follow-up study. In 1998 a Vietnamese doctor claimed that some seventy thousand suffered from illnesses caused by Agent Orange.[1] The following year Seth Mydans reported that a Canadian environmental research group, Hatfield Consultants, conducted a five-year study of the highland A Luoi valley (in the Katu country where Special Forces had a camp in 1965). They found high levels of dioxin in the soil, in fish and animal tissue, and in the blood of people born after the war.[2] The same article noted that the Veterans Association in Washington was offering veterans compensation for ten diseases and the birth defect spina bifida linked or possibly linked to spraying in Vietnam. In March 2000 an air force report said there was "particularly strong evidence" tying Agent Orange to the onset of diabetes in veterans who were involved in spraying in Vietnam.[3]

When I sailed from Saigon on 1 April 1973, it was all too apparent that the continuing war had irreversibly shifted in favor of the North Vietnamese Communists. But my odyssey had not ended because in many respects odysseys never end.

In the quiet of Cornell University I kept in touch with my highlander friends, Touneh Han Tho, Nay Luett, Pierre K'Briuh, and Y Thih Eban who in their letters expressed a sense of having been abandoned by the Americans, which they had. Y Thih Eban wrote on 10 August 1973 that "the situation at the ministry is getting worse by the day." He added that the government wanted to do away with the ministry and also rescind the 9 November 1970 law that called for each highland village to receive title to a village-owned territory.

Before leaving Vietnam I had tried to find out who in Washington or Saigon successfully advocated total support of President Thieu, a weak and corrupt leader without a trace of popularity among the Vietnamese. Washington remained silent while Thieu trampled on nationalism, systematically cracking down on any opposition and closing newspapers. Some felt that because of unqualified American backing, Thieu thought he had license to do what he wanted. This was not the view of Ngo Dong Duc, an anti-Thieu publisher and former member of the lower house who was forced to leave Vietnam. Mr. Duc visited the Cornell University Southeast Asia Program on 5 February 1975 where he met with the staff and students. He was an organizer in Paris of a "Third Force," composed of leaders among the Buddhists, Catholics, Hoa Hao and Cao Daists, and representatives of nationalist parties as well as former military officers and political exiles. The Third Force advocated "reconciliation" and was in the process of making an accommodation with the NLF. Mr. Duc said that in the coming months Thieu would be toppled and a council of representatives drawn from the Third Force would take over and name a chief of state. They would immediately call a cease-fire and open negotiations with the NLF to hold elections. The new government would have the total support of the Vietnamese people who wanted to end the bloodshed and destruction. In Mr. Duc's view, Thieu's iron-fisted behavior was a pose to create the illusion of strength when it really was a reflection of his desperation. His grip on power was weakening and the American Congress was slashing military aid. Mr. Duc concluded with the dire prediction that if Thieu were to face defeat he would try to bring South Vietnam down with him.

I found it most interesting that now with the Americans out of South Vietnam, nationalists felt free to come forward and realize their desire for accommodation with the NLF leading to a coalition and an end to the war.

Sadly, this attempt was too late. On 29 April 1975, Gen. Duong Van Minh, now president (Thieu had fled to Taiwan), asked his troops to lay down their arms as Communist troops entered Saigon. The first day of May marked the end of the Vietnam War.

Ironically, the series of events that led to the collapse of the South Viet-namese government began with the 12 March 1975 fall of Ban Me Thuot. The failure of the Saigon government to reach any accommodation with the FULRO movement between 1964 and 1975 contributed directly to this loss. Around 1970, with Y Bham Enuol under house arrest in Phnom Penh and negotiations with the Saigon government stalled, FULRO lacked strong leadership. One result was internal fragmentation. In 1972 a splin-ter FULRO group in the Ban Me Thuot area became involved in a search for missing Americans (which had been launched with offers of money by John Paul Vann before his death in June 1972). Leaders of this FULRO group also eyed profits to be made by selling timber to the Vietnamese. This led in November 1973 to collaboration with local Viet Cong forces who by March 1974 began using FULRO as a front to gain Rhadé vil-lagers' support. With four North Vietnamese divisions in the highlands, Gen. Van Tien Dung decided to move on Ban Me Thuot. The FULRO group which did not inform the province chief knew the build-up of Com-munist forces. The city fell on 12 March 1975.

With this, President Thieu made the fateful decision to abandon Pleiku and Kontum and withdraw his forces to the coast. The govern-ment's abandonment of the highlands also was ironic. Long convinced that the Vietnamese would never defend the mountain country, highland leaders had time and again asked the government and the Americans to allow them to form a fifty thousand–man defense force. The request was never honored. Thieu's evacuation of the highlands turned into a rout that earned for the Communists the dubious distinction of having inflicted the worst blood bath of the Vietnam War as they viciously attacked military and civilians fleeing the region. ARVN fought but the Communist forces rolled ahead.

By 3 April 1975, Hue, Danang, Qui Nhon, and Nhatrang had fallen, and the following day, Nay Luett, Touneh Han Tho, Ksor Rot, Touprong Ya Ba, Pierre K'Briuh, and Nay Alep met with officials of the American Embassy who assured them the South Vietnamese army would defend Saigon. Nay Luett asked the officials to include the highland leaders and their families in the American evacuation plans. On 28 April as the Com-munists were closing in on Saigon, highland leaders with their families gathered at Nay Luett's house to be evacuated. No evacuation buses came. Touneh Han Tho wisely returned to his own house, and on 29

April got his family to the former MACV headquarters where they boarded helicopters (as they flew away, Han Tho looked down to see Pentagon East burning after American marines threw thermal grenades into
the offices). Onboard the aircraft carrier, Midway, officers took Han Tho's
Cham sabers that had been in his family for generations (I subsequently wrote letters to the Navy Department to retrieve the sabers, but the
response was that they had been thrown overboard, something I do not
believe).

Meanwhile in neighboring Cambodia, Phnom Penh fell to the Khmer
Rouge on 17 April 1975. FULRO leaders Y Bham Enuol, Ksor Dhuat,
Kpa Doh, and Bun Sur were in the city (young leader Ksor Kok was in
the United States for military training) and took refuge in the French
Embassy as the population was forced into the countryside. FULRO leaders, along with Cambodian officials and officers, were removed from the
French Embassy by the Khmer Rouge and taken to Lambert Stadium. As
a colonel in the Khmer army, Bun Sur was taken away on a truck and
probably executed. The other FULRO leaders were moved in trucks north
of the city, but none was heard from again.

In Saigon, the MDEM was abolished in June. As highland leaders
returned to their native areas they were arrested and sent to jails where
under harsh conditions Nay Luett, Paul Nur, and others died while Y Thih
Eban and Ksor Rot were executed. Pierre K'Briuh (who spent nine years in
the Communist prisons) and Nay Alep (who was imprisoned fifteen years)
survived and eventually left Vietnam for the United States.

Soon after the fall of South Vietnam, my friend Pham Xuan An
emerged as a high-ranking Viet Cong officer. I never suspected he was
playing a double role, but then I had not given it any thought because one
never knew which side anyone was on.

After the fall of Ban Me Thuot a large number of FULRO followers,
now calling themselves Dega-FULRO, most of them Rhadé, went into the
forests to organize resistance to Communist rule. When large Vietnamese
Communist forces moved against them, only temporary support came
from the Khmer Rouge. According to my friend Y Yok Ayun in 1984 some
307 Dega-FULRO members, discouraged by lack of outside support, elected to move across Cambodia to reach Thailand. Using their skills at surviving in the forest, they reached the Thai border. In November 1986, two
hundred of these refugees were sent to North Carolina.

In late August 1992, Nate Thayer reported in the *Far Eastern Economic Review* that he had visited a redoubt of four hundred FULRO troops deep in the forests of the Cambodian province of Mondolkiri.[4] Living in five riverine villages, their adaptation was based on small gardens, hunting, and gathering. At the end of 1991, the United Nations mandated that foreign forces be repatriated, resettled in Cambodia, or removed to a third country as refugees. FULRO leader Y Hin Nie realized their only recourse was to go to the United States as refugees. They contacted the United Nations and the American Embassy in Phnom Penh arranged to bring Pierre K'Briuh from North Carolina to serve as intermediary with the "Lost Army." The FULRO troops (the Vietnamese government had put a price on their heads) were moved to a tent city near Phnom Penh, guarded by U.N. forces. In mid November 1992 the first group of FULRO troops boarded planes to leave for North Carolina.

These events marked the end of a very effective highlander leadership that had dealt admirably with the Saigon government and the American mission. The highland people were now left with no one to represent them.

Following their 1975 victory, the Communists' programs and policies have had varied effects in the two places where my ethnographic field work had been conducted—the Mekong River delta village of Khanh Hau and the central highlands.

In June 1979 I received a letter from an editor at *Encyclopaedia Britannica* about writing an article on the reunited Vietnam, and I accepted.[5] When in 1970 I had researched an earlier *Britannica* article I had found that despite the disruptions of the Vietnam War, capitalism was on the move in South Vietnam. For the 1980 article, research indicated that the Hanoi government was having problems with the capitalist South. The 1977 decision to accelerate the pace of southern integration into the socialist sphere was momentous and the effects were immediate. Southern private enterprise collapsed, and there was a massive exodus of ethnic Chinese. There also was a serious decline in agricultural production, particularly in the Mekong River delta where agrarian reform was running into problems. "In the rich Mekong River delta, the government had to deal not with large landlords, but with their former tenants who had become individual proprietors. The majority of the southern farmers in the late 1970s were middle-income peasants who owned enough land and

implements to farm successfully without relying on outside labor. With
their skill and experience in farm management, they were central figures
in the rural economy of the south." I had also found that among factors
cited for the decline in paddy production after 1976 were "the southern
farmers' reaction against collectivization and their unwillingness to produce a surplus for the markets while money and consumer goods were
in short supply."

"Preliminary research" in Khanh Hau during the summer of 1992 by
American anthropologist Hy Van Luong indicates that Khanh Hau in
many respects presented a microcosmic view of the government's failure
at collectivization which I had mentioned in the *Britannica* article.[6] He
reports that the Communists in 1977 had launched a land reform program to eliminate private agriculture and establish sale and credit cooperatives to reduce the role of private enterprise in industry and commerce.
In Khanh Hau (whose population which in 1958 was 3,241 had by 1992
increased to 8,734) the Communists classified twenty households as landlords, most them listed as traitors because they were supposed to have
collaborated with the Saigon government. The local government redistributed seventy hectares of their land to fifty village households. It
"encouraged" one hundred middle peasant households in the village to
donate more than one hundred hectares of "surplus" land to one hundred
landless families. Also in 1977 the local government assisted in formation of thirty-five solidarity production teams. At the end of 1978, rice
land was collectivized with formation of seventeen cooperative teams that
controlled all of the village farmland, including pagoda and communal-
temple (*đình*) lands.

Hy Van Luong reports that the cooperative movement in Khanh Hau
did not proceed smoothly. The village government reported acts of overt
and covert resistance. These included distribution of leaflets denouncing
cooperative team leaders, exertion of social pressure on their family
members, and even physical violence against them. Anti-cooperative slogans appeared on public walls, and 125 petitions were delivered to higher authorities for permission to leave cooperative teams. When authorities failed to act positively on these petitions, some villagers lay in the
path of tractors in fields they claimed. Of the estimated 1,300 village
households, 284 seized their land, causing the collapse of three cooperative teams. The government arrested a few ringleaders in order to exert

pressure on the dissident households. By 1980 most of these households returned to the cooperatives, but nine of them remained outside.

By and large, religious beliefs and practices were tolerated. While the local government withdrew its symbolic support for the Cult of the Guardian Spirit in Khanh Hau, the cult continued to be observed. The communal temple, although reduced to only the main sanctuary and allowed to deteriorate, remained the site of annual rituals which were curtailed and simplified (rather than offering pigs and cattle, chickens became the sacrificial animals). Although attacked as having been hostile to the Communists, Cao Daism continued to function in the village as did the cult of Marshal Nguyen Huynh Duc, a Khanh Hau deity.

The floundering situation I had described in the 1980 encyclopaedia article forced some basic changes in Vietnam. With the 1986 appointment of Nguyen Van Linh as Communist Party secretary general, a new program of economic renovation (called đổi mới) was launched to introduce elements of a free market and private enterprise while dismantling farm cooperatives.

Hy Van Luong reports that local village and provincial authorities faced an open challenge to their "collectivistic ideology." A year before implementation of the economic renovation, a few hundred Khanh Hau villagers demonstrated in Tan An, the provincial capital, to demand that their land be returned to them.[7] In 1987, all but two of Khanh Hau "landlords" were reclassified as "rich peasants" or "middle peasants." One result was that around four hundred village households became landless again, so the province government offered each of them 1.1 hectares of land in the Plain of Reeds where draining projects had increased the amount of arable land. These families maintained residence in Khanh Hau and sent male members to farm in the Plain of Reeds.

Agricultural production increased. In Khanh Hau the landowners began in 1987 to triple-crop paddy fields and they increased cash cropping. Hy Van Luong notes that "in 1992, the households of Khanh Hau were incorporated into the world system more than at any point in village history because village farmers purchased large amounts of chemical fertilizer and produced rice mainly for the international market."

Economic innovation also produced a proliferation of private enterprises. Hy Van Luong reports that in 1991–92 there were seven large restaurants; three sex bars (prostitution, alcohol, and coffee); 114 small shops; sixteen buses and trucks; six motorized three-wheeled vehicles and eight non-motorized ones; about a dozen informal middlemen for trade in paddy, handicraft products, and livestock; at least a dozen small-food processors; and 70–80 petty traders.

A sign of the greater prosperity was the spread of television. Even among the twenty households in the poorest quarter of the main hamlet, four owned television sets, one with color.

In 1988 the local government returned the two communal temple complexes to their cult committees, and rituals became better attended and more elaborate. Attendance also increased in the Buddhist, Caodaist, and Catholic places of worship. Family rituals associated with the Cult of the Ancestors and rites of passage such as marriages drew increased numbers of guests (who were no longer concerned about wearing traditional tunics).

As Hy Van Luong observes, "By 1992, the premises of capitalism had again saliently shaped the socioeconomic life in Khanh Hau!"

Khanh Hau has survived wars and sweeping political changes and now in the wake of economic innovation the village has entered a new era of globalization that is having widespread effects on the whole village society.

In 1958 Khanh Hau found an economy based solidly on rice cultivation with most villagers directly involved in it. Village society was characterized by homogeneity in attitudes and values with a cosmological view deeply rooted in the Taoist-Buddhist-Confucianist tradition. There also was homogeneity in the villagers' style of life, in social expectations, and in livelihood activities. There was manifest moral order. The village still was a small world that jealously guarded its way of life and disregarded (if not disdained) the outside world. But we also found that the relative isolation of the village was lessening, and the ways of the village were increasingly being encroached on by the ways of the modern world.

The 1991–92 research by Hy Van Luong strongly suggests this process of globalization and change has accelerated.[8] For one thing, it would appear that the previous relative isolation of Khanh Hau has vanished. Village population has more than doubled. Whereas in 1958 Khanh Hau had six battery-operated radios, by 1991–92 villagers had continuous contact with the outside world through the proliferation of modern communications. Furthermore, with Khanh Hau now producing rice mainly for the international market, livelihood activities have become more differentiated with an array of new enterprises many of which involve non-farming specializations. Some traditional religious rituals and rites of passage such as weddings and funerals have continued, but the appearance of three "sex bars" raises questions about moral order.

Changes described by Hy Van Luong indicate that one price Khanh Hau is paying for the material benefits brought by globalization is the dwindling of its little-community qualities. The corporate character we found in 1958 is being lost with a diminishment of homogeneity in style of life, attitudes and values, social expectations, and livelihood activities.

On 28 April 2000, two days before the anniversary of the end of the Vietnam War and reunification of the country under Communist rule, *New York Times* journalist Seth Mydans visited Khanh Hau.[9] At the shrine of Marshal Nguyen Huynh Duc (built in 1959, our team had contributed money and carried symbolic baskets of earth for the foundation) he encountered an eighty-year-old descendant, Bui Thi Van, who declared, "We still work in the fields. We still worship here. We have water and electricity now, but actually nothing has changed." Then she added, "I don't go anywhere, so how can I see any changes." Mydans notes that if she went the short distance to National Route 4 she would see the "forward edge of advancing development" in the form of new factories manufacturing textiles, ceramics, plastics, and aluminium plates along with billboards advertising tires, pesticides, face cream, and family planning that line the road.

Since 1975 the fate of the highland people has been radically different. The history of the highlanders has been one of tragedy. My odyssey among them taught me that their way of life, attuned as it is to nature and cosmic forces, could never withstand the crushing onslaught of a modern world attuned to power and money.

In some areas of the highlands, French economic colonialism brought changes in the physical environment with rubber and coffee estates, but by and large the French respected highlanders' ways, centered as they were in village communities. Furthermore, in 1923, French administrators Léopold Sabatier and Pierre Pasquier sought to protect the highlanders' land rights in the face of inroads by French commercial forces.[10]

Sadly, this was the last time any such official attempt was made.

The ethnocentrism and chauvinism of the Ngo Dinh Diem era would have wrought changes in village communities by Vietnamizing them, but the advent of insurgency and the Vietnam War prevented this. Nonetheless, the 1957 Land Development Program of the Diem government set a tone for all subsequent "development" schemes (whether Vietnamese, non-Vietnamese, Communist, or non-Communist) in ignoring the potential role of the highland people as participants because they were not sufficiently "advanced."

Following their 1975 victory, the Communists have brought to bear the same mix of Vietnamese ethnocentrism and chauvinism as the Saigon governments, but now they added the Marxist-Leninist perspective which deprecated highland people as "primitive" (in the worst sense), their rites of passage as "backward," and their religious beliefs and practices as "superstitions." This has led to the worst oppression the surviving highlanders have ever experienced. It also has contributed to wanton destruction of the highland physical environment.

Masters of deception, the Communists with their rhetoric, policies, and programs for the highlanders convey the impression that the upland region will be developed socially and economically with the highlanders fully participating. This is a clever ruse to mask the fact that Hanoi is engaged in terrible violations of the highlanders' human rights. The Communists have succeeded in hoodwinking the United Nations (which probably was unnecessary since in June 1976, a visiting United Nations team headed by Dr. Victor Umbricht, a Swiss Red Cross official, recommended that 8 million Vietnamese be resettled in the highlands[11]), the World Bank, Washington, and other supposed champions of human rights into believing that the massive resettlement of millions of lowland Vietnamese in the highlands is "economic development" from which the "nomadic" highlanders moved into "permanent communities" will benefit. Hanoi's repression of the highlanders' successful adaptation to the mountains by banning their traditional farming and ignoring their claims to land are justified as "saving the environment" when it is land-grabbing of the most blatant variety. The "permanent communities" ploy masks a ruthless program wherein highlanders have been forced to abandon their traditional habitations (very well suited to the mountain environment) as they have been dispersed into Vietnamese settlements. The goal has been to break up highlanders' clans and lineages (particularly the matrilineages) as one means of systematically erasing their ethnic identity while they are forced into the Vietnamese cultural sphere as second-class citizens at best.

In the central highlands, the 1986 economic renovation has had the effect of worsening the already disastrous effects of Hanoi's programs and policies by opening the doors to globalization which has made coffee production profitable. One result has been the Hanoi regime's seizure of highlanders' lands for state coffee estates. Another result has been a vast increase in land-grabbing squatters.

In mid 2001, Mike Benge, who has spent many years working in the central highlands, interviewed a large number of highlander refugees in two U.N. camps in Cambodia. He reports that "the government confiscated the Montagnards' ancestral lands to create vast state-run coffee plantations financed by the Asian Development Bank and the World Bank."[12] Consequently, "the Montagnards have been relegated to small parcels of land too small to grow enough food to feed their families." (There is no information on the fate of the 326 Rhadé coffee planters who in 1970 cultivated 513 hectares.)

Benge notes that "Vietnam has become the world's largest exporter of Robusta coffee and has dumped coffee on the international market, causing prices to plummet and impoverishing millions of coffee farmers in Latin America and elsewhere."

Benge's last point was echoed in a 6 September 2001 Associated Press dispatch from Nicaragua by Niko Price who observes that "politics and economics have left residents of Los Milagros without jobs, without food and without much hope."[13] He explains that this situation was caused "unwittingly more than a decade ago by bankers in Washington and politicians in Paris." In an effort to help Vietnamese peasants develop a new cash crop, the World Bank and the French government invested heavily in Vietnam's coffee industry. An 8 November 2001 article in the *New York Times* blamed the coffee glut on "a surge in production in Vietnam, where coffee is cheap because of labor costs and subsidies."

Benge warned in his August 2001 article that "the pending U.S.–Vietnam Bilateral Trade Agreement will only exacerbate this problem." Ratification of this agreement by the U.S. Congress took place in October and in Hanoi the following month. Seth Mydans reported in the *New York*

Times on 20 November 2001 that "in announcing the ratification today, the official Vietnam News Agency made reference to 'nonintervention in each other's internal affairs,' a phrase that responds in particular to American criticism of human rights standards in Vietnam."[14] Mydans added that "the Vietnamese government has reacted angrily [*sic*] to the recent passage in the House of Representatives of a Vietnam Human Rights Act that would tie future non-humanitarian aid to improvements in Hanoi's record on human rights. The measure is now before the Senate."

In December 2001, Gregory Stock, who has been closely monitoring the highlander situation in Washington, reported that in the press of legislation that followed by the 11 September attacks, "Congress found time to push through the U.S.–Vietnam Bilateral Trade Agreement. Immediately thereafter, President Bush signed the agreement. Even more troubling was the fact that Senator John Kerry, a major proponent of the trade bill, used the opportunity to block the Vietnam Human Rights Act, HR 2833, from coming to the floor for a vote."[15]

Meanwhile, although government-sponsored resettlement of lowland people ceased, the possibility of profits in cash crops (particularly coffee) in a renovation free market has brought to the highlands vast numbers of outsiders. Most are Vietnamese but in recent years they have been joined by northern Tai-speaking Nung and Tay as well as Hmong. This is particularly true in Dak Lak province, heart of the Rhadé country, where in the 1920s the "terres rouge," reddish brown latosols of the Darlac plateau, attracted French coffee and rubber estates. Highlander refugees describe how with economic renovation, grabbing of Rhadé lands by Vietnamese (including the military) had increased and the clearing of beautiful hardwood forests by settlers and illegal loggers has become more widespread (even extending to northeastern Cambodia) creating dire shortages of wood for fires, construction, and artifacts. Water sources have been seriously depleted.

Apart from the question of what the glut on the world market will mean for increased coffee production in Vietnam, there is the matter of soil fertility. Most of the central highlands is dominated by "mountain soils," which are relatively infertile and have a low water-holding capacity, causing them to become very dry in the dry season and susceptible to erosion. Ironically, such soils lend themselves to the swidden farming traditionally practiced by the highland people but now barred by Hanoi.[16]

Given the marked lack of success in growing coffee and rubber in the Diem-era Land Development Centers, one wonders how these smaller holdings will fare in the hands of inexperienced planters.

In April 1995 there appeared in the *Bangkok Post* an account of an extensive tour of the mountain country titled "Central Highlands in the Sunflower Season," written by Nguyen Ngoc, a prominent Vietnamese novelist and former editor of *Van-chuong* (Literature) magazine.[17] The account was the result of a month-long scouting mission for locations to shoot a movie based on one of his novels. With the eye of a novelist, Nguyen Ngoc saw the sunflower as a metaphor for the region. "Sunflowers belong to Tay Nguyen. They embody something profound and discrete about the mountains, forests, people, and the culture of Tay Nguyen, which at first glance seem wild and primitive. Yet when observed with respectful and soulful eyes, they offer a noble culture built on many beautiful and delicate layers."

Nguyen Ngoc observed, "We are doing great things there. We have covered tens of thousands of hectares along a strip of south Truong Son range with rubber plantation and we have planted tens of thousands of hectares of coffee plants."

But, traveling thousands of kilometers, Nguyen Ngoc found that the sunflower cultural qualities he so much admired had become elusive in the highlands. "Nearly a month had passed, but we could not find a real, virgin village to use in our film. We found some villages, but they were either in horrible condition or too hybrid." This raised in his mind the efficacy of changes the government's policies and programs have wrought. "It is true that because the highland used to have a nomadic lifestyle and mobile agriculture, we must enlist campaigns promoting a sedentary life for them. Please, allow me to say: I have doubts about this."

Nguyen Ngoc's misgivings are justified. As a result of Hanoi's policies and the advent of globalization, highland people now find themselves reduced to a fringe population in their own mountain country, a people more between zero and infinity than they had been at any previous period.

But the resilience and courage they displayed during the Vietnam War had not abandoned them. On 29 January 2001, there erupted angry demonstrations by thousands of highlanders. According to an 8 February article (based on a 6 February 2001 Reuters dispatch) in the *New York Times,* "Two important coffee-growing provinces of Vietnam's central highlands were tense today after several days of sometime violent land and rights protests by thousands of ethnic-minority people."[18] The protests were started "by disputes including land encroachment by Vietnamese," and "religious rights," problems "exacerbated by corruption among officials." A *New York Times* article (drawing on a 7 February 2001 *Agence France-Presse* dispatch) observed that "Vietnam's authorities acknowledged today that a wave of unrest in the Central Highlands had been more extensive than they had previously admitted, leading to several injuries and 20 arrests."[19] This article noted that "members of outlawed Protestant churches which have a large following among the ethnic minorities, have joined the protests in large numbers out of anger over the confiscation of their churches and the breakup of religious services."

Agence France-Presse reported on 8 February that the authorities closed off the central highlands while troops, riot police, and helicopters were deployed in the areas of unrest adding that "as the authorities intensified their clampdown, they moved to ensure that there would be as few independent witnesses as possible."[20]

A 27 March Associated Press article noted that the Vietnamese government accused a "U.S.-based group, the Montagnard Foundation, of instigating the unrest."[21] A 5 April 2001 dispatch reported that Vietnam accused the United States of attempting "to destabilize the region by offering asylum to 24 Vietnamese hill tribespeople being held in neighboring Cambodia, and asked Cambodia to send them home."[22] A 26 June 2001 article by Jacqueline Becker and Mark Lioi, journalists in Cambodia, reports that "human rights groups working in eastern Cambodia say both Vietnamese and Cambodian authorities have sealed off the border to prevent more [highlander] refugees from reaching Cambodia. They also assert that Vietnamese police are directing Cambodian security forces in a large-scale manhunt inside Cambodia."[23]

On 5 May 2001, the *New York Times* reported that some three hundred highlanders, who had boarded buses in North Carolina, staged a protest in New York at the American Stock Exchange and later at the United Nations.[24] Among them were twenty-four Rhadé who in February had take refuge in Cambodia where they had been turned over by the Cambodian authorities to the United Nations High Commission for Refugees in Phnom Penh. The U.S. Embassy then arranged for them to be flown to North Carolina. They and the other highlanders carried signs in Vietnamese, Chinese, French, and English calling on the United Nations to demand that they, "the hill regions' earliest settlers, of Mon-Khmer and Malayo-Polynesian descent, be recognized as 'endangered people.'"

The protests were clearly a desperate *cri de coeur* to call attention to the Communist government's blatant violations of their human rights. Initially it appeared that beyond the mountain country the highlanders' cry would be lost. But now the cry has been heard on the streets of New York. Furthermore, other developments at this time revealed that the demonstrations were a manifestation of widespread and politically significant unrest which could not be ignored, particularly in Hanoi. In reporting these events, the *Indochina Chronology* noted that authorities in Hanoi punished thirteen members of the Ethnic Affairs Department, including chairman Hoan Duc Nghi.[25]

So now in the new century and new millenium it is all too apparent that the worlds of the highlanders and Khanh Hau that I had seen through the window between 1956 and 1973 are rapidly vanishing. We who knew and admired those worlds in the twentieth century can only lament their passing. We might reflect on how poor the new millennium will be without them, but that would be unrealistic. The inescapable reality is that as everyone in the coming years is swept along by globalization, no one will remember that those vanished worlds ever existed at all.

CHAPTER 1. A BREATH OF PEACE AND HOPE

1. Gerald C. Hickey, ed. *Area Handbook on Laos*. HRAF Subcontractor's Monograph No. 23.

2. This botanical planning is reflected in Direction des Eaux et Forêts de l'Indochine, Service des Recherches et de l'Enseignement Forestiers, *Guide botanique de la ville de Saigon*.

3. Bao Dai's role in the central highlands is discussed in Gerald Cannon Hickey, *Sons of the Mountains: Ethnohistory of the Vietnamese Central Highlands to 1954*, pp. 367–69, 401, 404, 406, 410–13, 425–26. A different treatment of Bao Dai in the highlands can be found in Gerald Cannon Hickey, *Kingdom in the Morning Mist: Mayrena in the Highlands of Vietnam*, pp. 188–96.

CHAPTER 2. RUMBLINGS

1. This situation is discussed in detail in Gerald Cannon Hickey, *Free in the Forest: Ethnohistory of the Vietnamese Central Highlands, 1954–1976*.

2. Nguyen Huu Chau, the secretary of state at the presidency, to the chief advisor of MSUG, memorandum, Saigon, 2 April 1957.

3. J. Price Gittinger, "Tenure in Ban Me Thuot Land Development Projects: Situation and Recommendations (Summary)," mimeographed, Saigon, 18 June 1957.

4. Gerald C. Hickey, "Research Report on the PMS." Saigon: Michigan State University Vietnam Advisory Group, June 1957.

5. For further information on the highlander, Cham, and Khmer ethnonationalistic movements see Hickey, *Free in the Forest,* pp. 60–62, 92, 98, 118, 205.

6. Katu ethnography can be found in Gerald Cannon Hickey, *Shattered World: Adaptation and Survival among Vietnam's Highland Peoples during the Vietnam War,* pp. 107–40.

7. J. Le Pichon, "Les chasseurs de sang," *Bulletin des Amis de Vieux Hué* 25, no. 4 (1938): 362.

8. Léopold Cadière, *Croyances et pratiques religieuses des Vietnamiens,* 2d ed., 1:6–7.

9. This finding is discussed more fully in Gerald Cannon Hickey, *Sons of the Mountains: Ethnohistory of the Vietnamese Central Highlands to 1954,* pp. 5–7, 61–63.

10. James B. Hendry, *The Study of a Vietnamese Rural Community: Economic Activities*; Gerald C. Hickey, *The Study of a Vietnamese Rural Community: Sociology*; Lloyd W. Woodruff, *A Study of a Vietnamese Rural Community: Administrative Activity,* 2 vols.

11. H. G. Creel, *Chinese Thought from Confucius to Mao Tse-tung,* pp. 106–26.

CHAPTER 3. INSURGENCY

1. Robert Shaplen, *The Road from War: Vietnam 1965–1970,* pp. 4–6.

2. Bernard Fall, *Viet-Nam Witness, 1953–1966,* pp. 144–46, 152–54.

3. John C. Donnell and Gerald C. Hickey, *The Vietnamese "Strategic Hamlets": A Preliminary Report.*

4. Steve Hosmer, *Maintaining the Independence of RAND's Research Product,* RAND Alumni Bulletin Supplement.

5. Published in Paris by Editions du Seuil in 1952.

6. Frank M. Lebar, Gerald C. Hickey, and John K. Musgrave, *Ethnic Groups of Southeast Asia.*

7. Gerald Cannon Hickey, *Village in Vietnam*; James B. Hendry, *The Small World of Khanh Hau.*

8. Ethnographic information on the Stieng is included in Gerald Cannon Hickey, *Shattered World: Adaptation and Survival among Vietnam's Highland Peoples during the Vietnam War,* pp. 77–106.

9. Léopold Cadière, *Croyances et pratiques religieuses des Viêtnamiens* 2:236–39; G. Langrand, *Vie sociale et religieuse en Annam: Monographie d'un village de la côte Sud-Annam.*

10. Ethnographic data on the Bru and Pacoh are included in Hickey, *Shattered World,* pp. 141–74.

CHAPTER 4. VICTORY AT NAM DONG

1. Capt. Roger Donlon as told to Warren Roger with a foreword by Senator Robert F. Kennedy, *Outpost of Freedom.* A condensed version was published in Capt. Roger H. C. Donlon as told to Warren Rogers, "Outpost of Freedom, A Condensation of the Book," *Reader's Digest Condensed Books,* vol. 1, 1966, pp. 7–83. Accounts of the Nam Dong battle itself were excerpted for Capt. Roger H. C. Donlon, U.S. Army, as told to Warren

Rogers, "The Battle for Nam Dong," *Post,* October 28, 1965, pp. 38–53; and Detachment A-726, "Captain Roger H. C. Donlon, Vietnam Hero," *Coronet,* December 1965, pp. 58–65.

CHAPTER 5. THUNDERHEADS

1. Howard Sochurek, "American Special Forces in Action in Vietnam," *National Geographic* 127, no. 1 (1965): 38–65.

2. Neil Shcchan et al., *The Pentagon Papers: As Published by the New York Times,* pp. 311–15.

3. George W. Ball, "Top Secret: The Prophecy the President Rejected," *Atlantic Monthly* 230, no. 1 (1972): 36–50.

4. W. C. Westmoreland, "Report on Operations in South Vietnam: January 1964–June 1968," in U. S. G. Sharp and W. C. Westmoreland, eds., *Report on the War in Vietnam: As of 30 June 1968,* section 2, p. 107.

5. Gerald C. Hickey and W. Davison, *The American Military Adviser and His Foreign Counterpart: The Case of Vietnam.*

6. Charles Meyer, *Derrière le sourire Khmer,* pp. 269–71.

7. Gerald C. Hickey, "Memorandum on the Refugee and Montagnard Situation in Pleiku Province," Saigon, RAND Corporation, 25 August 1965.

CHAPTER 6. THE VIETNAM WAR

1. These findings are discussed in Gerald Cannon Hickey, *Sons of the Mountains: Ethnohistory of the Vietnamese Central Highlands to 1954,* pp. 126–43, 164–81.

2. Ward Just, *To What End: Report from Vietnam,* pp. 167–91.

3. Such solidarity would be similar to the "organic solidarity" envisaged by Emile Durkheim in his work, *The Division of Labor in Society.* This solidarity arises out of the interdependence and need to cooperate as the division of labor in society becomes more specialized and diverse.

4. Gerald C. Hickey, *Accommodation in South Vietnam: The Key to Sociopolitical Solidarity.*

5. South Vietnam National Front for Liberation, *Political Programme of The South Viet Nam National Front for Liberation,* pp. 29–30.

6. Gerald C. Hickey, *The Highland People of South Vietnam: Social and Economic Development.*

7. Zalin Grant, "Counting on Strength That's Not There," *New Republic,* June 15, 1968.

8. Discussion of the import of ethnography on epidemiological research among the Stieng, Rhadé, and Sedang can be found in Gerald Cannon Hickey, *Shattered World: Adaptation and Survival among Vietnam's Highland Peoples during the Vietnam War,* pp. xxi–xxii, xxiv, 79, 247, 283–84.

CHAPTER 7. THE TET OFFENSIVE

1. Raymond R. Coffey, "Even Hints of Coalition Rattle Saigon," *Chicago Daily News,* 13 January 1968.

2. Robert Shaplen, *The Road from War: Vietnam 1965–1970,* pp. 182–84.

3. Ibid., p. 209.

4. Keyes Beech, "Heavy Red Losses: War's Turning Point?" *Chicago Daily News* 8 February 1968.

5. An account of the Tet Offensive throughout the highlands is contained in Gerald Cannon Hickey, *Free in the Forest: Ethnohistory of the Vietnamese Central Highlands, 1954–1976,* pp. 168–86.

6. Carl Mydans, "Refugees on the Bridge to Nowhere" *Life,* 26 April 1968.

CHAPTER 8. AFTERMATH

1. Gerald C. Hickey, "Memorandum on the Current Situation in the Highlands," Saigon, RAND Corporation, 3 May 1968.

2. W. E. Colby, "To Report on the Current Status of the Edap Enang Resettlement Project," Saigon, 8 May 1968.

3. Alice Hsieh, RAND Corporation, letter to The Honorable William F. Bundy, assistant secretary for East Asian and Pacific Affairs, Department of State, Santa Monica, Calif., 19 June 1968.

4. Bernard Weinraub, "U.S. Impact on Vietnam Life Called Devastating," *New York Times,* 11 June 1968.

5. Headquarters, Military Assistance Command, Vietnam, Operations and Analysis Division, *Revised Hamlet Evaluation Handbook,* p. 5. The Hamlet Evaluation System was a computerized program for measuring development and security in rural areas. Using a standard form programmed for computers, American military advisers in collaboration with their counterparts recorded accomplishments (e.g., how many hamlets had become secure) and incidents (e.g., ambushes). The monthly reports were compiled in Saigon and were supposed to reflect the situation in the rural areas throughout the country.

6. Gerald C. Hickey, "Myths Concerning the Highlanders," Saigon, RAND Corporation, 11 January 1969.

7. W. E. Colby, personal correspondence to author, 21 January 1969.

8. U.S. Embassy Committee on Montagnard Affairs, "Statement Concerning Resettlement of Highland Villages," Saigon, 20 February 1969.

9. Gerald C. Hickey, "Population Relocation in the Highlands," Saigon, RAND Corporation, 20 March 1969.

10. Joint Development Group, *The Postwar Development of the Republic of Vietnam: Policies and Programs* 2: 465–90 and Summary, pp. 61–66.

11. Marquis Childs, "The U.S. in Vietnam: A Gulliver Made Helpless by Lilliputians," *Washington Post,* 2 April 1969.

12. C. L. Sulzberger, "Foreign Affairs: The Third Level," *New York Times,* 11 April 1969.

13. Maynard Parker, "The Illusion of Vietnamization," *Newsweek,* 29 September 1969.

14. Gerald C. Hickey, *Accommodation and Coalition in South Vietnam.*

15. Daniel Southerland, "Sharing Called Viet Solution," *Christian Science Monitor* 12 February 1970.

16. Gerald C. Hickey, *The Highland People of South Vietnam: Social and Economic Development.*

17. Gerald C. Hickey, *Some Recommendations Affecting the Prospective Role of Vietnamese Highlanders in Economic Development.*

18. Hickey, *The Highland People of South Vietnam,* pp. 91–93.

19. For a classical source on Cambodian peasant society, see Jean Delvert, *Le paysan Cambodgien.*

20. Daniel Southerland, "Why Cambodia Didn't Fall," *Christian Science Monitor,* 9 November 1970.

21. I recorded observations of the situation in Cambodia during this period in *The War in Cambodia: Focus on Some of the Internal Forces Involved.*

22. Cf. "Vietnam, South," *Encyclopaedia Britannica,* 1974, pp. 138–44.

CHAPTER 9. AMERICAN WITHDRAWAL

1. Richard Nixon, letter to author, the Western White House, San Clemente, 22 August 1970.

2. Gerald C. Hickey, "Memorandum on Montagnard Land Ownership and Area Defense," Saigon, RAND Corporation, 20 July 1970.

3. R. W. Komer, RAND Corporation, letter to author, Santa Monica, Calif., 28 July 1970 (emphasis his).

4. Eugene Knez, personal correspondence, 19 February 1970.

5. Gerald C. Hickey, "Memorandum on the Uncertain Future of Montagnard Refugees in Cam Lam District, Khanh Hoa Province," Saigon, RAND Corporation, 9 September 1970.

6. Gerald C. Hickey, "Memorandum on the Unlearned Lessons of History: Relocation of Montagnards," Saigon, RAND Corporation, 13 February 1971.

7. Gloria Emerson, "Anthropologist in Vietnam Seeks Montagnard Gain," *New York Times,* 25 April 1971; Peter Osnos, "Security a Disaster for Montagnards," *Washington Post,* 25 April 1971.

8. Kevin Buckley, "The War in Indochina, Departing Words," *Newsweek,* 3 May 1971.

9. U.S. Congress, Senate, Committee on Foreign Relations, *Legislative Proposals Relating to the War in Southeast Asia,* 92d Cong., 1st sess., pp. 425–84.

10. Fred Eggan to author, personal correspondence, 17 December 1970.

11. Norton Ginsburg to author, personal correspondence, 3 March 1971.

12. Ibid., 22 March 1971.

13. Fred Eggan to Bernard S. Cohn, Chairman, Department of Anthropology, memorandum, regarding Gerald C. Hickey, 11 March 1971.

14. Fred Eggan to author, personal correspondence, 15 March 1971.

15. Arthur T. Hadley to author, personal correspondence, 27 March 1971.

16. Fred Eggan to author, personal correspondence, 5 April 1971.

17. Israel Shenker, "Anthropologists Clash Over Their Colleagues' Ethics in Thailand," *New York Times,* 21 November 1971.

18. Everett Martin to author, personal correspondence, 20 October 1971.

19. William Braden, "Levi Denies U. of C. Blackballed Scholar over Viet Link," *Chicago Sun-Times,* 8 December 1971.

20. Arthur R. Nayer, University of Chicago Alumni Association to Dear Alumnus, Chicago, Illinois, 13 December 1971.

21. Joseph A. Morris, chairman, Students for Capitalism and Freedom at the University of Chicago to William F. Kirby, president, *Wall Street Journal,* University of Chicago, 6 December 1971.

22. Everett Martin to author, personal correspondence, 8 December 1971.

23. Andrew H. Malcolm, "Vietnam Expert's Bid Stirs Chicago U.," *New York Times,* 12 December 1971.

24. Norton Ginsburg, "What the Center Is/Is Not," *Center Report,* February 1972, pp. 11–12.

25. Harry C. Holloway, M.D., to author, personal correspondence, 8 December 1971.

26. Denis Warner, *Certain Victory: How Hanoi Won the War,* p. 182.

27. Charles F. Keyes, "Tribal Ethnicity and the State in Vietnam," *American Ethnologist* 11, no. 1 (1984): 176–82.

28. Eugene Knez to author, personal correspondence, 6 December 1971.

29. Ibid., 16 February 1972.

30. Clifford Evans, chairman, Department of Anthropology, National Museum of Natural History, Smithsonian Institution, to Mr. Gerald C. Hickey, RAND Corporation, Washington, D.C., 6 September 1972.

CHAPTER 10. LAST DAYS

1. Harry Rowen, RAND Corporation, letter to author, Santa Monica, Calif., 24 May 1968.

2. John P. White, vice president, RAND Corporation, letter to author, Santa Monica, Calif., 25 April 1972.

3. Vann's place among other outsiders who sought power and authority in the central highlands is discussed in Gerald Cannon Hickey, *Kingdom in the Morning Mist: Mayrena in the Highlands of Vietnam,* pp. 199–206.

4. I used this incident as a lead in an op-ed piece, "The Lost Montagnards," that, thanks to Gloria Emerson, the *New York Times* published on 26 August 1973.

5. Daniel Southerland, "U.S. Pullout Leaves Viet Highlanders in the Lurch," *Christian Science Monitor,* 19 July 1972.

6. The information in the documents and other data supplied by Martine Piat were used in Gerald C. Hickey, *Sons of the Mountains: Ethnohistory of the Vietnamese Central Highlands to 1954,* pp. 140–42.

7. Hugh A. Mulligan, "Saigon Old-timer Looks at the War," Associated Press, 28 January 1973. The full-page article was also published in the *Washington Post* and even in the *Pacific Stars and Stripes* on 31 January 1973.

8. National Academy of Sciences, Committee on the Effects of Herbicides in Vietnam, *The Effects of Herbicides in South Vietnam;* Part A, *Summary and Conclusions,* p. x. My findings were more objectively treated in an article by John Finney, "Vietnam Defoliants Study Sees Effect of 100 Years," *New York Times,* 22 February 1974.

9. "Can South Vietnam Make It On Its Own?" *U.S. News and World Report,* 13 August 1973.

EPILOGUE

1. Philip M. Boffey, "Agent Orange in Vietnam, 30 Years Later," *New York Times,* 8 September 1998.

2. Seth Mydans, "Vietnam Sees War's Legacy in Its Young," *New York Times,* 16 May 1999.

3. Philip Shenon, "Air Force Report Links Agent Orange to Diabetes," *New York Times,* 29 March 2000.

4. Nate Thayer, "The Forgotten Army," and "Trail of Tears: 'Lost' Montagnard Army Vows to Fight On," *Far Eastern Economic Review,* 10 September 1992, pp. 16–22.

5. *Encyclopaedia Britannica,* 1980, s.v. "Vietnam, Socialist Republic of."

6. Hy V. Luong, "The Marxist State and the Diaglogic Re-Structuration of Culture in Rural Vietnam," in *Indochina: Social and Cultural Change,* ed. David W. P. Elliott, Ben Kiernan, Hy Van Luong, and Therese M. Mahoney, pp. 79–111.

7. Ibid., pp. 101–108.

8. Ibid., pp. 100–108.

9. Seth Mydans, "As Vietnamese Modernize, Villages Cleave to the Past," *New York Times,* 30 April 2000.

10. This protection is discussed in Gerald C. Hickey, *Sons of the Mountains: Ethnohistory of the Vietnamese Central Highlands to 1954,* pp. 297–308.

11. Gerald C. Hickey, *Free in the Forest: Ethnohistory of the Vietnamese Central Highlands, 1954–1976,* p. 88.

12. Mike Benge, "Persecution of the Montagnards," *Washington Post,* 20 August 2001.

13. Niko Price, "Coffee glut has bitter taste to workers," Associated Press, 6 September 2001.

14. Seth Mydans, "Relations at Last Normal, Vietnam Signs U.S. Trade Pact," *New York Times,* 29 November 2001.

15. Greg Stock, "Abandoned Allies, the Montagnard People," *Air Commando Newsletter,* December 2001, pp. 29–32.

16. F. R. Moorman, *The Soils of the Republic of Vietnam,* pp. 6–11.

17. Nguyen Ngoc, "Central Highlands in the Sunflower Season: Tay Nguyen Will Remain Tay Nguyen, Modern and Traditional, Civilized and Virgin," *Bangkok Post,* 30 April 1995.

18. "Minority Protests in Vietnam Focus on Land and Rights Issues," *New York Times,* 8 February 2001.

19. "Vietnam Admits to More Unrest Among Minorities in Highlands," *New York Times,* 9 February 2001.

20. *Agence France-Presse* 8 February 2001.

21. Tini Tran, "Vietnamese Villagers Clash with Cops," Associated Press, 27 March 2001.

22. David Thurber, "Vietnam Accuses U.S. over Asylum," Associated Press, 5 April 2001.

23. Jacqueline Becker and Mark Lioi, "Flight from Vietnam," *San Francisco Chronicle,* 26 June 2001.

24. Barbara Crossette, "New Protests Against Vietnam: Montagnards Rally Over Land, Coffee and Rights," *New York Times,* 5 May 2001.

25. "Bulky Public," *Indochina Chronology, 7.*

BIBLIOGRAPHY

UNPUBLISHED WORKS

Colby, W. E. "To Report on the Current Status of the Edap Enang Resettlement Project." CORDS Report, Saigon, 8 May 1968.

Gittinger, J. Price. "Tenure in Ban Me Thuot Land Development Projects: Situation and Recommendations (Summary)." Mimeographed. Saigon, 18 June 1957

Hickey, Gerald C. "Memorandum on the Current Situation in the Highlands." RAND Corporation, Saigon, 3 May 1968."

———. "Memorandum on Montagnard Land Ownership and Area Defense." RAND Corporation, Saigon, 20 July 1970.

———. "Memorandum on the Refugee and Montagnard Situation in Pleiku Province." RAND Corporation, Saigon, 25 August 1965.

———. "Memorandum on the Uncertain Future of Montagnard Refugees in Cam Lam District, Khanh Hoa Province." RAND Corporation, Saigon, 9 September 1970.

———. "Memorandum on the Unlearned Lessons of History: Relocation of Montagnards." RAND Corporation, Saigon, 13 February 1971.

GOVERNMENT DOCUMENTS

France, Service des Recherches et de l'Enseignement Forestiers, Direction des Eaux et Forêts de l'Indochine. *Guide botanique de la ville de Saigon.* Saigon: REF, 1949.

South Vietnam National Front for Liberation. *Political Programme of the South Viet Nam National Front for Liberation.* South Vietnam: Giai Phong Publishing House, 1967.

U.S. Army, Headquarters, Military Assistance Command Vietnam, Operations and Analysis Division. *Revised Hamlet Evaluation Handbook.* Saigon: MACV, 1968.

U.S. Congress, Senate, Committee on Foreign Relations. *Legislative Proposals Relating to the War in Southeast Asia.* 92d Cong., 1st sess., 1971, pp. 425–84.

U.S. State Department, Embassy to the Republic of South Vietnam, Committee on Montagnard Affairs. "Statement Concerning Resettlement of Highland Villages," Saigon, 20 February 1969.

PUBLISHED WORKS

Agence France-Presse, 8 February 2001.

"Balky Public." *Indochina Chronology* 19, no. 4 (2000): 7.

Ball, George W. "Top Secret: The Prophecy the President Rejected." *Atlantic Monthly* 230, no. 1 (1972): 36–50.

Becker, Jacqueline and Mark Lioi. "Flight from Vietnam." *San Francisco Chronicle,* 26 June 2001.

Beech, Keyes. "Heavy Red Losses: War's Turning Point?" *Chicago Daily News,* 8 February 1968.

Benge, Mike. "Persecution of the Montagnards." *Washington Post,* 20 August 2001.

Boffey, Philip M. "Agent Orange in Vietnam, 30 Years Later." *New York Times,* 8 September 1998.

Braden, William. "Levi Denies U. of C. Blackballed Scholar over Viet Link." *Chicago Sun-Times,* 8 December 1971.

Buckley, Kevin. "The War in Indochina, Departing Words." *Newsweek,* 3 May 1971.

Cadière, Léopold. *Croyances et pratiques religieuses des Vietnamiens.* 2d ed. 3 vols. Saigon: Nouvelle Imprimerie d'Extreme-Orient, 1958.

"Can South Vietnam Make It on Its Own?" *U.S. News and World Report,* August 13, 1973.

"Captain Roger H. C. Donlon, Vietnam Hero." *Coronet,* December 1965, pp. 58–65.

Childs, Marquis. "The U.S. in Vietnam: A Gulliver Made Helpless by Lilliputians." *Washington Post,* 2 April 1969.

Cochod, Louis. *Hué la mystérieuse.* Paris: Mercure de France, 1943.

Coffey, Raymond R. "Even Hints of Coalition Rattle Saigon." *Chicago Daily News,* 13 January 1968.

Creel, H. G. *Chinese Thought from Confucius to Mao Tse-tung.* London: Eyre & Spottiswoode, 1954.

Crossette, Barbara. "New Protests against Vietnam: Montagnards Rally over Land, Coffee and Rights." *New York Times,* 5 May 2001.

Delvert, Jean. *Le paysan Cambodgien.* Paris: Mouton, 1961.

Donlon, Roger H. C., and Warren Rogers, "The Battle for Nam Dong." *Post,* October 28, 1965, pp. 38–53.

———. *Outpost of Freedom.* New York: McGraw-Hill Book Company, 1965.

Donnell, John C., and Gerald C. Hickey. *The Vietnamese "Strategic Hamlets": A Preliminary Report.* Santa Monica, Calif.: RAND Corporation, 1962.

Durkheim, Emile. *The Division of Labor in Society.* Trans. George Simpson. New York: Free Press of Glencoe, 1964.

Emerson, Gloria. "Anthropologist in Vietnam Seeks Montagnard Gain." *New York Times,* 25 April 1971.

Fall, Bernard. *Viet-Nam Witness, 1953–1966*. New York: Frederick A. Praeger, 1966.

Finney, John. "Vietnam Defoliants Study Sees Effect of 100 Years." *New York Times,* 22 February 1974.

Ginsburg, Norton. "What the Center Is/Is Not." *Center Report,* February 1972, pp. 11–12.

Grant, Zalin. "Counting on Strength That's Not There." *New Republic,* June 15, 1968.

Hendry, James B. *The Small World of Khanh Hau.* Chicago: Aldine Publishing Company, 1964.

———. *The Study of a Vietnamese Rural Community: Economic Activities.* Saigon: Michigan State University Advisory Group, 1959.

Hickey, Gerald C. *Accommodation and Coalition in South Vietnam.* Santa Monica, Calif.: RAND Corporation, 1970.

———. *Accommodation in South Vietnam: The Key to Sociopolitical Solidarity.* Santa Monica, Calif.: RAND Corporation, 1967.

———. *Free in the Forest: Ethnohistory of the Vietnamese Central Highlands, 1954–1976.* New Haven: Yale University Press, 1982; reissue, CD-ROM, Houston: RADIX Press, 2003

———. *The Highland People of South Vietnam: Social and Economic Development.* Santa Monica, Calif.: RAND Corporation, 1967.

———. *Kingdom in the Morning Mist: Mayrena in the Highlands of Vietnam.* Philadelphia: University of Pennsylvania Press, 1988; reissue, CD-ROM, Houston: RADIX Press, 2003

———. "The Lost Montagnards." *New York Times,* 26 August 1973.

———. "Myths Concerning the Highlanders." Saigon: RAND Corporation, 11 January 1969.

———. "Population Relocation in the Highlands." Saigon: RAND Corporation, 20 March 1969.

———. "Preliminary Research Report on PMS." Michigan State University Advisory Group, Saigon, June, 1957.

———. *Shattered World: Adaptation and Survival among Vietnam's Highland Peoples during the Vietnam War.* Philadelphia: University of Pennsylvania Press, 1993; reissue, CD-ROM, Houston: RADIX Press, 2003

———. *Some Recommendations Affecting the Prospective Role of Vietnamese Highlanders in Economic Development.* Santa Monica, Calif.: RAND Corporation, 1971.

———. *Sons of the Mountains: Ethnohistory of the Vietnamese Central Highlands to 1954.* New Haven: Yale University Press, 1982; reissue, CD-ROM, Houston: RADIX Press, 2003

———. *The Study of a Vietnamese Rural Community: Sociology.* Saigon: Michigan State University Advisory Group, 1960.

———. *Village in Vietnam.* New Haven: Yale University Press, 1964; reissue, CD-ROM, Houston: RADIX Press, 2003

———. *The War in Cambodia: Focus on Some of the Internal Forces Involved.* Santa Monica, Calif.: RAND Corporation, 1970.

————, and W. Davison. *The American Military Adviser and His Foreign Counterpart: The Case of Vietnam.* Santa Monica, Calif.: RAND Corporation, 1965.

————, ed. *Area Handbook on Laos.* HRAF Subcontractor's Monograph No. 23. Chicago: University of Chicago, 1955.

Hosmer, Steve. *Maintaining the Independence of RAND's Research Product.* RAND Alumni Bulletin Supplement. Santa Monica, Calif.: RAND Corporation, 1998.

Hy V. Luong. "The Marxist State and the Dialogic Re-Structuration of Culture in Rural Vietnam." In *Indochina: Social and Cultural Change.* Edited by David W. P. Elliott, Ben Kiernan, Hy Van Luong, and Therese M. Mahoney. Claremont McKenna College Monograph Series, No. 7. Claremont, Calif.: Keck Center for International and Strategic Studies, Claremont McKenna College, 1994.

Joint Development Group. *The Postwar Development of the Republic of Vietnam: Policies and Programs.* 3 vols. and Summary. Saigon and New York: Postwar Planning Group, Development and Resources Corporation, 1969.

Just, Ward. *To What End: Report from Vietnam.* Boston: Houghton Mifflin Company, 1968.

Keyes, Charles F. "Tribal Ethnicity and the State in Vietnam." *American Ethnologist* 11, no. 1 (1984): 176–82.

Langrand, G. *Vie sociale et religieuse en Annam: Monographie d'un village de la côte Sud-Annam.* Lille: Editions Univers, 1945.

Lebar, Frank M., Gerald C. Hickey, and John K. Musgrave. *Ethnic Groups of Southeast Asia.* New Haven: Human Relations Area Files Press, 1964.

Le Pichon, J. "Les chasseurs de sang." *Bulletin des Amis de Vieux Hué* 25, no. 4 (1938): 362.

Malcolm, Andrew H. "Vietnam Expert's Bid Stirs Chicago U." *New York Times,* 12 December 1971.

Meyer, Charles. *Derrière le sourire Khmer.* Paris: Plon, 1971.

"Minority Protests in Vietnam Focus on Land and Rights Issues." *New York Times,* 8 February 2001.

Moorman, F. R. *The Soils of the Republic of Vietnam.* (Saigon: Republic of Vietnam, Ministry of Agriculture, 1961), pp. 6–11.

Mulligan, Hugh A. "Saigon Old-timer Looks at the War." *Washington Post,* 8 January 1973; Associated Press, 28 January 1973; *Pacific Stars and Stripes,* 31 January 1973.

Mus, Paul. *Viêt-Nam: sociologie d'une guerre.* Paris: Editions du Seuil, 1952.

Mydans, Carl. "Refugees on the Bridge to Nowhere." *Life,* 26 April 1968.

Mydans, Seth. "As Vietnamese Modernize, Villages Cleave to the Past." *New York Times,* 30 April 2000.

————. "Relations at Last Normal, Vietnam Signs U.S. Trade Pact." *New York Times,* 29 November 2001.

————. "Vietnam Sees War's Legacy in Its Young." *New York Times,* 16 May 1999.

National Academy of Sciences, Committee on the Effects of Herbicides in Vietnam. *The Effects of Herbicides in South Vietnam,* Part A, *Summary and Conclusions.* Washington, D.C.: NAS, 1974.

"New Leader in Vietnam." *New York Times,* 22 April 2001.

Nguyen Ngoc. "Central Highlands in the Sunflower Season: Tay Nguyen Will Remain Tay Nguyen, Modern and Traditional, Civilized and Virgin." *Bangkok Post,* 30 April 1995.

Osnos, Peter. "Security a Disaster for Montagnards." *Washington Post,* 25 April 1971.

Parker, Maynard. "The Illusion of Vietnamization." *Newsweek,* 29 September 1969.

Price, Niko. "Coffee glut has bitter taste to workers." Associated Press, 6 September 2001.

Shaplen, Robert. *The Road From War: Vietnam 1965–1970.* New York: Harper & Row, 1970.

Sheehan, Neil et al. *The Pentagon Papers: As Published by the New York Times.* Toronto, New York, and London: Bantam Books.

Shenker, Israel. "Anthropologists Clash Over Their Colleagues' Ethics in Thailand." *New York Times,* 21 November 1971.

Shenon, Philip. "Air Force Report Links Agent Orange to Diabetes." *New York Times,* 29 March 2000.

Sochurek, Howard. "American Special Forces in Action in Vietnam." *National Geographic* 127, no. 1 (1965): 38–65.

Southerland, Daniel. "Sharing Called Viet Solution." *Christian Science Monitor* 12 February 1970.

———. "U.S. Pullout Leaves Viet Highlanders in the Lurch." *Christian Science Monitor,* 19 July 1972.

———. "Why Cambodia Didn't Fall." *Christian Science Monitor,* 9 November 1970.

Stock, Greg. "Abandoned Allies, the Montagnard People," *Air Commando Newsletter,* December 2001, pp. 29–32.

Sulzberger, C. L. "Foreign Affairs: The Third Level." *New York Times,* 11 April 1969.

Thayer, Nate. "The Forgotten Army" and "Trail of Tears: 'Lost' Montagnard Army Vows to Fight On." *Far Eastern Economic Review,* 10 September 1992, pp. 16–22.

Thurber, David. "Vietnam Accuses U.S. over Asylum." Associated Press, 5 April 2001.

Tran, Tini. "Vietnam Communists Pick Moderate to Lead the Nation." *Chicago Tribune,* 23 April 2001.

———. "Vietnamese Villagers Clash with Cops," Associated Press, 27 March 2001.

"Vietnam Admits to More Unrest among Minorities in Highlands." *New York Times,* 9 February 2001.

Warner, Denis. *Certain Victory: How Hanoi Won the War.* Kansas City: Sheed Andrews and McMeel, 1978.

Weinraub, Bernard. "U.S. Impact on Vietnam Life Called Devastating." *New York Times,* 11 June 1968.

Westmoreland, W. C. "Report on Operations in South Vietnam: January 1964–June 1968." In *Report on the War in Vietnam: As of 30 June 1968.* Ed. U. S. G. Sharp and W. C. Westmoreland. 2 sections. Washington, D.C.: GPO, 1969.

Woodruff, Lloyd W. *A Study of a Vietnamese Rural Community: Administrative Activity.* 2 vols. Saigon: Michigan State University Advisory Group, 1960.

INDEX

Abrams, Gen. Creighton, W., Long Range Planning Project of, 260, 264; and highlander resettlement policy, 263, 284

Apple, R. W. "Johnny," 220

administration, highlands: French, 54; prejudiced Vietnamese officials, 58, 61–2; neglect of health and education, 60; corvée for highlanders, 63. *See also* Ministry for Ethnic Minorities Development

Agency for International Development (AID). *See* U.S. Agency for International Development (USAID)

agriculture:

—highlander, swidden, 32, 57, 61, 65, 364; field crops, 32; tool complex, 65; paddy, 36; innovations in, 267–8; cash crops in globalization, 365–7. *See also* Coffee; Land Tenure

—Vietnamese, wet-rice farming, 76–7, 97; artifacts, 76; rain-fed rice, 93; tobacco, 93; tractors, 97; and Communist collectivization, 360–1; and economic renovation/globalization, 361–2. *See also* Khanh Hau

Alamo, M. Sgt. Gabriel, 122, 125, 127, 130, 134–6, 138, 144, 148

Allen, Joan, 250, 253–4, 278, 287, 308

American Anthropological Association: and use of herbicides in Vietnam, 296, 305; Thailand controversy, 297, 299–301. *See also* Mead, Margaret

Angkor Wat and "Dap Chhuon affair," 83–4

architecture: French colonial, 21–2, 25, 29, 32, 37; highlander, 32–3; Luang Prabang, 47; in Hue, 49–51. *See also* Rhadé; Bahnar

Army of the Republic of Vietnam (ARVN): in counterinsurgency, 9; highlanders' complaints against, 61; and Viet Cong, 197, and forced relocations, 211, 288; and "Free Strike Zones," 211; Operation Lam Son, 719, 292; 1972 Offensive, 316–7, 321–2; and Minh Qui Hospital, 333. *See also* North Vietnamese Army

Arnett, Peter, 220, 285

Asia Development Bank, 365

Atwood, Tracy: 152–3, 325–6, 328–30

Austronesian linguistic stock: highland languages, 6; and Vietnamese language, 8

Bahnar, linguistic affiliation, 37; descent, 37–8 ; men's houses, 38; permanent field farming, 62–3; relations with Vietnamese, 62–3

383